Sunderla
/Headways

for return on or before the
that sanctions are
Renew o   33
HαL

REFERENCE ONLY

Othello

Recent Titles in
Greenwood Guides to Shakespeare

Henry V: A Guide to the Play
Joan Lord Hall

Macbeth: A Guide to the Play
H. R. Coursen

Hamlet: A Guide to the Play
W. Thomas MacCary

Julius Caesar: A Guide to the Play
Jo McMurtry

Romeo and Juliet: A Guide to the Play
Jay L. Halio

OTHELLO

A Guide to the Play

JOAN LORD HALL

Greenwood Guides to Shakespeare

Greenwood Press
Westport, Connecticut • London

Library of Congress Cataloging-in-Publication Data

Hall, Joan Lord.
    Othello : a guide to the play / Joan Lord Hall.
       p.   cm. — (Greenwood guides to Shakespeare)
       Includes bibliographical references (p.   ) and index.
       ISBN 0–313–30263–4 (alk. paper)
       1. Shakespeare, William, 1564–1616.   Othello—Examinations—Study
    guides.   2. Muslims in literature—Examinations—Study guides.
    3. Tragedy—Examinations—Study guides.   I. Title.   II. Series.
    PR2829.H35   1999
    822.3'3—dc21   98–46817

British Library Cataloguing in Publication Data is available.

Library of Congress Catalog Card Number: 98–46817
ISBN: 0–313–30263–4

First published in 1999

Greenwood Press, 88 Post Road West, Westport, CT 06881
An imprint of Greenwood Publishing Group, Inc.
www.greenwood.com

Printed in the United States of America

The paper used in this book complies with the
Permanent Paper Standard issued by the National
Information Standards Organization (Z39.48–1984).

P

In order to keep this title in print and available to the academic community, this edition
was produced using digital reprint technology in a relatively short print run. This would
not have been attainable using traditional methods. Although the cover has been changed
from its original appearance, the text remains the same and all materials and methods
used still conform to the highest book-making standards.

To Cliff

CONTENTS

PREFACE

Othello may not take the palm as the greatest of William Shakespeare's tragedies, but many readers have found it the most "painfully exciting,"[1] coherent, and intense of all of them. When performed, the play is relentless in its drive toward disaster, drawing audiences into the horrifying spectacle of a husband quickly driven to murder his innocent wife. What is more, the black warrior Othello—the only African hero in Shakespeare—is married to a white woman. The tragedy touches on sensitive issues that have acquired fresh resonance in our own age: racial prejudice and fascination with the "Other," the nature of sexual jealousy, and the difficulty of knowing anything or anyone definitively.

Othello: *A Guide to the Play* is a reference work that aims to open up *Othello* to students as well as to interested readers and spectators. Chapters and chapter sections are designed to be consulted independently, so that users can discover more about various facets of this tragedy and the critical discussion they have generated. The guide begins with an overview of *Othello*'s complicated textual history (Chapter 1) and then considers the historical contexts and source materials that inform the play (Chapter 2). Chapter 3 covers *Othello*'s dramatic structure—its assimilation of different genres, its formal design and patterns of language—as a prelude to the central fourth chapter on the play's three main characters. These have long been the subject of heated debate. Is the tragic protagonist Othello an admirable, "noble" hero or a self-deceived egoist? Worse still, might he strike audiences as a fool in a melodrama engineered by the brilliant word-spinner Iago? Is it possible to penetrate Iago's mystery, or is he pure villain—a skillful amalgam of various dramatic conventions or an embodiment of evil that requires no credible motives? In recent years, commentators have insisted that Desdemona, once relegated to the symbolic status of angel to balance Iago's devil, is a presence as "intensely felt"[2] as that of Othello and Iago. Among feminist critics, in particular, this erstwhile saint is now analyzed as a product of both cultural discourses and dramaturgical expectations, to assess how subversive or submissive are her roles within the developing play.

Chapter 5 explores the themes of the play. Chapter 6 discusses how different schools of criticism, ranging from early character analysis to recent ideologist theory, have approached the tragedy. *Othello* continues to rivet audiences when it is performed, and Chapter 7 examines stage presentations from the seventeenth to the twentieth century, paying particular attention to how the play has been artfully reinvented in film and television productions. While the multifaceted Iago remains a gift for talented thespians, the role of Othello, now more often played by a black man than a white in blackface, has stretched actors to the height of their powers; perhaps none has encompassed its full range. As with the actor in the theater, there is, of course, no single way for the scholar to interpret the text of *Othello* or respond to its challenges and subtleties. Othello: *A Guide to the Play* tries to do justice to diverse critical approaches, encouraging the reader to enter the ongoing debate on this dramatic masterpiece.

All quotations from *Othello* are taken from Alvin Kernan (ed.), *The Signet Classic Shakespeare* (1963; New York: Penguin Books, 1986; 1998). Quotations from Shakespeare's other plays are from G. Blakemore Evans (ed.), *The Riverside Shakespeare* (1976; Boston: Houghton Mifflin, 1997).

My thanks go to the Writing Program and the College of Arts and Sciences at the University of Colorado, Boulder, both of which helped to fund part of this project; to Reg Saner, colleague in English, who supplied the *Variorum* edition of *Othello* when it was inexplicably out of print; and, once more, to Nancy Mann for her fine editing skills. This book is dedicated to Clifton Hall, whose many talents include charming the computer and magic on the Web.

NOTES

1. A. C. Bradley, *Shakespearean Tragedy* (1904; London: Macmillan, 1962), p. 143.

2. James Earl Jones, "Foreword," *Othello, The Everyman Shakespeare* (London and Vermont: J. M. Dent and Charles E. Tuttle, 1995), p. xv.

JOURNAL ABBREVIATIONS

RenD	*Renaissance Drama*
RenQ	*Renaissance Quarterly*
SEL	*Studies in English Literature*
ShS	*Shakespeare Survey*
ShStud	*Shakespeare Studies*
Sight&S	*Sight and Sound*
SLitI	*Studies in Literary Imagination*
SP	*Studies in Philology*
SQ	*Shakespeare Quarterly*
SWR	*Southwest Review*
TLS	*Times Literary Supplement*
TSLL	*Texas Studies in Literature and Language*
UCrow	*Upstart Crow*
UTQ	*University of Toronto Quarterly*
WMQ	*William and Mary Quarterly*
WS	*Women's Studies*
YR	*Yale Review*

1

TEXTUAL HISTORY

DIFFERENT TEXTS: QUARTO AND FOLIO

Because of its complex textual history, *Othello* has proved a challenge for editors.
It exists in two reliable but somewhat different versions: the Quarto (Q), published
in 1622, and the Folio (F), the collection of thirty-six of Shakespeare's plays published in 1623. (In a quarto edition, each sheet is folded twice, creating four leaves,
or eight pages; in the larger folio, each sheet is folded once to produce two leaves,
or four pages.) As the Quarto version of *Othello* is a "good" one, not a "bad"
memorial reconstruction of the text or a shortened acting version, it has some
claim to be used as the copy-text—the undisputed basis for an edition of the play.
But because the Folio version has 160 more lines than the Quarto, F is usually
taken as the copy-text and then collated with Q. The second Quarto (Q2), published in 1630, has no authority as an independent text; it is a conflation of Q and
F with some editorial emendations.[1]

The Quarto was published by Thomas Walkley in 1622, after being entered in
the *Stationer's Register* (to block any other printing of the play) on October 6,
1621. The title page testifies to the play's popularity on the stage:

> THE Tragœdy of Othello, the Moore of Venice. *As it hath beene diuerse times*
> *acted at the* Globe, and at the Black-Friers, by *his Maiesties Seruants. Writ-*
> *ten* by VVilliam Shakespeare. LONDON, Printed by N. O. [Nicholas Okes]
> for *Thomas Walkley,* and are to be sold at his shop, at the Eagle and Child, in
> Brittans Bursse. 1622.

Textual scholars think that Q was based either on the acting company's stage
promptbook (Alice Walker's theory)[2] or, according to M. R. Ridley and more recent editors, on a scribal copy of Shakespeare's "foul papers"—the version of his
manuscript that he handed over to his company, the King's Men, to be used in the
theater. The date of the Quarto is unusual, in that it was printed about eighteen

years after the play's first performance (1604) and when work on the Folio was already going forward. Possibly it was made for a private collector. Shakespeare's own papers must have been copied sometime during these eighteen years, probably after 1609 if the act divisions were marked in the manuscript of the Quarto (the first among the "good" quartos of Shakespeare's plays to provide them), since that is when breaks between the acts were first observed in the public theater.[3]

Earlier scholars, who felt that the 160 lines missing from the Quarto were deliberate cuts rather than passages added to the Folio version, argued that Q was based on a script that had been modified for theatrical performance. W. W. Greg comments that "a cut text more usually goes back to prompt-copy,"[4] or a manuscript streamlined for the actors. Yet these cuts would have saved barely ten minutes of playing time[5]—not much benefit!—and the more obvious passages for exclusion, such as the Clown sequences, have remained intact. It is possible that these exclusions in Q, if indeed they are cuts, took place in the printing house in order to accommodate a set number of pages.[6]

Some evidence points strongly to Shakespeare's foul papers, and not the company's promptbook, as the manuscript behind Q. The Quarto's stage directions are much fuller than the Folio's. A few are fairly nonspecific, as in "*Exit two or three*" (1. 3. 121) and "*Enter* Desdemona, Iago, *and the rest*" (1. 3. 169), where an author might leave the exact number of characters open; but many are visualized very concretely, as in "Enter Brabantio *in his night gown, and Servants with torches*" (1. 1. 156) and "*Enter Duke and Senators, set at a table with lights and Attendants*" (at the opening of 1. 3), where the details of nightgown and table are missing from F. "Oth. *falls on the bed*" (5. 2. 194) and "Iago *kills his wife*" (5. 2. 232) are helpful pointers for the staging that appear in Q only. Although the uninitiated might expect the company's promptbook to offer full stage directions of this kind, such details are in fact more typical of an author's script, or a reading copy, than one used by a bookkeeper, who, as prompter and stage manager, is likely to improvise a little according to the needs of the actors. Certain spellings characteristic of Shakespeare, such as "gardage" (1. 2. 69) and "ghesse" (3. 3. 145), as well as his favored contractions " 'twere," " 'twill," and " 'twould," also suggest that the scribe was copying from foul papers.[7] Ridley, editor of the second *New Arden Othello* and a staunch supporter of the Quarto text above the Folio in many instances, concludes that Q was not copied by the bookkeeper, but (with the addition of the cut passages) is "as near an approximation as we are likely to get to the play as Shakespeare first wrote it."[8] Inevitably, errors would creep in first from scribal carelessness (the manuscript may have been copied by two scribes working hurriedly) and then from misreadings and accidental cuts when the three compositors set up the manuscript for printing on Nicholas Okes's press.[9] Nevertheless, there appears to have been less substitution and normalization of words in Q than in F.

Until fairly recently, most textual scholars thought that the Folio derived from the same source as the Quarto—a version of either the promptbook or Shakespeare's foul papers. They assumed that F was a copy of Q that had been corrected against the original promptbook[10] or author's manuscript.[11] In judging F to be closer to what

Shakespeare first wrote, or to the play as he left it after revisions in the playhouse, bibliographers considered it a more reliable text overall than Q. Ideas about the origins of F then changed radically with the "revision-theory" critics. Since the early 1980s, it has been widely accepted that Shakespeare's *King Lear* exists in two independent versions (Quarto and Folio), each of which represents a subtly different conception of the play by the author.[12] There is no "pure" or single text. Nevill Coghill, a forerunner of the revision theorists,[13] and E. A. J. Honigmann[14] have postulated a similar situation for *Othello*. As a result, most editors now accept the Folio version as a scribal copy of Shakespeare's own revised transcript of the play. Whether, as Honigmann contended in 1997, Shakespeare made no "large-scale revision" in this new "fair copy"[15] of *Othello*, or whether he did make substantial changes, the manuscript underlying F is significantly different from Q. Possibly Shakespeare made his revisions by jotting down his "second thoughts" in the promptbook, which was then used by John Heminge and Henry Condell (Shakespeare's colleagues from his acting company, the King's Men) when they prepared their copy for the Folio. Alternatively, Stanley Wells and Gary Taylor, editors of the *New Oxford Shakespeare*, contend that "there must have existed a transcript by Shakespeare himself."[16] They go on to point out how the scribe who copied it apparently made some changes that deviated from this transcript. In particular, the stage directions are pared down and there are none of the music cues or offstage noises from Q, such as "*A shot*" (2. 1. 55), "*Trumpets within*" (2. 1. 175), and "*A bell rung*" (2. 3. 158). The punctuation seems heavier than is usual in foul papers, and F gives in full some expressions (e.g., "I would" for "I'ld" [3. 4. 189]) that are colloquial abbreviations in Q. To compound the changes from the author's "difficult to read"[17] manuscript, there appears to be more editorial intervention and regularization (presumably from Heminge and Condell and their assistants)[18] than in the Quarto. And inevitably, there are errors from Compositor B and especially from Compositor E, the "inexpert workman"[19] who set up the early part of the script. Obviously, there can be no claims that the Folio version represents word for word, with any high degree of consistency, what Shakespeare actually wrote.

The scribal, abbreviated stage directions constitute one important difference between F and Q; another is that some fifty-three of the oaths in the Quarto ("Zoun[d]s," "God," "Faith," etc.) have been cut from the Folio. Sometimes "God" is replaced by "Heaven" (as in 3. 4. 77 and 4. 3. 107). This almost certainly followed Parliament's act in May 1606 to "restrain abuses of players" by prohibiting swearing or profanity onstage.[20] Presumably, those modifications of the foul papers that resulted in the Folio text took place after 1606.

Faced with two significantly varying texts, neither of which is clearly authoritative, what decisions do editors make? They have often resorted to an eclectic or conflated text. Taking F, the longer version, as the copy-text, they add some of the color—the oaths and stage directions—from Q and evaluate the mechanical correctness or stylistic appropriateness of the shorter variants. While accepting, for the last two decades, that "the two texts reflect two stages of composition for both of which Shakespeare himself was responsible,"[21] recent editors have understandably found it impractical to offer dual texts. Wells and Taylor, like Ridley, see a case for using Q as the copy-text and grafting on the passages that appear in F only. Nevertheless, the *Oxford* editors commit themselves to the other text, deciding to "follow F in all readings which make acceptable sense, whether or not we prefer them to Q1's, unless we suspect them of corruption."[22] Norman Sanders, editor of the *New Cambridge Othello,* frankly admits to conflating the two texts to produce a new, hybrid version of the play: "Providing the editor supplies sufficient collation for the reader to reconstruct Q1 and F in the original form, he is free to offer what he thinks to be a 'best' version of the play in the full knowledge that in fact he is making a third version of it."[23] The fact that editors have felt the need to defend their often eclectic approaches, and to admit to some subjective editing, indicates the difficulty of reproducing a single text of *Othello.*

Since there are about a thousand variants between the Quarto and Folio texts of *Othello*[24]—far too many to discuss comprehensively—it is most helpful to concentrate on the ones that might significantly alter our perception of the play. We can begin with the longer passages that appear in F only. The earlier assumption, that these lines were deliberately omitted from Q, seemed plausible in that the action of the play holds firm without them. Also, Honigmann finds that metrical irregularities at the site of some of the passages missing in Q suggest that "at least some of the disputed longer passages" were cut from Q rather than added to F.[25] Yet in an earlier study, Honigmann showed that a few of the extra passages in F also break continuity in verse (Emilia's speech in 4. 3. 89–106 begins in prose, but F's amplification is in verse) or continuity in syntax (the seventeen-line addition to Roderigo's speech that begins "If't be your pleasure" [1. 1. 118] fits awkwardly with the preceding "I beseech you").[26] This suggests that they are interpolations in the Folio copy rather than cuts in the Quarto.

If we assume that these passages were added at a later stage by the author, what patterns can we discern? Sometimes the extra passages serve for exposition, or to make the play's action more intelligible. Roderigo's long speech to Brabantio (1. 1. 118–34) clarifies the details of Desdemona's elopement. The First Senator's amplified speech in 1. 3. 24–30 on why Cyprus is more important than Rhodes to the Turks helps to explain their decoy tactics. Other additions build the mood and dramatic tension of scenes. The extension of Othello's outburst in prose before he falls in a fit (culminating in "Confess?—Handkerchief?—O devil!" [4. 1. 39–45]) reinforces the agony of his sexual jealousy, while Desdemona's "willow song" and surrounding passages (4. 3. 31–54, 56–58), absent from Q, build up a poignant and thematically charged interlude before the murder.

Other changes suggest that Shakespeare worked to enhance the texture and metaphoric intensity of his poetry. When Cassio hyberbolically praises Desdemona in the storm scene, he describes her in Q as

> One that excels the blazoning pens,
> And in th' essential vesture of creation
> Does bear all excellency.   (2. 1. 63–65)

Folio's version is much tighter, adding "quirks" and the "ingener" reference:

> One that excels the quirks of blazoning pens,
> And in th' essential vesture of creation
> Does tire the ingener [Ingeniuer].

The image is now one of nature (Desdemona in her "essential" state) surpassing art, or exhausting the skills of the artist ("ingener") who attempts to capture her beauty. In the same scene, F adds to Montano's speech, on how those on shore will watch for a glimpse of Othello, the lines "Even till we make the main and th' aerial blue / An indistinct regard" (39–40): the anxious onlookers will strain their eyes until the sea and the horizon blur. Here again, F provides a more complex poetic image.

Another group of additions, occurring in Act 1, reinforces the idea that Desdemona's choice appears so unnatural that her father can explain it only as bewitchment. If we include Roderigo's long speech to Brabantio, a case can surely be made that these passages underscore the Venetians' racist attitude toward Othello. Roderigo stereotypes him as a "lascivious Moor" and "an extravagant and wheeling stranger" (1. 1. 133). Brabantio's added claims that the Moor has "practiced" witchcraft on Desdemona and "Abused her delicate youth with drugs and minerals" (1. 2. 71–76) expand on his earlier (F only) parenthetical hypothesis that she could not possibly have been attracted to Othello "If she in chains of magic were not bound" (64). These extra lines, plus the added "Being not deficient, blind, or lame of sense" (1. 3. 63), support Brabantio's accusation (in both Q and F, 1. 3. 60–64, 101–6) that his daughter has been "abus'd, stol'n from [him]" through Othello's "practices of cunning hell." Othello's own awareness of his blackness and his alien status, as well as his concern for "reputation," feeds into his agonized plea for "proof" and satisfaction in the lines of F only, where he tells Iago, "My name, that was as fresh / As Dian's visage, is now begrimed and black / As mine own face" (3. 3. 380–87). Except for Roderigo's speech, none of these passages is necessary to propel or explain the action. Rather, each reinforces the idea of Othello as the outsider in Venice, the black man associated with devilish arts.

Other passages only in F serve to delineate the characters of the play more finely. Desdemona's moving speech where she kneels to Iago and swears that her love for Othello will never be destroyed by "unkindness" or "divorce" (4. 2. 150–63) provides a compelling stage image to balance that of Iago and Othello kneeling together at the end of Act 3, scene 3,[27] while it underlines her absolute loyalty to her husband, whom she would not betray for the whole world. And Coghill is surely correct in discerning a pattern of lines that complicate and deepen the character of Emilia. In particular, her spirited eighteen-line defense of wives as being like husbands in their "affections" and "desires for sport" (4. 3. 89–106) can hardly be dismissed as an "undramatic disquisition."[28] A gift for the actress playing Emilia, it establishes her pragmatism in contrast to Desdemona's idealism. Hers is the one voice in the play that defends women's right to be vindictive as well as tolerant in their sexual relationships: "and though we have some grace, / Yet have we some revenge" (95–96). Emilia's part is also strengthened in the final scene of the play, with her incredulous "My husband say she was false?" even as Othello reiterates his trust in "honest, honest Iago" (5. 2. 149–151). Her anguished recognition of "Villainy, villainy, villainy! / I think upon't—I think I smell't / . . . I'll kill myself for grief" (187–88) puts her firmly on the side of goodness and integrity. Finally, at least two passages only in F work to amplify the character of Othello. His eloquent Pontic Sea speech (3. 3. 450–57), through its rhythms and imagery (the "icy current" that "nev'r feels retiring ebb"), enacts Othello's total commitment to a "wide" revenge that will "ne'er ebb to humble love." In the last scene, his dignified promise not to try to escape even though he is "weapon'd" reassures the audience that he stoically accepts his fate:

> Here is my journey's end, here is my butt,
> And very seamark of my utmost sail.   (5. 2. 264–65)

His sense of having reached his final destination, in this F-only passage, is couched in the sea imagery that pervades the play.

Honigmann has argued that some of the changes in F are more "sexually specific,"[29] emphasizing the physical and not just the spiritual nature of the play's central love relationship. Cassio's hope (in F) that Othello will soon "Make love's quick pants in Desdemona's arms" (2. 1. 80) is certainly franker than Q's "swiftly come to Desdemona's arms," while Desdemona's insistence on her "storm of fortunes" (1. 3. 244) comes across more strongly than "scorn" of fortunes (Q). But most editors sense that F's line where Othello is describing Desdemona's role in the courtship, "She gave me for my pains a world of kisses" (1. 3. 158), is a copyist's slip, and hence they prefer Q's more restrained "world of sighs." And sensuality seems to be toned down when F replaces Desdemona's declaration in Q that "My heart's subdued / Even to the utmost pleasure of my lord" (246) with "the very quality of my lord."[30] In the same scene, F cuts Desdemona's "Tonight, my lord?" (273), which might suggest the bride's disappointment, even resentment, that her nuptials are being cut so short. In addition, F replaces Q's "heat" in "Upon this heat I spoke" (1. 3. 165) with the moderate "hint" (Othello is explaining how he took his cue to propose marriage from Desdemona's strong response to his life's "story"). In short, it is difficult to find a consistent pattern here. Quite possibly in this scene, "F retouches Q to protect Desdemona"[31] from the charge of being too importunate in her love for the Moor.

From the shorter variants—a word or phrase—we cannot establish any design that would affect the meaning of the play, and editors have disagreed over whether or not the Folio's variants are superior. At times F clearly corrects scribal or compositorial misreadings that appear in Q, as when it replaces the nonsensical "resterine" with "restem" (where the Turkish galleys "restem / Their backward course" [1. 3. 37–38]) and "youth" with "vouch" ("To vouch this is no proof" [1. 3. 106]). But sometimes F replaces an unusual word in Q with a more ordinary one; we find "bitter" for "acerb" (1. 3. 345), "in the interim" for "in the nick" (5. 2. 313), and "loading [of this bed]" for "lodging" (5. 2. 359). The regularization of Q's "greatest abuse" to "least misuse," when Desdemona is asking how she could have behaved to encourage her husband to "stick / The small'st opinion, on my greatest abuse" (4. 2. 107–8), misses the strong point in the Quarto text; even her most terrible fault, Desdemona feels, could not provoke suspicion in Othello. F's "slow, and moving finger" of the time (4. 2. 54), which Othello feels is pointing scornfully at him, tidies up Q's apparently illogical "slow unmoving fingers" but has been judged "pedestrian."[32] We cannot be sure whether such regularization stemmed from Shakespeare, the scribe or scribes who copied his manuscript, the compositors who set up the type, or the editors of the Folio.[33]

Often, though, the word choice in F appears more incisive or more stylistically appropriate. Ridley, who regards F's "simplificatory or sophisticating methods" with the "utmost suspicion,"[34] seems unprepared to concede that some of F's more sophisticated word choices do work. Iago's decision to "plume up" his "will" (1. 3. 384) by plotting against Othello is more evocative than Q's "make up my will." Othello's recognition that he cannot "relume" Desdemona's light if he snuffs it out develops the life as light metaphor more precisely than does Q's "return" (5. 2. 13). Likewise, in Iago's urging Cassio to "entreat" Desdemona to "splinter" ("splint" in modern English) his relationship with Othello (2. 3. 322), F's "broken joint" develops the image more consistently than does Q's "brawl." In Act 3, scene 3, when Othello is categorizing Iago's hesitations as "close denotements, working from the heart, / That passion cannot rule" (3. 3. 123–24), Q's "denotements" is more straightforward than F's "dilations"; Ridley glosses "denotements" as "indications of something shut up and secret," carefully contained within a "just" heart that is not governed by passion. But F's "dilations" is more thought-provoking. The word could mean either delays or amplifications, while "delations" (Samuel Johnson's minor emendation) meant secret accusations; one critic finds it a "freighted term suggestive of all three of those resonances—amplification, accusation, delay— which are so much a part of the unfolding of this particular tragedy."[35] "Dilation" might also describe the expansion of the arteries around the heart, a graphic way of suggesting that Iago's pauses are (according to Sanders in the *New Cambridge* edition) "the involuntary swellings of the heart in a just man who is not normally a slave of his passions."[36]

On other occasions, Q and F offer "equally appropriate"[37] readings, as with Cassio's elaborate description of the rocks (in F) as "Traitors ensteeped to enclog the guiltless keel" (2. 1. 70), which reads "Traitors enscerped" in Q. Or the readings may be equally difficult to untangle. Iago's question in Q when he blames Bianca for the assault on Cassio, "Do you perceive the gestures [ieastures] of her eye?" (5. 1. 106), seems to refer to the prostitute's tactics for soliciting a client, while F's "gastness" emphasizes the expression of terror in Bianca's eyes. "Crush" in Iago's description of Roderigo in Q as "this poor trash of Venice, whom I crush / For his quick hunting" (2. 1. 303–4) is as baffling to editors as F's "trace," meaning to "follow the footprints or traces of" or to "track."[38] Iago is not crushing or crowding

Roderigo. Nor is he actively chasing Roderigo because of his "quick hunting" of Desdemona. He is, however, exploiting Roderigo's desire for Desdemona, so that, assuming that "For" means "in order to (make him)" and not "because of," the line from F might be glossed as "whose steps I pursue in order to make him hunt more quickly."[39]

Perhaps the most famous single word crux in *Othello* is the "Indian"/"Judean" variant in Othello's final speech. The hero describes himself in Q as "one whose hand, / Like the base Indian, threw a pearl away / Richer than all his tribe" (5. 2. 342–44); F reads "base Judean [Iudean]." At first this might seem to be a straightforward printing error, with an initial confusion of "n" and "u" (where the compositor could have accidentally turned a letter on the printing press), followed by an "e" instead of an "i." Yet "Indian" is never printed with "-ean" in the rest of the Folio, so that a double error becomes less likely. Scholars who support F's reading as an authorial alternative are divided over whether "Judean" refers to Herod the Great or to Judas Iscariot. Herod murdered his wife, Mariamne, after she had been falsely accused of infidelity and then bitterly regretted his action; this mirrors Othello's situation.[40] Herod provides a somewhat closer parallel than the morally "base" Judas who betrayed Christ (a pearl of great price), since Othello is not portrayed in the tragedy as a calculating deceiver.[41]

Debate rages on, but a majority of scholars favor Q's "Indian." Richard Levin points out that the adjective "Judean" is unusual, although a few instances have now been found before the 1652 usage cited as the first by the *Oxford English Dictionary*;[42] he also notes that Q2, which collates Q carefully against F, prefers the Quarto reading.[43] "Indian" certainly fits the tenor of Othello's speech. The assumption that (American) Indians undervalued and discarded their precious natural resources appears in other writings of the period, such as Thomas Nashe's *Pierce Penniless* (1592), where artists are called "base-minded," like Indians who are "ignorant" of the value of their plentiful gold and jewels.[44] Othello's image of himself as the "base Indian" points up his tragic ignorance in destroying a human being as precious and unique as Desdemona.

NOTES

1. Thomas L. Berger, "The Second Quarto of *Othello* and the Question of Textual 'Authority,'" *Analytical and Enumerative Bibliography*, 2.4 (1988): 141–59, makes a good case for considering some of the choices made by the "active, alert editorial intelligence" behind Q2, as this editor was closer to Shakespeare's language than we are. (Reprinted in Anthony Gerard Barthelemy [ed.], *Critical Essays on Shakespeare's* Othello [New York: Macmillan, 1994], pp. 144–61, quote at p. 151.) Indeed, some of Q2's emendations have been quietly adopted by most editors, as with "Her name" instead of "My name" (3. 3. 383).

2. Alice Walker, *Textual Problems of the First Folio* (Cambridge: Cambridge University Press, 1953), pp. 138–61.

3. See Stanley Wells and Gary Taylor (eds.), *William Shakespeare: A Textual Companion* (Oxford: Oxford University Press, 1987), p. 476.

4. W. W. Greg, *The Shakespeare First Folio* (Oxford: Clarendon Press, 1955), p. 361.

5. See Nevill Coghill, "Revision after Performance," *Shakespeare's Professional Skills* (Cambridge: Cambridge University Press, 1964), p. 178.

6. See David Bevington (ed.), *Othello, Bantam Classic* (New York: Scott, Foresman, and Co., 1988), p. 128.

7. See Norman Sanders (ed.), *Othello, New Cambridge Shakespeare* (Cambridge: Cambridge University Press, 1984), p. 196.

8. M. R. Ridley (ed.), *Othello, The New Arden Shakespeare* (1958; London and New York: Routledge, 1992), p. xliii.

9. See E. A. J. Honigmann, *The Stability of Shakespeare's Text* (Lincoln: University of Nebraska Press, 1965), pp. 13–14, 120. One case of accidental cutting through eye-skipping apparently occurred at Act 4, scene 2, lines 72–75, where Othello's decrying of Desdemona as a "public commoner" between two instances of "Committed?" is left out.

10. Greg, *Shakespeare First Folio*, p. 370.

11. Alice Walker and J. Dover Wilson (eds.), *Othello, New Cambridge Shakespeare*, 1st ed. (Cambridge: Cambridge University Press, 1957), consider that F results from Q "hand-corrected with an authoritative manuscript" (p. 121).

12. See Gary Taylor and Michael Warren (eds.), *The Division of the Kingdoms: Shakespeare's Two Versions of* King Lear (Oxford: Clarendon Press, 1983).

13. Coghill, "Revision after Performance," pp. 164–202.

14. E. A. J. Honigman, "Shakespeare's Revised Plays: *King Lear* and *Othello," Library,* 6.4 (1982): 156–73.

15. E. A. J. Honigmann (ed.), *Othello, The Arden Shakespeare,* 3rd ed. (Walton-on-Thames: Thomas Nelson and Sons, Ltd., 1997), p. 354.

16. Wells and Taylor (eds.), *A Textual Companion,* p. 477.

17. Honigmann (ed.), *Othello,* app. 2, "The Textual Problem," p. 355.

18. In *The Texts of* Othello *and Shakespearian Revision* (London and New York: Routledge, 1996), E. A. J. Honigmann postulates that the scribe Ralph Crane was one of these influential assistants (p. 73).

19. Sanders (ed.), *Othello,* p. 197.

20. E. K. Chambers (ed.), *The Elizabethan Stage* (Oxford: Clarendon Press, 1923), vol. 4, pp. 338–39. Honigmann offers an alternative explanation for the missing oaths in F by pointing out that Crane often omitted profanity when copying manuscripts (*Texts of* Othello, pp. 78–79), while Greg comments on the "literary tradition of expurgation" established by 1623 (*Shakespeare First Folio*, p. 152).

21. Sanders (ed.), *Othello,* p. 206.

22. Wells and Taylor (eds.), *A Textual Companion,* p. 478.

23. Sanders (ed.), *Othello,* p. 207.

24. Only a few passages appear in Q but not in F. The four extra lines of conversation between Iago and Roderigo (1. 3. 373ff.) that are replaced by Roderigo's "I'll sell all my land" in F are not crucial, although they do offer a vignette of Roderigo as one of the landed gentry who is prepared, like others in the Jacobean age, to sell off his estate for ready cash. Desdemona's line in Q only, "O Lord, Lord, Lord" (5. 2. 84), after Othello smothers her, may be more significant. As these words are very similar to Emilia's "My lord, my lord!" immediately following, the omission of Desdemona's line could be a case of eye-skipping by one of F's compositors; and Harley Granville Barker has defended the dying woman's "agonized cry" to God, echoed by Emilia's frantic cry "My lord, my lord!" to Othello, as part of a "macabre duet" between the women (*Prefaces to Shakespeare* [Princeton, N.J.: Princeton University Press, 1947], vol. 2, p. 80 n.52). If Desdemona *does*

speak here, her words lead naturally into Othello's "What noise is this? Not dead? Not yet quite dead?" (5. 2. 85).

25. Honigmann, *Texts of* Othello, p. 16. Honigmann now theorizes that "the manuscript behind Q was 'marked up' to indicate possible cuts by someone asked to shorten the play" and that the printer implemented only some of the cuts (p. 13).

26. Honigmann, "Shakespeare's Revised Plays," pp. 161–62.

27. Coghill calls this a "stroke of stage-craft of great visual force and point" ("Revision after Performance," pp. 189–90).

28. Ridley (ed.), *Othello,* p. 201.

29. Honigmann, "Shakespeare's Revised Plays," p. 162.

30. Barthelemy, in his "Introduction" to his *Critical Essays on Shakespeare's* Othello, finds Q's sexually frank reading here crucial to Othello's disclaimer of "appetite" that follows (p. 5).

31. Honigmann, *Texts of* Othello, p. 18.

32. Ridley (ed.), *Othello,* p. 153.

33. See Charlton Hinman, *The Printing and Proof-Reading of the First Folio,* 2 vols. (Oxford: Oxford University Press, 1963); and Honigmann, *Texts of* Othello, pp. 59–76.

34. Ridley (ed.), *Othello,* p. 85.

35. Patricia Parker, "Shakespeare and Rhetoric: 'Dilation' and 'Delation' in *Othello,*" in Patricia Parker and Geoffrey Hartman (eds.), *Shakespeare and the Question of Theory* (New York and London: Methuen, 1985), pp. 54–74, quote at p. 56.

36. Sanders (ed.), *Othello,* p. 190.

37. Ibid.

38. The definition is from the *Oxford English Dictionary* (*OED*) (Oxford: Oxford University Press, 1971), $v.^1$ II.5, p. 3368. George Steevens (followed by many other editors) emends this to "trash" (meaning "to check by weights") and Walker to "leash" (see Sanders [ed.], *Othello,* p. 190). But T. S. Dorsch, "This Poor Trash of Venice," *SQ,* 6 (1955): 359–61, points out that Roderigo, as the "weak and unhappy tool of Iago," needs no restraining (p. 361).

39. As in Barbara A. Mowat and Paul Werstine (eds.), *Othello, New Folger Library Shakespeare* (New York: Washington Square Press, 1993), p. 78. Dorsch supports the *OED*'s "to pursue, to dog" as the meaning of "trace" because Roderigo needs "hounding on, perpetual chasing, to make him hunt at all" ("This Poor Trash," p. 261).

40. See Nathan Cervo, "Shakespeare's *Othello,*" *Expli* (Summer 1995): 189–91.

41. See Richard Levin, "The Indian/Judean Crux in *Othello,*" *SQ,* 33 (1982): 60–67.

42. In "The Indian/Iudean Crux in *Othello:* An Addendum," *SQ,* 34.1 (1983): 72, Levin discovers an instance of "Iudeian" in the 1607 tragedy *Tiberius.* George Walton Williams in "Yet Another Early Use of Iudean," in ibid., finds one in Elizabeth Cary's 1613 play *Miriam.*

43. Levin, "The Indian/Judean Crux," p. 61.

44. Thomas Nashe, *The Unfortunate Traveller and Other Works,* ed. J. B. Steane (Harmondsworth: Penguin, 1972), p. 141.

2

CONTEXTS AND SOURCES

THE DATE OF THE PLAY

Othello was performed by the King's Men at the court of James I on November 1, 1604. The "Accounts of the Master of the Revels" (once suspected of being a forgery but now accepted as genuine) record "A play in the Banketinge house att Whithall called the Moor of Venis" by "Shaxberd," a variation on Shakespeare's name. We need not assume that this court production was the first performance of the play. But since the public theaters were closed between March 1603 and April 1604 because of bubonic plague, 1604 is the most likely year for the play's debut at the Globe Theatre.[1] *Othello* may have been designed to appeal to the new king, who succeeded Elizabeth to the throne in 1603, as James I was fascinated by Turkish history and the events leading up to the 1571 Battle of Lepanto in which the Christians were victorious.[2] The Quarto text, published in 1622, mentions that *Othello* was frequently performed at both the Globe and the Blackfriars, the indoor theater that Shakespeare's company used as their winter home after 1608. Records show that as well as being staged at the Globe and in Oxford in 1610, the play was presented again at court in 1612–1613 as part of the celebrations when Princess Elizabeth married the Elector Palatine.

Othello is the second of the four major tragedies, appearing after *Hamlet* and before *King Lear* and *Macbeth*. Written close in date to *Measure for Measure,* which was also performed at court during the same season, on December 26, 1604, *Othello* shows a similar preoccupation with the darker side of sexuality and with accuracy of judgment when human beings try to impose "justice." Like the tragedies, *Measure for Measure* explores the theme of treachery and "seeming" that culminates in Iago, the Machiavellian villain of *Othello.* This "problem play" also resembles *Othello* in being based on a story from Giraldi Cinthio's *Hecatommithi* (1566).

One possible topical allusion that has caught the eye of date detectives surfaces in Othello's comment to Desdemona, "The hearts of old gave hands, / But our new heraldry is hands, not hearts" (3. 4. 46–47). In 1611, James instituted a new order, the baronetage, whose members were entitled to add the red (gules) hand of Ulster to their coat of arms; Othello's words seem to gesture toward this heraldic badge. If so, the lines, which appear in both the Quarto and the Folio, must have been a later interpolation. They cannot be used to argue for a dating of the play later than 1603–1604.

Although no scholar now argues that *Othello* premiered after 1604, E. A. J. Honigmann revives arguments for dating the play in late 1601 or early 1602.[3] In his *Arden* edition of the play, he draws attention to some possible echoes of *Othello* in the "bad" Quarto of *Hamlet,*[4] published in 1603: "Olympus high" occurs in both texts; and Montano, a character in *Othello,* replaces Reynaldo in the *Hamlet* Quarto. Honigmann also points out that *Othello* has some casting requirements very similar to those of *Twelfth Night,* written in 1601–1602. In particular, the boy actor of Viola, for whom the "Come away death" song in *Twelfth Night* seems to have been originally intended, might also have been scheduled to sing the willow song as Desdemona in *Othello*. Honigmann guesses that because the boy's voice broke sooner than anticipated, Shakespeare marked these "willow" passages for cutting in the manuscript (foul papers) that underlies the Quarto text. While Honigmann's speculations are plausible—Othello may have been composed by early 1602—there is no evidence that would date the play in performance before 1603–1604.

HISTORICAL AND CULTURAL CONTEXTS

Among Shakespeare's tragedies, *Othello* is probably the least implicated in social or political change; it does not appear to have been written in response to a particular historical event or social movement in the early 1600s. As a domestic tragedy, it exposes power plays within patriarchal society—specifically, in father-daughter and husband-wife relationships. But unlike *King Lear,* which insistently questions received "authority" as the king's status is eroded, *Othello* does not treat the wider political ramifications of this patriarchal power. Nor does it deal with rifts in state power, as do Shakespeare's history plays and *Coriolanus*. Although Othello is highborn, he is not the actual or potential leader of a kingdom (as are Lear, Macbeth, and Hamlet), upon whose fate depends that of the whole nation.[5] Performed shortly after the 1603 publication of Richard Knolles's *The Generall Historie of the Turkes,* dedicated to James I, the play reveals some interest in the relatively recent clashes between Turks and Christians. But the initially pressing question of whether the Ottoman Empire (the Turks) will conquer the Venetian Christian fortress of Cyprus, as happened historically in 1570, is quickly deflected after Act 1 when the political military crisis is superseded by Othello's marital one.

Othello is nevertheless grounded in important cultural issues, ones that concern us as historians of an earlier age and as members of late-twentieth-century society. Othello's exact color—whether he is an olive-skinned Moor or a darker African with negroid features—has been much debated, sometimes with racist overtones.[6] What matters is that Othello is a black man, probably from North Africa (Mauritania is mentioned by Iago in 4. 2. 224), and now living in a white European community; the issue of racial difference is embedded in the play and is especially visible in performance. How would the hero have been perceived by the Jacobean audience, and how is he viewed today?[7] Does the play incorporate or reject racist stereotypes? To what extent does Desdemona, a white upper-class woman, transgress the norms of her society by choosing to marry a black man, and does the play endorse or repudiate her defiance? Frequently, there are no simple answers to these questions. Cultural materialists emphasize how dramatic literature participates in the shifting ideology and cultural beliefs of its time and also how it illuminates and is illuminated by our own ideological struggles.[8] Following their lead, we can examine ways in which *Othello* contributes to the discourse on two groups—black Africans and women—that were often marginalized in the early seventeenth century.

Although it cannot be equated with today's racial discrimination,[9] color prejudice as a kind of xenophobia appears to have flourished in England under Queen Elizabeth and King James. In 1600–1601, two or three years before *Othello* was first staged, an embassy from Barbary visited London, led by Abd el-Ouahed ben Messaoud.[10] There was some talk of a joint invasion by England and Morocco (Barbary) against their common enemy, Spain. The North Africans were described as "very strangely attired and behauiored,"[11] and these cultural differences, together with their parsimony—in their six-month stay, they cost the city over £230 and offered no presents at court—led to an attitude of distrust and muted hostility among the English. Contemporary accounts refer to them as "Barbarians": literally inhabitants of Barbary, but a loaded term. When it came time for them to leave, several English mariners, not wanting to be "friendlie or familiar with Infidells," refused to transport them.[12] Queen Elizabeth herself instigated some ethnic cleansing. She had written to the Lord Mayor of London in 1596 about the spread of "diverse blackmoores brought into this realm" (presumably slaves originally bound for Spanish and Portuguese colonies in the New World but then captured by English sailors)[13] and had arranged for them to be shipped back to Spain and Portugal. In January 1601, she licensed the same merchant, Caspar van Senden, to deport such Moors[14] "out of this her majesty's realm."[15]

Her edicts reflect a certain insularity (the Moors are "Infidells") and concern about overpopulation (she explains that "God hath blessed this land with great increase of people of our own nation") rather than a conviction that nonwhites were racially inferior. Nor would English people in the early 1600s necessarily have identified Africans as servants or slaves, since the slave trade, developing through Portuguese inroads into Africa, was not fully established until later in the seventeenth century;[16] Othello's reference to how he was "sold to slavery" and then rescued (1. 3. 137) seems more one of his heroic adventures than an account of "shameful servitude."[17] Rather than automatically associating black people with slavery, the Jacobean audience based their impressions on limited exposure to West and North Africans living in London, on geographical accounts of Africa, and on exotic travelers' tales.[18] It was inevitable, though, that ignorance and distrust of the black alien, together with the categorization of Moors as Muslim infidels,[19] would lead to hostile stereotyping as a way of confirming the "assumed superiority of European values."[20] Thomas Middleton's London pageant *The Triumph of Truth* (1613) pointedly dramatizes this stock response to the unfamiliar. It features a Moorish king who comments on the "amazement" that his color produces among the spectators:

> does my complexion draw
> So many Christian eyes, that never saw
> A king so black before?[21]

"Amazement" at his appearance, the king recognizes, is closely linked to prejudice about his moral status. For although (like Othello) he is a Christian, he knows that English onlookers will equate his blackness with sinfulness: "I being a Moor, then, in opinion's lightness, / As far from sanctity as my face from whiteness."[22]

Travelers encountering strange customs among Africans reveal the same Eurocentric suspicion that anything culturally different constitutes "beastly living."[23] Black men were often stereotyped as sexually overactive; John Pory, translating Leo Africanus's *The History and Description of Africa* in 1600, calls them "prone to venerie."[24] According to one biblical tradition, Chus (the grandson of Noah) was born "blacke and lothsome" because his father, Cham, defied the edict against sexual intercourse on Noah's ark: "of this blacke and cursed Chus came all those blacke Moores which are in Africa."[25] Discussing North Africans, Pory also observes that "no nation in the world is so subiect vnto iealousie"[26]—a classification that lies behind Rosalind's words as, playing the role of the youth Ganymede in *As You Like It,* she promises Orlando: "I will be more jealous of thee than a Barbary cock-pigeon over his hen" (IV. i. 149–51). Because of the stock identification of black with evil,[27] Westerners also continued to associate Africans' dark skins with the devil. This is the casual association that Portia makes in *The Merchant of Venice* when she refers to the African prince of Morocco as having the "complexion of a devil" (I. ii. 130) and later hopes that none "of his complexion" will win her hand (II. vii. 79).

This typecasting of the black man as lustful and devilish is dominant in dramatic characters of the period, such as the treacherous villain Muly Hamet in George Peele's *The Battle of Alcazar* (1588) and the vengeful, lecherous Eleazar in Thomas Heywood's *Lust's Dominion* (1600).[28] It is especially pronounced in Shakespeare's depiction of Aaron the Moor in *Titus Andronicus* (c. 1592). Queen Tamora keeps Aaron as her adulterous partner, and his sexual prowess is exceeded only by his "villainy" when he resolves, in accordance with the stereotype of black men as devils, that "Aaron will have his soul black like his face" (III. i. 205). In his opportunism and Machiavellian strategy as he disposes of two of Titus's sons, Aaron is a forerunner of Iago. His strong defense of his infant son, who is as black as he is despite having a white mother,[29] and of his skin color ("is black so base a hue?" [IV. ii. 71]) takes him beyond the stereotype of the coldhearted villain; but he has little in common with the "noble Moor" Othello.

In view of the prejudices of the time and the literary legacy of Moors as villains, it is remarkable that Shakespeare chooses to make his tragic hero a black man and his villain the white Iago. Many recent critics consider that Shakespeare introduces the standard preconceptions about Africans through the racist discourse of Iago and Brabantio—Iago glibly slanders Othello as "lusty Moor" (2. 1. 295) and "devil" (1. 1. 88), while Brabantio, who "lov'd" Othello as a warrior, accuses him of winning his daughter's love through "damned" witchcraft (1. 2. 62)[30]—but that he does so only to explode these prejudices in the course of the play. In this reading, Othello's error is a universal human weakness rather than a flaw arising from his race; the tragedy is emphatically not a "study of a civilized barbarian reverting to type," for Iago is the true savage.[31] G. K. Hunter acknowledges the long-established medieval tradition, literary and pictorial, that associated the black man with inferiority and damnation. He argues, though, that a countercurrent of religious discourse and art, such as the emphasis on inner sanctity over outward appearance and the depiction of Balthazar, one of the Magi bearing gifts for the infant Christ, as a black man, enabled Shakespeare to develop Othello as a "great Christian gentleman."[32] Hunter finds no evidence in the play that the hero is truly savage, since he recovers his nobility after his tragic loss of faith in Desdemona.[33] Martin Orkin, a South African critic keenly aware of how Shakespeare's *Othello* invites racist responses, is in basic agreement with Hunter's conclusions. He thinks that Shakespeare works "consciously against the color prejudice reflected in the language of Iago, Roderigo, and Brabantio" to refute such preconceptions and to emphasize the "limitations" of "human judgment" in general as the real cause of Othello's tragedy.[34]

All this is true on one level: Shakespeare develops his characterization of "valiant Othello" far beyond that of the conventional stereotype. Yet there are moments when Othello's actions do fulfill the "erring barbarian" image.[35] This is particularly the case in Act 4, where he loses consciousness in a frenzy of jealousy ("savage madness" is how Iago describes it in 4. 1. 57), vows to "chop" Desdemona into "messes" after listening in on the conversation between Iago and Cassio, and behaves viciously by striking Desdemona in public. Does Shakespeare, as Laurence Lerner contends, exhibit "colour prejudice" by making Othello revert to the expected image of "black savage"?[36] One defense of Othello's behavior here is to say that it is a triumph of Iago's callous manipulation of him, combined with the Moor's "tragic readiness to accept the negative, oversimplified stereotype of himself";[37] but Othello's degrading performance is almost bound to alienate the audience, Jacobean or modern. By the finale of the play, Othello is split between the identity he has tried to maintain as an "honorary white"[38] in Venice—where the Senate has appropriated his military "services" and even, in opposition to Brabantio, condoned his marriage to a white woman—and his pervasive sense of himself as an African outsider. In succumbing to jealousy and murdering his wife, Othello finally describes himself as more akin to the "base Judean [or Indian]" and the "malignant" Muslim Turk[39] than to the civilized Christian (5. 2. 343, 349). Some readers and audiences feel that Othello recoups his dignity as an admirable tragic hero in the denouement; others disagree.

And while it is fair to say that *Othello* does not endorse the rooted prejudices of an Iago, how does the audience respond to Emilia's racist comments in the final scene? Emilia becomes the center of dramatic attention when she exposes Othello's dreadful mistake and dismantles any "just grounds" for his thinking that Desdemona committed adultery. Identifying with her frank truth-telling, the audience is encouraged to become complicit in her views even though they are charged with racial hatred: she calls Othello the "blacker devil" who is as "ignorant as dirt" and regrets that Desdemona was "too fond of her most filthy bargain" (5. 2. 130, 161, 154). This illustrates the difficulty of deciding exactly where the play stands on the issue of Othello's blackness. Since the balance of dramatic sympathies shifts from moment to moment, we are likely to accept Emilia's angry unleashing of prejudice while rejecting Iago's coldly virulent racism, despite the close relationship he has established with the audience. Just as Shakespeare's *The Merchant of Venice* may simultaneously undermine anti-Semitic prejudice (through Shylock's probing speech "Hath not a Jew eyes?" [3. 1. 59–67]) and reinforce it (with Shylock's grotesque wish that his daughter "were hears'd at my foot, and the ducats in her coffin!" [89–90]), it can be argued that *Othello* "challenges the racist stereotypes of the sixteenth-century stage even as it confirms them."[40] It is also the case, as Virginia Mason Vaughan points out, that "to be totally free of racism, one would have to invent a new language with no loaded words, no color discriminations, and no associations of blackness with evil, whiteness with good."[41] In other words, *Othello* cannot transcend the language and presuppositions of its culture.

If black-skinned men were regarded as the "Other" in Renaissance Europe—a difference to be uneasily contained within or rejected by a white community—then women were also a troublesome Other in patriarchal society. The Reformation in England is sometimes perceived as an era when attitudes toward women's roles, at least within marriage, were becoming more liberal.[42] Puritans promoted an equal wedded partnership, rather than the unquestioned subordination of wife to husband, and lauded married chastity above celibacy; yet, as Valerie Wayne has suggested, this elevation of the married state might have served as a strategy to contain women's unruly desire rather than to promote a measure of real independence for them.[43] Desdemona is obviously committed to the ideal of married chastity, but she is also a rebel; her daring repudiation of her father's wishes (and, by extension, those of the Venetian ruling class) in order to marry a black man and her frank desire to fulfill the "rites" for which she married Othello (1. 3. 252) constitute highly unconventional behavior. They are doubly "transgressive" acts,[44] in that she has stepped beyond the boundaries of her race—"Against all rules of nature," as Brabantio sees it (1. 3. 101)—and the modesty expected of her gender.

Shakespeare nevertheless presents the rebellious Desdemona as an admirable character. Her eloquence in explaining why she chose Othello despite her father's opposition, her courageous passion for the Moor, and her spirited (though misguided) defense of Cassio are all likely to win the sympathies of the audience. Her boldness, as well as Othello's initial welcoming of it (he calls her his "fair warrior" when he arrives in Cyprus [2. 1. 180]), points toward a marriage of mutual love and respect. In Cyprus, however, Desdemona becomes more isolated and vulnerable. Once Othello absorbs Iago's misogynistic views, interpreting Desdemona as a faithless and promiscuous woman, she has no means of resisting her husband's violent need to control her. It would seem, then, that there are mixed messages in the play about what behavior is appropriate for women. The unruly female who challenges her place in the male-dominated society is given some scope but is then punished, primarily because Othello misreads her, but also, the drama may suggest, because of her transgressive desires.[45]

As with the issue of racism in *Othello*, Emilia's role heightens the ambivalent treatment of women in the play. Her strong defense of wives in Act 4 explodes the double sexual standard by which men and women are judged:

> And have not we affections?
> Desires for sport? and frailty? as men have?
> Then let them use us well; else let them know,
> The ills we do, their ills instruct us so.   (4. 3. 103–6)

Since Emilia insists that women are men's equals in desire and have the right to behave like their husbands, her manifesto is potentially subversive in its denial of gender differences that work only to the advantage of males. Nevertheless, the context of the speech, as well as what we know of the speaker herself, tends to diffuse the power of the message. Emilia has gender in common with Desdemona but not class; therefore, Shakespeare's audience might downplay the significance of her comments, rationalizing them as appropriate for servingwomen but not for upper-class ladies.[46] Desdemona herself rejects such a philosophy of female retaliation— Emilia's "Yet have we some revenge" (96)—when she closes the scene by resolving "Not to pick bad from bad." And because Emilia has compromised her integrity by appropriating the handkerchief and then covering up, the audience may discount her as a reliable spokesperson for equality. Perhaps more importantly, Emilia has capitulated to her husband's "fantasy"—subordinated herself to his whim and contradicted her philosophy of independence—by giving him the keepsake. Only in the final scene is Emilia able to stand against her mate ("Perchance, Iago, I will ne'er go home" [5. 2. 194]). Her show of female assertiveness, as she speaks "liberal as the north" to condemn Iago, is heroic but too late to divert the tragedy.

SOURCES AND ANALOGUES

Shakespeare's main source for *Othello* is a story from Giraldi Cinthio's *Hecatommithi,* a collection of a hundred realistic tales on the theme of marriage that was first published in Venice in 1566.[47] Using the seventh novella in the third decade, the dramatist follows most of Cinthio's plot fairly closely, especially in

Acts 3 and 4 of the play. A comparison of the Italian tale with *Othello* reveals Shakespeare's skill in transforming a leisurely narrative into tightly knit drama. The playwright modifies some parts of the story to heighten dramatic immediacy and sharpen character presentation, and he also makes significant changes— leaves out or adds material—to ennoble his hero and turn a melodramatic tale into compelling tragedy.

Shakespeare appropriates four main characters from Cinthio: the Moor (who becomes Othello), the Ensign (Iago), the Captain (Cassio), and the Moor's wife Disdemona, the only character Cinthio names. Cinthio's Disdemona, like *Othello*'s heroine, is a beautiful and virtuous woman of Venice who falls in love with the Moor because of his "valor."[48] When he is put in command of the garrison in Cyprus, she insists on accompanying him to share any "toils and perils"[49] with her husband. The Moor's Ensign, who sails to Cyprus with them, is described as a malicious man—"of the most depraved nature in the world"[50]—who disguises his villainy under persuasive language and a fine exterior. His wife is a close friend of Disdemona's. Knowing that he must use "artful fraud"[51] to turn the Moor against his wife, he hits on the plan of accusing Disdemona of an affair with the Captain. Soon afterward, when the Captain is deprived of his rank for wounding another soldier, the Ensign is able to hint that Disdemona's kind efforts to reinstate the Captain have an ulterior motive; he also tells the Moor that Disdemona has taken an "aversion"[52] to his blackness. As in Shakespeare's play, he remains diffident about revealing too much until the Moor angrily demands visual proof of his wife's adultery. The Ensign then acquires the handkerchief ("precious"[53] to Disdemona because her husband gave it to her) and makes it seem, through a conversation he arranges for the Moor to overhear, that Disdemona has given it to the Captain at their last meeting. When the Moor challenges his wife about the lost handkerchief, she is unable to produce it. Subsequently, the Ensign and the Moor arrange to kill the Captain, but the Ensign, attacking in the dark, succeeds only in severing the Captain's leg. Later, he collaborates with the Moor in killing Disdemona.

Using this outline of events, Shakespeare makes important modifications to propel his characters into swift crisis. Desdemona and Othello are given no chance to live in "harmony and peace in Venice"[54] as their counterparts in Cinthio do; instead, the Turkish threat to Venice forces them to leave for Cyprus immediately, even before they have consummated their marriage. Whereas in Cinthio's tale Disdemona gains the reluctant consent of her relatives to marry the Moor, Brabantio's opposition to Othello as a son-in-law is virulent. His antagonism reinforces the racist element in the play and introduces the topic of witchcraft; it also allows Shakespeare's Desdemona to offer a spirited defense of her love for Othello in the Senate scene (1. 3). In Cinthio, Disdemona comments on the "hot" temperament of Moors[55] when her husband reacts angrily to her pleading the Captain's cause, and later she also points up the moral of the tale by speculating that Italian women will learn from her marriage never to wed men from alien cultures against their parents' wishes.[56] Shakespeare's Desdemona, on the other hand, never openly impugns Othello and regrets briefly "Arraigning his unkindness with [her] soul"

(3. 4. 152). Brabantio and Iago are the ones who single out black Othello as an outsider. And it is Emilia, not Othello's bride, who wishes that Desdemona had "never seen him" (4. 3. 18).

Shakespeare also complicates Iago's motivation and strategy. In Cinthio, the Ensign's reason for vilifying the Moor's wife is his own unrequited love for her. When she barely notices his attentions, he assumes that she prefers the Captain, and once his passionate love has turned to animosity, he resolves to kill the Captain and destroy the Moor's love for Disdemona. Shakespeare's Iago mentions, in passing, an attraction to Desdemona—"Now I do love her too" (2. 1. 291)—but this is never developed. Instead, he outlines his overt motives and strategy at the beginning of the play: that he hates Othello because Cassio has been promoted to lieutenant while Iago is passed over (1. 1. 24–30) and that he will take his revenge on both general and lieutenant by making Othello believe that his wife is in love with Cassio (1. 3. 386–89). Additional motives suggesting Iago's warped nature—sexual paranoia in suspecting that Othello has slept with his wife, as well as racial hatred—are also introduced in his soliloquy in Act 1, scene 3 (377–81).

From Cinthio's assertion that the Ensign "cloaked" his malevolence with a fair "outward show,"[57] Shakespeare develops Iago into the most sinister of his Machiavellian villains. It is Iago who suggests to Cassio that he use Desdemona as his advocate, so that he can exploit this as evidence of their close relationship. Cinthio's Ensign is evasive, "feigning at first great reluctance to say aught that might displease the Moor";[58] Shakespeare expands this simple description into Iago's masterpiece of understatement and insinuation in Act 3, scene 3. Whereas the Ensign steals the handkerchief after the Moor demands eyewitness evidence, Iago is fortunate enough to gain possession of it (and keep it as ammunition to produce when the right moment arrives) before Othello demands "ocular proof." In Cinthio's tale, the Ensign steals the handkerchief from Disdemona's girdle while she is playing with his three-year-old daughter; in *Othello,* Emilia retrieves the handkerchief and gives it to her "wayward husband" after Desdemona accidentally drops it. The modification is both practical and consistent with character portrayal. It serves to eliminate an awkward complication—not only would the very young child be difficult to stage, but it is almost impossible to imagine Iago in the role of caring father!—and it excuses Desdemona's moment of carelessness in losing her "precious" handkerchief as concern over Othello's headache.[59] Meanwhile, Emilia becomes another unwitting pawn in her husband's opportunistic schemes.

The Ensign's wife in Cinthio's tale knows of her husband's plot but is too frightened to reveal it to her close friend Disdemona. Shakespeare's Emilia, in contrast, remains ignorant of her husband's "villainy" until the final scene. Shakespeare also changes the way that the handkerchief is used as "ocular proof." In Cinthio, a seamstress[60] who lives in the Captain's house decides to copy the embroidery on the handkerchief; and when the Moor sees her at work on it by the window, he regards this as proof that the Captain has obtained it as a love token from Disdemona. In *Othello,* it is Bianca, Cassio's mistress, who angrily confronts Cassio with the handkerchief at the end of Act 4, scene 1, refusing to copy the pattern of what she imagines to be some other woman's gift. Witnessing this confrontation fuels Othello's sense of degradation; he assumes that Desdemona has passed the love token on to Cassio and "he hath giv'n it his whore" (179).

The narrative sequence of Cinthio's tale progresses much more slowly than does the action in *Othello*. After the period of wedded bliss in Venice, events in Cyprus apparently cover weeks or months rather than days, as the author uses nonspecific time pointers to move from one happening to the next. After the Ensign promises to deliver proof, the Moor awaits "the day" when the evidence will come. Disdemona discovers the loss of her handkerchief "a few days" after it has been stolen. "One day" the Ensign arranges the conversation on which the Moor eavesdrops, and sometime afterward (again the vague "one day" is used), the Moor challenges his wife about the handkerchief. Only "at length" does the Moor persuade the Ensign to try to kill the Captain; then they have to wait to murder Disdemona until "one night"[61] the opportunity presents itself. In contrast, Iago's undermining of Othello's faith in Desdemona, the loss of the handkerchief, Othello's eavesdropping, and Bianca's returning of the handkerchief (3. 3–4.1) all appear to take place within the space of a morning and an afternoon, with the murder on that same night. The success of Iago's plan depends on the speed with which it gains momentum to destroy Othello's peace of mind; no time can be allowed for quiet reflection or rational questioning.

Shakespeare's amplification of Cinthio's tale early in the play builds Iago's role and heightens dramatic tension, as well as more fully establishing Othello as a tragic hero. Roderigo, introduced in the first scene of Act 1, is Shakespeare's invention; as Iago's first dupe, he affords the audience a fuller view of the ensign's manipulative tactics. Shakespeare adds to the plot not only the Turkish threat, but the storm that separates the newlyweds, heightens their ecstatic reunion, and foreshadows their marital conflict; in Cinthio, the Venetians reach Cyprus on a "perfectly tranquil"[62] sea. Othello's dignified speeches to the Senate and, more particularly, the calm authority with which he handles the armed clash in the street (1. 2) demonstrate what Cinthio merely asserts to be the Moor's "great skill and prudence" in war.[63]

It is at the end of his play that Shakespeare deviates most from his source in *Hecatommithi*. Whereas Cinthio's conclusion becomes drawn-out and melodramatic, Shakespeare's denouement is swift and, to some extent, restores Othello to the image of nobility he projects in the first two acts of the play. In Cinthio, the Moor and the Ensign hatch a grotesque plan to murder Disdemona. Concealed in the closet one night, the Ensign leaps out and batters her to death with a stocking filled with sand when she gets out of bed to investigate a noise. To fake an accidental death, the two conspirators then pull down part of the ceiling onto the corpse, so that Disdemona appears to have been crushed to death by a rafter. When the Moor, regretting his actions, cashiers the Ensign, this villain seeks revenge by telling the Captain (now equipped with a wooden leg) that the Moor is responsible for his maiming. After the Captain's revelations in Venice, the Moor is arrested and tortured; eventually he is killed in exile by Disdemona's relatives. Some time afterward, the Ensign's plot against one of his comrades backfires, so that he, too, is tortured and then dies a "miserable death"[64] from his injuries. Shakespeare avoids any narrative details that make Othello's behavior overly ignominious. Deciding against bloodshed, Othello strangles Desdemona without Iago's help and attempts to make the murder "honorable." Moreover, Othello then takes responsibility for his terrible error and administers retribution by killing himself. It is Iago, the arch-villain, who must submit to degrading torture, although he vows to remain silent, just as Cinthio's Moor refuses to confess.

Since no sixteenth-century English translation of the *Hecatommithi* has been found, scholars conclude that Shakespeare read it in the original Italian or used the French translation of Gabriel Chappuys, published in 1584. A few verbal parallels connect *Othello* with the original text. Othello's demand for "ocular proof" (3. 3. 357) echoes a phrase in the Italian, *"se non mi fai . . . vedere cogl'occhi,"* and Quarto's "acerbe," meaning "bitter," is reminiscent of Cinthio's *"in acerbissimo odio,"* recounting how the Ensign's love for Disdemona turned into "bitterest hate." (Shakespeare may also have read Ludovico Ariosto's *Orlando Furioso* in the original Italian, as the phrase *"il furo profetico,"* not in John Harrington's 1591 translation, finds an echo in the "prophetic fury" with which the Sibyl sewed the Moor's handkerchief.)[65] The strongest evidence that Shakespeare consulted the French translation of Cinthio's tale is the phrase *"tirer le patron"* (take out the pattern), which Chappuys adds to describe how the woman in Cassio's house embroiders a handkerchief similar to Disdemona's. The phrases in *Othello,* "I'll have the work ta'en out" (3. 3. 295), "Take me this work out" (3. 4. 179), and "I must take out the work?" (4. 1. 153–54)—a verbal construction found nowhere else in Shakespeare—echo the French *"tirer."*[66]

Cinthio's tale in the *Hecatommithi* is clearly the primary source for *Othello.* It is possible, though, that Shakespeare used another story about jealousy that he found in François de Belleforest's *Histoires Tragiques* (1561), translated by Geoffrey Fenton in *Certaine Tragicall Discourses* (1567). When Don Spado's loyal wife promises that she will not outlive him, the jealous Don stabs both of them to death in a frenzy—but not before (as Fenton writes) "he embraced and kissed her, in such sorte as Judas kissed our Lorde the same night he betraied him."[67] It is tempting to speculate that this analogy lies behind the Folio's reading "base Judean" (5. 2. 343).[68] The tragedy of Don Spado and his wife, like *Othello,* is also set against a background of Turkish invasion.

Shakespeare and his contemporaries absorbed accounts of Africa and Africans from popular travelogues such as Richard Hakluyt's *Principal Navigations* (1589). The playwright's presentation of Othello most likely draws on Pory's 1600 translation of Africanus's *History and Description of Africa,* or Shakespeare may have consulted the Latin original.[69] Africanus distinguishes the "white and tawnie Moors" from the "Negroes or blacke Moors"[70] (references to Othello's "sooty bosom" [1. 2. 69] and "thick-lips" [1. 1. 63] ally him with "blacke Moors," although Iago's designation "Barbary horse" [1. 1. 108–9] suggests Arabian traits), and he delineates some characteristics that prove relevant to Othello or to the stereotypes on which the play draws: how Moors love "simplicitie and truth"[71] and are especially prone to sexual passion and jealousy. Shakespeare may have picked up the reference, in Pory's translation, to cave dwellers who live below the deserts of North Africa and used it in Othello's description of "anters vast and deserts idle" (1. 3. 139).[72] The playwright almost certainly assimilated other exotic details from Pliny's *Natural History,* translated by Philemon Holland in 1601. In particular, he incorporates the man-eating Anthropophagi (1. 3. 143), the "chrysolite" for which Othello would not trade Desdemona (5. 2. 142), the gum-dropping Arabian trees (346–47), and the movement of the Pontic Sea (3. 3. 450–53). Othello's protestation that he has never used witchcraft apparently owes something to Pliny's account of C. Furius Cresnus, a former bond slave who is accused of using black magic to acquire great wealth. Pointing to his plow and farm utensils, Cresnus tells his "masters" that "there are all the sorceries, charmes, and all the inchauntments that I use," just as Othello, explaining how he won Desdemona's love by recounting the story of his life, tells his "noble and approved good masters" (1. 3. 77) in the Senate that "This only is the witchcraft I have used" (168).[73]

In constructing Othello's defense, Shakespeare may also have drawn on Sir Lewis Lewkenor's 1599 translation of Cardinal Gasparo Contarini's *The Commonwealth and Government of Venice* (1543). Discussing travelers' tales, Lewkenor writes that he was "euer . . . ready to receive their discourses with an attentive eare" and "would willingly endure to haue [his] eares enclined" to their tales; Desdemona, too, devoured Othello's discourse with a "greedy ear" and "seriously incline[d]" to listen to his stories (1. 3. 148, 145).[74] This source would also have furnished information about Venice and its government. From Knolles's *Generall Historie of the Turkes,* Shakespeare probably obtained details about the Venetian-Turkish wars: the controversy over where the Turks are heading (1. 3. 19–30), the number of Turkish galleys,[75] and the puzzling reference to "Signior Angelo" (16) that could point back to Angelus Sorianus, a commander of the galleys mentioned in *Historie of the Turkes.*[76] Othoman, the founder of the Turkish dynasty discussed by Knolles, may have influenced the name of Shakespeare's hero; it seems more than coincidence that that Othoman had a trusted Christian captain called Michael Cossi.[77]

NOTES

1. J. Leeds Barroll, *Politics, Plague, and Shakespeare's Theater* (London and Ithaca, N.Y.: Cornell University Press, 1991), argues that the autumn of 1604 was a likely time for the play's debut at the Globe, since the plague was still a threat in London throughout the summer months (p. 123).

2. Emrys Jones, "*Othello, Lepanto,* and the Cyprus Wars," *ShS,* 21 (1968): 47–52, points out the popularity of King James's poem "Lepanto" and how the action of *Othello* (the invasion of Cyprus) appears to take place the year before the Battle of Lepanto, in 1570 (p. 49).

3. E. A. J. Honigmann (ed.), *Othello, The Arden Shakespeare,* 3rd ed. (Walton-on-Thames: Thomas Nelson and Sons, Ltd., 1997), points out that if we assume that *Othello* is

indebted to Philemon Holland's translation of Pliny's *Natural History*, published in June 1601, the play cannot be dated before this (p. 344).

4. Echoes of the *Hamlet* "bad" Quarto in *Othello* were first observed by Alfred Hart, "The Date of *Othello*," *TLS*, 10 (October 10, 1935): 631.

5. G. R. Hibbard, "*Othello* and the Pattern of Shakespearian Tragedy," *ShS*, 21 (1968): 39–46, points out that the "public" and "private" worlds are not closely interconnected in *Othello*.

6. See the appendix on "Othello's Colour," in Horace Howard Furness (ed.), *A New Variorum Edition of Shakespeare: Othello* (New York: Dover Publications, 1963; rpt. of the 1886 Lippincott edition), pp. 389–96. Nineteenth-century discomfort with Othello's blackness ranges from Samuel Taylor Coleridge's conviction that Othello was not a "veritable Negro" to Mary Preston's conclusion (in *Studies in Shakespeare*, 1869, p. 71) that "Othello *was* a *white* man!"

7. Whereas earlier critics of the play tended to ignore Othello's color or offer apologies for it, Othello's blackness has been thoroughly discussed in recent literary criticism, as the references in this chapter will illustrate. For instance, Jane Coles (ed.), *The Cambridge School Shakespeare: Othello* (Cambridge: Cambridge University Press, 1992), frankly raises the question for pupils: "Is *Othello* a racist play?" She points out that "Othello's main action in the play is to strangle a white woman. He is black" (p. 227).

8. See Jonathan Dollimore and Alan Sinfield (eds.), *Political Shakespeare: New Essays in Cultural Materialism* (London and Ithaca, N.Y.: Cornell University Press, 1985), pp. 2–17.

9. Lynda E. Boose, "'The Getting of a Lawful Race': Racial Discourse in Early Modern England and the Unrepresentable Black Woman," in Margo Hendricks and Patricia Parker (eds.), *Woman, "Race," and Writing in the Early Modern Period* (London and New York: Routledge, 1994), pp. 35–54, points out that "it was late in the century—well after Shakespeare wrote *Othello*—that black Africans were conceptually reduced in the popular imagination to commodified objects of trade" (p. 36).

10. His portrait, that of a shrewd, hawk-faced Arabic man, is reproduced in Norman Sanders (ed.), *Othello, New Cambridge Shakespeare* (Cambridge: Cambridge University Press, 1984), p. 12, and in Bernard Harris, "A Portrait of a Moor," *ShS*, 11 (1958): 89–97. Honigmann, dating the play to 1601–1602, thinks that Shakespeare would have encountered this ambassador when the King's Men performed at court and speculates that "this very face" may have "inspired the writing of his tragedy" (*Othello*, p. 4).

11. Letter from Rowland White (August 1600) to Sir Robert Sidney, quoted in Harris, "A Portrait of a Moor," p. 92.

12. Letter from John Chamberlain to Dudley Carleton (October 15, 1600), quoted in ibid., p. 94.

13. See Virginia Mason Vaughan, Othello: *A Contextual History* (Cambridge: Cambridge University Press, 1994), p. 58.

14. In "'Spanish Othello': The Making of Shakespeare's Moor," *ShS*, 35 (1982): 101–12, Barbara Everett argues that these were olive-skinned Spanish Moors and not Negroes (p. 104). But as Mythili Kaul points out in "Background: Black or Tawny? Stage Presentations of Othello from 1604 to the Present," in Mythili Kaul (ed.), Othello: *New Essays by Black Writers* (Washington, D.C.: Howard University Press, 1997), pp. 1–19, "Moor" often meant "blackamoor, or a person of black or very swarthy color" (p. 2).

15. In Paul L. Hughes and James F. Larkin (eds.), *Tudor Royal Proclamations* (New Haven, Conn.: Yale University Press, 1969), vol. 3, pp. 221–22.

16. See G. M. Matthews, "*Othello* and the Dignity of Man," in Arnold Kettle (ed.), *Shakespeare in a Changing World* (New York: International Publishers, 1964), p. 124; and Peter Erickson, "Representations of Blacks and Blackness in the Renaissance," *Criticism*, 35.4 (Fall 1993): 499–527, who points out that 1444 marks "the beginning of the Portuguese importation of African slaves to Europe," while black slaves reached the American mainland of Virginia only in 1619 (p. 500). Emily C. Bartels, "*Othello* and Africa: Postcolonialism Reconsidered," *WMQ*, 54.1 (January 1997): 45–64, cites evidence that "Africa was not, like the Americas, a crux of English expansion" in the late Renaissance (p. 57).

17. Camille Wells Slights, "Slaves and Subjects in *Othello*," *SQ*, 48 (Winter 1997): 377–90, quote at 382. Slights discusses how English culture at the time of *Othello* "simultaneously promoted and denied slavery" (p. 381).

18. See Eldred Jones, *Othello's Countrymen: The African in English Renaissance Drama* (London: Oxford University Press, 1965), pp. 1–26.

19. Anthony Gerard Barthlelemy, *Black Face, Maligned Race: The Representation of Blacks in English Drama from Shakespeare to Southerne* (Baton Rouge and London: Louisiana University Press, 1987), points out that the term "Moor" covered a "rather general category of alien"; it could refer to a black (Negro or Arab) or to a Muslim (pp. 6–7).

20. Jack D'Amico, *The Moor in English Renaissance Drama* (Tampa: University of South Florida Press, 1991), p. 36.

21. A. H. Bullen, *The Works of Thomas Middleton* (London: John C. Nimmo, 1886), vol. 7, pp. 247–48.

22. Ibid., p. 248.

23. Mentioned in Richard Eden's voyages, published in Richard Hakluyt's *Principal Navigations* (1589), and quoted in Jones, *Othello's Countrymen*, p. 11.

24. Leo Africanus, *The History and Description of Africa*, ed. Robert Brown, trans. John Pory (1600; London: Hakluyt Society, 1896), vol. 1, p. 180.

25. George Best, in Richard Hakluyt, *The Principal Navigations* (Glasgow: James Macehose and Sons, 1904), vol. 7, p. 264, cited at length in Vaughan, Othello: *A Contextual History*, p. 53. David Gillies, *Shakespeare and the Geography of Difference* (Cambridge: Cambridge University Press, 1994), also finds that the Renaissance concept of the Moor as "sexually polluting" informs *Othello* (p. 33).

26. Africanus, *The History and Description of Africa*, vol. 1, p. 180.

27. On the negative associations (moral and aesthetic) that "black" carries in Western culture, see Winthrop D. Jordan, *White over Black: American Attitudes towards the Negro, 1550–1812* (Chapel Hill: University of North Carolina Press, 1968), p. 7; Doris Adler, "The Rhetoric of 'Black' and 'White' in *Othello*," *SQ*, 25.2 (1974): 248–57; and Elliot H. Tokson, *The Popular Image of the Black Man in English Drama, 1550–1688* (Boston: G. K. Hall and Co., 1982), p. 7.

28. D'Amico, *The Moor in English Renaissance Drama*, discusses how the presentation of Eleazar both reinforces and complicates the stereotype of the Moor (pp. 106–19). See also Emily C. Bartels, "Making More of the Moor: Aaron, Othello, and Renaissance Refashionings of Race," *SQ*, 41 (1990): 433–54.

29. Richard Eden (in *Hakluyt's Voyages*, 1600) touches on miscegenation when he mentions an Ethiopian who took a "fair English woman to wife" and "begat a sonne . . . as blacke as the father was"; he rationalizes this dominant blackness as a "natural infection" of that man (quoted by Karen Newman, "'To Wash the Ethiop White': Femininity and the Monstrous in *Othello*," in *Fashioning Femininity and English Renaissance Drama* [Chicago and London: University of Chicago Press, 1991], p. 78).

30. See John Salway, "Veritable Negroes and Circumcised Dogs: Racial Disturbances in Shakespeare," in Lesley Aers and Nigel Wheale (eds.), *Shakespeare in the Changing Curriculum* (London and New York: Routledge, 1991), pp. 108–24, quote at p. 110.

31. Matthews, "*Othello* and the Dignity of Man," p. 133. See also Ruth Cowhig, "The Importance of Othello's Race," *JCL,* 12.2 (December 1977): 153–61.

32. G. K. Hunter, "*Othello* and Color Prejudice," in *Dramatic Identities and Cultural Tradition* (New York: Barnes and Noble, 1978), pp. 31–59, quote at p. 45.

33. Ibid., pp. 55–56.

34. Martin Orkin, "Othello and the Plain Face of Racism," *SQ,* 38.2 (1987): 166–88, quotes at 170 and 181.

35. K. W. Evans, "The Racial Factor in Othello," *ShStud,* 5 (1969): 124–39, finds that Othello behaves "like the traditional black Moor" throughout much of the second phase of the play. Arthur J. Little, Jr., "An Essence That's Not Seen: The Primal Scene of Racism in *Othello,*" *SQ,* 44 (1993): 304–24, comments on how Othello "becomes the literal embodiment of a metaphorical blackness" (p. 322).

36. Laurence Lerner, "The Machiavel and the Moor," *EIC,* 9.4 (October 1959): 339–60, quote at 358. More recently, several authors in Kaul (ed.), Othello: *New Essays by Black Writers* have found this to be the case: Jacquelyn Y. McLendon, "'A Round Unvarnished Tale': (Mis)Reading *Othello* or African American Strategies of Dissent," finds in the play "prevailing negative images of blackness" once Othello succumbs to jealousy (p. 124), while S. E. Ogude, "Literature and Racism: The Example of *Othello,*" considers that Othello is "preeminently a caricature of the black man" (p. 163).

37. D'Amico, *The Moor in English Renaissance Drama,* p. 196.

38. Ania Loomba, "Sexuality and Racial Difference," in *Gender, Race, and Renaissance Drama* (Manchester: Manchester University Press, 1989), pp. 38–64, uses this term (p. 52). Jyotsna Singh, "Othello's Identity, Postcolonial Theory, and Contemporary African Rewritings of *Othello,*" in Hendricks and Parker (eds.), *Women, "Race," and Writing,* pp. 287–99, points out how Othello reflects the "divided subjectivity" of the black man who "mimics" white society (p. 293). In "Othello's Alienation," *SEL,* 30 (1990): 315–33, Edward Berry also finds that Othello has no authentic self because he has internalized a "false dichotomy" between "exotic European" and "brutal savage" (p. 330).

39. Daniel J. Vitkus, "Turning Turk in *Othello:* The Conversion and Damnation of the Moor," *SQ,* 48.2 (Summer 1997): 145–76, contends that Othello "damns himself by killing the Turk he has become" (p. 176). Melvin Seiden, "The Wound and the Covenant," *Humanist,* 56 (July/August 1996): 28–30, also speculates that Othello finally recognizes himself as "pledged by inherited religion to Islam and not to the Christianity of white Europeans" (p. 29).

40. Anthony Gerard Barthelemy (ed.), "Introduction," *Critical Essays on Shakespeare's* Othello (New York: Macmillan, 1994), p. 2. Julie Hankey, "Introduction," Othello: *Plays in Performance* (Bristol: Bristol Classical Press, 1987), touches on the possibility, "uncomfortable to white liberal-minded audiences, that Shakespeare was pointing to something basically un-English in Othello's descent into murderous sexual jealousy" (p. 15).

41. Vaughan, Othello: *A Contextual History,* p. 70.

42. Discussed by Juliet Dusinberre, *Shakespeare and the Nature of Women* (London and Basingstoke: Macmillan, 1976), pp. 3–5.

43. "Historical Differences: Misogyny and *Othello,*" in Valerie Wayne (ed.), *The Matter of Difference: Materialist Criticism of Shakespeare* (Ithaca, N.Y.: Cornell University Press, 1991), p. 159. Mary Beth Rose, *The Expense of Spirit: Love and Sexuality in English*

Renaissance Drama (Ithaca, N.Y.: Cornell University Press, 1988), also points out how the Puritans, while arguing for "female equality" in sexual relations, continued to insist on "wifely obedience, silence, and subjection" (pp. 148–49).

44. Loomba, "Sexuality and Racial Difference," emphasizes that "Desdemona's desire is especially transgressive because its object is black" (p. 56).

45. See Dympna Callaghan, "Woman, Tragedy, and Transgression," in *Women and Gender in Renaissance Tragedy* (Atlantic Highlands, N.J.: Humanities Press International, 1989), pp. 47–97.

46. See Kenneth Burke, "*Othello:* An Essay to Illuminate a Method," *HudR,* 4 (Autumn 1951): 165–203, on how the "low" status of Emilia affects the reception of her speech (p. 185).

47. See Kenneth Muir, *Shakespeare's Sources I* (London: Methuen, 1957), pp. 122–27, 129–36, for an illuminating discussion of this story and how Shakespeare modifies it in *Othello.*

48. In Alvin Kernan (ed.), *Othello, The Signet Classic Shakespeare* (1963; New York: Penguin Books, 1986; 1998), p. 135. All quotations are taken from this translation of the tale from *Hecatommithi.*

49. Ibid., p. 136.

50. Ibid.

51. Ibid., p. 137.

52. Ibid., p. 138.

53. Ibid., p. 139.

54. Ibid., p. 135.

55. Ibid., p. 138.

56. Ibid., p. 142.

57. Ibid., p. 136.

58. Ibid., p. 138.

59. Max Bluestone, *From Story to Stage* (The Hague and Paris: Mouton, 1974), points out the "rich complexity" of the loss of the handkerchief in the play—in particular, how Shakespeare makes "Desdemona's good intentions rather than Iago's thievery operative in the moment of loss" (p. 20).

60. Kernan (ed.), *Othello,* translates "donna" as "wife" (p. 142); more usually the term is interpreted to mean a woman (a seamstress) living in Cassio's house.

61. Ibid., pp. 139, 140, 141, 142–43, 144.

62. Ibid., p. 136.

63. Ibid., p. 134.

64. Ibid., p. 146.

65. See Muir, *Shakespeare's Sources,* vol. 1, p. 123.

66. See Sanders (ed.), *Othello,* p. 3.

67. See Geoffrey Bullough (ed.), *Narrative and Dramatic Sources of Shakespeare* (London: Routledge, 1973), vol. 2, p. 204.

68. For arguments against this, see Richard Levin, "The Indian/Judean Crux in *Othello,*" *SQ,* 33 (1982): 65–67.

69. See Lois Whitney, "Did Shakespeare Know Leo Africanus?", *PMLA,* 37 (1922): 470–88. Rosalind Johnson, "African Presence in Shakespearean Drama: Parallels between Othello and the Historical Leo Africanus," *Journal of African Civilizations,* 7 (1985): 276–87, points out similarities between Leo's adventures (as described in his preface) and those of Othello.

70. Africanus, *History and Description of Africa,* vol. 1, p. 20.

71. Ibid., vol. 1, p. 183.

72. See Bullough, *Narrative and Dramatic Sources,* vol. 2, p. 210.

73. Ibid., p. 211; and Muir, *Shakespeare's Sources,* vol. 1, p. 127.

74. See Muir, *Shakespeare's Sources,* vol. 1, pp. 128–29.

75. See Jones, "*Othello, Lepanto,* and the Cyprus Wars," p. 51.

76. Bullough, *Narrative and Dramatic Sources,* vol. 2, p. 213.

77. This and other parallels to Othoman in Knolles's narrative are outlined by F. N. Lees, "Othello's Name," *N&Q,* 211 (April 1961): 139–41.

3

DRAMATIC STRUCTURE

THE TWO SETTINGS: VENICE AND CYPRUS

Othello is not built on the cosmic scale of Shakespeare's other major tragedies.[1] It has neither the supernatural dimensions of *Hamlet* and *Macbeth,* with their Ghost and Witches, nor *King Lear*'s insistent questioning of "Nature" and the gods; yet it is the only one of the four plays to offer two separate countries as locations. After Act 1, the action of the play moves from the highly civilized world of Renaissance Venice to the island of Cyprus. Venice is home to all of the characters except Cassio, who comes from Florence (1. 1. 17), and Othello, the mercenary soldier who has lived in Venice for only the past nine months. Cyprus, unfamiliar to the Venetian city dwellers, is a more threatening milieu. Geographically, it was a military outpost on the edge of the Christian world, controlled by the Turks after 1570; symbolically, it represents a liminal area where apparently secure values may be challenged or overthrown. Whereas *Antony and Cleopatra* oscillates between Rome and Egypt, constantly modifying the audience's perceptions of each society, *Othello*'s action remains on the island of Cyprus after the first act. Venice and Cyprus are divided by the ocean, and the sea storm that opens Act 2 severs crucial links with the city and foreshadows the violent personal upheavals that erupt on the island.

For the Elizabethan-Jacobean audience, the image of Venice was multifaceted.[2] As depicted in Shakespeare's *The Merchant of Venice,* the city was a thriving Mediterannean seaport, a hub of commerce in sixteenth-century Europe. To protect its shipping routes with the East, Venice built up a strong military force (its Arsenal was noteworthy)[3] and maintained garrisons, such as Cyprus, throughout the Mediterranean.[4] The military side of Venice's trading empire features prominently in *Othello,* as does Venice's reputation as a free state, a commonwealth with an impressive judicial system and government. The sixteenth-century translator Lewis Lewkenor praises the "pure and uncorrupted" justice of the noble city.[5] Indeed, in

Act 1, scene 3, the Senate (Signiory) maintains its objectivity by giving both parties, the aggrieved Brabantio and the accused Othello, a fair hearing.[6] The Duke has already shown "judgment" in determining that the Turkish fleet is headed for Cyprus, and now he wisely refuses to accept at face value Brabantio's assertion that Othello has used witchcraft: "To vouch this is no proof" (106). In the final scene, Lodovico restores the Venetian sense of measured judgment by proposing to keep Othello prisoner until his "fault" is made "known / To the Venetian state" (5. 2. 332–33). Then, after Othello's suicide, he rapidly reestablishes social order in Cyprus.

Rich in art and architecture, Venice represented the glory of Renaissance Italy. With splendor, however, came the possibility of decadence, and Italy was fascinating to the English because of its dualities. On the one hand, it had produced *The Courtier* (1528; translated into English by Sir Thomas Hoby in 1561), Baldassare Castiglione's testament to the importance of orderly, decorous behavior. At the other extreme was Niccolò Machiavelli's *The Prince* (1514), recommending that the effective leader combine the traits of the strong lion with those of the wily fox. In a debased version of this political creed, the Machiavellian villain of Elizabethan drama sprang into life as a monster of deviousness, skilled in the art of poisoning. If Michael Cassio's "courtesy" owes something to Castiglione, Iago's tactics are those of the deceitful Machiavel. As part of his strategy, he exploits the image of an oversophisticated, morally decadent Venice when he glibly labels Desdemona a "supersubtle Venetian" (1. 3. 352). The city was indeed renowned for prostitutes. In his travelogue *Coryat's Crudities* (1611), Thomas Coryat estimated that there were between 10,000 and 20,000 courtesans in Venice—almost certainly an exaggeration, but the number was very high.[7] Iago draws on this darker side of Venice's reputation by telling Othello that

> In Venice they do let heaven see the pranks
> They dare not show their husbands.   (3. 3. 202–3)

Once his faith is poisoned, Othello translates Desdemona into a "cunning whore of Venice" (4. 2. 87). While on one level Venice represents the ideal city, or what Alvin Kernan terms "the ageless image of government, of reason, of law, and of social concord,"[8] it can also be perceived as ripe for subversion: an overcivilized society, prone to insularity, that carries the seeds of destruction.

Cyprus is the perfect setting for this undermining. As a "frontier between barbarism and *The City*,"[9] it is physically more vulnerable to Turkish invasion than is Venice. Once the actual Turks have been drowned in the storm, Iago carries on the battle between infidel and Christian on a psychological level;[10] by attacking Othello's faith in Desdemona, he destroys Othello as a moral human being. The play's protagonists are especially vulnerable to Iago's attack because they are enclosed in a "wild" setting where the "people's hearts" are still "brimful of fear," as Othello emphasizes when he denounces the brawl between Cassio and Montano (2. 3. 213). Michael Neill comments on how well the "cramping confines of a besieged citadel" lend themselves to the "vicious psychological circumscription"[11] engineered by Iago.

Although Cyprus is a fortified military garrison, the island was also renowned as the seat of Venus, goddess of love. According to Greek legend, Aphrodite was born in the ocean foam and then wafted ashore at Cyprus, so that her rites were established on the island.[12] It is ironic, then, that in *Othello* the "war-world" so completely "invades the love-world."[13] Part of the tragedy is the way that the military ethic of swift decision and absolute honor supersedes a more lengthy, complex, and compassionate judgment. Such an evaluation might have been made in peaceful, civil Venice. But Othello's marriage is never consummated there, only on the "warlike isle" (2. 1. 43). As an esteemed warrior, Othello competently takes charge of Cyprus and establishes social order; as a lover and husband, he is vulnerable to the subtle tactics of the Venetian Iago.

LINEAR PLOT AND DOUBLE-TIME SCHEME

A. C. Bradley finds *Othello* the most "masterly" of Shakespeare's tragedies in its construction.[14] There are virtually no delaying tactics to slow down the action, as in *Hamlet* where the hero defers revenge, and no subplot to ramify the complications, as happens in *King Lear.* Acts 2–5, set in Cyprus, form a continuous sequence. While there are some variations in pace—the slower tempo of the willow scene (4. 3), where Desdemona and Emilia take stock of the situation, balances the low-key sequence in Act 2, scene 1, where Iago exercises his wit before the climactic arrival of Othello in Cyprus—the momentum in these four acts develops steadily to fulfill Iago's adage "Dull not device by coldness and delay" (2. 3. 388).

Although *Othello*'s dramatic narrative builds convincingly, critics have noted certain inconsistencies in the play's time sequence. John Wilson, writing in *Blackwood's Magazine* (1849–1850) under the pseudonym Christopher North, was the first to develop a theory of double time to account for these apparent contradictions: a "short" time in which Desdemona is murdered on her second night in Cyprus, and a "long" time scheme in which weeks or even months might have passed on the island before the murder takes place. The first two acts pose no problem. The duration of events in Act 1 is close to stage time, with the rousing of Brabantio, his confrontation with Othello in the street, and Othello's defense in the council chamber all happening in quick succession. Othello and his entourage leave for Cyprus that "very night." Act 2 covers the second half of a single day: following the Venetians' arrival, the Herald announces, at five o'clock in the afternoon, that the populace is free to celebrate the demise of the Turks and Othello's "nuptial" (2. 2. 7); then the scene where Cassio is cashiered begins late in the evening (Iago informs us "'tis not yet ten o'th'clock" [2. 3. 13–14]) and takes the audience through most of that night.

Early the next morning, Cassio arranges to visit Desdemona (3. 1), and at the beginning of Act 3, scene 3, she offers to intercede for him. This long scene builds slowly as Iago first provokes suspicion within Othello and then, during the second phase (330–476), works him into a crescendo of vowed revenge, in which he asks Iago to kill Cassio within "these three days" (469). Sandwiched between their two encounters is the short conversation between Desdemona and Othello (278–88) and the sequence where Desdemona drops her handkerchief, Emilia picks it up, and Iago takes possession of it. Possibly there is a break in time between the end of Act 3, scene 3 and the beginning of Act 3, scene 4, where Desdemona converses briefly with the Clown and then with Emilia about her loss of the handkerchief.[15] But unless the director chooses to place an interval here, the audience will assume that Desdemona, Emilia, and the Clown enter the stage immediately after Othello and Iago have solemnly left it.

Likewise, because Act 4 starts up in midconversation ("Will you think so?"), Othello and Iago seem to be picking up the threads of their urgent conversation from the last scene but one (3. 3). When Bianca fortuitously arrives at the end of the eavesdropping sequence (4. 1. 145), angrily confronting Cassio with the hand-kerchief, she refers to it as "that same handkerchief you gave me even now" (149–50), thus establishing a strong continuity between this scene and the end of Act 3, scene 4, where Cassio gives her the token and asks her to copy its design. In Act 3, scene 3, line 279, Desdemona calls Othello in for "dinner" (the midday meal) with the islanders, while at Act 4, scene 1, line 262, Othello invites the embassy from Vienna to "sup" with him. The ensuing brothel scene, where Othello insults Desdemona as a prostitute, ends at "high supper time" (4. 2. 242). The meal has presumably taken place by the beginning of the third scene in Act 4, when Othello instructs Desdemona, "Get you to bed on th' instant" (7). These unobtrusive time pointers, plus the increasing dramatic tension, encourage the audience to view the events of Acts 3 and 4 as all happening within the space of one day.

Act 5 opens with Iago advising Roderigo how to kill Cassio in the dark street. We assume it is now late the same night, as Iago tells Roderigo, when they part at the end of Act 4, scene 2, that he will "fashion" Cassio's visit to Bianca "to fall out between twelve and one" (236). Othello hears Cassio being wounded and, soon afterward, strangles Desdemona. The denouement, we conclude, occurs about twenty-six hours after the consummation of the nuptials and less than thirty-six hours after Desdemona and Othello first reach Cyprus. This is "short" time indeed!

Nevertheless, some references in the text may indicate that the action of *Othello* covers a longer time span.[16] Othello meditates on Desdemona's "stol'n hours of lust" (3. 3. 335) and, justifying his killing of her to Emilia, remarks that his wife has committed the "act of shame" a "thousand times" with Cassio (5. 2. 208–9). How could this be possible? Calculating on short time, we quickly realize that Desdemona has had no opportunity to become intimate with Cassio after they arrive at Cyprus. Nor, since they traveled on separate ships, could they have slept together on the voyage from Venice. Iago's recounting of Cassio's "dream" about Desdemona, prefaced by "I lay with Cassio lately" (3. 3. 410), also suggests a longer time span than that afforded by a single night on Cyprus. And Bianca's chiding accusation to Cassio, "What, keep a week away? Seven days and nights?" (3. 4. 172), presupposes a relatively long-term relationship with him, as does Cassio's jesting allusion to her embarrassing public show of affection toward him "the other day" on the quayside (4. 1. 134). Chronologically, too, it is impossible for Lodovico and the messengers from Venice to arrive in Act 4, scene 1—barely one day after the storm that has destroyed the Turkish fleet—already bringing instructions for Othello to return home!

Bradley finds it difficult to account for the "extraordinary contradiction"[17] in time schemes, while Ned B. Allen conjectures that the references to long time, mainly in Acts 3–5, are the result of Shakespeare's following Giraldi Cinthio's slow-paced narrative more closely there than he does in Acts 1 and 2.[18] Contending that "double time" is an ingenious device to enhance the credibility of the action, M. R. Ridley praises Shakespeare's "astonishing skill"[19] in juxtaposing allusions to long time with a strong impression of a thirty-three-hour time span on Cyprus. It is, he thinks, a means of lulling the audience into thinking that more time has passed than the action warrants, so that they do not question why, logically, Othello would be murdering his wife for her supposed adultery the very night after he has consummated their marriage.

Other critics have disputed the whole theory of double time or have regarded it as a nonissue. Emrys Jones sensibly notes that Shakespeare's "prime concern is not duration but continuity."[20] Brusquely dismissing double-time theory as "nonsense," Graham Bradshaw argues that "short" time is adequate to explain the apparent discrepancies that have bothered readers of *Othello*.[21] Bianca's complaint that Cassio has been absent for a whole week makes sense if we assume that she knew him in Venice and has traveled over to Cyprus as a camp follower. Even Iago's early description of the bachelor Cassio as "almost damned in a fair wife" (1. 1. 18), which most editors assume to be carelessness on Shakespeare's part, could refer to Bianca's determination to marry her lover; Cassio, in Iago's view, has "almost" been trapped into marriage with her. And if we postulate that Desdemona's "stol'n hours" of lust took place in Venice—not *after* the marriage, but during the courtship when Cassio acted as a go-between—then Othello's assumptions need not be ruled chronologically absurd. But this last hypothesis lessens the immediacy of Othello's humiliation.[22] Also, if Othello has just consummated his nuptials, would he not be reassured that his wife was a virgin when she married him?

Speculation along these lines tends to become slightly absurd and inconclusive,[23] going too far beyond what the play offers for our inspection. In any case, spectators in the theater are less concerned with temporal discrepancies than is the leisurely reader in her study. Iago's observation at the end of Act 2 that "Pleasure and action make the hours seem short" (2. 3. 379) provides an apt comment on how the audience, caught up in the momentum of events, responds to the accelerating pace of the drama. Another reason for our accepting "short" time is that Shakespeare presents Othello as a man with an irrational obsession. Once Iago has sown the seed, Othello's hyperactive imagination needs little stimulation before it burgeons into the vision of not only Cassio but possibly "pioners and all" enjoying Desdemona's body. On a practical level, this is virtually impossible (what opportunity has Desdemona had to become promiscuous?); yet psychologically,

Othello's ignoring of chronological considerations is perfectly plausible. In Shakespeare's *The Winter's Tale,* Leontes makes a further leap when he is convinced that the child his wife is carrying (almost at full term) was conceived by his friend Polixenes, who has been in Bohemia just nine months. His obsessive jealousy, like that of Othello, is not bound by considerations of time and probability.

The occasional tendency to treat the play as a detective story, or a realistic novel in which details of time and place are paramount, has spawned another question related to plot: is the marriage between Othello and Desdemona ever actually consummated? Certainly it appears that the couple, rushed off on the military expedition, postpone their wedding "rites" until Cyprus. Othello's words as he leads off his bride, "The purchase made, the fruits are to ensue" (2. 3. 9), strongly imply that the marriage has not yet been consummated. Granted, the drunken quarrel then develops fairly quickly (in stage time), and Othello is summoned to the scene by the "dreadful bell"; still, his words as he returns to bed with Desdemona—"'tis the soldiers' life / To have their balmy slumbers waked with strife" (256–57)—offer no indication of interrupted coitus. Given the play's focus on how quickly the "monster" of jealousy works its mischief, it seems needlessly strained to attribute Othello's cruelty to "frustrated desire."[24] Such a reading also risks turning him into the ludicrous figure of the elderly, impotent husband. To argue that "the murder is indeed this marriage's only consummation"[25] adds a maudlin twist that is not convincingly supported by the text.

DOMESTIC TRAGEDY AND THE INVERSION OF ROMANCE

Othello enacts the downfall of a man who is beyond the ordinary, and the play culminates in his death; unquestionably, it is a tragedy. The tragic categories that Aristotle outlines in his *Poetics* would not have been binding for Jacobean playwrights—they read the *Poetics* filtered through the moralizing of Italian commentators[26]—but the play does, in fact, conform to Aristotle's criteria for tragedy. Othello's error (hamartia) is to believe Iago and murder Desdemona on the assumption that she is unfaithful; the plot reversal (peripeteia) and Othello's recognition of what he has done (anagnorisis) occur swiftly once Iago's villainy is unmasked. Aristotle's comments on the purging (catharsis) of pity and fear in the audience are more open to interpretation.[27] But most readers or spectators would agree that the events of the play are likely to produce in the audience the emotions of pity—because a potentially great man has murdered an innocent woman and destroyed himself—and fear that the cosmos allows such evil creatures as Iago to wreak their havoc.

Shakespeare's play is partly modeled on Renaissance revenge tragedy. In this genre, the murderous intrigue is precipitated by jealousy (as in John Ford's *'Tis Pity She's a Whore* [c. 1625]) or by the need to avenge the killing of a blood relative or loved one (the pattern of *Hamlet* [1601] and *The Revenger's Tragedy* [1606]). Whereas most revenge tragedies are set in the Italian court or in an aristocratic milieu, *Othello* more closely follows the pattern of domestic tragedy. It is true that neither Othello nor Desdemona belongs to the middle class often associated with this genre—the African Othello claims ancestors of "royal" status (1. 2. 21), while Desdemona is the daughter of a magnifico—but from the second act on, the couple is presented within a domestic context. Despite being courted by the "wealthy, curlèd darlings" of her city, Desdemona must attend to the "house affairs" when Othello visits Brabantio in Venice (1. 2. 67; 1. 3. 146). Once married, she promises to plead Cassio's cause by nagging her husband until his "bed shall seem a school, his board a shrift" (3. 3. 24). Again, she finds a strong voice through homely analogies when she assures Othello

> Why, this is not a boon;
> 'Tis as I should entreat you wear your gloves,
> Or feed on nourishing dishes, or keep you warm.   (76–78)

In the Senate scene, Othello is so confident that the pleasures of marriage will never "taint" the important "business" of being a soldier that he offers to "Let housewives make a skillet of [his] helm" if the god of love ever unmans him (1. 3. 267). Ironically, once he becomes a husband obsessed with his wife's alleged infidelity, he can no longer pursue the role of warrior that has been central to his existence. Declaring "Othello's occupation's gone!" (3. 3. 354), he voluntarily renounces his military profession in favor of domestic revenge.

Iago and Emilia, lower in social status, provide a second husband-and-wife team in the play. The misogynistic Iago taunts women as "Players in your housewifery, and housewives in your beds," as spendthrift domestically as they are niggardly in their sexual favors (2. 1. 111). To him Emilia is no more than a "common thing," promiscuous in her appetites and a "foolish wife" (3. 3. 300–302). Just as Othello destroys his wife for supposed infidelity, so Iago is suspicious of Emilia and tries to silence her by stabbing her to death; unlike Desdemona, though, Emilia finally refuses to play the role of subservient spouse, protesting " 'Tis proper I obey him, but not now" (5. 2. 193). In the closing tableau of this domestic tragedy, the bodies of two murdered wives and of one husband are displayed on the bed—an emblem of conjugal union now transformed into a bier.

Initially, the handkerchief that features so prominently in the plot of *Othello* may strike the audience as material for "*comic* misunderstanding,"[28] the stuff of citizen comedy rather than tragedy. Yet Shakespeare contrives to make the accident of Desdemona's dropping it a fatal link in the play's causation and also endows it, through Othello's discussion of its "magic," with talismanic, almost "fate-guided" properties.[29] Writing in the late seventeenth century, Thomas Rymer ignored the complex role of the handkerchief when he scoffed that the play has a clear moral: to teach all "good wives" to "look well to their linen."[30] Nevertheless, Rymer's comment draws attention to what Rosalie L. Colie calls the playwright's technical difficulties in making the "domestic problems of love"[31] sufficiently serious as tragedy.

One of these potential difficulties is that many of the play's characters share affinities with comic "types" from the Roman plays of Terence and Plautus, which in turn found their way into contemporary Italian learned comedy[32] and commedia dell'arte.[33] Brabantio resembles the *senex iratus* or pantalone in the commedia, who opposes the lovers, while Iago, called "slave" in the denouement (5. 2. 288), is one of the *zanni,* or the wily servant (*servus callidus*) constantly improvising to trick his master. Most importantly, Othello comes uncomfortably close to the "gull of comic tradition"[34]—a combination of the *miles gloriosus* or braggart soldier[35] ("bragging" and telling "fantastical lies," according to Iago [2. 1. 221–22]) and the absurdly jealous husband. With his diseased imagination and extravagant behavior, the Othello of Acts 3 and 4 parallels the husbands of comic tradition who fear they have been cuckolded, such as Ford in *Merry Wives of Windsor* (c. 1600) or Thorello (almost an anagram of Othello) in Ben Jonson's first version of *Everyman in His Humor* (1598). Emilia, reviling Othello as "O gull! O dolt!" in the final scene (5. 2. 160), finds her master criminally foolish. Through another analogue, the underlying structure of the play has been interpreted as a charivari, or "carnivalesque derangement of marriage," in which Iago acts as "erotic nemesis" to the grotesque bridegroom Othello.[36] Only our awareness that Othello is being entrapped by the malevolent Iago and the sheer scope of his anguish prevent a sequence such as the eavesdropping interlude in Act 4, scene 1 (where Othello assumes that Cassio and Iago are crudely discussing Desdemona when they are actually speaking of Bianca) from coming off as farce. Shakespeare daringly draws on these comic conventions, not to undercut his hero, but to increase the "tragic impact"[37] when potentially absurd characters become brutal and domestic misunderstandings inexorably turn disastrous.

Enhancing the tragic irony is another key feature: the play's structural inversion of romantic comedy. The conclusion of Act 1 seems to promise a resolution to family difficulties the lovers have encountered; Brabantio, the blocking father, cannot stop their marriage, and the only impediment to social and domestic happiness is the Turkish fleet bearing down on Cyprus. Once the storm has destroyed this fleet and Othello's ship comes safe to harbor (2. 1), it might seem that the "heavens," or comic providence, will allow the "loves and comforts" of Desdemona and Othello to "increase" in a successful union (191–92). But Othello's welcoming speech to his wife marks the high point of his "absolute" contentment. Iago counterpoints the couple's kiss with his resolve to "set down the pegs that make this music" (198), modulating the action into a tragic key with his malicious resolve to humiliate his master and bring him out of tune.[38] From this point in Act 2, Shakespeare explores the fatal consequences of a possessive passion,[39] not the comic values of forgiveness and tolerance.[40] Whereas the action in *A Midsummer Night's Dream* and *As You Like It* moves from the inflexible court to the energizing "green world,"[41] *Othello* shifts from the civil world of Venice to "warlike" Cyprus, where Iago can work his destructive mischief.

Othello is also the only Shakespearean play in which the slandered woman, falsely accused of infidelity, is murdered. In *Much Ado about Nothing,* Claudio leaves his fiancée, Hero, for dead at the altar, but she is restored to him once her name is cleared and he is penitent.[42] And in the romances *Cymbeline* and *The Win-*

ter's Tale, which explore the healing of fractured families, wives are reconciled with their husbands by the end of the play. In contrast, *Othello* carries to an ultimate, tragic conclusion its hero's insight into how any breach of his love for Desdemona will have terrifying, apocalyptic consequences:

> Perdition catch my soul
> But I do love thee! And when I love thee not,
> Chaos is come again.   (3. 3. 90–92)

THE SCHEMATIC MORALITY PLAY

In the 1950s, it was usual to stress the religious framework of *Othello,* even to interpret the play as a Christian allegory. Secular audiences may now be liable to go to the opposite extreme, bypassing this dimension altogether or paying little attention to it. Since the play is indeed steeped in Christian symbolism—heaven and hell, angels and devils—it is important to recognize how morality play underpinnings extend the tragedy's significance. That Christian iconography is part of the play's basic texture (and more than a subdued metaphor for the Renaissance audience) is underscored by a remark Gratiano makes near the end, on how the murder of Desdemona would have made her father "desperate" had he lived to hear of it. Such a horrible outcome, says Gratiano, would have led Brabantio to "curse his better angel from his side, / And fall to reprobation" (5. 2. 204–6). And it is surely significant that the words "devil" and "devils" occur twenty-two times in *Othello,* whereas *Hamlet* and *Macbeth,* two other Shakespearean tragedies that are full of Christian imagery, contain only eight and seven instances, respectively.[43] Iago is the main source of the devil references; he often associates himself with hell and devils (as in 1. 2. 394 and 2. 3. 350–52) and is viewed as "demi-devil" by the end of the play (5. 2. 297). Under his influence, Othello takes slanderous report for truth and confuses fair with foul, mistaking Desdemona for a "devil" by the end of Act 3.

The devil figure, or Vice, vying against the forces of good to ensnare the soul of Everyman: this is the conflict that characterizes the morality play. Elizabethan-Jacobean tragedies are firmly rooted in this late medieval, early Tudor dramatic form; Christopher Marlowe's *Doctor Faustus* (c. 1589), for instance, retains Good and Bad Angels who offer conflicting advice to the scholar-hero (1. 1. 69–76).[44] Within this schema, Iago closely resembles the Vice figure of the late moralities,[45] a comic deceiver who tries to lure the Mankind figure (here Othello) into evil. Desdemona, referred to as "blessed" (2. 1. 250) and "heavenly true" (5. 2. 134), and calling on "every spirit sanctified" (3. 4. 126), represents the forces of good in the *Othello* world. At the opening of the play, Othello's "free" disposition (1. 3. 390) perfectly matches her goodness and generous nature; she is literally his "soul's joy" (2. 1. 182). The hero, as the Duke observes, is morally "far more fair than black" (1. 3. 285). Yet this human being, susceptible to both good and evil, falls into "perdition" (3. 3. 90) once he is ensnared by the devilish Iago. Casting aside his saving love for Desdemona means trading Christian virtue—"All seals and symbols of redeemèd sin" (2. 3. 344), as Iago puts it—for "chaos" (3. 3. 92).

Act 3, scene 3, where Iago first plants suspicion in Othello, is often called the "temptation scene." The second half especially gains resonance as a battle between good and evil, salvation and damnation. Torn between doubt and faith, Othello takes Iago by the throat to impress on him the high stakes for both of them: by the "worth of [Othello's] eternal soul," Iago can "nothing . . . to damnation add / Greater" than slandering Desdemona and tormenting Othello (3. 3. 358, 369–70). Earlier, Iago explained to the audience that when "devils will the blackest sins put on, / They do suggest at first with heavenly shows" (2. 3. 351–52). Now, angling for Othello's soul, he convinces his master that he is "honest" by allying himself with the forces of good: "O grace! O heaven forgive me!" (3. 3. 370). As soon as Iago eliminates Othello's remaining doubts with flimsy circumstantial evidence, Othello is prepared to "damn" both Desdemona and himself. Othello's vow of revenge, backed by Iago's "Witness, you ever-burning lights above" (460), contains a terrible irony: while addressing "yond marble heaven" (457), Othello is actually consigning himself to hell, since that is where "black vengeance" (444) inevitably leads.[46]

Othello's choice of damnation over salvation here is an ironic twist on the morality play's usual comic outcome. As René E. Fortin comments, the tragedy provides a "remarkable inversion" of the usual patten of moral allegory, so that instead of progressing from evil to repentance and contrition, Othello becomes "identified with the Tempter and . . . kills Desdemona, the Good Angel-Mercy figure who would redeem him."[47] Throughout his "pilgrimage" (1. 3. 152), Othello continually foregrounds the morality play pattern by vividly dramatizing his own situation in terms of eternal realities. Not only does he address Emilia as the madam of a brothel when he visits her in Act 4, scene 2; he also envisages her as keeper of the gates of hell. Encouraging Desdemona to play the role of fair deceiver, so angelically beautiful that devils in hell may "fear to seize" her (36), he histrionically invites her to double damn herself by swearing that she is chaste. Othello's reversal of perception in this brothel scenario is completed when he tells his wife, "Heaven truly knows that thou art false as hell" (38).

In having adopted Christianity, Othello counteracts the stereotype of the Muhammadan Moor. Indeed, as a Christian, he seems particularly preoccupied with the afterlife. Because he is reluctant to "kill" Desdemona's immortal soul, he at first urges her to pray before she dies (5. 2. 32) and later accepts that he will be "damned beneath all depth in hell" if he has murdered her without just cause (136). Realizing too late that she is innocent, he fears that when husband and wife meet at Judgment Day ("compt"), Desdemona's chaste expression, her angelic look, "will hurl [his] soul from heaven, / And fiends will snatch at it" (270–72); he even begs the devils to "whip" him "From possession of this heavenly sight" to ensure his utter damnation (274–75). Other characters, too, contemplate the state of their souls. Cassio's Calvinist musing that "there be souls must be saved, and there be souls must not be saved" (2. 3. 100–101), which culminates in his hope to be one of the elect, is picked up in Emilia's dying wish, after unmasking Iago: "So come my soul to bliss as I speak true" (5. 2. 247). Earlier, Emilia provided some middle ground in a world of moral absolutes when she speculated, "who would not make her husband a cuckold to make him a monarch? I should venture purgatory for't" (4. 3. 77–79). But there is no question about the fate of the demi-devil Iago. Roderigo delivers his epitaph with "damned Iago! O inhuman dog!" (5. 1. 62).

Echoing Othello's deep concern at the end of the play with his spiritual state, earlier critics have speculated on whether or not the hero of this tragedy is damned. In a recent new historicist reading, Daniel J. Vitkus finds Othello "'doubly damned' for backsliding" because he reverts from Christianity to his Islamic roots.[48] It is a mistake, however, to try to judge the play or its characters by theological criteria. Suicide, a sin of despair according to Christian doctrine, is treated as a fitting conclusion to Shakespeare's other tragedies of love, *Romeo and Juliet* and *Antony and Cleopatra,* and here it is part of Othello's self-administered justice. Tragedy does not invite us to ponder the protagonist's afterlife, or whether Othello might receive divine punishment or forgiveness. To decide that Othello will "roast . . . in sulphur" is as inappropriate as wondering whether flights of angels are actually singing Hamlet to his eternal rest at the end of his tragedy. To be sure, feeling damned forever adds to Othello's conviction of total loss; audiences, though, whether Christian or otherwise, must suspend belief in Judgment Day if they are fully to experience the tragic waste of the catastrophe. As Robert H. West comments, *Othello* is no "stamped and certified *exemplum* of Christian sin and punishment."[49] While the morality play substructure is an integral part of the play's form and meaning, alerting us to the eschatological myth underlying this domestic tragedy, Shakespeare's naturalistic treatment of character and situation goes well beyond abstract schemes or symbols. *Othello* succeeds as a complex, realistically conceived drama, played out by multifaceted characters who cannot be explained simply as representations of Vice, Virtue, or Everyman.

CHARACTER GROUPINGS AND COUNTERPOINTS

One of the delights of reading or watching Shakespeare's plays is becoming aware of a complex web of correspondences involving the characters, their language, and their situations. The forward momentum of the linear plot is artfully counterpointed by reiterated images and characters in changing combinations— echoings and visual groupings that create a dynamic spatial design. In *Othello,* the interplay of characters is particularly close. The affair between Cassio and Bianca, for instance, hardly counts as a separate subplot because it is fully integrated with the main action, contributing to and modifying our impressions of other male-female relationships in the play.

Repetition, with variation, of certain character clusters and stage formations knits the action together more tightly. This dramatic "rhyming"[50] often generates ironic parallels, as when Iago, kneeling with Othello to swear a vow of revenge by the "ever-burning lights" (3. 3. 460), is mirrored by Desdemona on her knees as a suppliant to Iago, swearing her love for Othello "by this light of heaven" (4. 2. 149). The crucial "temptation scene" (3. 3) is flanked by two visits from Cassio to Desdemona, whose ability to intercede for him is fatally undermined in the interim, so that in their second scene it is ironically she, even more than Cassio, who now stands in the "blank of [Othello's] displeasure" (3. 4. 128). Bianca's rage when she returns the handkerchief to Cassio as "some minx's token" (4. 1. 153) is a mirror image of Othello's obsessive "Fetch me the handkerchief!" when he challenges Desdemona in Act 3 (4. 90). Othello's perverted "cause" of punishing Desdemona in Act 5 matches Brabantio's determination ("Mine's not an idle cause" [1. 2. 94]) to bring Othello to justice at the beginning of the play.[51] Even the report of Roderigo's speaking "After long seeming dead" (5. 2. 324) becomes a maudlin twist on Desdemona's revival to "speak again" twenty-eight lines after she has been smothered. Unlike Roderigo, who insists that "Iago hurt him, / Iago set him on" (324–25), Desdemona altruistically protects her killer with the words "Nobody—I myself" (123). Instances could be multiplied; these are only some of the chiming situations that build up the intricate pattern of *Othello*.

Characters are sometimes paired as foils (contrasts to) or mirrorings[52] of each other in the thematic development of the play. We are invited to contrast the refined Cassio with the practical soldier Iago, who maintains a blunt, apparently "honest" exterior, but whose Machiavellian strategy in Act 2, scene 3 undoes the "thrice-gentle" Cassio (3. 4. 122). With his low tolerance for alcohol, Cassio perceives wine as a "devil"; the devilish Iago is more willing to accept wine as a "good familiar creature" (2. 3. 308–9). When Desdemona defends Cassio as a man "That errs in ignorance, and not in cunning" (3. 3. 49), she points to a parallel between Othello and his lieutenant and a contrast with Iago. Desdemona herself, "heavenly true," manifests idealism in marriage, while Emilia, the tough-minded realist, is prepared to compromise, justifying women's "galls" as appropriate retaliation for men's mistreatment of them (4. 3. 95). The helpless old father, Brabantio, at first seems the antithesis of the successful warrior and lover, Othello, but they are ultimately linked through their disillusionment in Desdemona and their conviction that she is deceitful.[53] Othello and Iago, who begin by representing such opposed views of life (romantic idealism set against reductive cynicism) and contrasting character traits (generous openness contrasting with mean-spirited hypocrisy), converge as Othello takes over both Iago's destructively negative viewpoint and his habit of seeing the act of love in coarse, bestial terms.

More often than twosomes, we perceive characters in groups of three.[54] Two Gentlemen are joined by a third to report on the storm (2. 1), and the eavesdropping sequence (4. 1) juxtaposes three characters—Cassio and Iago conversing on the main stage, with Othello as a concealed onlooker. (Even the fatal handkerchief puts in three appearances: when it is transferred from Desdemona to Iago via Emilia [3. 3], when Cassio gives it to Bianca [3. 4], and when she returns it to him [4. 1].) The play's major triangle, of course, is Iago-Othello-Desdemona, in which evil Iago successfully undermines the bond between husband and wife by winning Othello's trust and, in a sense, substituting for the good Desdemona in Othello's affections.

As well as exemplifying this morality play pattern, the three can be seen locked in what Kenneth Burke calls a "tragic trinity of ownership," representing the "principles of possession, possessor and estrangement,"[55] as Othello futilely tries to take absolute possession of another human being. We apprehend their triangle as part of an abstract design, the play of ideas in *Othello*. For although Iago, Othello, and Desdemona appear together as part of a larger ensemble in five scenes (1. 3, 2. 1, 2. 3, 3. 3, and 4. 1), they never interact together physically as a threesome onstage. In Act 1, scene 3, for instance, Iago brings Desdemona into the Senate meeting but remains a spectator while she publicly offers a defense of her marriage to match Othello's. In fact, it is Iago and Othello, not Desdemona and Othello, who communicate most in private, in the two long sequences of the temptation scene (3. 3) and in Act 4, scene 1. Ironically, Desdemona and Othello are truly alone together onstage only in the scene where he murders her (5. 2). Creating another threesome, Emilia accompanies them during their two conversations in Act 3, scene 3 and when Othello challenges his wife over the missing handkerchief in the very next scene. And although Othello dismisses Emilia in Act 4, scene 2 to guard the door, she apparently overhears his conversation with Desdemona, since she tells Iago in the following sequence, "He called her whore" (119). Fittingly, it is Emilia who breaks up the twosome of the death scene when she insists on being admitted into the bedchamber immediately after Desdemona has been strangled.

On two occasions, Iago, Desdemona, and Emilia are the characters who make up a trio onstage. Their grouping in Act 2, scene 1, centering on Iago's satiric banter against women as they wait at the quayside for news of Othello, chimes with that of the second part of Act 4, scene 2, where Emilia (no longer as silent) expresses outrage at Othello's verbal abuse of his wife, and Desdemona appeals to Iago to help her win back her lord. Although Desdemona chides Iago as "slanderer" for his antifeminist vignettes in Act 2, scene 1, she is fooled into thinking they belong to his persona as bluff soldier. What should have been a warning for her is not received as such; Desdemona naively turns to her archenemy for support in Act 4, scene 2.

In a play that focuses on sexual jealousy, the three female characters offer a spectrum of approaches to sexual love. Desdemona, who sees "Othello's visage in his mind" but also claims her nuptial "rites" (1. 3. 247, 252), combines spiritual with physical love for her husband; her total loyalty to him and belief in married chastity shine through in her statement that nothing, even Othello's mistreatment of her, can ever "taint" her love for him (4. 2. 160). Her incredulity that any woman could "abuse" her husband by being unfaithful to him is counterbalanced by her waiting-woman's worldliness. Emilia judges adultery a "small vice" if it means winning the "whole world" (4. 3. 71, 77). Even though there is no hard evidence in the play that she has strayed from her husband (she reviles the unknown "scurvy fellow" who made Iago suspect her of an affair with the Moor [4. 2. 139–46]), she promotes a tit-for-tat sexual philosophy that does not rule out the option: "I do think it is their husbands' faults / If wives do fall" (4. 3. 89–90). Bianca, the third female, at first appears to be a type character, the prostitute set up as a foil to the chaste Desdemona who is later mistaken by Othello for a "public commoner" (4. 2. 72). Iago describes Bianca as "A huswife that by selling her desires / Buys herself bread and cloth" (4. 1. 96–97). Yet she is devoted to Cassio and open in her affection for him; she rushes to help her "sweet Cassio" (5. 1. 76) when he is wounded. When Emilia stereotypes her with "O fie upon thee, strumpet," Bianca has a surprising retort:

> I am no strumpet, but of life as honest
> As you that thus abuse me.   (122–23)

Loyal to her man, Bianca may qualify as more chaste than Emilia, who condones infidelity if the reward is high enough. Revising our initial judgments, we may ultimately conclude that Bianca is a sexually free woman who is nevertheless pure (her name signifies whiteness) in spirit. Portraits of chastity and licentiousness that at first seem to be clearly polarized—Desdemona and Bianca, with Emilia as the midpoint between them—dissolve in the total design, reassembling as a more complicated exploration of what it means to be sexually "honest."

The three male partners to these women occupy rungs on the military ladder: general, lieutenant, and ancient (or ensign). Immune from envy himself, though sensitive, like Othello, to "reputation," Cassio is set up as a rival to both Iago and Othello. Bitter that Cassio has been promoted to second-in-command ahead of him, the practical Iago nevertheless succeeds in replacing the newcomer when Othello pledges at the end of Act 3, scene 3, "Now art thou my lieutenant." Connecting military position with sexual power,[56] Iago imagines that at some point, both Othello and Cassio have "done [his] office" (1. 3. 379) and "leaped into [his] seat" (2. 1. 296) by sleeping with Emilia. Part of his revenge now is to make his general perceive a sexual rivalry with Cassio where none actually exists. Othello's later discovery that the Venetians are "deputing Cassio" to take over his post in Cyprus (4. 1. 237) adds salt to his imaginary wound: that having been replaced by Cassio in Desdemona's bed, he is now being ousted by his ex-lieutenant in the chain of military command.[57] Ironically, the displacement that Othello fears takes place visually in the storm scene, when Cassio is the first to greet Desdemona on Cyprus and his rapturous welcome ("Hail to thee lady!" [2. 1. 84]) preempts Othello's joy in seeing her again. The pattern of substitutions continues when Iago, having promised Othello that he will kill the deputy, makes Roderigo his proxy in the "removing" of Cassio (4. 2. 227).

As with the female characters, the men offer a variety of attitudes toward sexual love and women in general. Othello, the romantic lover, at first believes devoutly in Desdemona's purity and loyalty ("My life upon her faith!" [1. 3. 289]); yet he swings to the opposite extreme as soon as he is infected by Iago's poisonous attitude toward women. Iago, who sneers that even the most "deserving woman" is good only to "suckle fools and chronicle small beer" (2. 1. 158), voices his misogynist cynicism and disdain for noble feelings at every opportunity. Lovemaking in his book is no spiritual or emotional consummation, but the outcome of "salt and

... loose affection" (2. 1. 239–40), a coupling of rampant goats or monkeys. His assumption that all women are promiscuous, given the chance, activates in Othello the same fear, so that the Moor switches from idealizing Desdemona to denigrating her as a "cunning whore of Venice" (4. 2. 88). Cassio's approach to women is frankly dualistic; some women (such as the "divine" Desdemona) are to be revered, while others (the "customer" Bianca) are to be used for sexual pleasure. To Iago's coarse suggestion that Desdemona is "full of game," Cassio responds protectively that she is a "most fresh and delicate creature" (2. 3. 19–20), and, like a courtly lover, he later assures Desdemona that "He's never anything but [her] true servant" (3. 3. 9). In harsh contrast, he rebukes his sexual partner Bianca for her jealousy with "Go to, woman! / Throw your vile guesses in the devil's teeth" (3. 4. 182–83) and laughs behind her back at her "monkey's" tricks (4. 1. 129).[58]

The fourth man who is given a substantial part in the play, Roderigo, is viewed primarily as Iago's first dupe, but structural parallels are also established between him and Othello. Othello, Iago's prize prey and his third dupe (after Cassio), is ironically the only one of the three who does not immediately defend Desdemona against Iago's damaging insinuations, for Roderigo protests that she is "full of most blessed condition" (2. 1. 249–50) while Cassio terms her "right modest" (2. 3. 23). Roderigo's stance toward Desdemona is a curious combination of idolatry (at first he cannot believe Iago's assertion that she has "found" Cassio sexually) and crude eagerness to bribe her into an adulterous liaison. This contradictory mixture is a pale reflection of Othello's veering between his intuition of Desdemona as "A fine woman, a fair woman, a sweet woman" and his new perception of her as "Devil" (4. 1. 180–81, 240).[59] When Roderigo reluctantly agrees to try to kill Cassio, he confides to the audience that Iago "has given [him] satisfying reasons" (5. 1. 9)—an exact parallel with Othello's being convinced by Iago that Desdemona is unfaithful and should therefore be murdered.[60]

LANGUAGE AND STYLE

Written just over halfway through his career, *Othello* displays the full range of Shakespeare's expertise; the play's language is both subtle and versatile. It is also economical, perfectly geared to the dramatic business at hand. Apart from two sequences in rhyming couplets (the *sententiae* spoken by the Duke and Brabantio in the council scene [1. 3. 197–216] and Iago's performance at the quayside [2. 1. 127–58]), the play contains almost no set speeches or purely decorative images. Complex image patterns—figures of the cosmos, light and dark, animals and trapping—create *Othello*'s tone and texture and feed into the play's dominant themes. Above all, as is the mark of Shakespeare's mature dramatic style, diction, syntax, and imagery are all tied into the presentation of character. Each of *Othello*'s main dramatic characters possesses a distinct idiom and pattern of language; we gauge these speakers not only by what they say, but how they say it.

Whether a character speaks in low-key prose or high-toned verse is one determinant of his or her style, but the character's manipulation of a particular image, or choice of an elaborate or plain form of English, is equally important. Images of the sea, for instance, arise naturally in a play set in the commercial port of Venice and in Cyprus, an island fortress situated in the stormy Mediterranean. Beyond this, though, Iago's use of a nautical metaphor to describe Othello's union with Desdemona as the boarding of a "land carack" (the piracy of a treasure ship [1. 2. 49]) tells us that his mind-set is vulgar, mercenary, and potentially predatory. Othello, by contrast, reveals an emotional expansiveness, a way of valuing personal freedom in elemental terms, when he admits that but for his love of Desdemona, he would not have given up his independence for the "seas' worth" (1. 2. 27). Cassio's extravagantly idealized view of Desdemona is conveyed through elaborate, hyperbolic phrases (she "excels the quirks of blazoning pens" [2. 1. 63]), whereas the cynical Iago punctures any illusion about her divinity when he tells Roderigo, in his pithy, down-to-earth idiom, "Blessed fig's-end! The wine she drinks is made of grapes" (2. 1. 251–52). Similarly, Emilia's coarsely physical assessment of men—"They eat us hungerly, and when they are full, / They belch us" (3. 4. 105–6)—contrasts with Desdemona's more reluctant and refined disillusionment, in an image evoking the attentiveness of a new spouse before the honeymoon period is over:

> Nay, we must think men are not gods,
> Nor of them look for such observancy
> As fits the bridal.   (3. 4. 148–50)

Through such juxtapositions, *Othello* produces no single melodic line, but a range of counterpointed motifs that build up the dramatic score.

Prose

Most of *Othello* consists of blank verse; only about 17 percent of the play is written in prose.[61] The two comic sequences in Act 3 that include the Clown appear in prose, which affords a suitable vehicle for the lewd joke on "wind instrument" and "tale"/tail (3. 1. 10)—perhaps an oblique comment on Othello's long-windedness in his "tale" in Act 1, scene 3!—and for the insistent pun on "lie," meaning both to lie down and to tell an untruth (3. 4. 1–13). This word "lie" is picked up in Act 4, scene 1, where Iago's salacious picture of Cassio with Desdemona ("Lie— . . . With her, on her; what you will" [34–35]) prompts in Othello an eruption of disjointed ideas too horrible to be contemplated steadily: "Lie on her?—We say lie on her when they belie her" (36–37). As his finely modulated verse fragments into prose, Othello even echoes "Pish," which Iago has used earlier to conjure up the sex act to Roderigo, in "Pish! Noses, ears, and lips?" (43–44).[62]

Prose is a crucial medium for Iago. It suits his vulgar, often reductive view of life and the pragmatic persona with which he gulls his victims. While he uses the convention of the verse soliloquy to confide his motives and plan of action to the audience,[63] he usually converses with his dupes in prose. After the formal verse of the council scene (1. 3), Iago drops into prose to persuade Roderigo he can still win Desdemona and should "put money in [his] purse" if he is to succeed in Cyprus. The pattern is similar in Act 2, scene 1. After the high point of Othello's "wonder" at finding Desdemona already in Cyprus comes Iago's low-key prose conversation with Roderigo on how to pick a fight with Cassio (211–84). Iago also moves into prose in his advice to Cassio after the brawl (2. 3. 258–335) and when he reencounters Roderigo toward the end of Act 4, scene 2, this time to persuade him to kill Cassio (170–245). He draws Othello down to his own banal, prosy level after the eavesdropping sequence (4. 1. 171–214), although Othello's cadences— as in the chiasmic balance of "But yet the pity of it, Iago. O Iago, the pity of it" (197–98)—often raise the level of the dialogue. Two exceptions are the opening scene (1. 1. 1–156), where Iago's self-revelations, like his soliloquies, are couched in blank verse, and his speech at the end of Act 2, scene 3, "How poor are they that have not patience!" (370–82). As this speech is sandwiched between his two soliloquies for the audience, it does not seem out of character for him to go on speaking in blank verse rather than switch briefly into prose (for twelve lines only) to match Roderigo's.

Iago, a master manipulator, is able "to vary his argument to suit the nature of his listener,"[64] shifting not only his viewpoint and message (painting Desdemona to Roderigo as fickle and sensual but to Cassio as virtuous and generous), but also his linguistic register and strategy. As T. McAlindon points out, Iago can "ape the stately style of an Othello or the foppish euphuism of a Roderigo."[65] To Othello (speaking now in verse), Iago chooses elevated images—of a bride and groom "Devesting them for bed" and of losing limbs in "action glorious" (2. 3. 180, 185)—that will appeal to the newly married general. To Roderigo, he is the plain speaker ("Virtue? A fig!") who can nevertheless support his argument with glib eloquence. When he wants to convince the gull that Cassio and Desdemona are already involved sexually, he concludes his grandiose, alliterated phrases, "mutualities . . . marshall the way" and "incorporate conclusion," with the vulgar (and graphic) expletive "Pish!" (2. 1. 261–63). The language of the experienced, worldly man of reason coalesces with the blunt idiom of the soldier. His balanced syntax (symmetrical noun phrases) in fact underscores a cynical view of human emotions and values, one that dismisses love as "merely a lust of the blood and a permission of the will" (1. 3. 330–31). To reach this reductive conclusion, he counters the apparent logic of Roderigo's despairing "It is silliness to live when to live is a torment" (303) with the formal, extended analogy of the human body as a garden cultivated and controlled by the will. This leads to his persuasive proposition (buttressed with the neat antithesis of "reason" and "sensuality" and the symmetry of "blood and baseness") that "If the balance of our lives had not one scale of reason to poise another of sensuality, the blood and baseness of our natures would conduct us to most prepost'rous conclusions" (321–25). Killing oneself, he strongly implies, would be one of these preposterous conclusions.

This habit of convincing his hearer by way of a seemingly viable "if/then" proposition ("If thou wilt needs damn thyself, do it a more delicate way than drowning" [348–50]) is another trick of Iago's. The premise in the "if" clause often remains purely speculative, however, as when he promises his gull, "If sanctimony and a frail vow betwixt an erring barbarian and supersubtle Venetian be not too hard for my wits, and all the tribe of hell, thou shalt enjoy her" (350–54). In his final conversation with Roderigo, he sets up a series of conditionals, such as "If you dare do yourself a profit" and "If you will watch [Cassio's] going hence," to support the outrageous conclusion (which Roderigo somehow swallows) that "If thou the next night following enjoy not Desdemona, take me from this world . . . and devise engines for my life" (4. 2. 215–17). Iago perfects this tactic in the temptation scene. Now speaking in verse, he proposes that Othello will acquire proof of Desdemona's adultery "If imputation and strong circumstances / Which lead directly to the door of truth / Will give you satisfaction" (3. 3. 403–5). "Imputation" is not the same as empirical evidence or "truth," but Iago makes it seem so through the relative clause ("which") embedded in the "if" clause. Later, he opens a floodgate of anguish in Othello by throwing in a reminder of possible consequences: "But if I give my wife a handkerchief—" (4. 1. 10). As Madeleine Doran points out, Iago is able to create monstrous deceptions by trading on the "false relations of a condition to its conclusion."[66] He also has a sinister way of turning plain statement of fact—"He holds me well"—into future probability: "The better shall my purpose work on him" (1. 3. 381–82).[67]

Iago is an adept organizer and manager—often he acts by proxy, telling other people what they should do—and this is reflected in his frequent imperatives, or "speech acts of command."[68] In Act 1, scene 3, he repeats his instruction to Roderigo, "Put money in thy purse," or a variation on that, no less than ten times in thirty-two lines (335–67). Telling Roderigo "be you ruled by me" in Act 2, scene 1, he proceeds to teach him how to pick a quarrel with Cassio: "Watch you tonight," "find some occasion to anger Cassio," "Provoke him that he may [strike at you]" (264–65, 267–68, 273). He adopts the same tactic, "I tell you what you shall do," with Cassio in the third scene of the same act, quickly mapping out a strategy for the demoted lieutenant to win Desdemona as his advocate: "Confess yourself freely to her; importune her to put you in your place again" (314–19). This is the hortatory mode that Iago finally adopts with Othello in the temptation scene; once he gathers momentum, he moves from the tactful "I do beseech you" to the bald imperatives "Look to your wife; observe her well with Cassio" (3. 3. 197) and "Look to't" (200).

Verse

Since the norm of poetry in *Othello* is blank verse (iambic pentameter), the few sustained passages of rhymed couplets are foregrounded as philosophical set pieces. As he concludes the "trial" of Othello in Act 1, scene 3, the Duke modulates into *sententiae* to advocate to Brabantio a stoical acceptance of what cannot be changed. But the aggrieved father quickly caps them, slicing through the fatuousness of such consolations with a bitterly ironic couplet on how the Duke's sentiments might be applied to the military crisis:

> So let the Turk of Cyprus us beguile:
> We lose it not so long as we can smile.   (207–8)

Iago, too, frames his "old fond paradoxes" in rhymed couplets, while Desdemona counterpoints them in prose. Calculated for effect as a one-off performance, the couplets at the harbor highlight Iago's glib facility for reducing women to sexual objects:

> She never yet was foolish that was fair,
> For even her folly helped her to an heir.   (2. 1. 134–35)

Several scenes end with a terse couplet—such as Iago's "Hell and night / Must bring this monstrous birth to the world's light" (1. 3. 394–95) and his clinching lines at the end of the first and third scenes of Act 2—while Othello dies with an epigrammatic neatness in the chiasmic balance of his couplet "I kissed thee ere I killed thee. No way but this, / Killing myself, to die upon a kiss" (5. 2. 354–55). The play's blank verse offers a more versatile vehicle of expression; it ranges from Othello's highly patterned oration "Farewell the tranquil mind" (3. 3. 345–54) to the down-to-earth analysis of Iago's "Let me see now: / To get his place, and to plume up my will / In double knavery" (1. 3. 383–85)—verse that mirrors the slick operations of a cunning mind.

"*Language* most shewes a man: speake that I may see thee," exhorts Jonson in his *Discoveries*.[69] Desdemona's speech, unadorned and lucid, is what Eamon Grennan calls an "exact embodiment of self" and an index of her "moral conviction."[70] Whereas Iago's "words" and "performances," Roderigo observes, are "no kin together" (4. 2. 180–81), Desdemona's words reflect the honesty, tough-mindedness, and purity she demonstrates in her actions. Forthright in wanting to "trumpet to the world" her "downright violence, and storm of fortunes" (1. 3. 244–45), she proudly introduces her passionate union with Othello through this martial image. In front of the Senate, she straightforwardly proclaims, "here's my husband" and states her desire with the simple request, "Let me go with him" (1. 3. 254). Desdemona prefaces her one interlude of jesting at the harbor with the disclaimer that she is "not merry" and is only "seeming otherwise" (2. 1. 120–21); on other occasions, her words are a clear reflection of her feelings. To Othello's high-flown fear of "unknown fate," she responds with a more down-to-earth image of natural growth, simply expressed in the assured rhythms of

> The heavens forbid
> But that our loves and comforts should increase
> Even as our days do grow.   (2. 1. 192–94)

She can be direct to the point of insistence, speaking "stoutly" (though never rudely) when she presses Othello to reinstate Cassio—"I prithee name the time, but let it not / Exceed three days"—and amplifies her frank "Why, this is not a

boon" with the domestic imagery of wearing gloves and eating wholesome dishes
(3. 3. 62–63, 76–78). Desdemona's language remains in touch with the ordinary
world of the senses; her conversation with Emilia in the willow scene is punctu-
ated by the simple physicality of "Prithee unpin me" and "Mine eyes do itch"
(4. 3. 21, 59). Whereas Iago's mode of speech is hortatory, Desdemona's is often
interrogatory, for she wants to communicate with Othello and to discover the
truth. Although she regrets being chided for her "free speech" (3. 4. 129), she
continues to confront Othello with direct questions in the "brothel scene" ("what
is your will?", "How am I false?", "Alas, what ignorant sin have I committed?"
[4. 2. 24, 39, 69]) and reinforces her moral integrity with strong denials when he
calls her strumpet: "No, as I am a Christian!", "No, as I shall be saved!" (81, 85).
Even in the murder scene, she is still, guilelessly, seeking the reason for Othello's
displeasure with her passionate question "What's the matter?" (5. 2. 47). Her directness persists to the end, as she indignantly cuts through Othello's assumption
that she has given the handkerchief to Cassio with a commonsense approach:
"No, by my life and soul! / Send for the man and ask him" (49–50). Unlike
Othello's often self-centered expression, Desdemona's speech is truly other-
directed. The one time that she does focus on herself, in her dying words "Nobody—I myself" (123), constitutes, paradoxically, a selfless gesture; she takes
the blame for a violent act she has not committed.

Othello's language is set in a higher key than Desdemona's. Measured, colorful,
and exotic, it has a "soaring cosmic allusiveness"[71]—at least before Othello falls
under Iago's spell. How we react to his dominant speech patterns is closely tied to
how we interpret his character. An audience may register Othello's expansive,
slightly orotund verse as the utterance of a confident and "noble" leader of men,
a bold adventurer. Alternatively, they might find in the formal phrasing and decla-
mation a hint of self-display, a "straining after magnificence" not to be "confused
with real gold"[72] or an ostentatiousness that could register a "secret insecurity" because he is a Moor in Venice.[73] When Othello, hunted by Brabantio, tells Iago that
"my demerits / May speak unbonneted to as proud a fortune / As this that I have
reached" (1. 2. 21–23), he uses a rather grand image, of not needing to doff his hat
to a social superior, to assert (with just a hint of arrogance?) that he deserves the
pinnacle of success he has reached in marrying Desdemona. Whatever else it may
be, this is not the "rude" or "round unvarnished" speech that he claims as his own
when he addresses the Senate (1. 3. 81, 90). Iago is undoubtedly exaggerating
when he sneers at the Moor's "bombast" (1. 1. 12); yet Othello's speech *is* artfully
constructed, for he knows that he must impress the Senators. Certainly the oration
in which he justifies his marriage to Desdemona (127–69) is a powerful piece of
narrative spellbinding. It mixes abstract noun phrases (the balanced "disastrous
chances" and "moving accidents") with concrete detail, juxtaposing the strange
"men whose heads / Grew beneath their shoulders" with the personification of
"hills whose heads touch heaven." Othello's tongue rolls sonorously around the
exotic "Anthropophagi," as later around "chrysolite" and the "med'cinable gum"
of Arabian trees (5. 2. 142, 346–47). Through anaphora with amplification (re-

peated adjectives that are then qualified), he creates the surge of Desdemona's feelings for him:

> She swore in faith 'twas strange, 'twas passing strange;
> 'Twas pitiful, 'twas wondrous pitiful.   (1. 3. 159–60)

His defense of his wooing culminates in the strong declaration (with the stress falling on the inverted "only"), "This only is the witchcraft I have used" (168). Othello's is not the verbal trickery or witchcraft that Iago employs, but it is a potent kind of word magic, nonetheless.

The leisurely, often mannered effect of Othello's verse is partly the result of frequent doublets—a stylistic habit of using two words when one would do, which Iago cruelly terms being "Horribly stuffed with epithets" (1. 1. 13).[74] Early in the play, Othello expands on his previously "unhousèd free condition" (1. 2. 25) and still welcomes the "flinty and steel" couch of war (1. 3. 227); he claims to deserve all "indign and base" adversities (268) if he allows marital pleasures to "corrupt and taint" (266) his professional duties. Later, he derides as "exsufflicate and blown" the "surmises" that Iago offers him (3. 3. 182). This trick of amplification, foregrounded in his pointedly deferential address to the "Most potent, grave, and reverend signiors, / My very noble and approved good masters" (1. 3. 76–77), stays with him through Act 5, where, with dignified expansiveness, he provides three versions of having reached the end of his life:

> Here is my journey's end, here is my butt,
> And very seamark of my utmost sail.   (5. 2. 264–65)

As so often in Othello's speeches, the stately rhythm is enhanced by repeated sounds—here the alliteration on "s" and the assonance on "u." Patterned repetition turns shrilly histrionic, though, at the end of this speech, in the insistent imperatives[75] of "Blow me about in winds! roast me in sulphur! / Wash me in steep-down gulfs of liquid fire!" (276–77).

Counterbalancing Othello's grand, sometimes overinflated and turgid style is what E. A. J. Honigmann calls his "'business' voice,"[76] as in "To his conveyance I assign my wife" (1. 3. 280) and "Our wars are done; the Turks are drowned" (2. 1. 200). There are also moments of simple directness—"Keep up your bright swords" (1. 2. 58), "it is too much of joy" (2. 1. 195), "Cassio, I love thee; / But never more be officer of mine" (2. 3. 247–48)—that reflect his need for unambiguous explanations or decisive, soldierly actions. Othello's mind is not that of a simpleton,[77] but his tendency to react emotionally rather than to think deeply is mirrored in his language. Under stress, he repeats words and phrases, no longer for elegant variation, but as the expression of intense feeling. He laments the loss of Desdemona as a "fine woman, a fair woman, a sweet woman" (4. 1. 180–81) and builds his savage public harangue of her through repetition (with variation) of "turn," "weep," and "obedient":

> Sir, she can turn, and turn, and yet go on
> And turn again; and she can weep, sir, weep;
> And she's obedient; as you say, obedient.
> Very obedient.   (253–56)

It is also through repeated clauses, now with a strong monosyllabic beat,[78] that Othello convinces himself that he is justified in murdering Desdemona: "It is the cause, it is the cause, my soul" (5. 2. 1). In this calmly paced soliloquy, Othello apprehends Desdemona (as he prepares to kill her) in a visual and tactile way: her skin is whiter than snow, smoother than alabaster; her life is a light that may be snuffed out forever, unlike the candle that Othello can "relume"; and her body, with its beauty and its "balmy breath," is like a fresh, sweet-smelling rose that will wither forever once it is plucked. These similes and metaphors celebrate the unique preciousness of Desdemona even as Othello plans, perversely (and with his usual trick of repetition), to "Put out the light, and then put out the light" (7). Here, as in his justification to the Senate and his "farewell to war" speech, where he hears war in the "shrill trump" and the "ear-piercing fife" and sees it in the "plumèd troops" and the "royal banner" (3. 3. 345–50), Othello registers the world through his senses. It is ironic that he intuits the purity as well as the beauty of Desdemona through strong sensory impressions yet still tries to justify her murder intellectually: "she must die, else she'll betray more men" (6).

Image Patterns

G. Wilson Knight, analyzing the "Othello music" created in the verse, observes that the play's "beautiful effects of style are all expressions of Othello's personal passion."[79] This is an overgeneralization; Montano, for instance, describes the sea storm energetically, evoking the fury of an ocean where "mountains melt" on "ribs of oak," while the Second Gentleman envisages the retaliation of the elements when "The chidden billow seems to pelt the clouds" (2. 1. 8, 12). But it is Othello's cosmic images that help to create a certain spaciousness in this domestic tragedy. Othello's references to the elements and the cosmos are less morally charged than the allusions to devils and angels that establish the play's Christian context; they suggest, rather, a breadth of imagination activated by strong passion. To express his absolute joy in meeting Desdemona at Cyprus, Othello combines a nautical analogy with a hyperbolical image of vast cosmic space (height and depth):

> let the laboring bark climb hills of seas
> Olympus-high, and duck again as low
> As hell's from heaven.   (2. 1. 185–87)

With the noun "Olympus," Othello ventures into the mythological realm; his eclectic imagination moves easily from a Christian world to the classical allusions of "feathered Cupid" (1. 3. 264), "Dian's visage" (3. 3. 384), and "Jove's dread clamors" (353). When he next elaborates a maritime image, it is the simile of the Pontic Sea, whose "icy current and compulsive course" he ironically compares with the "violent pace" of his hot, "bloody thoughts" (3. 3. 451–54)—an echo of how Brabantio, too, finds his grief of "so floodgate and o'erbearing nature" that it "engluts and swallows other sorrows" (1. 3. 56–57). Still evoking a sense of far-reaching adventure through his metaphor, Othello calmly envisages the end of his life's journey as the very "seamark of [his] utmost sail" (5. 2. 265).

Wolfgang Clemen remarks that in his images, Othello "always takes *himself* as the point of departure."[80] Indeed, Othello often expands and generalizes his own dilemma into cosmic proportions. He warns Iago that he would need to "Do deeds to make heaven weep, all earth amazed" to try to match the horror of slandering Desdemona (3. 3. 368), and he finds Desdemona's conjectured adultery so offensive and disgusting that "Heaven stops the nose at it, and the moon winks," while even the "bawdy wind" is shocked into silence by it (4. 2. 76–77). After the murder, Othello looks for a universal catastrophe to match his own "heavy" sense of having destroyed his wife:

> Methinks it should be now a huge eclipse
> Of sun and moon, and that th' affrighted globe
> Should yawn at alteration. (5. 2. 98–100)

Whereas in the world of *King Lear*, cosmic disorder extends from the microcosm to the macrocosm, in *Othello,* allusions to the universe remain "silhouetted, defined, concrete"[81] because they are restricted to the hero; he alone finds that "Chaos is come again." These images of cosmic upheaval offer a window into Othello's solipsism, enabling the audience to apprehend the intensity with which he experiences personal loss.

While Othello's images put human beings in touch with higher cosmic forces, Iago's duck down as low as hell's from heaven; he is the cynic who continually reduces humans to their animal natures, the "bestial" level to which Cassio feels consigned once he has ruined his "immortal part" (2. 3. 262–63). As far as Iago is concerned, Othello is a gullible ass (1. 3. 393) and Roderigo a snipe—a long-beaked bird (376)—as well as a hound (2. 1. 303–4). With coarse vulgarity, he envisages Othello as an "old black ram" tupping a "white ewe" (Desdemona) and a Barbary horse making the "beast with two backs" (1. 1. 85–86, 108–14). Later, he inflames Othello's imagination by comparing Cassio and Desdemona, "as prime as goats, as hot as monkeys" (3. 3. 400), to the most sexually rampant of animals. Iago himself claims that he would "change [his] humanity with a baboon" before he would drown himself "for the love of a guinea hen" (1. 3. 310–11)—a slang term for prostitute. It is fitting that by the end of the play, Iago himself is equated with an "inhuman dog" (5. 1. 62). He is obsessed, too, with trapping his animal victims. He plans to "ensnare" the "fly" Cassio in the "web" of his own courtesy (2. 1. 166–67) and to utilize Desdemona's "goodness," and the fact that Othello's soul is "enfettered" to her love, as a "net" to "enmesh them all" (2. 3. 361–62). And in the denouement, Othello does indeed demand to know why Iago has "thus ensnared [his] soul and body" (5. 2. 298).

Under Iago's reductive influence, Othello begins to perceive human beings as animals. The expletive "Goats and monkeys!" that Othello spits out as he leaves the shocked ambassadors (4. 1. 263) is a clear echo of Iago's "prime as goats . . . hot as monkeys" (3. 3. 400) two scenes earlier. Just as Othello superimposes the image of devil onto the angelic Desdemona once Iago has poisoned his mind, so from Act 3, scene 3 onward he begins to envisage his wife in bestial images. She is a hawk that has proved "haggard" or untrainable (3. 3. 259), her body has turned into a cistern for "foul toads / To knot and gender in" (4. 2. 60–61), and Othello himself would rather be a "toad" than possess only part of her. In a significant transference, Othello dramatizes his suicide by remembering how he once "took by the throat" a "circumcisèd dog"—the Turk in Aleppo (5. 2. 351)—and stabbed him. Listening to the speech, the audience might expect him to kill the "Spartan dog" Iago (357); instead, Othello turns the sword on himself.

Iago has also become a "viper" by the final scene (5. 2. 281), a concrete realization of his own imagery of poison. Early in the play, he describes his own sexual jealousy as a "poisonous mineral" burning his entrails (2. 1. 297) and plans to "pour" the "pestilence" of false suggestion into Othello's ear to make him suffer the same kind of acute pain (2. 3. 356). By the middle of Act 3, scene 3, he boasts that "the Moor already changes with [his] poison," which, in his diabolical guise as the concerned friend, Iago applies like a helpful physician administering remedies ("My med'cine works!" he gloats [4. 1. 47]).[82] The "dangerous conceits" that he sows in Othello's mind will burn "like the mines of sulphur" (3. 3. 323–26). By the play's finale, the marriage bed loaded with Iago's victims has become an object that "poisons sight" for the survivor, Lodovico (5. 2. 360).

Images of stealing and entrapping, like those of poison, define Iago's nature as Machiavellian. Iago is a thief; he owns Roderigo's purse strings and bilks him of his jewels, and he has begged his wife "a thousand times" to steal Desdemona's handkerchief. Expert in the art of suggestion, Iago twice cries out, "Thieves! thieves!" (1. 1. 76–78) to bolster Brabantio's own perception of Othello as a "foul thief" who has stolen his daughter (1. 2. 61). Iago's strategy with Othello is to disclaim any mercenary interest—"Who steals my purse steals trash" (3. 3. 157)—and then to convince his lord that being robbed of one's "good name" is to lose something truly precious, the "immediate jewel" of one's soul. Accordingly, Othello feels that he has been "robbed" by Desdemona's "stol'n hours of lust" (335–39) and treats her like "trash" in the brothel scene, hurling down "money for your pains" to Emilia (4. 2. 92). Only at the close of the play does he appreciate the rich "pearl" he has thrown away (5. 2. 343–44).

Symbols

It is noticeable how often verbal images crystallize into stage emblems in *Othello*. Recurrent images of light and darkness (fair and foul) translate into actual props in the theater, when the lighted torches of the three groups in the nighttime street scenes in Venice (1. 1, 2) narrow to the single light that Othello brings to Desdemona's bedside on her final night in Cyprus, which comes to be associated with the light of a life to be extinguished forever.[83] Iago, the embodiment of satanic darkness who secretly commits the "blackest sins" (2. 3. 351), ironically swears his loyalty to Othello by the "ever-burning lights above" (3. 3. 460) and enters the dark street "with a light" after Cassio and Roderigo have been wounded (5. 1. 46). Light and darkness are archetypal symbols of good and evil; yet the apparent antithesis of white and black, echoed in the play's language, turns out to be a false or shifting one. Black Othello mistakes the "lovely fair" Desdemona for a "black weed" (Quarto reading) who is "false as hell" (4. 2. 66–67, 38); only in the play's final scene is she reestablished in his eyes as both beautiful and "heavenly true," one case where appearances are not deceptive. In Desdemona's murder, too, the underlined legal terms "cause,"[84] "perjury," "article," and "confess" frame this as a trial, with Othello as plaintiff, prosecuting attorney, judge, and executioner. Thus it echoes and inverts the actually staged trial before the Senate in Act 1, scene 3, where Othello is the defendant.

The dominant stage prop that also becomes a central symbol is Desdemona's strawberry-spotted handkerchief. Such an apparently inconsequential object is appropriate in a dramatic context characterized by domestic items; references to skillets, gloves, fans, embroidery, and nourishing dishes all help to create the world of the newly married couple. Derided by Thomas Rymer as "so remote a trifle"[85] as to constitute a ludicrous plot mechanism, the handkerchief is far from trivial to Othello; it is rooted in his Eastern lineage.[86] Woven by an ancient sibyl and dyed in the blood of "maidens' hearts," this talisman was given to Othello's mother by an Egyptian "charmer"; on her deathbed, the mother bequeathed it to her son to give to his future wife. As such, it may symbolize women's "civilizing power" to contain and control men's sexuality.[87] Othello, though, prizes it almost as a fetish that has power in itself, for he believes that as long as a wife guards it zealously, the handkerchief can magically prevent her husband from straying to "other fancies" (3. 4. 55–63).[88] That Othello then projects his own feelings of betrayal[89] onto the hankerchief is suggested by his second account of its origins at the end of the play, where he describes it as an "antique token / My father gave my mother" (5. 2. 213–14). Since he believes that Desdemona has given away his "pledge of love" (211) to Cassio, he reinterprets the history of the napkin to parallel his own situation; just as he gave the handkerchief to his wife, so he now imagines that his father, and not an Egyptian magician, gave it to his mother.

The audience may well feel, as Desdemona apparently does ("It is not lost. But what an if it were?" [3. 4. 83]), that Othello has invested the handkerchief with too much magical significance. His grim warning that losing it would be "such perdition / As nothing else could match" (67–68) suggests that he views it in a deeply superstitious way, akin to the witchcraft that he has disavowed in Act 1, scene 3.[90] It is telling that Desdemona drops it in the loving act of trying to ease her husband's apparent headache. As Robert B. Heilman comments, Othello rejects the truly "magical powers"[91] of Desdemona's love (when she moves to comfort him, he complains "Your napkin is too little" [3. 3. 286]) and instead becomes fixated on the "magic in the web" of the mere token (3. 4. 69). It shifts from being a symbol of his love for Desdemona—a gift freely given—to a representation of her chastity once he becomes obsessed with thoughts of her being unfaithful. When Othello warns her to "Make it a darling like your precious eye" (66), where "eye" is an Elizabethan-Jacobean double entendre for vagina,[92] he is insisting that her sexuality be kept closely guarded. With its design of red on white, the strawberry-spotted handkerchief may also serve as a visual reminder of the blood-spotted sheets on their wedding night.[93] Yet Othello focuses not on the virginity of his bride, but on how their marriage bed "shall with lust's blood be spotted" by the killing of Desdemona (5. 1. 36).

The handkerchief is not just an emblem or a personal symbol, of course, but a tangible object, subject to loss and chance encounters. Because Othello associates this piece of linen so closely with his wife's "honor"—an abstract essence that (unlike the handkerchief) is "not seen" (4. 1. 16)—he is terribly vulnerable to making the wrong inferences about Desdemona's fidelity. For the handkerchief travels promiscuously, from Emilia, to Iago, to Cassio, and then to Bianca, once Desdemona accidentally drops it. Strictly speaking, Othello does not need the circumstantial evidence of the handkerchief; by Act 4, scene 1, he would "gladly have forgot it!" (19) and has to ask Iago if the napkin in Bianca's hand is in fact the one he gave Desdemona. Nevertheless, by the end of the play, he twice refers to the concrete object—"I saw my handkerchief in's hand" and "I saw it in his hand" (5. 2. 62, 212)—as proof of his wife's unfaithfulness. In a play that scrutinizes the flimsiness of "poor likelihoods" (1. 3. 108), the handkerchief comes to represent the fallibility of jumping to hasty conclusions or applying inappropriate criteria to the testing of love relationships. Fidelity is not susceptible to empirical proof,[94] and apparent signs of infidelity may be misleading. Seeing the handkerchief in Bianca's hand should not constitute, for Othello, believing that Desdemona is unchaste.

The Free Play of Signifiers

Iago's verbal manipulation of Othello goes beyond a brilliant temptation or a complex interchange between two characters; it is a searching commentary on how words, notoriously unstable signifiers, can "create and re-create" their "own contexts of reference."[95] When Brabantio denies that mere phrases are capable of assuaging grief or changing one's perception of reality ("But words are words" [1. 3. 215]) and Othello, just before he falls into a trance, claims, "It is not words that shakes me thus" (4. 1. 42–43), they both underestimate the power of language. The often repeated question in *Othello*—"What's the matter?"—might be answered with Hamlet's response to a similar query from Polonius: "Words, words, words" (*Hamlet,* II. ii. 192). Just as Montaigne (in John Florio's 1603 translation of the *Essais*) comments on how words "signifie more th[a]n they utter,"[96] Iago, too, knows that words hint at much more—or, as he uses them, something much worse—than they state. He mobilizes the indeterminacy of language, the lack of correspondence between sign and referent (signifier and signified) to bring into being hidden doubts and frightening possibilities for Othello.

In this respect, the play demonstrates what poststructuralist and deconstructive critics have emphasized about language as it has evolved. Since there is only an arbitrary relation between the signifier and what is signified, absolute meaning, or "presence," is forever deferred; words offer, instead, a relatively free play of meanings. Iago, the ensign, appropriately becomes the agent of this destabilizing tendency in language. In himself he is the sign[97] whose true meaning is hidden (he shows a "flag and sign of love" [1. 1. 153] but really hates Othello), or possibly, as some critics have sensed about his overdetermined explication of his motives, this Iago/ego may spin out alternatives to the point where he cancels out his essential self, like his meanings, altogether: "I am not what I am" (1. 1. 62). In order to undermine Othello, he exploits the instability of the sign, as with the key word "honest." Earlier, he has confounded distinctions by collocating "honest" with "knaves" ("Whip me such honest knaves!" [1. 1. 46]).[98] Now, in the temptation scene, he iterates the word ("Honest, my lord?") that Othello first introduces, calling into play other possible meanings of honesty—sexual chastity as well as integrity or veracity—to muddy the image Othello has of Cassio and Desdemona.

What is more, Iago carries his strategy beyond simply manipulating the slipperiness of the sign. He also appeals to Othello's yearning for a stable (almost magical) union of words and things[99] by arbitrarily closing the gap between them when he engineers "ocular proof" through the handkerchief. He knows that "honor" is open to various interpretations—"They have it very oft that have it not" (4. 1. 17), just as "reputation" is often "got without merit and lost without deserving" (2. 3. 267–69)—and yet he induces Othello to equate this nebulous concept with a tangible piece of cloth.[100] Othello is susceptible to this kind of association, for he already regards Desdemona's safekeeping of the handkerchief as a guarantee that the love between husband and wife will remain secure. Watching Cassio handle the love token, Othello now takes it as a sign of Desdemona's unchastity—proof that she has given away her "honor."

Iago is an arch-deconstructor of meaning.[101] His "Virtue? A fig! 'Tis in ourselves that we are thus, or thus" (1. 3. 314–15) begins his destabilizing of traditional categories. Thus he emphasizes the importance of money to Roderigo ("Put money in thy purse" [1. 3. 339]) but dismisses it as "trash" when he is promoting the value of reputation instead to Othello (3. 3. 157). In effect, Iago empties "purse" of all meaning—"'Tis something, nothing"—just as he transforms "good name" from a precious "jewel" for Othello into "an idle and most false imposition" for Cassio (2. 3. 267–68). As *Othello* progresses, Iago works on a broader level both to undermine (for Othello) and then to reconstitute the traditional polarities—the semiotic clusters of light/white/fair and dark/black/foul[102]—through which European society formulates many of its moral distinctions. Sensing that the fair Desdemona embodies purity, Iago resolves to "turn her virtue into pitch" (2. 3. 360). His talent for collapsing what seem to be essential differences between dark and light, fair and foul, is revealed in his quayside witticisms, where he indiscriminately brands all women as sexual schemers: "If she be black, and thereto have a wit, / She'll find a white that shall her blackness fit" (2. 1. 130–31). He is subsequently able to make Othello view Desdemona as a "radically ambiguous sign,"[103] a beautiful woman who may be a "fair devil" because she is disguising her evil (3. 3. 475). Iago himself is the whited sepulcher, the deceiving appearance that Christ refers to when he chastises the Pharisees as "hypocrites" (Mark 23:27), while Othello represents the anomalous "noble Moor"—in the Duke's eyes, "far more fair than black" (1. 3. 285). By a reverse deconstruction, however, Iago precipitates in Othello the evil symbolically figured by darkness, together with the jealousy and uncontrollable passion that were common stereotypes, in Renaissance discourse, of ethnic blackness. Iago's juggling with semiotic codes is part of how he fragments Othello's ontological security, sullying and decomposing the "fair" identity that his master has built up in Venice.

While two-faced Iago swears by the god Janus, the play's language is sometimes Janus-like in its doubleness. The traditional distinction between black and white, fair and foul, is further subverted through the presentation of Bianca, the prostitute who is devoted to Cassio. What's in a name? Bianca's means whiteness;[104] but does the audience perceive her as "light" in the sense of being sexually promiscuous, or as representing a certain integrity, even a purity, in her loyalty to her lover? Is she a deceiving appearance (a white devil), or is she the opposite of Iago: a character whom everyone categorizes as corrupt but who reveals an honest side? Other words in the play also suggest an ambivalence or equivocation at the heart of existence, a baffling confusion between what is pure and impure. In Elizabethan English, "liberal," like "free," could mean generous—firmly established as a good quality—but also sexually open or licentious, an attribute frowned on for women in *Othello*'s society.[105] Iago assesses Othello's nature as "free and open" (1. 3. 390) and admits that Desdemona is "framed as fruitful / As the free elements" (2. 3. 341–42). But when Othello, transformed by Iago's skepticism, examines Desdemona's "moist palm" in Act 3, scene 4, he finds "fruitfulness and liberal heart"— now construed as reprehensible.[106] He warns her that her "liberal hand" requires a "sequester from liberty" (46, 40). The ambiguous word "frank" also points toward sexual looseness as well as open truthfulness, so that when Othello calls Desdemona's hand a "frank one," he is again implying that she is sexually unguarded, even promiscuous. Centered only on Othello and her love for him, Desdemona interprets "frank" favorably:

> You may, indeed, say so;
> For 'twas that hand that gave away my heart.   (44–45)

Her association of frankness with generosity brings us back to Iago and his hypocritical promise to show his love for Othello "with franker spirit" (3. 3. 195). This is the man who trades on the signifier "honest" but repeatedly reveals the yawning gap between sign and substance, verbal suggestion and material thing. Indeed, it is by means of the spoken word, the "pestilence" that he pours into Othello's ear, that Iago constructs an alternative (and false) reality for Othello, substituting "that name" of "whore" (4. 2. 117–19) for the "good name" of Desdemona.

NOTES

1. A. C. Bradley, *Shakespearean Tragedy* (1904; London: Macmillan, 1962), stresses the "comparative confinement of the imaginative atmosphere" in *Othello* (p. 150).

2. David C. McPherson, *Shakespeare, Jonson, and the Myth of Venice* (Newark: University of Delaware Press, 1990), discusses the Renaissance image of Venice under four headings: Venice the Rich, Venice the Wise, Venice the Just, and Venice città galante (city of pleasure).

3. Ibid., p. 29.

4. See Virginia Mason Vaughan, Othello: *A Contextual History* (Cambridge: Cambridge University Press, 1994), p. 14.

5. Lewis Lewkenor's translation of Cardinal Gasparo Contarini's *The Commonwealth and Government of Venice* (1599), sign. A2 verso, cited in McPherson, *Shakespeare, Jonson, and the Myth of Venice*, p. 37.

6. Murray J. Levith, *Shakespeare's Italian Settings and Plays* (New York: St. Martin's Press, 1989), does point out some slight deviations from "actual Venetian practice," such as the Duke's pardon of his general after "only an informal hearing" (p. 33).

7. Discussed by McPherson, *Shakespeare, Jonson, and the Myth of Venice*, p. 43.

8. Alvin Kernan (ed.), *Othello, The Signet Classic Shakespeare* (1963; New York: Penguin Books, 1986; 1998), p. lxvi.

9. Ibid., p. lxvii.

10. T. McAlindon, *Shakespeare's Tragic Cosmos* (Cambridge: Cambridge University Press, 1997), points out that the private conflicts in the play might strike the Jacobean audience as a "microcosm" of the Christians' loss of Cyprus to the Turks in 1570 (p. 129).

11. Michael Neill, "Changing Places in *Othello*," *ShS*, 37 (1984): 115–31, quote at 118.

12. Rosalie L. Colie, *Shakespeare's Living Art* (Princeton, N.J.: Princeton University Press, 1974), points this out (p. 150).

13. Ibid., p. 152.

14. Bradley, *Shakespearean Tragedy*, p. 144.

15. Emrys Jones, *Scenic Form in Shakespeare* (Oxford: Clarendon Press, 1971), argues that Act 3 could logically end here (p. 134). Lending support to this argument is the parallel between the comic relief opening of Act 4, scene 3, where the Clown appears with Desdemona, and the opening of Act 3, which begins with Cassio's brief conversation with the musicians and the Clown.

16. Max Bluestone, *From Story to Stage* (The Hague and Paris: Mouton, 1974), points out that while Shakespeare omits the period of domestic tranquillity between the Moor and his wife, the domestic allusions—images of gloves, skillets, and parlors—"create an aura of settled domesticity implying long time" (p. 222).

17. Bradley, *Shakespearean Tragedy*, p. 362.

18. Ned B. Allen, "The Two Parts of *Othello*," *ShS*, 21 (1968): 13–29.

19. M. R. Ridley (ed.), *Othello, The New Arden Shakespeare* (London: Methuen, 1958), p. lxx. In a subtle analysis, Joel B. Altman, "'Preposterous Conclusions': Eros, *Enargeia*, and the Composition of *Othello*," *Representations*, 18 (Spring 1987), 129–57, argues that Shakespeare is deliberately using the rhetorical figure of *hysteron proteron* ("the latter part put before the former") to introduce the element of literal improbability into the represented action of the play (p. 133).

20. Jones, *Scenic Form in Shakespeare*, p. 41.

21. Graham Bradshaw, *Misrepresentations: Shakespeare and the Materialists* (London and Ithaca, N.Y.: Cornell University Press, 1993), pp. 155–63.

22. Ridley (ed.), *Othello*, also comments that "Othello's poisoned fear is that he has been cuckolded, not that he has been merely anticipated" (p. lxix).

23. It is just as plausible, for instance, to deduce that Desdemona wants to display her wedding sheets as evidence that she was a virgin when the marriage was consummated (implied, though not stated, in Lynda E. Boose, "Othello's Handkerchief: The Recognizance and Pledge of Love," *ELR*, 5 [1975]: 360–74) as to assert that the cleanliness of the sheets must mean that they are "as yet unstained with virgin blood" (T. G. A. Nelson and Charles Haines, "Othello's Unconsummated Marriage," *EIC*, 33.1 [1983]: 1–18, quote at 9).

24. Nelson and Haines, "Othello's Unconsummated Marriage," p. 1. Maynard Mack, " 'Speak of Me as I Am,' " in *Everybody's Shakespeare* (Lincoln and London: University of Nebraska Press, 1993), points out that to regard Othello as a "sexual cripple" reduces the impact of the play (p. 140).

25. Bradshaw, *Misrepresentations*, p. 167.

26. As in Lodovico Castelvetro, *Poetica d'Aritotele* (1576), discussed in Madeleine Doran, *Endeavors of Art: A Study of Form in Elizabethan Drama* (Madison: University of Wisconsin Press, 1954), p. 7.

27. Harley Granville Barker, *Prefaces to Shakespeare* (Princeton, N.J.: Princeton University Press, 1947), vol. 2, p. 100, declares that the ending of *Othello* "does not so much purge us with pity and terror as fill us with horror and with anger."

28. R. S. White, *Innocent Victims: Poetic Injustice in Shakespearean Tragedy* (1982; London: Athlone Press, 1986), p. 90.

29. See Kenneth Burke, "*Othello:* An Essay to Illustrate a Method," *HudR*, 4 (1951): 165–203, quote at 197.

30. Thomas Rymer, *A Short View of Tragedy* (1693; Menston, Yorkshire: Scholar Press, 1970), p. 89.

31. Colie, *Shakespeare's Living Art*, p. 135.

32. See Barbara Everett, "Spanish Othello: The Making of Shakespeare's Moor," *ShS*, 35 (1982): 101–12.

33. Explored by Barbara Heliodora C. De Mendonca, "*Othello:* A Tragedy Built on a Comic Structure," *ShS*, 21 (1968): 31–38.

34. See Russ McDonald, "Othello, Thorello, and the Foolish Hero," *SQ*, 30.1 (1979): 51–58, quote at 58.

35. See Stephen Rogers, "*Othello:* Comedy in Reverse," *SQ*, 24 (1973): 210–220. Francis Teague, "*Othello* and New Comedy," *CompD*, 20.1 (Spring 1986): 54–64, analyzes Othello as a "tragic inversion of the *miles gloriosus*," a "soldier whose emotions are manipulated by a clever underling," the *servus callidus* (pp. 59, 55).

36. Michael D. Bristol, "Charivari and the Comedy of Abjection in *Othello*," *RenD*, n.s. 21 (1990): 3–21, quotes at 4 and 13.

37. McDonald, "Othello, Thorello, and the Foolish Hero," p. 57.

38. On this aspect of the play, see Rosalind King, " 'Then Murder's Out of Tune': The Music and Structure of *Othello*," *ShS*, 39 (1987): 149–58.

39. In "Othello's Occupation: Shakespeare and the Romance of Chivalry," *ELR*, 15 (1985): 293–311, Mark Rose discusses the play's conversion of Elizabethan romance into tragedy at a time when "the feudal world of honor, fidelity, and service is becoming the bourgeois world of property and contractual relations."

40. Susan Snyder, "Beyond Comedy: *Romeo and Juliet* and *Othello*," in *The Comic Matrix of Shakespeare's Tragedies* (Princeton, N.J.: Princeton University Press, 1979), pp. 56–90, discusses how "the love that in comedies was a strength in *Othello* is vulnerable to attacks of reason, arguments from nature" (p. 81). Carol Thomas Neely, "Women and Men in *Othello*," in Carolyn Lenz, Gayle Greene, and Carol Thomas Neely (eds.), *The Woman's Part: Feminist Criticism of Shakespeare* (Urbana: University of Illinois Press, 1980), pp. 211–39, points out that *Othello* ends like "cankered comedy" with no "comic resolution of male with female" (p. 234).

41. Northrop Frye, *Anatomy of Criticism* (1957; Princeton, N.J.: Princeton University Press, 1971), p. 182.

42. For other plot similarities between *Othello* and *Much Ado about Nothing*, see Jones, *Scenic Form in Shakespeare*, pp. 120–23.

43. The sixty-three instances of "Heaven" in *Othello* (as opposed to the fifty-one in *Hamlet*) are less significant, as "Heaven" was used as a substitute for "God" in plays published after 1606.

44. *Christopher Marlowe: The Complete Plays*, ed. J. B. Steane (Harmondsworth: Penguin, 1969), p. 268.

45. Bernard Spivack, *Shakespeare and the Allegory of Evil* (New York: Columbia University Press, 1958), concludes that we can best understand Iago as a "hybrid" creation—part Vice (from the older homiletic tradition) and part naturalistic character (pp. 33ff.).

46. That the bloodthirsty revenger was damned is strongly implied in the tragedies of the period, most notably in the character of Vindice in *The Revenger's Tragedy* (1606).

47. René E. Fortin, "Allegory and Genre in *Othello*," *Genre*, 4.2 (July 1971): 153–72, quote at 168.

48. Daniel J. Vitkus, "Turning Turk in *Othello:* The Conversion and Damnation of the Moor," *SQ*, 48.2 (1997): 145–76, quote at 176.

49. Robert H. West, "The Christianness of *Othello*," *SQ*, 15 (1964): 333–43, quote at 343. See also Edward Hubler, "The Damnation of Othello: Some Limitations on the Christian View of the Play," *SQ*, 9 (1958): 295–300.

50. Bradshaw uses this term in *Misrepresentations*, p. 171.

51. Pointed out by T. McAlindon, *Shakespeare and Decorum* (London and Basingstoke: Macmillan, 1973), pp. 92–93.

52. These terms are helpfully discussed by Maynard Mack, "The Jacobean Shakespeare: Some Observations on the Construction of the Tragedies," in Kernan (ed.), *Othello*, pp. 190–226.

53. Martha Widmayer, "Brabantio and Othello," *ES*, 77.2 (1996): 113–26, pushes this similarity further, arguing that each character is "crushed by his desire for absolute goodness in the person of Desdemona" (p. 126).

54. A. P. Rossiter, *Angel with Horns* (London: Longman, 1961), notes a "highly complex pattern of incongruent triangles in the play" (pp. 206–8), including the wished-for (by Roderigo) Roderigo-Desdemona-Othello triangle.

55. Burke, "*Othello*," pp. 166–67.

56. Julia Genster, "Lieutenancy, Standing in, and *Othello*," *ELH*, 57.4 (1990): 785–809, explores how in *Othello* "arrangements of social and sexual power are played out particularly close to the terms of office, of place" (p. 785).

57. Neill, "Changing Places in *Othello*," comments in detail on the "double displacement" that Iago feels he has suffered himself and now creates for Othello (p. 128).

58. Robert Rogers, "Endopsychic Drama in *Othello*," *SQ*, 20 (1969): 205–15, points out

how the "sexual double standard is perceptible in Othello, obvious in Cassio, and symbolized in extreme pathological form by Othello-Iago" (p. 213).

59. John Bayley, *The Characters of Love* (New York: Basic Books, 1960), notes that Roderigo functions as a "feeble echo" of Othello's passion (p. 164).

60. Noted by Ralph Berry, "Pattern in *Othello*," *SQ*, 23 (1972): 3–19.

61. Brian Vickers, *The Artistry of Shakespeare's Prose* (London: Methuen, 1968), p. 433.

62. Giorgio Melchiori, "The Rhetoric of Character Construction: Othello," *ShS*, 34 (1981): 61–72, observes the progressive disintegration of Othello's speech through his earlier picking up of "Zounds" and "Ha!" from Iago.

63. One exception is Iago's eleven-line aside in prose in Act 2 (scene 1, 165–76), when he is watching Cassio with Desdemona—"He takes her by the palm"—and plotting his downfall. Foregrounded because it comes straight after Iago's witty couplets, this speech is more a voicing of private thoughts than a direct address to the audience.

64. Vickers, *The Artistry of Shakespeare's Prose*, p. 336. Wolfgang Clemen, *The Development of Shakespeare's Imagery* (London: Methuen, 1951), comments on how Iago's prose style combines "skilful ingenuity with calculation" and links it with the euphuistic style (pp. 122–23).

65. McAlindon, *Shakespeare and Decorum*, p. 107.

66. Madeleine Doran, "Iago's '*If*'—Conditional and Subjunctive in *Othello*," in *Shakespeare's Dramatic Language* (Madison: University of Wisconsin Press, 1976), p. 90.

67. Noted by Brian Vickers, *Appropriating Shakespeare* (London and New Haven, Conn.: Yale University Press, 1993), p. 79.

68. Joseph A. Porter, "Complement Extern: Iago's Speech Acts," in Virginia Mason Vaughan and Kent Cartwright (eds.), Othello: *New Perspectives* (London and Toronto: Associated University Presses, 1991), pp. 74–88, notes how both Iago's imperatives and his "performatives," such as "I do beseech you," are "intended to induce some action or behavior" (p. 78).

69. In C. H. Herford, Percy Simpson, and Evelyn Simpson (eds.), *Ben Jonson* (Oxford: Clarendon Press, 1947), vol. 8, p. 625.

70. Eamon Grennan, "The Women's Voices in *Othello*: Speech, Song, Silence," *SQ*, 38 (1987): 275–92, quotes at 289 and 288.

71. Norman Sanders (ed.), *Othello, New Cambridge Shakespeare* (Cambridge: Cambridge University Press, 1984), p. 31.

72. E. A. J. Honigmann, "Shakespeare's 'Bombast,'" in Philip Edwards, Inga-Stina Ewbank, and G. K. Hunter (eds.), *Shakespeare's Styles* (Cambridge: Cambridge University Press, 1980), p. 159. Robert Heilman, *Magic in the Web: Language and Action in* Othello (Lexington: University of Kentucky Press, 1956), also finds an ambiguity in Othello's style—magniloquence that "suggests largeness and freedom of spirit" coexisting with "self-deception, limitedness of feeling, and egotism" (p. 138).

73. E. A. J. Honigmann, "Secret Motives in *Othello*," *Shakespeare: Seven Tragedies* (New York: Barnes and Noble, 1976), p. 95.

74. Philip A. Smith, "Othello's Diction," *SQ*, 9 (1958): 428–30, thinks that this is part of the eccentric, "foreign nature" of Othello's language, a "compensatory posturing" because he is "culturally unassimilated" (p. 429).

75. Anthony Hecht, *Obbligati: Essays in Criticism* (New York: Atheneum, 1986), notes how often Othello's self-conscious style includes apostrophes and vocatives (pp. 71–72).

76. Honigmann, *Shakespeare: Seven Tragedies*, p. 91.

77. In "'Egregiously an Ass': The Dark Side of the Moor. A View of Othello's Mind," *ShS*, 10 (1957): 98–106, Albert Gerard contends instead that the tragedy springs from "the shortcomings of [Othello's] intellect" (p. 105).

78. For a close reading of this soliloquy, see John Money, "Othello's 'It Is the Cause . . . ': An Analysis," *ShS*, 6 (1953): 94–105.

79. G. Wilson Knight, "The *Othello* Music," in *The Wheel of Fire: Interpretations of Shakespeare's Sombre Tragedies* (London: Oxford University Press, 1930), p. 97.

80. Clemen, *The Development of Shakespeare's Imagery*, p. 121.

81. Knight, "The *Othello* Music," p. 104.

82. See Heilman, *Magic in the Web*, pp. 86–98.

83. See J. L. Styan, *Shakespeare's Stagecraft* (Cambridge: Cambridge University Press, 1967), p. 33.

84. Winifred M. T. Nowottny, "Justice and Love in *Othello*," *UTQ*, 21 (July 1952): 330–44, analyzes in detail how the word "cause," complex in its meanings, unites "the personal, the social, and the religious aspects" of justice (p. 341).

85. Rymer, *A Short View of Tragedy*, p. 140.

86. James A. McPherson, "Three Great Ones of the City and One Perfect Soul: Well Met at Cyprus," in Mythili Kaul (ed.), Othello: *New Essays by Black Writers* (Washington, D.C.: Howard University Press, 1997), points out that the token, invested with "all the potent emotional powers of the mysterious 'East,'" is a symbol of Othello's bond with Desdemona "*in his own ancestral terms*" (pp. 65–66).

87. See Neely, "Women and Men in *Othello*," p. 228. In her later "Circumscriptedness and Unhousedness: *Othello* in the Borderlands," in Deborah Barker and Ivo Kemps (eds.), *Shakespeare and Gender: A History* (London and New York: Verso, 1995), pp. 302–15, Carol Thomas Neely finds in the handkerchief an emblem of "Moorish female sexuality," so that Desdemona is caught between "contradictory prescriptions"—sexual "power" and "the wifely duty her mother models" (p. 309).

88. Michael C. Andrews, "Honest Othello: The Handkerchief Once More," *SEL*, 13.2 (Spring 1973): 273–84, who deduces that the first version of the handkerchief's origins is authentic and not Othello's attempt to intimidate Desdemona, stresses how Othello regards the talisman as "ensuring the continuance of his love for Desdemona" (pp. 281–82).

89. Arthur Kirsch, *Shakespeare and the Experience of Love* (Cambridge: Cambridge University Press, 1981), points out how the origins of the handkerchief suggest Othello's sense of "primal betrayal" as the child separates from his mother (pp. 34, 24–26).

90. David Kaula, "Othello Possessed: Notes on Shakespeare's Use of Magic and Witchcraft," *ShStud*, 2 (1966): 112–32, argues that when Othello becomes fixated on the handkerchief, he is in the grip of a delusion, "hallowing rather than recoiling from the demonic" (p. 126). Less judgmentally, Linda Woodbridge, *The Scythe of Saturn: Shakespeare and Magical Thinking* (Urbana and Chicago: University of Illinois Press, 1994), finds that in losing the handkerchief, Desdemona may forfeit a "magical protection against the evil eye" (p. 26).

91. Heilman, *Magic in the Web*, p. 213.

92. Peter Stallybrass, "Patriarchal Territories: The Body Enclosed," in Margaret W. Ferguson, Maureen Quilligan, and Nancy J. Vickers (eds.), *Rewriting the Renaissance* (Chicago: University of Chicago Press, 1986), pp. 123–42, comments on how the handkerchief "is metaphorically substituted for the body's apertures" (p. 139).

93. John Pory, translator of Leo Africanus, *The History and Description of Africa* (1600), ed. Robert Brown (London: Hakluyt Society, 1896), notes one African custom of

checking for blood-spotted sheets after the nuptials as proof of the bride's virginity (vol. 2, p. 450). Boose, "Othello's Handkerchief," 360–74, thinks that this "blood pledge" leads to Othello's role as judicial executioner; he bases his rationale for killing Desdemona on Deuteronomy 22:20–22, which justifies killing a bride if she cannot prove her virginity on the wedding night (pp. 372–73).

94. Katherine S. Stockholder, "Egregiously an Ass: Chance and Accident in *Othello*," *SEL*, 13.2 (Spring 1973): 256–72, emphasizes that it is dangerous for Othello to "confuse the handkerchief, which can be lost, copied, stolen, with the human love it represents" (p. 265).

95. Thomas Moisan, "Repetition and Interrogation in *Othello:* 'What Needs This Iterance?' or 'Can Anything Be Made of This?'", in Vaughan and Cartwright (eds.), Othello: *New Perspectives,* p. 61.

96. Michel Eyquem de Montaigne, *Montaigne's Essays,* trans. John Florio (1603), introd. L. C. Harmer (London: Dent, 1965), vol. 3, chap. 5, "Upon Some Verses of Virgil," p. 101.

97. See James L. Calderwood, "Signs, Speech, and Self," in *The Properties of* Othello (Amherst: University of Massachusetts Press, 1989), pp. 59–61.

98. McAlindon, *Shakespeare and Decorum,* includes this in his perceptive analysis of verbal witchcraft and semantic flux in *Othello* (pp. 121–30).

99. In "An Enemy in Their Mouths: The Closure of Language in *Othello,*" *UCrow,* 10 (1990): 69–85, Sharon Beehler comments on how Iago exploits Othello's naivete in "ceasing to respect the plurality of language" (pp. 71–72).

100. See Randolph Splitter, "Language, Sexual Conflict, and 'Symbiosis Anxiety' in *Othello,*" *Mosaic,* 15.3 (1982): 17–26.

101. Karl F. Zender, "The Humiliation of Iago," *SEL,* 34 (1994): 323–39, discusses how Iago "asserts his complete freedom to make any signifier mean anything," although he ultimately twists language in the service of his own "anger-driven discourse" (pp. 327–28).

102. See David Lucking's cogent analysis, "Putting Out the Light: Semantic Indeterminacy and the Deconstitution of Self in *Othello,*" *ES,* 75.2 (1994): 110–22.

103. Ibid., p. 118.

104. Dympna Callaghan, "'Othello Was a White Man': Properties of Race on Shakespeare's Stage," in Terence Hawkes (ed.), *Alternative Shakespeares* (London and New York: Routledge, 1996), vol. 2, pp. 192–215, points out how Bianca might be made up in exaggerated whiteface on the Renaissance stage and thereby associated with "the derogated cosmetic arts" (p. 206).

105. See also Felicity Rosslyn, "Nature Erring from Itself: *Othello* Again," *CQ,* 18.3 (1989): 289–302.

106. Stallybrass, "Patriarchal Territories," comments on the "linguistic wantonness that ceaselessly elides [for Othello] the cultural opposition between the woman who married him and the category of 'woman' constructed within misogynist discourse" (p. 136).

4

THE MAJOR CHARACTERS

DESEMONA

Characters in a play cannot truly be considered as independent units. We build our responses to them not only from what a character says and does, but also from what other persons in the play say about the character and how he or she interacts with these other dramatis personae. During the course of the action, as E. A. J. Honigmann notes, these impressions may have to be "cancelled or modified," for dramatic characters, like real people, often "appear to be a mass of contradictions."[1] And in the play's dialectic, characters continuously reflect on one another, so that Desdemona's innocence is highlighted by Iago's evil machinations and counterpointed by Emilia's worldliness. They also trade on one another's strengths or vulnerabilities; Desdemona's naivete and warm loyalty to those she loves, revealed in her spirited defense of Cassio, makes Iago's deception of Othello easier. As Iago triumphantly tells the audience, he can "turn her virtue into pitch, / And out of her own goodness make the net / That shall enmesh them all" (2. 3. 360–62).

The complexity of the three main protagonists has led to opposed views of them and thus to significantly different interpretations of *Othello*. So, even though characters in this play are bound to one another in what Barbara Everett calls a "curious degree of close relationship,"[2] it is helpful to isolate these major ones for analysis, to assess how plausible are the critical evaluations of them. Like Iago and Othello, Desdemona has proved elusive. While most readers will interpret her as a realistically developed character, it is worth remembering that she began, on the most material level, as a "female artifact created by a male imagination and objectified in a boy actor's body."[3] And to a large extent, she turns out to be constructed by the men in the play—Brabantio, Roderigo, Cassio, Iago, and, of course, Othello—who all read her somewhat differently.[4] Critics have been more extreme in their judgments. In the late seventeenth century, Thomas Rymer found her coarse, while John Quincy Adams, writing in the nineteenth century, judged her harshly as a "wanton" who received her just deserts.[5] Early-twentieth-century commentators, such as A. C.

Bradley, tended to overidealize her. "Criticized for her rebelliousness" by a few crit-ics, she has also been "blamed for her passivity"[6] when she becomes increasingly subdued by Othello's brutal treatment. Certainly she has struck discerning readers as more than a pathetic, "nearly-blank sheet."[7] But who is she?

The Demonized Female

When Iago, under cover of his witty discourse at the Cyprus harbor, accuses women of being "Saints in your injuries, devils being offended" (2. 1. 110), he is drawing on a long medieval and Renaissance tradition of misogynist satire related to women's allegedly unruly sexuality.[8] It trades on the male's fear that if a woman's sexual appetite is released, she will become insatiable or promiscuous and, in an era without reliable contraception, on the patriarchal husband's anxiety that his wife's children may be fathered by another man. The "divine" Desdemona, the totally unblemished woman that Cassio describes, is the other side of that coin. But Iago is able to exploit the husband Othello's ingrained fear that wives in gen-eral are prone to "stol'n hours of lust."

Iago is cynical enough to regard every woman, not just lubricious Venetian wives with their hidden "pranks," as a whore. "Fair and wise" women, he jokes, are as capable of the same "foul pranks" as ugly and foolish ones (2. 1. 127, 140). Iago may be arguing self-interestedly when he tells Roderigo that Desdemona will soon "disrelish and abhor the Moor" and find a partner more suited to her youth and race (2. 1. 232); yet even in soliloquy, he seems sincerely convinced "That she loves [Cassio], 'tis apt and of great credit" (287), and we know that he does not dis-tinguish love as platonic friendship from "lust of the blood." In his "profane" satire, he puts down even the most "deserving woman" (143) as fit only to "suckle fools and chronicle small beer" (158)—that is, if she exists at all.

Iago consciously demonizes women, and his quest is to make Othello do the same. He does indeed turn Desdemona's "virtue" into "pitch" in the eyes of Othello, unleashing in his master a deep distrust of women's sexuality,[9] a fear that Desde-mona's desires may be insatiable: "That we may call these delicate creatures ours, / And not their appetites!" (3. 3. 268–69). Just as the mad King Lear retches at the thought of the "burning, scalding, / Stench, consumption" of women's genitalia, the "sulphurous pit" of darkness that fiends inherit (*King Lear* IV. vi. 128–29), so Othello envisages his most beloved treasure, Desdemona's body, as soiled and overused, a "cistern for foul toads / To knot and gender in" (4. 2. 60–61).

Shakespeare did not invent the name of his heroine; he found it in Giraldi Cinthio's narrative, and it means, appropriately, "misfortune" in Greek. Yet once he is influenced by Iago, it is noticeable that Ot-hell-o projects the demonic onto Des-demon-a. It may be, as several commentators have suggested, that Othello's "blackening" of Desdemona is a projection of his own self-loathing onto her—an underlying fear, induced by Iago, that "his blackness has in fact contaminated her"[10] so that she becomes (in the Quarto text) a "black weed" (4. 2. 66) to him. Whatever the causes, by the end of the temptation scene, he sees her as a "fair devil" (3. 3. 475); soon afterward, he claims to have conjured up a "young and sweating devil" in the palm of Desdemona's hand (3. 4. 42). When he hits his wife in front of the Venetian embassy, he curses her as "devil" (4. 1. 240) and connects her supposed falseness with the antifeminist cliché that women often fake tears: "O devil, devil! / If that the earth could teem with woman's tears, / Each drop she falls would prove a crocodile" (245–46). In the brothel scene, he brands her "false as hell" (4. 2. 38). Pursuing this connection of devil with promiscuous woman, he inscribes Desdemona as a strumpet in an image that ironically suggests how Othello, writing on her blank page, is the real author of her whoredom: "Was this fair paper, this most goodly book, / Made to write 'whore' upon?" (70–71). For her part, Desdemona is stunned by his abuse; she "cannot say whore," let alone act the part. Emilia redresses the balance, shattering the construct of Desdemona as whore and demon when she affirms to Othello, after the murder, that his wife was chaste and angelic, while he is "the blacker devil" (5. 2. 130).

Although Brabantio discerns a warped "nature" in his daughter (1. 3. 62) and Iago postulates a "will most rank" in Desdemona's choice of the Moor, Othello is the only character in the play who openly castigates Desdemona as devilish; the audience is always aware of and appalled by his mistake. Critics have not demonized her outright, even though they have sometimes, in reaction to the earlier idealized readings of her character, sought to find fault with her. Margaret Loftus Ranald chides Desdemona for failing to be "the ideal young lady of the precept books,"[11] as though her freedom from such a stereotype makes her partially responsible for her terrible fate.[12] Taking a psychoanalytical approach, Robert Dickes finds Desdemona's capitulation to death an "alleviation of guilt" for the oedipal conflict that makes her choose "as a love object a representative of her father."[13] Attempts to disparage Desdemona, or to find deep-seated psychological reasons for her welcoming a violent death, appear a perverse attempt to blame the victim—an unwillingness to face up to the shocking injustice of her killing.[14]

The "Divine" Desdemona

The phrase is Cassio's; he virtually deifies Desdemona when she arrives in Cyprus, viewing her as a goddess or a figure of the Virgin Mary:

> Hail to thee, lady! and the grace of heaven,
> Before, behind thee, and on every hand,
> Enwheel thee round.   (2. 1. 84–86)

With similar hyberbole, he defends her to Iago as "perfection" (2. 3. 26). Her father uses the same term; finding in his white daughter a paragon of virtue, he is incredulous that her "perfection so could err / Against all rules of nature" (1. 3. 100–101) as to choose a black husband. Unwilling to believe that this ideal daughter could defy him, Brabantio convinces himself that Othello's witchcraft, or "practices of cunning hell," must be to blame for her defection.

Roderigo also acknowledges Desdemona's saintliness when he responds to Iago's suggestion of her fickleness with "she's full of most blessed condition" (2. 1. 249–50). Emilia perceives her as "heavenly true" (5. 2. 134). Even Iago is impressed by Desdemona's extraordinary generosity—he tells us that "she's framed as fruitful / As the free elements" (2. 3. 341–42)—although he remains cynical about all women, including this one. Despite being susceptible to Iago's insinuations in Act 3, scene 3, Othello remains intuitively convinced of Desdemona's heaven-sanctioned purity when she returns to the stage in that scene and he exclaims, "If she be false, heaven mocked itself! / I'll not believe it" (277–78); that is, heaven would have travestied ("mocked") its own values had it created a woman who appears so pure but is in fact corrupt. After the murder, Othello again glances at Desdemona's perfection by affirming that, had she remained faithful to him, he would not have traded her for a world "Of one entire and perfect chrysolite" (5. 2. 142).[15]

It is partly this perception by other characters that empowers Desdemona as a symbol of moral beauty, enabling her to act as good angel to Iago's devil in the underlying morality play scheme. Do Desdemona's own words and actions live up to this "divine" image? Or does viewing her as "divine" submit her to unrealistic expectations, putting her on a pedestal from which she is bound to fall once we approach the play as naturalistic drama and not as a schematic allegory?

The second part of the play provides several instances of Desdemona's almost superhuman charity. Her courageous unselfishness is pointed in her promise to help Cassio, even after Othello proves hostile: "What I can do I will; and more I will / Than for myself I dare" (3. 4. 130–31). In Act 4, as Othello turns brutal, Desdemona becomes increasingly self-effacing. Apparently recognizing that her "impulsiveness"[16] has had a disastrous effect on her husband, she "suppresses" it in the interests of repairing the relationship. She is, as Othello snarls, "very obedient" after he strikes her in public, where his sarcasm provides an ironic echo of her sincere pledge in Act 3, scene 3, "Whate'er you be, I am obedient" (89). Obeying when he summons her back, and turning the other cheek in exemplary Christian fashion, she allows herself only the mild protest "I have not deserved this" (4. 1. 241). Yet her self-denial is less a passive capitulation than a signal of her active love for her husband. When he abuses her as a whore in the following scene, she retorts, "By heaven, you do me wrong!" (4. 2. 80), and afterward she is eager to find out from Iago "What shall I do to win my lord again?" (148).[17] The words that follow are an incandescent tribute to the purity of her love and her absolute commitment to this man, regardless of his behavior toward her:

> Unkindness may do much,
> And his unkindness may defeat my life,
> But never taint my love.   (4. 2. 158–60)

She reaffirms this unconditional loyalty—she would not betray Othello for "all the world"—in the willow scene (4. 3. 65); to her amazingly forgiving eyes, even his "checks" and "frowns" have "grace and favor" (20–21). The most supreme proof of her self-sacrificing nature comes when she exonerates her husband from any blame in her death. As long as there is hope for them both, she pleads with him, "Kill me tomorrow; let me live tonight!" (5. 2. 80). But after the strangling, her principal concern is for his safety. Responding to Emilia's question "Who hath done this?" she proclaims a "sublime falsehood"[18] with her dying breath: "Nobody—I myself" (123). And her final request, "Commend me to my kind lord" (124), fulfills her earlier vow that Othello's "unkindness" will never "taint" her love or destroy her belief in his essential goodness. Other interpreters of her last words have unearthed more subtle possibilities. Jane Adamson finds in them "a kind of (innocent) suicide," part of Desdemona's "apathetic submission"[19] in the last part of the play that has troubled several feminist critics, while S. N. Garner reads them as a mature appraisal of her situation, in which Desdemona takes "full responsibility"[20] for her marriage and its consequences. On the stage, though, Desdemona's words come across as utterly altruistic.[21]

Desdemona is the epitome of unselfish Christian goodness here. She illustrates the "fruit of the Spirit," defined by St. Paul as "generosity, faithfulness, gentleness" in opposition to the "works of the flesh," which include "strife, jealousy, anger" (Galatians 5:19–33).[22] Early-twentieth-century critics, concentrating on the qualities she displays near the end of the play, have sometimes turned her into a saint. Bradley expounds at length on her "heavenly sweetness and self-surrender,"[23] while G. Wilson Knight finds that she embodies the "divine principle"[24] in the last act of the play. Yet this is to ignore her more human, fallible traits. We need not condemn the men in the play for responding, as several male critics do, to the dimension of Desdemona that Emilia terms "heavenly true." Rather, their difficulty lies in accommodating this facet of her with Shakespeare's presentation of a flesh-and-blood character who is surprisingly willful, sexually aware, and independent in her judgments. Above all, it is Othello who cannot modify his idealized image of Desdemona once he suspects that she is less than perfect; he veers from one extreme to the other, from viewing Desdemona as saint to seeing her as strumpet or "fair devil."

"She Speaks . . . Stoutly"

What the audience sees in Desdemona, particularly during the first three acts, is a woman who combines spiritual with physical love for Othello and who is courageous and independent in her judgments, often stubbornly so. Brabantio has clearly underestimated his daughter when he calls her a "maiden never bold" (1. 3. 94). It is true, as Ann Jenalie Cook points out, that the audience is initially impressed with the "downright violence" of Desdemona's attachment to the Moor; we discover that she is "strong willed, openly passionate, highly unconventional"[25] long before we are assured of her uncompromising integrity. In fact, some readers may find it difficult to reconcile the strong-willed woman of the first half of the play—the one who crosses her father and persists in her outspoken support of Cassio—with the self-abnegating Desdemona of the final two acts. Even the traits of the flesh-and-blood woman, the one who speaks "stoutly" (3. 1. 43), have given rise to quite different interpretations. Does she appear headstrong and insensitive in her defense of Cassio, courting disaster by harping on his reinstatement, or is she attractive in her warm loyalty to a friend and her candid pursuit of what she regards as a good cause?

Desdemona makes mistakes; she is not, after all, a perfect human being. When Othello confronts her with the loss of the handkerchief, she tells a lie: "It is not lost" (3. 4. 83). This defensive reaction, though, is provoked by Othello's grim warning about the token's origins. And Desdemona's immediate rejoinder "But what an if it were?" suggests an immunity to fetishes, a confidence that her love for Othello is worth more than any external emblem of it. Four other sequences where Desdemona shows her mettle have proved controversial and need to be re-examined: her defiance of her father in eloping with Othello; her comic banter with Iago on the quayside; her championing of Cassio after he has been demoted; and her admiring reference to Lodovico in Act 4, scene 3.

Critics writing in a less feminist age than ours remind readers that in Shakespeare's time, a young woman's deceiving her father to marry against his will was a serious business. G. Bonnard maintains that "none of Brabantio's exclamations on discovering that Desdemona had gone could sound exaggerated or comical in the ears of a Jacobean audience," for "Shakespeare meant his spectators to take quite seriously Desdemona's guilt as a rebellious child."[26] Brabantio's sense of betrayal is acute—he warns Othello "She has deceived her father, and may thee" (1. 3. 288)—and by the end of the play, he has died of a broken heart. It is certainly unfortunate that Desdemona has to trick her father and is either unwilling or unable to cushion the blow; in view of Brabantio's intransigently racist attitudes, though, she may have good reasons for keeping her wedding secret. Her opening speech to the Senate is a superb justification of her marriage, showing delicacy of feeling as well as firmness. Admitting a "divided duty," Desdemona is careful not to flaunt her newly married status to her grieving father. Instead, she respectfully reminds him that a woman inevitably transfers her loyalty once she chooses a husband:

> You are the lord of duty,
> I am hitherto your daughter. But here's my husband,
> And so much duty as my mother showed
> To you, preferring you before her father,
> So much I challenge that I may profess
> Due to the Moor my lord.   (1. 3. 182–87)

Desdemona's echo of St. Paul's "let the wife be [subject] to the husband" (Ephesians 5:1, 25) is a much more tactful version of Cordelia's blunt reminder to King Lear: "Sure, I shall never marry like my sisters, / To love my father all" (*King Lear* I. i. 103–4). It is up to the individual actress to convey the dominant emotion here, but there need be nothing callous or complacent about Desdemona's words.

Desdemona's speech seeking permission to accompany her husband to Cyprus reveals her courage—in front of the Senate, she is proud that her "downright violence" can "trumpet to the world" her physical passion for Othello—as well as her total devotion to him: "My heart's subdued / Even to the very quality of my lord" (1. 3. 244–46). A similar combination of physical frankness and joyful compliance emerges from Othello's description of how Desdemona fell in love with him and became "half the wooer." She listened to the story of his life with a "greedy ear," wept in compassion for his hardships, and gave him a "world of sighs" (Quarto reading; the Folio offers "kisses"). Afterward, she is the one who hints that she would like to marry him:

> She wished she had not heard it; yet she wished
> That heaven had made her such a man.   (161–62)

The lines are subtly ambiguous—does Desdemona wish she had been born a male like Othello, or does she want the gift of Othello as her man?—but in either case, they suggest an independent will coexisting with a desire for union. The same kind of paradox, of being "subdu'd" to her lord while retaining a stubborn integrity, is implied in the willow scene (4. 3. 26), where Desdemona identifies herself with the "maid" (chaste woman) "called Barbary" (the part of Africa from which Othello originated). It is true that Desdemona is very young and does not know Othello well when she marries him. Yet her romantic attachment to him is based on a strong appreciation of, and yearning to identify with, his courage and dignity in exotic, life-threatening situations. The audience is more likely to be impressed by the freedom from conventional social judgments demonstrated in Desdemona's "I saw Othello's visage in his mind" (1. 3. 247) than to dismiss her passion for him as what W. H. Auden terms "the romantic crush of a silly school girl."[27]

Desdemona's spiritedness is revealed in the second controversial sequence—her banter with Iago when she is waiting for the arrival of her husband in Cyprus. Critics who idealize Desdemona are alarmed because she appears worldly and sexually knowing here, producing repartee that fails to jibe with their image of her. M. R. Ridley, for instance, finds it unnatural that she would indulge in such "cheap backchat" with Iago.[28] Granted, by taunting Iago with "Come, how wouldst thou praise me?" (2. 1. 122), Desdemona goads him into delivering what she then derides as his "lame and impotent" antifeminist riposte. Surely, though, she does not cheapen herself, just as Shakespeare's comic heroines (Rosalind in *As You Like It*, for example) gain rather than lose the audience's respect by sharpening their wits on the men.

Psychologically, too, Desdemona's prolonging of the exchange works as a strategy to deflect her anxiety over Othello's safety. As she explains to the audience, or to the company at large, "I am not merry; but I do beguile / The thing I am by seeming otherwise" (120–21). This is determined cheerfulness in the quest to stay upbeat. The audience is more disposed to approve her self-possession in a situation that could induce panic than to criticize her for vulgarity or insensitivity.

The one instance of insensitivity on Desdemona's part is her continuing to defend Cassio "stoutly" even after Othello has signaled his strong wish to terminate this discussion. Strictly speaking, Desdemona does not need to play the advocate at all. Emilia reports that Othello himself intends to reinstate his lieutenant before long, when she reassures Cassio,

> But he protests he loves you,
> And needs no other suitor but his likings
> To bring you in again.   (3. 1. 46–48)

Yet the warm-hearted Desdemona makes it her cause—"If I do vow a friendship I'll perform it / To the last article" (3. 3. 21–22)—and outlines a campaign of attack that seems almost shrewish:

> My lord shall never rest;
> I'll watch him tame and talk him out of patience;
> His bed shall seem a school, his board a shrift.   (22–24)

Indeed, she does badger Othello for a quick response, demanding "shall't be shortly?", "Shall't be tonight at supper?", "Tomorrow dinner then?", and exclaiming, "By'r Lady, I could do much" (56–58, 74). Several critics have viewed Desdemona's driving insistence as unwarranted interference in military protocol.[29] Her motives, however, remain altruistic; she is convinced that Othello will suffer if he loses Cassio's services and that restoring the lieutenant to his military station will bring "peculiar profit / To [Othello's] own person," equivalent to feeding on "nourishing dishes" (79–80). Her metaphors of domestic well-being convey the same tender, affectionate concern that she displays when she later pulls out the handkerchief to apply to his forehead (285).

It is in Act 3, scene 4 that Desdemona's spirited determination to help Cassio takes a disastrous turn. Naively, she assumes that Othello's demand for the missing handkerchief (repeated three times) is a "trick" to distract her from her mission; consequently, she tries to face him down by reiterating Cassio's good qualities ("You'll never meet a more sufficient man" [92]). On one level, this is a tactless and insensitive move, but it also shows Desedmona's inexperience: she simply cannot grasp what is immediately obvious to Emilia—that "this man" is "jealous" (99). Although Desdemona quickly learns to make allowances for Othello's harshness, rationalizing that he is preoccupied with state affairs and that "we must think men are not gods" (148), she remains convinced that he is "made of no such baseness / As jealous creatures are" (27–28). This naivete need not be interpreted as a perverse need to "remain oblivious"[30] to the change in Othello's feelings for her. As Madeleine Doran comments, Desdemona's "very tactlessness is the best guarantee of her innocence."[31] Her innocent harping on what most inflames Othello's suspicions is evident again in Act 4, scene 1, when Desdemona tells Lodovico (within Othello's hearing) how her "love" for Cassio makes her want to heal the "unkind breach" between the ex-lieutenant and her husband (232, 226).

Finally, Desdemona's sexual loyalty has been questioned because she suddenly remarks to Emilia that "this Lodovico is a proper man" (4. 3. 36). Could the abused Desdemona be contemplating what Lodovico—a more appropriate suitor in Venetian eyes—might have been like as a husband in place of Othello? Not consciously, to be sure, for it is Emilia who turns the adjective "proper" into a springboard for sexual appraisal when she comments on how very "handsome" Lodovico is and how much a certain young woman in Venice would have valued "a touch of his nether lip" (37, 40). It has been suggested that Desdemona may be referring instead to Lodovico's exceptionally "proper" behavior in the social arena—his unwillingness to intervene even though he has seen Othello strike her in public.[32] Yet most critics have taken Desdemona's remark to be an admiring one. While Auden cynically deduces from the remark that "Given a few more years" she "might well, one feels, have taken a lover,"[33] Garner says, more charitably, that Desdemona "unconsciously longs for a man like Lodovico" only because the man she has risked everything for "has turned into a barbarian and a madman."[34] Speculation about Desdemona's unconscious desires is surely futile, though. Like the theories that she masochistically welcomes a violent death because of underlying guilt over rejecting her father, it is a way of bringing the amazing Desdemona down to earth: an unwillingness to believe (in our skeptical age) that her moral integrity and love for her husband could be unwavering. As W. D. Adamson points out, it is more relevant to consider what Desdemona "does *not* say about the eligible bachelor" Lodovico than to fault her for mentioning him.[35]

During the Cyprus scenes, Desdemona's very strengths—courageous loyalty, frankness in speaking "stoutly," and unworldly innocence—are disastrously misconstrued by Othello. That this can happen despite her manifest purity ("guiltiness I know not," she affirms as Othello prepares to kill her [5. 2. 39]) is one of the play's deepest ironies. Norman Sanders outlines how in Desdemona's character "independence of mind emerges as stubborn persistence; joyful erotic confidence leads to dangerous interference in her husband's professional life; innocent conviction precludes any apprehension of evil until it is too late."[36] The audience, though, continues to admire her spiritedness and to remain staunchly sympathetic to her plight; unlike the critics who snipe at her fallibility, theater viewers "care intensely" for this "passionate" woman.[37]

IAGO AS VILLAIN

F. R. Leavis, intent on dissecting the main protagonist Othello, sidelines Iago as "not much more than a necessary piece of dramatic mechanism."[38] This provocative judgment runs counter to most people's impressions of Iago as a fascinating, multifaceted study in evil. Unlike the Moor, he establishes a close relationship with the audience[39] when he confides his plans to them and, through several soliloquies, frankly displays his various dimensions—as villain and as arch-hypocrite.

As Julie Hankey remarks, Shakespeare must have had an "extraordinary confidence" in his chief tragedian, Richard Burbage (the actor of Othello), to risk juxtaposing two centers of interest in this way.[40] But Iago, built on a less grand scale than Othello, need not steal the show from the hero. Ideally, the two characters work in tandem. Especially in the temptation scene (3. 3), we become aware of their symbiotic relationship so that, as J. I. M. Stewart puts it, "Othello and Iago are felt less as individuals each with his own psychological integrity than as abstractions from a single . . . protagonist."[41]

Samuel Taylor Coleridge's influential assessment of Iago—that his deep-rooted malice is "motiveless malignity" questing for ways to explain itself—points toward the symbolic level of character: Iago as Vice or devil figure. Yet any actor who tried to portray him purely as a symbol of evil—an attempt almost certainly spelling disaster in the theater[42]—would have had to ignore parts of Shakespeare's complex characterization. An actor is more likely to work with, and not against, the "inwardness that seems to have gone into [the] creation"[43] of this character. While appreciating the different personae (the morality play's Vice among them) that Iago projects so skillfully, the audience is likely to respond to him as a naturalistically conceived character, driven to malicious action by psychologically credible motives and all the more sinister for choosing evil rather than simply representing it. Arguably, some of his motives remain unstated, offshoots of a warped and paranoid nature seething with jealousy and envy.

"Honest" Iago

In this play about treachery and deceiving appearances, the repeated word "honest" takes on a special piquancy; the arch-villain is masquerading as a truthful, helpful friend. Iago is called "honest" or associated with "honesty" some twenty-seven times. In fact, all of the play's characters except Roderigo and (to some extent) Emilia are convinced that Iago is a plain-dealing truth-teller: Cassio claims never to have known a Florentine who is "more kind and honest" (3. 1. 39); Desdemona commends him as an "honest fellow" (3. 3. 5); and only once before the denouement does Othello waver in his conviction that his comrade is "honest, honest Iago" (5. 2. 151). He attributes "honesty" to his ensign fourteen times while being fairly quick to doubt the "honesty" (in a secondary Renaissance meaning, sexual chastity) of his wife. Honesty as chastity is prominent in Iago's undermining of Othello's trust in both Cassio and Desdemona. It is less relevant to Iago himself, even though he does have an almost puritanical obsession with sexual dishonesty, or the "slime" of "filthy deeds" (5. 2. 145–46).

Iago's reputation for truthfulness hinges on his blunt speaking as a soldier. This is the kind of barracks-room frankness—tough realism often tipping over into cynicism—that Cassio observes at the harbor, when he discerns in Iago's satire more of the "soldier" than the "scholar" (2. 1. 164). Like Henry V wooing Princess Katherine (*Henry V* V. ii. 149), Iago speaks as "plain soldier." Montano warns Iago that he is "no soldier" if he delivers "more or less than truth" in his report of Cassio's drunken behavior (2. 3. 218–19), and Iago himself makes the same connection when Othello threatens him with the prospect of damnation if he is lying. Indignantly, Iago offers to resign his post (the ensign, or flag bearer, was supposed to represent the "value and vertue"[44] of the whole army) with "God b' wi' you! Take mine office," sagely protesting that "To be direct and honest is not safe" (3. 3. 372, 375). In his dealings with Roderigo, Iago exploits this honest soldier persona, with its license both to speak bluntly and to unmask underhanded dealings—to "blow the gaff"[45] on others, as William Empson puts it—before he perfects it in the temptation of Othello. For the original audience, Iago may have evoked Honesty in *A Knack to Know a Knave* (1594), a morality play character who has a talent for exposing evil. Seen in this context, Iago is not only a villain posing as an truthful man, but "a knave posing as Honesty, a hunter of knaves."[46]

"Honest" Iago is subtle enough to work with the truth when it suits his purposes. He boasts to the audience that the advice he gives to Cassio is "free" and "honest" (2. 3. 337), for he has merely reminded Cassio of Desdemona's "blessed" and generous disposition and suggested that the demoted lieutenant avail himself of it to regain his military rank. But Iago is like Janus, the two-faced god by whom he swears ("By Janus, I think no" [1. 2. 32]), in that he speaks with a double tongue. He alters his version of the truth to suit the occasion. To Roderigo he presents a Desdemona who is sexually susceptible, while to Cassio he offers a jaundiced view of "good name"—no longer the "jewel" of the soul that he praises to Othello (3. 3. 156)—when he asserts that "reputation" is an "idle and most false imposition" (2. 3. 267–68). Although Iago does tell a few direct lies,[47] such as the presumably fabricated "dream" of Cassio, his speciality is more often "false interpretations of factual data"[48] or the manipulation of empirical data to his advantage. Thus he puts a negative spin on Cassio's sudden departure from Desdemona at the beginning of Act 3, scene 3, making it seem "guilty-like" (39) rather than understandable embarrassment at encountering Othello so soon after being publicly disgraced.

Iago also poses as the honest man who is nevertheless reluctant to tell the whole truth when it may hurt a friend. This is a clever tactic, as it confirms the impression of his loyalty while making him seem, paradoxically, more trustworthy. When Montano suggests that it would be an "honest" action to tell Othello that his lieutenant, Cassio, is a drunkard, Iago replies, "Not I, for this fair island!" (2. 3. 139). Because Iago, playing the loyal friend, says he would rather have his tongue cut out than "do offense to Michael Cassio" (221), Othello assumes that the ensign's "honesty and love doth mince this matter, / Making it light to Cassio" (246–47). He promptly cashiers his lieutenant, the very outcome that Iago has worked hard to bring about. No wonder, then, that by Act 3, scene 3, Iago can accomplish so much by seeming hesitant to speak his "thoughts," compromising his frankness in order to protect Othello's "quiet" and "good" (152–54). As the scene progresses, Iago justifies the little that he is prepared to give away as a manifestation of his "love and duty" (194), evidence of his "too much loving" Othello (213). Othello, who "thinks men honest that but seem to be so" (1. 3. 391), does indeed believe that Iago is protecting him. And because he also regards his ensign as a candid and wise expert in human affairs, one who "knows all qualities, with a learnèd spirit / Of human dealings" (3. 3. 258–59), he assumes that Iago's diffidence masks a truth too horrible to be revealed:

> This honest creature doubtless
> Sees and knows more, much more, than he unfolds.   (242–43)

When Othello, soon afterward, briefly suspects Iago's veracity, Iago retorts, "I should be wise; for honesty's a fool / And loses that it works for" (379–80). Under the guise of injured innocence, he is uttering his real feelings, for he does indeed despise truthfulness. In Act 1, scene 1, he scoffs to Roderigo, "Whip me such honest knaves!" (46), contemptuous of servants who are genuinely devoted to their masters and who wear their hearts on their sleeves (61–62). In contrast to these fools, he boasts, he is is merely "trimmed in forms and visages of duty" (47), his inner self the very opposite of his "outward action" (58). Like the standard-bearer, Iago can "show out a flag and sign of love" (153), but this is a mere front or appearance; he admits, "I am not what I am" (62). This terse statement implies more than the classic boast of the Machiavellian villain who delights in disguise; it suggests that Iago is contradictory to the point of negating any true self. Can such a creature ever be entirely "honest," even when he is confiding in the audience? The dramatic convention of the soliloquy calls for truthfulness,[49] and indeed there is no evidence that Iago is deliberately pulling the wool over our eyes. But if we judge Iago as a "life-like" character[50]—and we are encouraged to do so by his extended confessional mode—then the difficulties inherent in any honest communication of self loom large. Insofar as it is impossible for complex characters ever to understand themselves fully or to know their own subconscious motives (not even a Hamlet can do that), and since Iago is also self-consciously playing the role of the villain for the audience, we cannot expect him to give complete explanations for his behavior. Audiences accept the sincerity of his explosive "I hate the Moor" (1. 3. 377), his resentment at being passed over for promotion to lieutenant despite his being senior to Cassio (1. 1. 32–33),[51] and his fear of being cuckolded (1. 3., 378–79; 2. 1. 307). At the same time, they probably intuit other motives that drive his campaign of hatred: an underlying racial animosity toward Othello[52] and bitterness at "class privilege,"[53] a pervasive envy[54] of anyone who is more successful than he is, and a need to assert himself through exercising power over the people who threaten his ego.[55]

"Honest" Iago, then, is as frank and self-revelatory as he can be to the audience. They are in a position to marvel at the scope of his hypocrisy as he deceives the other characters in the play—a diabolical villain posing as a blunt man who is trusted implicitly by most of those around him. The Victorian actor Edwin Booth stressed how important it was for Iago to be a perfect dissembler in public when he advised, "Don't *act* the villain, don't *look* it, or *speak* it . . . but *think* it all the time."[56] Iago himself exploits the dramatic irony of this double perspective. His wry aside "I'll set down the pegs that make this music, / As honest as I am" (2. 1.

198–99) exposes the falseness of his bluff persona, while the tag with which he describes himself to Cassio, "As I am an honest man, I had thought you had received some bodily wound" (2. 3. 265–66), convinces Cassio that he is well-meaning while underlining to the audience how disingenous Iago really is.

The Vice/Devil Figure and Shadow Side

"Honest" Iago, the subtle hypocrite who knows how to exploit his plain-dealing persona, emerges as a naturalistically developed character, not a personification of evil lacking psychological credibility. The symbolic stratum of his character—his role as an evil tempter trying to ensnare the soul of the hero—cannot be ignored, however; it stubbornly continues to surface.[57] This "diablo" (2. 3. 159)[58] frankly associates himself with the "divinity of hell" (350) and "all the tribe of hell" (1. 3. 353). His remark about Othello, "I hate him as I do hell-pains" (1. 1. 151), may express the same sense of being trapped in infernal torments that Mephistopheles does in Christopher Marlowe's play *Doctor Faustus;* when Faustus asks him why he is here on earth if he is one of the "damned," Mephostophilis replies, "Why this is hell, nor am I out of it" (1. 3. 76).[59] As devil figure, Iago represents the objective forces of evil existing outside man's control, or the diabolical "I am not what I am" set up to oppose the divine integrity of "I AM THAT I AM" (Exodus 3:14). And the deadly sin of envy, which Iago directs against both Cassio and Othello, is what Francis Bacon, in an essay first published in 1597, defines as the "proper attribute" of the devil, who is called *"the envious man."*[60]

While most twentieth-century commentators have viewed Iago's role as devil figure as an extra dimension, part of the wider Christian allegory, a few scholars have argued that Iago's character can be understood only as an evolution from the morality play. There, the Vice figure is a shape-shifting trickster, gloating in his triumph over Everyman and needing no motivation other than his rooted hatred of goodness. Bernard Spivack, in particular, views Iago as a hybrid creation in which the underlying Vice is only imperfectly grafted onto a more naturalistically conceived character. He finds that Iago's purported motive of sexual jealousy is presented frivolously in his soliloquies and lacks "emotional sincerity."[61] It is true that instead of making a forceful logical connection—that he hates Othello *because* it is rumored that the Moor has slept with Emilia—Iago presents the association much more loosely:

> I hate the Moor,
> And it is thought abroad that twixt my sheets
> H'as done my office.   (1. 3. 377–79)

This casual "And," thinks Spivack, betrays the "seam between the drama of allegory and the drama of nature."[62] Iago follows it up with the apparently nonchalant "I know not if it be true," while his later addition of Cassio to the list of possible adulterers—"(For I fear Cassio with my nightcap too)" (2. 1. 307)—might appear somewhat absurd, almost an afterthought. Whereas the original Vice sporting his "self-proclaimed, ebullient villainy"[63] does not need motives, Iago is not wholly convincing when he provides them.

Granted, Iago's soliloquies do pile on the motives. An actor, however, might supply the passions of seething disgust and paranoia that would make Iago's suspicions about Othello and Cassio seem more than idle speculation or unfocused hatred. The paratactic "And" and "For" in the speeches cited above could signal Iago's irrational leap from one idea to the next as he experiences jealousy afresh. Stanley Edgar Hyman also points out that Spivack overemphasizes Iago's Vice-like "jocularity."[64] Apart from a few moments of self-congratulatory glee ("And what's he then that says I play the villain?" [2. 3. 336]) and pride in his own artistry ("Pleasure and action make the hours seem short" [379]), Iago displays little of the joie de vivre and droll humor that animate an Edmund (in *King Lear*) or a Richard III. Constantly reminded of his negativity, we perceive him not as a sympathetic villain, but mainly as an extremely nasty piece of work, "conscienceless and sinister."[65]

We may reject the idea of Iago as a Vice or hybrid Vice figure but still find in him what the Jungian critic Maud Bodkin calls the "shadow-side of Othello, the devil-shape" generated by Othello's idealistic, romantic vision. Bodkin defines the devil, in psychological terms, as "our tendency to represent in personal form the forces within and without us that threaten our supreme values."[66] On a symbolic level, Iago serves as "the negative that shadows all positives."[67] More specifically, he is the repressed side of Othello, bringing "to Othello's consciousness what he has already guessed is there."[68] With his "absolute need to denigrate and undermine all that is true, good, and beautiful,"[69] he embodies a deeply corrosive cynicism.

Clearly, the cynic Iago taps into undercurrents that are all too ready to surface in Othello—his insecurities and distrust of women—and voices a universal truth when he points out how every person tends to harbor "foul" thoughts:

> Who has that breast so pure
> But some uncleanly apprehensions
> Keep leets and law days, and in sessions sit
> With meditations lawful?   (3. 3. 138–41)

The growing symbiotic relationship between Othello and Iago, with the sense of one feeding off the other, is palpable in the temptation scene. Since Othello is the first to enunciate the key words "honest" and "think,"[70] it is difficult to discern who is echoing whom, or which man is nurturing the "monstrous" thoughts. The Clown's word game at the opening of Act 3, "I hear not your honest friend. I hear you" (3. 1. 22), aptly reflects on the situation two scenes later, where "honest" Iago is merely a catalyst and what we hear are Othello's "uncleanly apprehensions." At the beginning of the play, Iago's seemingly redundant observation "Were I the Moor, I would not be Iago," succeeded by "In following him, I follow but myself" (1. 1. 54–55), has the effect of stressing the interchangeability of the two characters rather than their essential differences. And Iago's puzzling final words in the play, "What you know, you know. / From this time forth I never will speak word" (5. 2. 299–300), suggest that once he has completed the circle of Othello's knowledge, unleashed the evil in his host, he can stay forever silent. As the unrelenting spirit of negation ("I am not what I am"), his refusal to speak again makes him an antitype of the divine Logos evoked by St. John's gospel: "In the beginning was the Word. And the Word was with God, and the Word was God." Locked into silence, Iago nevertheless continues to exist. When Othello, striking out at his own "shadow projection,"[71] wounds Iago in the final scene, the ensign is seemingly as indestructible as the devil himself. He crows, "I bleed, sir, but not killed" (5. 2. 284). The audience may expect Othello to strike Iago when he talks of slaying the Turkish "dog"; instead, he destroys the dark side of his psyche by killing himself.

The Machiavellian Schemer and Artist in Evil

When E. E. Stoll argues that Iago must be viewed as the standard figure of the slanderous villain who is always believed,[72] and Wyndham Lewis categorizes Iago as "a variety of the recognized Machiavellian type,"[73] they are stressing Iago's conventional role in this Jacobean tragedy. Certainly, Iago's prime dramatic function is to play the villain who deceives the hero, but he cannot be simply reduced to this function, just as he cannot be explained away as Vice or a devil figure. Rather, this convention is what gives Shakespeare "a solid basis on which to build something more interesting."[74] The Machiavellian villain of Renaissance tragedy, popular from the 1590s on, was a gross distortion of Niccolò Machiavelli's pragmatic recommendations on statecraft in *The Prince*. Based more closely on Innocent Gentillet's *Contre Machiavel* (1576), this stereotyped character—such as the future Richard III, who boasts of how he can "set the murtherous Machevil to school" (*Henry VI, Part III* III. ii. 193)—delights in deceit, "policy," and ingenious murder, often by poison. Iago self-consciously employs Machiavellian strategies of deceit and verbal poison but goes one better than the standard villain in his artistry; with his facility for stage-managing characters and engineering plots, he becomes a surrogate playwright.

In metadramatic fashion, Iago pokes fun at his prime dramatic function. He boldly defies audience expectations when he asks, "And what's he then that says I play the villain?" (2. 3. 336), transforming himself from Machiavellian villain back into "honest" Iago by reminding us that he has just given sound advice ("free" and "honest") to Cassio. Later, he plays the detached chorus to his own villainous role when he muses (with his victim Othello lying at his feet in an epileptic trance), "Thus credulous fools are caught" (4. 1. 47). In a moment of supreme black humor, Iago responds to Emilia's detailed description of how an "eternal villain" and "insinuating rogue" has devised "slander" to get "some office"—terms that fit Iago to a T—with the sanctimonious, "Fie, there is no such man! It is impossible" (4. 2. 133).

Clever with words, Iago pours "pestilence" in Othello's "ear" (2. 3. 356) as if it were "med'cine" (4. 1. 47). Unlike the conventional Machiavel, Iago eschews literal poison. When Othello asks for poison to dispatch Desdemona, Iago deflects the request with "Do it not with poison. Strangle her in her bed, even the bed she hath contaminated" (4. 1. 209–10). This is a subtle Machiavel who allows characters to entrap themselves by turning their strong points—Cassio's "courtesy" or the Moor's "free and open nature"—into liabilities.

Iago takes pride in his ingenuity. Expanding on William Hazlitt's comments that Iago has an "untamable love of mischievous contrivance" and is an "amateur of tragedy in real life,"[75] Bradley discusses how Iago discovers the "joy of artistic creation"[76] in his manipulation of his dupes. Other critics have been impressed with Iago's "egotistic relish of his artistry in seduction"[77] and with his "playwright's delight in creating illusion and manipulating people by his powers of deception."[78] The puppet master making his creations dance and squirm is one apt image for this side of Iago. He has also been described as a "zestful athlete of deception"[79] (he urges Roderigo to offer him the "sport" of cuckolding Othello [1. 3. 365]) and the ultimate practical joker, an experimental scientist acting without any moral scruples.[80] Lewis compares Iago's provoking of Othello to the way a matador skillfully finesses the bull toward its destruction.[81] Certainly, Iago is superb at raising Othello to fever pitch and then cooling him down in order to repeat the process[82] ("Nay, this was but his dream" and "She may be honest yet" [3. 3. 424, 430]). Favored with much luck, Iago improvises brilliantly up to Act 5: he engineers Cassio's disgrace in Act 2, scene 3, provides seeming "ocular proof" when he stage-manages the encounter between Cassio and himself for Othello to witness in Act 4, scene 1; and persuades Roderigo to dispose of Cassio in Act 4, scene 2. Yet his skill seems to desert him at the end of the street scene (5. 1). Unless we posit a drive toward self-destruction[83] or the standard overreaching of the Machiavellian villain, it is difficult to understand why he sends Emilia off to report to Othello on what has happened after the botched murder of Cassio. A lack of detachment, a sense that "wind and stream" have pushed along his "boat" too quickly so that he is no longer in control of his master plan or "dream" (2. 3. 60–61), is foregrounded in his urgent words at the end of the street scene: "This is the night / That either makes me or fordoes me quite" (5. 1. 128–29). Harley Granville Barker points out that Iago has the intuition of an artist but also reveals a "radical stupidity"[84] or obtuseness. Iago fatally underestimates Emilia's love for her mistress, which, in the final scene, overrides any loyalty to her husband and leads to his unmasking.

"Eaten Up with Passion"

In defending Iago as an artist in evil, Bradley also perceives him as "decidedly cold by temperament."[85] Other critics have commented on Iago's inability to love, speculating that his need to destroy the passionate union of Othello and Desdemona springs from his own deep-seated fear that he is "lacking in worth" and "does not have the love and regard of others."[86] Envious of other people's happiness (he admits that Cassio has a "daily beauty in his life" that makes Iago himself appear "ugly" [5. 1. 19–20]), Iago is compelled, on a fundamental level, to prove that any notion of a fulfilling love is an illusion. His intrigues thus serve to shore up the terrible emptiness of his "inner abyss."[87] The actor of Iago, though, may prefer to portray him as a smoldering volcano of aggression and pathological jealousy rather than as an emotionally dead human being.[88]

There is indeed a strong case for an Iago who is not a cold-blooded snake or a "passionless creature,"[89] but someone "eaten up with passion"—words that he applies to Othello (3. 3. 388) but that, in the transference process frequent in this play, could be just as relevant to him. If we find in Iago's soliloquies interior development rather than casual motive-hunting,[90] then the character is suffering from acute jealousy and sexual paranoia. He appears to distrust his wife intensely. Resentful of Cassio's attentions to Emilia at the harbor, he later wonders if Cassio has usurped his "nightcap" (his place in bed). In his very first soliloquy, he broods on the rumor that Emilia has slept with Othello (1. 3. 378–79). This is not something he dreams up on the spur of the moment to justify his villainy to the audience; Emilia mentions it when she reminds her husband of how some malicious slanderer "turned your wit the seamy side without / And made you to suspect me with the Moor" (4. 2. 145–46). Above all, Iago wants to infect Othello with the same kind of painful suspicion that afflicts him. In his second soliloquy, he explains what fuels his desire for revenge on his master:

> For that I do suspect the lusty Moor
> Hath leaped into my seat; the thought whereof
> Doth, like a poisonous mineral, gnaw my inwards.   (2. 1. 295–97)

True, Iago does not get "evened with him, wife for wife" (299). But by convincing Othello that Cassio is committing adultery with Desdemona, he effects a double revenge, taking Cassio's "place" as lieutenant at the same time that he unhinges Othello.

In this second soliloquy, Iago offers no plan to kill Othello, Desdemona, and Cassio. Rather, he wants to triumph over the two men—have his military rival Michael Cassio "on the hip" (at his mercy) and make Othello "egregiously an ass" (2. 1. 305, 309). Yet he expresses a deeper malice when he sadistically plans to undermine Othello's "peace and quiet, / Even to madness" (310–11): "a jealousy so strong / That judgment cannot cure" (301–2). Iago's own susceptibility to this emotion lends resonance to his warning to Othello to be on guard against it. From his heartfelt description of "the green-eyed monster, which doth mock / The meat it feeds on" (3. 3. 166–67), we infer that Iago is well acquainted with the ravages of jealousy.

Because of his persona as a sage, worldly-wise fellow, Iago's speeches appear, superficially at least, to be eminently reasonable. He specializes in commonsense wisdom: "But men are men; the best sometimes forget" (2. 3. 240) and "How poor are they that have not patience!" (370). Yet it is certainly possible to view Iago as only a few steps away from "madness" himself. G. M. Matthews calls him a "superb study of an irrational mind, lucid and cunning on the surface but mad just underneath."[91] Iago's submerged but anarchic craziness is suggested in the open-ing scene, when he instructs Roderigo to "poison" Brabantio's peace of mind by rousing him with "timorous accent and dire yell" as if announcing fire in a city (1. 1. 65, 72–74),[92] just as in Act 2 he incites his stooge to "Go out and cry a mutiny!" (2. 3. 154–55). Much can also be conveyed by how the individual actor handles Iago's soliloquies, as when Ian McKellen in the Royal Shakespeare Company stage production, televised in 1990, draws on a deep well of passionate hatred, almost spewing up the words "I hate the Moor," or when Bob Hoskins in the 1980 BBC television production periodically breaks into manic laughter, submerged at first but reaching a crescendo when he is led offstage at the end of the play. Iago's sex-ual paranoia, his anger at women, also simmers beneath his controlled exterior. His mask of bonhomie slips a little when he is alone with Emilia in Act 3, scene 3, where the pointed sexual coarseness of his "You have a thing for me?" (300) echoes the blistering nastiness of his riposte on women—his assumption that their "fairness" is merely for sexual "use"—in the harbor scene (2. 1. 127–28). Finally, he kills Emilia in a passionate fury, calling her "Villainous whore" (5. 2. 226) when she unmasks him in the final scene.

Even Iago's compelling speech on how "Our bodies are our gardens, to the which our wills are gardeners" (1. 3. 315–16)—ostensibly arguing the triumph of the "autonomous will"[93] over passion—subverts itself once we take into account the other Jacobean meaning of "will" as sexual desire.[94] Iago's intention is to per-suade Roderigo that our "wills" give us "power" and "authority" over our mater-ial selves, and he allies conscious intention with "reason" when he insists that "If the balance of our lives had not one scale of reason to poise another of sensuality, the blood and baseness of our natures would conduct us to most prepost'rous con-clusions" (1. 3. 321–25). But Iago is less immune to "blood" (passion) and "base-ness" (animal nature) than his speech implies. In describing love as "merely a lust of the blood and a permission of the will," he may be setting up an equivalence rather than a contrast, since the concept of rational control is largely canceled out if we register that other meaning of will.[95] Lending support to this reading is the fact that Iago, just a few lines later, uses will to mean carnal desire or appetite when he asserts that "These Moors are changeable in their wills" (342–43). The image that follows—of how Othello will soon find the "luscious" food of Desde-mona's body as "bitter as coloquintida"—furthers the idea of fickle sexual attrac-tion. Iago's self-confessed desire to "plume up [his] will" in "double knavery" (384–85) also suggests that he finds manipulating others sexually arousing as well as gratifying to his ego. Bradley's observation that Iago manifests remarkable "strength of will"[96] overemphasizes Iago's rational control by ignoring the passion that both energizes and undermines him.

Where do Iago's sexual proclivities lie? He claims to feel some love for Desde-mona (more akin to "lust" than affection [2. 1. 292]) and is highly possessive about his wife. A few critics, adopting a psychoanalytic approach, have viewed Iago as a repressed homosexual, attracted to Othello[97]—and possibly Cassio, too[98]—in a love-hate dynamic. Hyman points out how, in recounting Cassio's "dream" to Othello, Iago turns himself into a Desdemona surrogate for Cassio to caress and even mount (he "laid his leg o'er my thigh" [3. 3. 421]); the pact between Othello and Iago at the end of Act 3, scene 3, where Iago vows "I am your own forever" (476), also darkly parodies the wedding vow.[99] To conclude from these instances that Iago has unconscious homosexual yearnings seems strained, however,[100] for the audience is surely more impressed with the virulence of the ensign's "hate" for his general than with any hidden, thwarted love for Othello. When Laurence Olivier, taking up a suggestion from the Freudian critic Ernest Jones, decided to portray Iago as sexually attracted to Othello in Tyrone Guthrie's 1937 production, the concept misfired on the stage: "Hardly anyone could tell what Olivier's Iago was doing and why."[101] Olivier later commented that since any homosexual motivation is "entirely in [Iago's] subconscious," there is no point in "touching on it in any detail of performance."[102] As with so many facets of Iago, the ultimate test of an interpretation is whether it makes sense in the theater.

OTHELLO AS TRAGIC HERO

We expect the hero of a tragedy to be a cut above the ordinary, possessing some stature that will make significant his change from "fortune to misfortune," as Aristotle defines the tragic fall in the *Poetics*. Othello is descended from "men of royal siege" (1. 2. 21), but more important, he is an accomplished leader who also proves himself to be, in Cassio's words, "great of heart" (5. 2. 357). And after he makes a fatal error (Aristotle's hamartia) or series of mistakes, trusting Iago instead of his wife and killing Desdemona after Iago works him into a frenzy of jealousy, he recognizes the enormity of what he has done (Aristotle's anagnorisis). But does Othello regain stature at the end of the play, or is his act of violence, the killing of an innocent woman, so terrible that he forfeits all pity? If audiences perceive him as deeply flawed—self-centered and deluded about his real motives for killing his wife rather than understandably susceptible to the evil insinuations of Iago because of his trusting, guileless nature—then they may well lose respect for Othello and find it difficult to regard his downfall as tragic.

The play is resistant to easy answers on these issues. It is not enough to state that Shakespeare probably intended to create in Othello a "Complete Man"[103] by Renaissance standards and leave it at that; we can only respond to the dramatic character as individual readers or audience members, informed about the play's original contexts but bound to make judgments from within our own cultural moment. Admittedly, none of Shakespeare's tragic protagonists is so ideal as never to behave in a way that alienates audience sympathies. Hamlet is cruel to Ophelia and Macbeth becomes a hardened murderer. But Othello may be a special case if he strikes us as more self-deceived than Shakespeare's other tragic heroes—finally unable to confront or come to terms with the deepest springs of his own nature. As so often in Shakespeare's drama, the evidence cuts two ways.

Racist Stereotypes

The other complicating factor in the presentation of Othello is his race and color. The audience is constantly reminded that Othello is a black African not only by his physical presence onstage, but also because almost all the other characters in the play, who are white, regard him as different from, and possibly inferior to, themselves.

There is a certain indirectness, even a misleading quality, about the way that Othello is introduced. When Roderigo and Iago enter in midconversation, the audience is mystified over the identity of the "him" they are talking about. To Roderigo's challenge, "Thou told'st me / Thou didst hold him in thy hate," Iago responds by recounting how "he, as loving his own pride and purposes," chose a different candidate for lieutenant (1. 1. 5–6, 11). Not until line 30 does Iago use a noun instead of a pronoun to refer to Othello, and then it is the derogatory "his Moorship" (an improvised variation on "his worship" that slyly undercuts Othello's social pretensions). In fact, Othello is not addressed by name until the Senate scene, when the Duke, paying tribute to his prowess as a soldier, greets him as "valiant Othello" (1. 3. 48). Before that, he is referred to as "the Moor" by Iago, Roderigo, and Brabantio a total of seven times in the opening scene. This automatic equation of the man with his race, coupled with the image that Iago and Roderigo project of Othello as a marauding seducer, sets up certain expectations in the audience. Iago graphically draws on one Renaissance stereotype of the black man as lecherous and bestial when he tells Brabantio that "an old black ram / Is tupping your white ewe" (1. 1. 85–86) and that "you'll have your daughter covered with a Barbary horse" (108–9). Iago's coarseness is echoed in the paler clichés of Roderigo, who imagines Desdemona in the "gross clasps of a lascivious Moor" (123). This tactic in presenting Othello is like the circuitous route the Turks take to Rhodes before heading for their real destination, Cyprus. It is a "pageant / To keep us in false gaze" (1. 3. 18–19).

Shortly after Othello appears onstage, allowing the audience to form some independent judgments on him, Brabantio bursts in to unleash his virulent racial hatred against the "foul thief" who has eloped with his daughter, a man he views as a "damned" enchanter, a (literally) black magician and "practicer / Of arts inhibited and out of warrant" (1. 2. 61–78). This association of a black man with the devil and "practices of cunning hell" is repeated when Brabantio appeals to the Duke in Act 1, scene 3. Even the Duke's consoling speech to the old father, "If virtue no delighted beauty lack, / Your son-in-law is far more fair than black" (1. 3. 284–85), contains more than a tinge of racism. The implication is that Othello's blackness, traditionally associated with moral turpitude, can now be effaced; he has become a "fair" honorary white man through his proven "virtue."

After this point, it is Iago who both crudely and subtly perpetuates the racist attitude toward Othello. He plays on the stereotype of black men as lecherous when he speculates on whether the "lusty Moor" has committed adultery with Emilia (2. 1. 295). Having identified the Moor with the satanic when he taunts Brabantio with "the devil will make a grandsire of you" (1. 1. 88), he assures Roderigo that Desdemona will soon tire of her husband, for "what delight shall she have to look on the devil?" (2. 1. 224–25). While he addresses Othello to his face as "my lord," in private it is almost always "the Moor." On one of the rare occasions when he does refer to his master by name, it is as "black Othello" (2. 3. 30). In Act 3, scene 3, he calls Desdemona's choice of Othello "Foul disproportions, thoughts unnatural" (233), again revealing his racial animosity by connecting blackness (or an attraction to blackness) with foulness. This prompts in Othello the brief speculation, in "Haply for I am black" (262), that Desdemona may have reverted to a less "unnatural" choice (the white Cassio) because she is repelled by Othello's color. Soon he is convinced that his reputation, or "name," is as "begrimed and black" as his "own face" (383–85, Folio text). At the end of the play, in a voice of righteous indignation shot through with racism, Emilia correlates the Moor's blackness with his sinful action, calling Othello Desdemona's "most filthy bargain" (5. 2. 154) and a "blacker devil" for killing her angelic mistress (130). Since many of the play's characters automatically associate blackness with dirt and sinfulness, Othello can never escape being seen through racist eyes. These stereotypes form part of the play's perspective, and because at certain stages of the play Othello seems to conform to them, it remains an open question whether the play itself endorses racist stereotypes of the black man or whether Othello's character, as a whole, escapes them.

"Noble" Hero or Self-Deluded Egoist?

Apart from one instance, where the Herald refers to Othello as "our noble and valiant general" (2. 2. 1–2), the epithet "noble," when it is used about the hero, is always collocated with "Moor." Montano finds it regrettable that the "noble Moor" would choose a habitual drunkard as his lieutenant (2. 3. 135); Desdemona refers to her husband as "my noble Moor" (3. 4. 26); and Lodovico is amazed that the "noble Moor" judged by the Venetian magnificos to be "all in all sufficient" (4. 1. 265) could treat his wife so brutally. It is as though Othello's primary identity remains his race, and epithets of praise denoting heroic qualities must be grafted onto this outsider to civilize his alien nature; unlike "noble Macbeth" (*Macbeth* I. ii. 67), he is never called "noble Othello." The collocation "noble Moor" may have struck Jacobean audiences as surprising and even slightly oxymoronic, conditioned as they were to type characters such as Aaron in *Titus Andronicus,* who is twice referrred to as the "barbarous Moor" (II. iii. 78; V. iii. 4).

How "noble" is Othello as a character? He reveals to Iago that he has royal ancestors but does not broadcast this information; instead, he has forged his reputation as a mercenary soldier before being furloughed in Venice for the past nine months (1. 3. 84). At the end of the play, Lodovico calls him "Othello that was once so good" (5. 2. 287); but "good" here may mean, not virtuous, but professionally "all in all sufficient" (just as when Shylock in *The Merchant of Venice* calls Antonio a "good man," he means simply that he is a financially secure or "sufficient" merchant [I. iii. 16–17]). Othello is indeed valued in Venice as a "worthy" general. Even Brabantio, evidently impressed with Othello's leadership qualities, "loved [him], oft invited [him]" (1. 3. 127) to his home—before discovering that the Moor has crossed the racial line by marrying his daughter.

Whenever he speaks and acts in the early part of the play, Othello successfully projects this sense of being "sufficient"; he is self-assured, dignified, and a natural leader, conveying what Helen Gardner calls an "immediate" impression of the "extraordinary."[104] His opening words, commending Iago's restraint in holding back from violence, suggest a mature unwillingness to inflame the situation: "'Tis better as it is" (1. 2. 6). Confident that his "services" to the Venetian Senate will override Brabantio's grievance against him, Othello is not afraid to "be found" by the enraged father. He is sure that his natural gifts, his social status, and his unsullied conscience will all speak for him:

> My parts, my title, and my perfect soul
> Shall manifest me rightly.   (30–31)

Although Brabantio's accusations are incendiary, Othello calmly issues commands to defuse the situation: "Keep up your bright swords" (58) and "Hold your hands, / Both you of my inclining and the rest" (80–81). The same courtesy and poise, combined with powerful eloquence, emerges from his appeal to the "gracious patience" of the "potent, grave, and reverend signiors" when he "dilate[s]" his tale—recapitulating both the "story" of his life and how he wooed, and was wooed by, Desdemona (1. 3. 127–69). The adventures he describes—"disastrous chances," "hairbreadth scapes," and release from slavery—evoke an image of him as both stoical and courageous. And although he is defensive about keeping his professional persona free from "light-winged toys" of love, he shows a generous impulse to be "free and bounteous" to Desdemona's "mind" (260–63) in arguing that she should accompany him to Cyprus.

The "noble" impression of Othello continues, on the whole, through Act 2. He experiences "wonder" and "absolute" happiness in finding Desdemona ahead of him in Cyprus, and his response to her as his "soul's joy" suggests a largeness of spirit, an extraordinary meeting of minds in their union. In Act 2, scene 3, again the strong leader, he takes swift action in quelling the drunken fight and punishing Cassio as the apparent instigator of violence. He is not as self-controlled as in the earlier scenes, however; he admits that "passion . . . / Assays to lead the way" (205–6) and threatens "If I once stir . . . the best of you / Shall sink in my rebuke" (206–8). Since his reputation, as Lodovico makes clear, is built on having a "nature" that "passion could not shake" (4. 1. 265–66), this may be the first chink in his stoic armor. Still, his noble nature is evident in his instinctive loathing of the "barbarous" brawl that undermines the "propriety" of the island (2. 3. 171–75).

The testimony of other characters, and their intuitive response to Othello as noble, also biases the audience toward the hero. True, these same characters are deceived into thinking that Iago is "honest," but whereas Iago puts out only a false "sign" of himself, Othello is always concerned to "manifest" himself rightly. If Othello has flaws, they are not immediately apparent to those who surround him. Brabantio is prejudiced against the black man who has "stol'n" his daughter, and the villain Iago hates him; but most of the play's characters instinctively admire Othello. Attracted to him as a heroic soldier and adventurer, Desdemona dedicates herself to his "valiant" qualities. Cassio, who admittedly tends to idealize his superiors, envisages Othello in almost godlike terms. In the storm scene, he prays to "great Jove" (syntactically parallel to his own "great" captain three lines above [2. 1. 74–77]) to guard this commander in chief, so that Othello may "bless this bay with his tall ship" and "Give renewed fire to our extinguished spirits" (79–81). After he has been cashiered, Cassio craves a return to the good graces of the leader he "entirely honor[s]" (3. 4. 114). Montano comments on Othello's "good nature" (2. 3. 130) and respects him as "worthy" and "brave" (2. 1. 30, 38). In Act 4, Lodovico is appalled that the general lauded by the Venetian Senate because no "dart of chance" could pierce his "solid virtue" (4. 1. 266–67) has now lost control to the point where he publicly strikes his wife. Even Iago concedes in soliloquy that the Moor "is of a constant, loving, noble nature" (2. 1. 289).

Samuel Johnson, a sensitive reader of Shakespeare, likewise responded to Othello as "magnanimous, artless, and credulous, boundless in his confidence,"[105] and Coleridge called him "noble, generous, open-hearted; unsuspicious and unsuspecting."[106] In the early twentieth century, Bradley concluded, "This character is so noble . . . and his sufferings are so heart-rending, that he stirs, I believe, in most readers a passion of mingled love and pity which they feel for no other hero in Shakespeare."[107]

Bradley undoubtedly overidealizes the hero. His enthusiasm is not based on a close analysis of individual dramatic speeches or perspectives offered outside Othello's consciousness; it is modeled on Othello's opinion of himself. Because Iago is not always a "reliable narrator," we approach what he says with caution. Yet he is a shrewd assessor of character traits (he discerns not only Othello's "free and open nature" [1. 3. 390], but also Cassio's "smooth dispose / To be suspected" [388–89] and Desdemona's disposition "as fruitful / As the free elements" [2. 3. 341–42]), and therefore we cannot entirely discount his verdict on Othello's method of choosing his lieutenant:

> But he, as loving his own pride and purposes,
> Evades them with a bombast circumstance. (1. 1. 11–12)

It is the "pride" and "bombast" that Leavis concentrates on in his essay "Diabolic Intellect and the Noble Hero," where he mercilessly exposes Othello's "habit of self-approving self-dramatization."[108] He notes how, in Othello's Pontic Sea speech, "Self-pride becomes stupidity . . . an insane and self-deceiving passion"; castigating Bradley's version of Othello as a "sentimental perversity," Leavis concedes only "the impressive manifestation of a noble egotism."[109]

Careful examination of Othello's speeches (some of which were also analyzed in the section on "Language and Style" in Chapter 3 above) reveals that they are double-edged. In their expansiveness, we hear the note of mature, dignified self-assurance; but we may also detect, as in the reference to "perfect soul," a touch of arrogance. Even his disclaimer of boastfulness, when he declines to reveal his own high birth—"'Tis yet to know— / Which when I know that boasting is a honor / I shall promulgate" (1. 2. 18–20)—manages to sound a shade too self-approving. By using the theatrical metaphor "Were it my cue to fight, I should have known it / Without a prompter" (82–83), he places himself center stage as an accomplished performer. His speech to the Senate is as much a personal "manifesto"[110] as a defense of his marriage to Desdemona, and his basis for falling in love with Desdemona—"She loved me for the dangers I had passed, / And I loved her that she did pity them" (1. 3. 166–67)—strikes a narcissistic note. He may, indeed, appreciate Desdemona's compassion, but the emphasis here falls on *his* "dangers" and how she validates "his existence as a romantic hero."[111] Everett comments that "A hatred and fear of the 'heroic,' the large, the universal, the self-sufficient, the grandiose, the rhetorical is a fundamental part of our own age."[112] Maybe so. At any rate, many contemporary readers have discerned ambivalence built into Othello's grand style, where (as Robert Heilman puts it) "largeness and freedom of spirit" seem to coexist with "self-deception, limitedness of feeling, and egotism."[113]

This pattern of nobility girded by what Leavis calls "self-pride" can be discerned throughout the play. In Act 4, scene 2, we pity Othello's terrible anguish when he feels betrayed by the woman who has become the very center of his being—"The fountain from the which my current runs / Or else dries up" (4. 2. 58–59)—and yet this noble suffering is undercut by his expression of wounded pride at becoming "The fixèd figure for the time of scorn / To point his slow and moving finger at" (53–54). His full, passionate acknowledgment of what has been lost, in "But yet the pity of it, Iago" (4. 1. 197–98), contrasts similarly with the petty vindictiveness of a threatened ego as he roars, "I will chop her into messes! Cuckold me!" (202). Othello, "great of heart" and imagination, grasps the cosmic significance of killing Desdemona when he declares, "Methinks it should be now a huge eclipse / Of sun and moon" (5. 2. 98–99). Yet he can slide from this into self-pitying masochism, as he begs,

> Whip me, ye devils,
> From the possession of this heavenly sight! . . .
> Wash me in steep-down gulfs of liquid fire!   (274–77)

Leavis also takes issue with the cornerstone of Bradley's case that Othello is noble—his contention that the hero is not prone to jealousy. Is Othello correct when he claims, at the end of the play, that he is "one not easily jealous, but, being wrought, / Perplexed in the extreme" (341–42)? If not, this lends support to Leavis's claim that he is self-deceived. As A. P. Rossiter remarks, "The integrity of the '*noble Othello*' depends enormously" on whether we can accept those lines;[114]

and it seems clear that, in them, Othello is referring primarily to sexual jealousy and not to the other Elizabethan sense of "jealous" as suspicious, or distrustful in general. Bradley finds no evidence of sexual jealousy in the hero in Act 3, scene 3 until Iago scores a hit by alluding to the hidden "pranks" of Venetian wives and the fact that Desdemona has already deceived another man, her father; only then, after dismissing his ensign, does Othello pose the devastating question "Why did I marry?" (3. 3. 242). This is about 147 lines into the "temptation" sequence. Leavis, on the other hand, detects Othello's capitulation to jealousy in "O misery!", less than 80 lines into Iago's attack.[115]

The issue of how quickly Othello takes the bait is complicated, inevitably, by dramatic exigencies; the undermining of the hero calls for compression since the play's tragic conclusion is due in another hour or so of stage time. But Othello appears sincere when he assures Iago that he gladly accepts his wife's outgoing nature, her feeding "well" and loving "company," because "she had eyes, and chose me" (184–89). What triggers Othello's insecurity is Iago's suggestion that only a white woman with a "will most rank" (232) could choose and then remain faithful to a black man. We may thus conclude that Othello is not being flagrantly evasive or self-deluded when he sums himself up as "not easily jealous," while conceding that Iago's plan works flawlessly not only because he is such a skillful con man, but because he is able to play on Othello's weak points—concern with self-image and an underlying distrust of women. To some extent, as Leavis puts it, "the essential traitor is within the gates."[116]

Bradley excuses Othello's egregious behavior in Act 4, contending that the hero "sees everything blurred through a mist of blood and tears" but that "his grandeur remains almost undiminished."[117] Most contemporary audiences, witnessing Othello's loss of self-control, ignominious eavesdropping, brutal vows of vengeance, and striking of Desdemona in front of the Venetian embassy, are unlikely to romanticize the protagonist in this way. In his jealous rage, Othello totally contradicts Iago's observation to Roderigo that "base men being in love have then a nobility in their natures more than is native to them" (2. 1. 213–14). More difficult to determine is whether the "noble" Othello triumphs over the "base" one in Act 5. Once again, Bradley takes the protagonist at his word, thinking that he kills Desdemona not in "hate," but as an act of justice (5. 2. 290–91). Nor (in keeping with most critics in a prefeminist age) does Bradley question Othello's determination to restore his honor as husband by killing a wife he believes to be unfaithful. His commentary closely echoes Othello's words to Desdemona, "[Thou] makst me call what I intend to do / A murder, which I thought a sacrifice" (64–65), when he writes, "The deed he is bound to do is no murder, but a sacrifice." Bradley finds "boundless sorrow"[118] in the protagonist but fails to detect the rationalization of wounded pride—a claim of altruism that rings false—in Othello's "she must die, else she'll betray more men" (6).

Audiences, too, may be carried along by the magnificent sweep of Othello's verse as he declaims, "It is the cause, it is the cause, my soul." But Othello's sensuous apprehension of Desdemona as a beautiful woman who is very much alive (her skin "smooth," her breath "balmy," her life like a "light" or a "rose") jars not only with his destructive drive to transform that life into death (underlined in "alabaster," "quench," "plucked," and "fatal"), but with his abstract notion of himself as an impersonal "justice" pursuing a sanctified "cause." His "concern for justice," as Leavis notes, "appears as self-deception";[119] his real motive for killing his wife, the affront to his pride expressed in "Cuckold me!", is apparent in his quick reversion to "bloody passion" when Desdemona awakes and challenges him. Othello's self-appointed roles as priest ("confess thee freely of thy sin" [53]) and spiritual savior ("I would not kill thy soul" [32]) collapse once she heatedly denies the charges against her. With his insistent "Down strumpet," Othello's calm persona of impersonal justice has vanished completely; in his brutal rage, he allows her not even "one prayer" (83).[120]

Can Othello regain stature after this? Again, the evidence is mixed. Almost immediately after smothering Desdemona, he recognizes the enormity of what he has done ("O heavy hour"), and later he does not shy away from the eternal consequences of murdering an innocent woman: "When we shall meet at compt, / This look of thine will hurl my soul from heaven" (270–71). As soon as the group of Venetians enters the bedchamber, he courageously faces up to his deed with "Nay, stare not, masters. It is true indeed" (185); and although he is a "weaponed" soldier, he does not try to bluster or fight his way out of the situation. "Here is my journey's end" (264) is spoken with quiet dignity. Coexisting with this, though, is the prolonged masochism of the "Blow me about in winds! roast me in sulphur!" lament (276). Moreover, Othello finds ways of subtly disowning ultimate responsibility for the "monstrous act" (187): murder is an "error of the moon" (108); Desdemona is not his victim, but merely an "ill-starred wench" (269); and he himself is "ensnared" by a demi-devil and unable to "control" his "fate" (298, 262), just as he accepted earlier that cuckoldry was a "destiny unshunnable" (3. 3. 274).

Concerned to defend himself as one who did "naught . . . in hate, but all in honor" (5. 2. 291), Othello has a strong desire to reestablish his "good name." Yet his phrase "honorable murderer" may strike the audience as both oxymoronic and self-deceiving, since Othello has acted in uncontrolled fury, as Desdemona observes (44), and not in the altruistic spirit of "sacrifice." While a few earlier critics, such as Curtis Brown Watson, consider that the play endorses Othello's masculine code of honor—the exacting of the highest penalty for a wife's presumed adultery because it dishonors the husband[121]—Brents Stirling finds that the murder springs from "an inverted, egoistic defensiveness of good name,"[122] and Richard S. Ide puts it more bluntly: "the Moor launches a frantic, passionate campaign to plume up his masculine ego."[123] Othello's question "why should honor outlive honesty?" as he prepares to "Let it all go" (242–43) carries some recognition, at least, that his attempt at honorable action has proved sadly defective. He knows that because any honest evaluation of him would discredit his reputation ("honor"), he deserves to die; or, if we read in the lines a reference to Desdemona, he is asking why his own good name, on which he has staked so much, should outlive his wife, whose chastity ("honesty") now stands fully vindicated.

Othello's suicide, too, is open to different interpretations. On one hand, it constitutes courageous self-punishment in full knowledge of the torments to ensue in the next life; yet it might also be construed as escapism, since Othello tells the survivor Iago, "'tis happiness to die" (286). He is concerned to salvage his reputation as a great public servant, commanding attention with

> Soft you, a word or two before you go.
> I have done the state some service, and they know't.   (334–35)

Othello is also reminding the Venetians of his former glories (part of "he that was Othello" [280]) when he requests them to "Speak of me as I am." True, Othello's final summing up falls within the dramatic convention of the tragic hero's noble exit from life; Hamlet, too, is anxious to avoid leaving a "wounded name" behind him as he dies, while Mark Antony justifies his suicide as the heroic action of "a Roman by a Roman / Valiantly vanquished" (*Antony and Cleopatra* IV. xv. 57–58). Even allowing for the convention, however, we detect more in the speech than what John Holloway calls a valid reestablishing of the "great man."[124] T. S. Eliot detects in Othello's words a determined effort at "*cheering himself up*" as he endeavors to "escape reality,"[125] a final piece of "self-publication"[126] that has the effect of distancing Othello somewhat from the horror of what he has done and what he has become. As Othello moves from the pronoun "I" to the impersonal "one" ("one that loved not wisely, but too well" [340]), we may question the objectivity of this verdict. Does loving "too well" entail murder? He dramatizes his predicament by comparing himself to the "base Judean" ["Indian" in the Quarto text] who has thrown away a priceless pearl and then identifies himself with the outsider—the "malignant" Turk—when he kills himself. Yet the heroism of his self-inflicted retribution is inevitably undercut by his own histrionic gesture, which ostentatiously reminds the audience of how he was once such a loyal and brave defender of Venice. The complexity of effects here—Othello's courageous effort to restore dignity and concede guilt partly vitiated by evasiveness and the impulse toward self-aggrandizement—makes it impossible to agree with Bradley that this Othello is even "greater and nobler" than the character at the start of the play.[127] Yet to view him simply as the proud, self-deceived man may be a trap, too, bringing us close to the reductiveness of Iago.[128] Othello remains a complex mixture of the "noble" hero and the self-deceiving egoist concerned with his "good name."

The Warrior in Love

One way to negotiate between those two extremes is to consider how the play presents the main protagonist as a soldier. After years of cultivating "hardness" in his chosen military profession, Othello falls in love with, and marries, Desdemona. His superb soldiership, part of what Reuben Brower calls his "heroic simplicity,"[129] does not equip him for complex shifts in personal relationships, however;[130] the swift martial decisions he has had to make, and continues to make when he cashiers

Cassio, prove disastrous when applied to his crisis of faith in his wife. Ironically, his professional role disintegrates ("Othello's occupation's gone!") once his romantic love for Desdemona gives way to obsessive jealousy, and only at the end of the play is he able to regain his persona as the "valiant," self-possessed warrior.

"The man commands / Like a full soldier," reports Montano in Act 2 (scene 1, 35–36). Through his poise, rational control, and courage, Othello has earned his appointment as commander in chief in the Venetian expedition and then governor of Cyprus, for (as even Iago admits) "another of his fathom they have none" (1. 1. 149). His courage is quickly established when he unhesitatingly confronts Brabantio and his armed followers ("I must be found") and when, in recounting the story of his life to the Senators, he privileges "battle, sieges" and "hairbreadth scapes i' th' imminent deadly breach" (1. 3. 129, 135) above his exotic travels. Iago, playing up Othello's reputation for stoicism, later asks, with mock incredulity, "Can he be angry?", recalling how Othello remained unmoved in battle even as the cannon blew "his ranks into the air" and annihilated his own brother (3. 4. 134–37). It is this "heroic self-sufficiency"[131] that makes Othello, even when he is married, yearn for some solitude as he asks Desdemona to "leave me but a little to myself" (3. 3. 85).

Othello's trance in Act 4, scene 1 is the antithesis of self-possession, and Iago taunts him by describing it as a "passion most unsuiting such a man" (79). In the play's denouement, however, Othello does return to the "full soldier" role. In a reversal of his first appearance onstage, where he commands, "Keep up your bright swords," Othello now initiates the swordplay. First defied by Emilia ("I care not for thy sword" [5. 2. 162]) and then disarmed after he has tried to wound Iago, Othello feels robbed of professional integrity and manliness: "I am not valiant neither; / But every puny whipster gets my sword" (240–41). Finding another weapon (a "sword of Spain") in the chamber, he revives the past image of himself as a terrific soldier as he threatens Gratiano:

> Behold, I have a weapon;
> A better never did itself sustain
> Upon a soldier's thigh. I have seen the day
> That with this little arm and this good sword
> I have made my way through more impediments
> Than twenty times your stop.   (256–61)

But Othello conjures up his former power only to renounce it. Like the warrior Coriolanus, who conquered the city of Corioli "alone" (*Coriolanus* V. vi. 116), Othello could presumably blaze his way through all the Venetians opposing him and escape from Cyprus. Instead, he assures them, "Be not afraid, though you do see me weaponed" (263). And, after wounding Iago before he is disarmed again (284), in his final moments he inflicts a military punishment on himself—executing himself, like the Turk, as a traitor to Venice—with yet another concealed weapon.

Othello then dies "upon a kiss," his martial self-punishment coalescing with a final confirmation of his love for Desdemona. Indeed, his whole concept of war, like his devotion to his lady, is romantic. It is the gorgeous trappings of military adventure—the "pride, pomp, and circumstance of glorious war"—that he responds to in his "farewell to war" speech, where he celebrates the "plumèd troops" and the "spirit-stirring drum" (3. 3. 345–49). When the Musicians play an aubade for the bridegroom, the Clown tellingly comments that "to hear music the general does not greatly care" (3. 1. 16–17); Othello is more attuned to the sounds of the "ear-piercing fife" and the "rude throat[s]" of the cannon on the battlefield, since they have brought him "content" and a "tranquil mind" in the past. The winning of Desdemona is, in one sense, the jewel in his military crown; like a medieval knight, he sees chivalry as including heroic dedication to a "fair damsel."[132]

Initially, then, Othello is able to absorb Desdemona and his devotion to her into his military world; he views her as his "fair warrior" (2. 1. 180), and she responds in kind, castigating herself as an "unhandsome warrior" after briefly becoming critical of her romantic hero (3. 4. 151). Othello believes that he can conduct battles against the Turks but still prove a most dear husband. Yet there is a trap building here in the inherent tension, if not dichotomy, between the worlds of love and war. As Gardner comments, "Othello's absolute soldiership is the symbol of his entire masculinity,"[133] and he is anxious to convince the Senate that this martial virtu will not be undermined by his marriage. Despite being very newly wed, he accepts with alacrity ("With all my heart") the command to leave for Cyprus the same night (1. 3. 273). He reminds the Venetian Senate, too, of his predilection for "hardness," the ascetic life of the soldier (230). Whereas Mark Antony is haunted by images of emasculation (*Antony and Cleopatra* III. x. 19; III. xiii, 7–8), Othello is confident that the "light-winged toys / Of feathered Cupid" will never "taint" his "business" as a warrior. If he proves to be anything less than a perfectly professional soldier, he dares "housewives" to make a "skillet of [his] helm" (263–67).[134]

Othello's choice of images here tends to downgrade his erotic relationship, making both it and the domesticity of marriage very secondary to the "serious and great" man's work of war. Othello also devalues married sexuality when he explains his reasons for wanting Desdemona to accompany him to Cyprus. In one of the most debated cruxes in *Othello,* the passage in the Folio text reads:

> I therefore beg it not
> To please the palate of my appetite,
> Nor to comply with heat the young affects
> In my defunct, and proper satisfaction.   (256–59)

The lines, possibly corrupt, are difficult to explicate. Othello appears to be renouncing physical "appetite," saying that he has no ardent need to gratify ("comply with") the passion ("heat") that "affects" the young. Is he also saying that the legitimate consummation of his marriage ("proper satisfaction") is dead ("defunct")? One minor change to clarify the meaning would be the emendation of "defunct" to "desumpt" (laid aside, since Othello has to postpone his wedding night) or "disjunct"[135] (separated from). More plausibly, if "defunct" were replaced by "distinct" (Lewis Theobald's suggestion, adopted by the editor of the *New Cambridge Othello*), Othello would be referring to the individual and legitimate ("distinct and proper") satisfaction of his marital rites. Since the Quarto text places a comma after "heat," many editors[136] have deduced from this that "young affects . . . defunct" is a phrase that applies to Othello himself and have accordingly emended "my" to "me." The lines then read

> Nor to comply with heat—the young affects
> In me defunct—and proper satisfaction.

Othello would now be saying that he does not feel compelled to gratify sexual desire ("comply with heat") or even to consummate the marriage (gain his legitimate "satisfaction") because he is a middle-aged man who no longer feels youthful passion. This reading, though, gives even more prominence to "defunct"; while Othello is hardly stating that he is impotent, he appears to protest too much that he has no pressing sexual needs. Possibly he is working hard to promote his professional image above the damaging stereotype of the Moor as "lascivious" or oversexed. Whichever reading we take, the speech comes across as excessively confident (*he* will not be undermined by sexual passion!) and even mildly insulting to Desdemona, who has been frank in seeking the "rites" for which she married Othello.

Othello then sends Desdemona off to Cyprus in a separate ship; as a soldier, he refuses to mix business with pleasure. The audience expects a heated confrontation between Turks and Christians on Cyprus, with Othello emerging triumphant. But when the storm suddenly destroys the Turks, the dramatic focus turns from war to peace with "Our wars are done; the Turks are drowned" (2. 1. 200). Othello's ecstasy over being reunited with Desdemona—"I prattle out of fashion, and I dote / In mine own comforts" (204–5)—suggests that he will not be quite as sovereign over married pleasures ("disports") as he promised to the Senate. Still, when he is forced to leave his wedding bed to contain the drunken brawl (2. 3), he continues to privilege the life of the warrior above that of the husband:

> Come, Desdemona: 'tis the soldiers' life
> To have their balmy slumbers waked with strife.   (256–57)

It is all too easy, though, as Cassio discovers to his chagrin, for a man to lose his military "reputation" to drunkenness (Othello has warned his lieutenant not to "outsport discretion" [33]) or to love;[137] Cassio later dismisses Bianca because he does not want his commander to see him "womaned" (3. 4. 194). Doubtless Iago is exaggerating when he tells Cassio, in Act 2, scene 3, that "Our general's wife is now the general" and, in soliloquy, when he predicts that Desdemona's "appetite shall play the god / With [Othello's] weak function" (314–15, 347–48). But Iago's song "A soldier's a man" (68) solidifies male camaraderie, obliquely suggesting that Othello must be on his guard against being emasculated by a wife who offers a dangerous distraction from barracks discipline.

In the event, Othello is unmanned not by Desdemona, but by the hypermilitary Iago, who exploits his "office" as an "honest" ensign to undermine his general's trust in Desdemona. Within a few scenes, Othello's pride in his wife—"Honey, you shall be well desired in Cyprus" (2. 1. 202)—has turned into his grotesque fantasy that the "general camp" of common soldiers may have "tasted her sweet body" (3. 3. 342–43). It is because his "fair warrior" has become central to his existence, the source where he "must live or bear no life" (4. 2. 57), that he feels compelled to renounce his profession once he thinks he has lost her. "Othello's occupation's gone!" (3. 3. 354) contains a pun on occupation as sexual intercourse;[138] since eros and soldiership have become inextricably joined for Othello, losing this claim on Desdemona means forfeiting his manly career as well. Although early in the play, the professional Othello elevates public military life above his private erotic and domestic happiness,[139] he has now discovered that his love for his wife validates all his other roles in life. Without that love, he can no longer be a terrific warrior.[140]

The speed with which Othello makes plans to murder both Cassio and Desdemona is an index of his martial decisiveness. In Act 2, scene 3, he threatens draconian punishment—"he dies upon his motion" (173)—if any brawler continues to fight. As military governor, Othello must take extreme disciplinary measures: "If I once stir . . . the best of you / Shall sink in my rebuke" (206–8). His declaration that whoever is responsible for the disruption of the peace will "lose" him, even if he were his twin, resembles the insistence of Captain Fluellen in *Henry V* that any British soldier looting in France should be executed, were he "my brother" (*Henry V* III. vi. 54). It is not surprising, then, that Othello behaves so single-mindedly when confronted with a delicate personal situation. To Iago he expounds the philosophy that "To be once in doubt / Is to be resolved" (3. 3. 179–80). But as soon as he actually experiences "doubt"—"I think my wife be honest, and think she is not" (381–82)—he finds the agony of uncertainty, of being unable to reconcile his conflicting images of Desdemona, unbearable. To restore order within his own emotional chaos, he seeks an extreme solution that would be appropriate in warfare: "If there be cords, or knives . . . I'll not endure it" (385–87). Like a soldier scouting out the territory, he demands the satisfaction of "ocular proof." Even the rhythms of the Pontic Sea speech, in which he commits himself absolutely to revenge, evoke a forced march; he will sweep on with "compulsive course" and "ne'er look back," subsuming his unswerving dedication to military valor within the "bloody thoughts" of a "capable and wide revenge" (451–56).

Othello's persona as a dedicated soldier helps to explain, if not to excuse for a modern audience,[141] the swiftness of his decisions and the brutality of his behavior once he becomes jealous. In choosing to resolve the issue quickly rather than to analyze and then pursue other possibilities—conversing more frankly with Desdemona, for instance!—he is the antithesis of Hamlet, who is also confronted with a revenge dilemma but postpones taking action. Othello, trained to action on the battlefield and not introspective by nature, declines to "unpack" his heart with "words" *(Hamlet* II. ii. 585). Instead, this commander in chief mistakenly moves to kill Desdemona at the end of their first full day in Cyprus. Whereas Hamlet, the reflective intellectual, is borne "like a soldier" onto the battlements at the end of his tragedy, one of *Othello*'s most biting ironies is that the hero's restored identity as a warrior is never acknowledged by the Venetians. They simply order that the bed on which this soldier-lover dies "be hid" (5. 2. 361).

NOTES

1. E. A. J. Honigmann (ed.), *Othello, The Arden Shakespeare,* 3rd ed. (Walton-on-Thames: Thomas Nelson and Sons, Ltd., 1977), pp. 25, 20.

2. Barbara Everett, "Reflections on the Sentimentalist's Othello," *CritQ,* 3.2 (Summer 1961): 127–39, quote at 130.

3. Michael D. Bristol, "Charivari and the Comedy of Abjection in *Othello,*" *RenD,* n.s. 20 (1990): 3–21, quote at 12.

4. Rochelle Smith, "Admirable Musicians: Women's Songs in *Othello* and *The Maid's Tragedy,*" *CompD,* 28.3 (Fall 1996): 311–24, points out that the willow scene (4. 3) is "the only time when our view is unmediated by the gaze of the men who surround [Desdemona]" (p. 313).

5. James Henry Hackett, *Notes, Criticism, and Correspondence upon Shakespeare Plays and Actors* (New York: Carleton, 1863), p. 224.

6. Ann Jenalie Cook, "The Design of Desdemona: Doubt Raised and Resolved," *ShStud,* 13 (1980): 187–96, quote at 187.

7. A. P. Rossiter, "*Othello:* A Moral Essay," in *Angel with Horns* (London: Longman, 1961), p. 206.

8. See Valerie Wayne, "Historical Differences: Misogyny and *Othello,*" in *The Matter of Difference: Materialist Feminist Criticism of Shakespeare* (Ithaca, N.Y.: Cornell University Press, 1991), pp. 153–79. Rodney Poisson, "The 'Calumniator Credited' and the Code of Honour in Shakespeare's *Othello,*" *ESC,* 11 (1976): 381–401, also explores the effects of Iago's "Italianate anti-feminism" (p. 382).

9. See, for example, Coppelia Kahn, *Man's Estate: Masculine Identity in Shakespeare* (Berkeley, Los Angeles, and London: University of California Press, 1981), pp. 127–146; and Edward A. Snow, "Sexual Anxiety and the Male Order of Things in *Othello,*" *ELR,* 10 (1980): 384–412.

10. See Janet Adelman, "Iago's Alter Ego: Race as Projection in *Othello,*" *SQ,* 48.3 (Summer 1997): 125–44, quote at 126. Edward Berry also suggests this in "Othello's Alienation," *SEL,* 30 (1990): 315–33, as does Snow, "Sexual Anxiety and the Male Order of Things," p. 401.

11. Margaret Loftus Ranald, "The Indiscretions of Desdemona," *SQ,* 14 (1963): 127–39, quote at 134.

12. Janet Overmyer, "Shakespeare's Desdemona: A Twentieth Century View," *University Review,* 37 (1971): 304–5, also considers that Desdemona is "partially responsible" for the tragic outcome; had she been "a bit more worldly-wise" and sophisticated, she might have been able to deflect Othello's suspicions (p. 304).

13. Robert Dickes, "Desdemona: An Innocent Victim?" *American Imago,* 27.3 (Fall 1970): 279–97, quotes at 295–96. Stephen Reid, "Desdemona's Guilt," *American Imago,* 27.3 (Fall 1970): 245–62, goes further, finding Desdemona's sense of guilt a consequence of trying to punish her father by marrying Othello.

14. Commented on by R. S. White, *Innocent Victims: Poetic Injustice in Shakespeare's Tragedy* (London: Athlone Press, 1986), p. 5. Evelyn Gajowski, "The Female Perspective in *Othello*," in Virginia Mason Vaughan and Kent Cartwright (eds.), Othello: *New Perspectives* (London and Toronto: Associated University Presses, 1991), pp. 97–114, also points out that it is "perverse" to try to find in Desdemona any "crimes" that would justify Othello's murdering her (p. 104).

15. John E. Seaman, "Othello's Pearl," *SQ,* 19 (1968): 81–85, points out that according to Revelation 21:20, chrysolite was one of the twelve precious stones in the walls of the heavenly city (p. 83).

16. Honigmann (ed.), *Othello,* p. 48.

17. Carol Thomas Neely, "Women and Men in *Othello*," in Carolyn Lenz, Gayle Greene, and Carol Thomas Neely (eds.), *The Woman's Part: Feminist Criticism of* Othello (Urbana: University of Illinois Press, 1980), pp. 211–39, stresses Desdemona's "energizing power" and how she makes every effort to "mend and renew the relationship" (p. 227).

18. Kenneth Muir (ed.), *Othello* (London and New York: Penguin, 1968), p. 41.

19. Jane Adamson, Othello *as Tragedy: Some Problems of Judgment and Feeling* (Cambridge: Cambridge University Press, 1985), pp. 262, 220. Mary Beth Rose, *The Expense of Spirit: Love and Sexuality in English Renaissance Drama* (Ithaca, N.Y.: Cornell University Press, 1988), finds in this final line an "act of self-assertion" that is simultaneously "an act of self-cancellation" (p. 152).

20. S. N. Garner, "Shakespeare's Desdemona," *ShStud,* 9 (1976): 233–52, quote at 249.

21. Robert B. Heilman, *Magic in the Web: Lanuage and Action in* Othello (Lexington: University of Kentucky Press, 1956), pp. 214–16, points out three stages in the "miracle" of Desdemona's love, from gesturing toward her wrongdoer in "O, falsely, falsely murdered!" (5. 2. 116), to exculpating herself in "A guiltless death I die" (121), to shielding and actually forgiving her wrongdoer in "Nobody—I myself. Farewell / Commend me to my kind lord" (123–24).

22. Pointed out by Robert V. Caro, "Ignatian Discernment and the World of *Othello*," *Crosscurrents,* 44 (Fall 1994): 332–44, quote at 342.

23. A. C. Bradley, *Shakespearean Tragedy* (1904; London: Macmillan, 1962), p. 165.

24. G. Wilson Knight, *The Wheel of Fire: Interpretation of Shakespeare's Sombre Tragedies* (London: Oxford University Press, 1930), p. 114.

25. Cook, "The Design of Desdemona," p. 190.

26. G. Bonnard, "Are Othello and Desdemona Innocent or Guilty?" *ES,* 30 (1949): 175–84, quotes at 176 and 183. John W. Draper, *The* Othello *of Shakespeare's Audience* (Paris: M. Didier, 1952), also emphasizes that Desdemona courts danger by her independent actions (p. 63).

27. W. H. Auden, "The Joker in the Pack," in *The Dyer's Hand* (New York: Random House, 1948), pp. 246–72, quote at 268.

28. M. R. Ridley (ed.), *Othello, The New Arden Shakespeare* (1958; New York: Routledge, 1987), p. 54.

29. Adamson, Othello *as Tragedy,* finds Desdemona somewhat "capricious" and "childish" here, turning what should be a "professional issue" into a "matrimonial power-struggle" (pp. 138–39). Graham Bradshaw, *Misrepresentations: Shakespeare and the Materialists* (London and Ithaca, N.Y.: Cornell University Press, 1993), emphasizes how Emilia's reassuring Cassio about Othello's intentions (3. 3. 46–48) makes Desdemona's subsequent appeals to Othello "redundant, and even offensive" (p. 174).

30. Suggested by Adamson, Othello *as Tragedy,* p. 231.

31. Madeleine Doran, "The Idea of Excellence in Shakespeare," *SQ*, 27 (1976): 133–49, quote at 148.

32. This is the interpretation of Ruth Vanita, "'Proper' Men and 'Fallen' Women: The Unprotectedness of Wives in *Othello*," *SEL*, 34 (1994): 341–56. Vanita offers a convincing analysis of how the play dramatizes "societal collusion in husbandly violence" (p. 349).

33. Auden, "The Joker in the Pack," p. 269.

34. Garner, "Shakespeare's Desdemona," 249. Reid, "Desdemona's Guilt," goes even further in asserting that the final clause of the willow song, "If I court moe women, you'll couch with moe men," represents Desdemona's "deepest wishes" to be unfaithful (p. 257).

35. W. D. Adamson, "Unpinned or Undone? Desdemona's Critics and the Problem of Sexual Innocence," *ShStud*, 13 (1980): 169–86, quote at 176.

36. Norman Sanders (ed.), *Othello, New Cambridge Shakespeare* (Cambridge: Cambridge University Press, 1984), p. 29.

37. Marvin Rosenberg, *The Masks of* Othello (Berkeley and Los Angeles: University of California Press, 1961), p. 209.

38. F. R. Leavis, "Diabolic Intellect and the Noble Hero," in *The Common Pursuit* (1952; Harmondsworth: Penguin Books, 1962), p. 138.

39. Peter Holland, "The Resources of Characterization in *Othello*," *ShS*, 41 (1989): 119–32, stresses how Iago "enforces a particular mode of close connection with the audience" (p. 129).

40. Julie Hankey (ed.), Othello: *Plays in Performance* (Bristol: Bristol Classical Press, 1987), pp. 11–12.

41. J. I. M. Stewart, *Character and Motive in Shakespeare* (London: Longman, 1949), p. 108.

42. G. Wilson Knight, *Shakespearian Production* (1964; London: Routledge and Kegan Paul, Ltd., 1968), p. 104.

43. Sanders (ed.), *Othello,* p. 25.

44. Leonard Digges, *An Arithmeticall Militare Treatise* (London, 1587), quoted in Julia Genster, "Lieutenancy, Standing in and Othello," *ELH*, 57.4 (1990): 785–809, quote at 793.

45. William Empson, "Honest in *Othello*," in *The Structure of Complex Words* (1951; London: Chatto and Windus, 1969), p. 235.

46. Paul Jorgensen, "*Honesty* in *Othello*," in *Redeeming Shakespeare's Words* (Berkeley, Los Angeles, and London: University of California Press, 1985), pp. 1–21, quote at p. 19.

47. Auden, "The Joker in the Pack," thinks that Roderigo is the only character to whom Iago tells direct lies (p. 260).

48. Ralph Berry, "Patterns in *Othello*," *SQ*, 23 (1972): 3–19, quote at 9.

49. See E. E. Stoll, *Art and Artifice* (New York: Barnes and Noble, 1951), p. 12.

50. See E. A. J. Honigmann, *Shakespeare: Seven Tragedies: The Dramatist's Manipulation of Response* (New York: Barnes and Noble, 1976), p. 4.

51. Muir (ed.), *Othello,* points out that this motive rapidly "fades into the background" (p. 15). But Michael Neill, "Changing Places in *Othello*," *ShS*, 37 (1984): 115–31, takes "resentment" to be Iago's defining personality trait and thinks that his bitterness at Cassio's promotion remains a prime motive for revenge (p. 121). From his own experience in the armed forces, Laurence Olivier found this motive crucial to an understanding of the role: "when someone gets a half-stripe more than you your soul can get bitten . . . with bitterness and envy" ("The Great Sir Laurence," *Life*, May 1, 1964, p. 88).

52. See G. M. Matthews, "Othello and the Dignity of Man," in Arnold Kettle (ed.), *Shakespeare in a Changing World* (New York: International Publishers, 1964), pp. 131–32.

53. Honigmann, *Shakespeare: Seven Tragedies,* discusses this as one of Iago's "secret motives," together with his "need to press distasteful images upon unwilling listeners" and his contemptuousness (pp. 88, 80). In his edition of *Othello,* Honigmann also notes Iago's "resentment of privilege"; when Iago apologizes to Gratiano for his inadequate "manners" (5. 1. 94), he is eager to be "accepted as an equal" (36–37).

54. Madeleine Doran, "Good Name in *Othello,*" *SEL,* 7 (1967): 195–217, explores Iago's "malicious envy" in terms of Renaissance personifications of this deadly sin (pp. 200–206). She points out how Envy in Thomas Nashe's *Pierce Penniless* (1592), like Iago, adopts an extremely honest persona (p. 206).

55. See Bradley, *Shakespearean Tragedy,* p. 187.

56. In Horace Howard Furness (ed.), *A New Variorum Edition of Shakespeare: Othello* (1886; New York: Dover Publications, 1963), p. 214.

57. Michael E. Mooney, "Location and Idiom in *Othello,*" in Vaughan and Cartwright (eds.), Othello: *New Perspectives,* pp. 115–34, draws on the *Figurenpositionen* established by Robert Weimann, *Shakespeare and the Popular Tradition in the Theater* (Baltimore and London: Johns Hopkins University Press, 1978), to suggest how Iago, in his realistic dimension, might converse with Roderigo on the main playing area while addressing the audience in his role as "dehumanized Vice" on the forefront of the stage (p. 132).

58. Eric Griffin, "Un-Sainting James; Or, *Othello* and the 'Spanish Spirits' of Shakespeare's Globe," *Representations,* 62 (Spring 1998): 58–99, points out that Iago's very name—a contraction of Santiago, or Saint James, the patron saint of Spain, may signal anti-Spanish, anti-Catholic sentiment in early-seventeenth-century England.

59. Christopher Marlowe, *Doctor Faustus,* in *Christopher Marlowe: The Complete Plays,* ed. J. B. Steane (Harmondsworth: Penguin, 1969).

60. Francis Bacon, *Essays* (1625; London: Dent, 1906, 1968), p. 28.

61. Bernard Spivack, *Shakespeare and the Allegory of Evil* (New York: Columbia University Press, 1958), p. 7.

62. Ibid., p. 448.

63. Ibid., p. 23.

64. Stanley Edgar Hyman, *Iago: Some Approaches to the Illusion of His Motivation* (New York: Atheneum, 1970), p. 26.

65. David Bevington (ed.), *Othello, New Bantam Shakespeare* (New York: Bantam Books, 1988), p. xxiv. Leah Scragg also challenges Spivack's thesis in "Iago—Vice or Devil?" *ShS,* 11 (1968): 53–64.

66. Maud Bodkin, *Archetypal Patterns in Poetry* (London, Oxford, and New York: Oxford University Press, 1934), pp. 245, 223. Stewart, *Character and Motive in Shakespeare,* similarly points out that "Othello *is* the human soul as it strives to be and Iago *is* that which corrodes or subverts it from within" (p. 108). See also Thomas F. Connolly, "Shakespeare and the Double Man," *SQ,* 1 (1950): 31–35.

67. James L. Calderwood, *The Properties of* Othello (Amherst: University of Massachusetts Press, 1989), p. 129.

68. Auden, "The Joker in the Pack," p. 266.

69. G. R. Hibbard, "*Othello* and Shakespearean Tragedy," *ShS,* 21 (1968): 39–46, quote at 44.

70. Pointed out by Arthur Kirsch, *Shakespeare and the Experience of Love* (Cambridge: Cambridge University Press, 1981), p. 28.

71. Leslie A. Fiedler, "The Moor as Stranger," in *The Stranger in Shakespeare* (1973; St. Albans, Hertfordshire: Paladin, 1974), p. 162.

72. E. E. Stoll refers to "the convention of the calumniator credited" in Othello: *An Historical and Comparative Study* (1915; New York: Gordian Press, Inc., 1967), p. 6.

73. Wyndham Lewis, *The Lion and the Fox* (London: Methuen, 1951), p. 193.

74. Empson, "'Honest' in *Othello*," p. 239.

75. From the *Examiner,* August 7, 1814, in William Hazlitt, *A View of the English Stage,* ed. W. Spencer Jackson (London: George Bell and Sons, 1906), p. 59.

76. Bradley, *Shakespearean Tragedy,* p. 188.

77. Heilman, *Magic in the Web,* p. 47.

78. Hyman, *Iago,* p. 61. Calderwood, *The Properties of* Othello, also finds Iago "aesthetically rather than realistically motivated" at times (p. 122).

79. Heilman, *Magic in the Web,* p. 48.

80. Auden, "The Joker in the Pack," p. 270.

81. In *The Lion and the Fox,* Lewis calls Iago "the *taurobolus* of this sacrificial bull" (p. 190). John Wain (ed.), "Introduction," Othello: *A Casebook* (London and Basingstoke: Macmillan, 1971), comments on how "Iago, the matador, succumbs to the excitement of his combat with the bull" (p. 13).

82. See Hyman, *Iago,* p. 66.

83. Auden explores this theory in "The Joker in the Pack," p. 252.

84. Harley Granville Barker, *Prefaces to Shakespeare* (Princeton, N.J.: Princeton University Press, 1947), vol. 2, p. 110.

85. Bradley, *Shakespearean Tragedy,* p. 177.

86. Michael Black, "Othello: A Study of the Self I," in *The Literature of Fidelity* (London: Chatto and Windus, 1975), p. 19. Adamson, Othello *as Tragedy,* discerns in Iago "a man who feels deeply threatened by others but is totally unable to acknowledge his fear" (p. 88). Auden, "The Joker in the Pack," also analyzes Iago's "feeling of self-insufficiency" (p. 256).

87. Black, "Othello," p. 20.

88. Rosenberg, *The Masks of* Othello, finds in Iago "a bottomless, consuming passion that feeds on all life around him" (p. 175) and an "internalized rage" (p. 177).

89. Granville Barker, *Prefaces to Shakespeare,* vol. 2, p. 108.

90. In *The Masks of* Othello, Rosenberg points out that these monologues are not a "necessary" part of the dramatic action (p.173).

91. Matthews, "Othello and the Dignity of Man," p. 134.

92. Harold C. Goddard, *The Meaning of Shakespeare* (Chicago: University of Chicago Press, 1951), terms Iago a "moral pyromaniac" with a "secret joy in being on the scene of the conflagration he has kindled" (p. 463).

93. Daniel Stempel, "The Silence of Iago," *PMLA,* 84 (1969): 252–63, finds that Iago is echoing "Jesuit Pelagianism" here: overemphasizing the freedom of the will. See also Ruth Levitsky, "All-in-All Sufficiency in Othello," *ShStud,* 6 (1970): 209–221.

94. This is the now archaic meaning of "will" as "carnal desire or appetite" (*Oxford English Dictionary, sb.*[1] 1.2) that the lover Troilus draws on when he laments that "the will is infinite and the execution confin'd" (*Troilus and Cressida* III. ii. 82).

95. Hugh Grady, "Iago and the Dialectic of Enlightenment: Reason, Will, and Desire in *Othello*," *Criticism,* 37.4 (Fall 1995): 537–58, also discusses how, in the play's exploration of "instrumental reason," "reason, desire, and will conflate into a single, undifferentiated will-to-power/pleasure whose locus is the frightening ego/id we call Iago" (pp. 552, 544).

96. Bradley, *Shakespearean Tragedy,* p. 178.

97. In particular, Martin Wangh, "*Othello:* The Tragedy of Iago," *Psychoanalytic Quarterly,* 19 (1950): 202–12.

98. Gordon Ross Smith, "Iago the Paranoiac," *American Imago,* 16 (Summer 1959): 155–67. Robert Rodgers, "Endopsychic Drama in *Othello,*" *SQ,* 20 (1969): 205–15, also analyzes *Othello* as an "endopsychic drama whose action symbolizes certain conflicting possibilities of sexual orientation" (p. 214).

99. Hyman (*Iago*) also stresses the "plurality" within the line, finding that it expresses a pinnacle of achievement for the stage villain, the Satan figure, the Machiavel, and the author-dramatist, as well as for the homosexual Iago (p. 139).

100. Jonathan Dollimore, "Forget Iago's Homosexuality," in *Sexual Dissidence* (Oxford: Clarendon Press, 1991), finds more important than any latent homosexuality the "homosocial alliance between Othello and Iago" as they vow vengeance against "the betraying feminine (Desdemona) and the usurping masculine (Cassio)" (p. 157).

101. Rosenberg, *The Masks of Othello*, p. 158.

102. Quoted in ibid., p. 182.

103. John Holloway, *The Story of the Night* (Lincoln: University of Nebraska Press, 1963), p. 47.

104. Helen Gardner, "The Noble Moor," *PBA,* 51 (1955): 189–205, quotes at 192 and 189.

105. Samuel Johnson, *Johnson on Shakespeare,* ed. Walter Raleigh (London: Oxford University Press, 1908), p. 200.

106. Samuel Taylor Coleridge, *Lectures at Bristol (1813–14),* vol. 2 of *Shakespearean Criticism,* ed. Thomas Middleton Raysor (London: Dent, 1960), p. 227.

107. Bradley, *Shakespearean Tragedy,* p. 155.

108. Leavis, "Diabolic Intellect," p. 142. Leo Kirschbaum, "The Modern Othello," *ELH,* 1 (1944): 283–96, also analyzed Othello's "trait of self-idealization" (p. 288) a few years after Leavis's essay was originally published in *Scrutiny* (1937).

109. Leavis, "Diabolic Intellect," pp. 146–47, 139, 142.

110. See Martin Elliott, *Shakespeare's Invention of Othello* (New York: St Martin's Press, 1988), p. 127.

111. Virginia Mason Vaughan, Othello: *A Contextual History* (Cambridge: Cambridge University Press, 1994), p. 47. Kirschbaum, "The Modern Othello," claims that "Othello loves not Desdemona *but his image of her*" (p. 292); and in *Flaming Minister: A Study of Othello* (New York: AMS Press, 1965), G. R. Elliott also finds that Othello manifests "pride and self-centeredness" in his love for Desdemona (p. 64).

112. Everett, "Reflections on the Sentimentalist's Othello," p. 132.

113. Heilman, *Magic in the Web,* p. 138. Matthew N. Proser, *The Heroic Image in Five Shakespearean Tragedies* (Princeton, N.J.: Princeton University Press, 1965), also comments on how Othello's language reveals "latent insecurity, self-protectiveness, and lack of self-possession" (p. 107).

114. Rossiter, "*Othello:* A Moral Essay," pp. 189–208, quote at 192. Rossiter goes on to explain how Othello may be "right and wrong at once" if we accept the two meanings of "jealous" in the speech (p. 192).

115. Holloway, *The Story of the Night,* points out that Leavis is inaccurate in claiming that this comes only seventy lines into Iago's attack (p. 156).

116. Leavis, "Diabolic Intellect," p. 141.

117. Bradley, *Shakespearean Tragedy,* pp. 159–60.

118. Ibid., p. 161.

119. Leavis, "Diabolic Intellect," p. 149.

120. Gardner, "The Noble Moor," still finds the "heroic" here, while conceding that "the godlike is mingled with the brutal" (p. 201).

121. In *Shakespeare and the Renaissance Concept of Honor* (Princeton, N.J.: Princeton University Press, 1960), Curtis Brown Watson comments that "revenge for adultery, by murder of both wife and adulterer, was tolerated in the early laws of every European country" (p. 160). Doran, "Good Name in *Othello*," also accepts that the reputation of the hero depends on the "'fame' he has by virtue of his wife's behavior" as well as the fame "inherent in his lineage" and the "fame he has won in action" (p. 200).

122. Brents Stirling, *Unity in Shakespearian Tragedy* (1956; New York: Gordian Press, Inc., 1966), p. 110. Norman Council, *When Honour's at the Stake* (London: George Allen and Unwin, Ltd., 1973), also contrasts Othello's initial identification of honor and virtuous action with his later "amoral compulsion to revenge the affront to his honour" (p. 127), while David L. Jeffrey and Patrick Grant, "Reputation in *Othello*," *ShStud*, 6 (1970): 197–208, analyze Othello's "mistaken allegiance" to earthly reputation, or "bad fame" (p. 206).

123. Richard S. Ide, *Possessed with Greatness: The Heroic Tragedies of Chapman and Shakespeare* (Chapel Hill: University of North Carolina Press, 1980), p. 50. John Fraser, "*Othello* and Honour," *CR*, 8 (1965): 59–70, also finds this "male ego-ideal" the villain of the play (p. 62).

124. Holloway, *The Story of the Night*, p. 55.

125. T. S. Eliot, "Shakespeare and the Stoicism of Seneca," *Selected Essays: 1917–1932* (1950; New York: Harcourt, Brace, and Co., 1932), p. 111.

126. Elliott, *Shakespeare's Invention of Othello*, p. 108.

127. Bradley, *Shakespearean Tragedy*, p. 161. Matthews, "*Othello* and the Dignity of Man," also finds a "complete recovery of [Othello's] integrity as a human being" at the end of the play (p. 145); James C. Bulman, *The Heroic Idiom of Shakespearean Tragedy* (London and Toronto: Associated University Presses, 1985), concludes that Othello's final "words and deeds are engaged in an absolute alliance" (p. 125); and T. McAlindon, *Shakespeare's Tragic Cosmos* (Cambridge: Cambridge University Press, 1991), argues that Othello regains "oneness with others and with his lost self" (p. 143).

128. Adamson, *Othello as Tragedy*, points out that when the hero moves quickly from brutal murder to administering justice on himself by committing suicide, it is impossible for us either to "identify" with him or to "remain wholly detached" from him (p. 265).

129. Reuben Brower, *Hero and Saint: Shakespeare and the Graeco-Roman Tradition* (Oxford: Clarendon Press, 1971), p. 10.

130. Proser, *The Heroic Image*, discusses how the soldier hero is placed in a situation "with which his military training cannot cope" (p. 192); to deal with Desdemona's supposed adultery, he resumes the role of "the good soldier fighting for a just cause" (p. 130).

131. Paul A. Cantor, "*Othello*: The Erring Barbarian and the Supersubtle Venetians," *SWR*, 75 (Summer 1990): 296–319, quote at 313.

132. Vaughan, Othello: *A Contextual History*, p. 35.

133. Helen Gardner, "'Othello': A Retrospect, 1900–67," *ShS*, 21 (1968): 1–11, quote at 6.

134. Elliott, *Shakespeare's Invention of Othello*, comments that Othello's word "disports," meaning "diversion from duties," also reduces marriage "to a physical and trivial function" (p. 12).

135. Edmond Malone's emendation; see Furness (ed.), *New Variorum Othello*, p. 73.

136. Samuel Johnson, following John Upton; see Furness (ed.), ibid., pp. 72–73.

137. Henry J. Webb, "The Military Background in *Othello*," *PQ*, 30.1 (June 1951): 40–52, is one critic who thinks that Othello's furlough has led to "soft living" and that he has begun to "disintegrate as an officer" (p. 50).

138. See Calderwood, *The Properties of* Othello, p. 89. Tom McBride, "Othello's Oro-tund Occupation," *TSLL,* 30 (1988): 412–30, also comments on how Othello's anxiety arises from the belief that someone else has "occupied his sexual territory" (p. 415).

139. Rose, *The Expense of Spirit,* comments perceptively on this (p. 140).

140. Cantor, "*Othello:* The Erring Barbarian," also comments on how once he is married, Othello derives "his sense of self-worth from Desdemona's admiration for him" (p. 311).

141. Gardner, "'Othello': A Retrospect," points out that we no longer regard military men as heroes in the way that the Renaissance did (p. 6).

5

THEMES

Because *Othello* is so obviously a play about sexual jealousy—the "bloody passion" that undermines the hero and turns him into a murderer—readers may take this to be the play's main theme. Or they may generalize *Othello*'s dramatic themes as reason versus passion[1] and good in conflict with evil. On a deeper level, though, the play explores important concerns arising from but not restricted to the central phenomenon of jealousy. Is Othello gullible, or does his status as an outsider in Venice make him—and, by extension, any stranger—uniquely vulnerable to evil insinuations by a social insider? How easy is it to attack emotional faith with reason or logical deduction, and should what appears to be objective proof always elicit belief that the loved one is false? Shakespeare shows how a deeply malicious man (Iago) can exploit the gap between intuitive belief and knowledge based on empirical evidence in order to subvert a husband's faith in his wife. Iago activates in Othello the "green-eyed monster" of jealousy. Still, the play goes on to ask, on what does the monster feed? *Othello* suggests that the human mind in itself is prone to nurture "monstrous" and "foul" imaginings and that people often act perversely, even without a demonic catalyst. The audience, too, becomes implicated in this theme; on one level, *Othello* encourages them to cultivate what Iago calls "Foul disproportions, thoughts unnatural" (3. 3. 233) through constructing as "monstrous" the sexual union of the black man and the white woman.

THE OUTSIDER

What are the repercussions of being a foreigner in a particular society? Through the character of its hero, *Othello* explores in some depth the theme of the outsider—how his integrity and secure identity can be undermined within an unfamiliar culture. Shakespeare's imagination may have been sparked by the opening sentence of Giraldi Cinthio's novella, "There once lived in Venice a Moor,"[2] for from the start of the play, Othello is foregrounded as a stranger in this city, cosmopolitan though it may be. Respected and utilized for his military prowess—the Venetians employ him to conquer a more threatening outsider, the Turk—he nevertheless remains an "uncharted stranger"[3] within the private world of Venice. Stranger beware. Above all, Shakespeare suggests, the subtle differences among cultures are what make the alien in a European city especially vulnerable. While Othello finds it difficult to "construe signs" within a strange culture, Iago is an "accomplished manipulator"[4] of these signs. Part of Othello's susceptibility to Iago's word-spinning is the fact that the ensign is an Italian insider, intimate with the ways of Venice. Iago is able to exploit Othello's limited knowledge of Venetian customs to undermine the African's confidence in his fitness to be Desdemona's husband and in the admirable persona he has constructed for himself in the city-state.

Even before we see Othello onstage, he is categorized by Roderigo as "an extravagant and wheeling stranger / Of here and everywhere" (1. 1. 133–34). Not only is he "estranged" from the ultracivilized city-state of Venice because of his black skin, but he lacks a "cultural identity"[5] in Africa; before residing in the city, he has lived as a peripatetic African warrior, traveling through exotic landscapes, being sold into slavery, and then freed for further adventures.[6] Respecting him for his outstanding soldiership, the Venetians appoint him commander in chief of the expedition to protect their outpost Cyprus. Historically, the policy of the Venetian free state was to use foreign mercenaries to protect its trading empire and to choose as its military leader a man who was not a citizen of Venice; Lewis Lewkenor (who translated Gasparo Contarini's work on Venice in 1599) comments that "The Captaine Generall of our Armie . . . is alwaies a straunger."[7] As such, Othello is given full power over the campaign and appointed governor of Cyprus. This does not inhibit racial slurs against him, however. In private and with Roderigo, Iago is the most virulently racist of the play's Venetians, but Brabantio slanders Othello in public as a "damned" heathen who uses black magic, and Roderigo, a landed gentleman of Venice, does not hesitate to term Othello "thicklips" and "lascivious Moor" (1. 1. 63, 123).

While Venice is a metropolis "open" to strangers "for the purposes of war and business,"[8] it remains conservative in its civic structure, maintaining a strict oligarchy. This becomes clear when the magnifico Brabantio, appalled that Othello has eloped with his daughter, finds the Moor's violation of decorum a threat to the entire structure of Venice: "For if such actions may have passage free, / Bondslaves and pagans shall our statesmen be" (1. 2. 97–98). Othello is no pagan or Muslim; he has been baptized a Christian.[9] But in Brabantio's eyes, the difference between the white Venetian aristocrat and the black alien is as acute as the gap separating Jew and Christian in *The Merchant of Venice*. There, Portia-Balthazar, turning the screws on the Jewish outsider Shylock in the trial scene, suddenly produces a draconian law (loss of all property and possible execution) that applies to any "alien" who seeks the "life of any citizen" of Venice (IV. 1. 349–51). The exclusion and scapegoating of the ethnic outsider could not be more pronounced. In Cinthio's *Hecatommithi,* too, the Venetian senators bestow "honor" on the Moor for his "bravery in arms" but reinforce the cultural gap after the murder; they force him back from Cyprus and torture him "when they hear[d] of the cruelty inflicted by a barbarian upon a lady of their city."[10]

On one level, Othello seems to be fairly well assimilated into Venetian society. Not only is he a Christian, but he is confident that the "service" he has "done the Signiory"—his acquired reputation as a valiant leader in battle[11]—will ensure the support of the Duke and the Senate for his marriage. Indeed, it does guarantee him a fair, perhaps even favorable, hearing from the Duke, who is much more determinedly color-blind than is Brabantio. It remains an open question, however, whether the assured rhythms of Othello's "My parts, my title, and my perfect soul / Shall manifest me rightly" (1. 2. 30–31) reflect a genuine confidence in his own worth or the overcompensations of an ego protecting itself within a mutedly hostile environment—what Richard S. Ide calls "the defensive posture of a racial and cultural alien."[12] When Othello insists in the Senate scene that his "offending" is limited to his marrying Desdemona—it "Hath this extent, no more" (81)—he almost seems, through a submerged pun, to be denying his unsophisticated Moorish origins, since the six-syllable half line echoes Brabantio's derisory address "This is the man—this Moor" just ten lines earlier.

Because they share a military background, Othello feels he can trust his comrade Iago, and he is resentful that the ensign would make his general a "stranger" to observations gleaned from civilian experience:

> Thou dost conspire against thy friend, Iago,
> If thou but think'st him wronged, and mak'st his ear
> A stranger to thy thoughts. (3. 3. 142–44)

When Iago chips away at Othello's defenses, it is on the assumption that Othello is, in fact, masking an inner core of vulnerability with grand words and gestures. Trading on his insider status and his reluctant agreement to reveal how Othello is "wronged," Iago plays his trump card in his speech "I know our country disposition well" (3. 3. 201) when he alludes to the Venetian wives'"pranks" that have escaped Othello's notice. Othello knows instinctively that he is inside the magic circle of Desdemona's devotion, for he stakes his "life upon her faith" (1. 3. 289). Yet within the space of half a scene, Iago convinces him that his color ("Haply for I am black"), his lack of Venetian social graces ("those soft parts of conversation / That chamberers have"), and his age (somewhat "declined / Into the vale of years," making him significantly older than his bride) have now placed him outside that circle: "She's gone. I am abused" (3. 3. 262–66). Feeling displaced, Othello relegates Desdemona to another inner circle of Venetian life—the courtesan culture. Tragically, he now interprets this extraordinary woman, the "cunning'st pattern of excelling nature" (5. 2. 11), as a "cunning whore of Venice" (4. 2. 88).

In Venice there are varying degrees of being alienated from the center of things— a series of concentric circles, with the Turks occupying the outermost rim.[13] As Muslim infidels, the Turks represent a threatening, warlike "Other" to the West (part of the sixteenth-century fear that the expanding Ottoman Empire might conquer Venice and lead to the fall of Christian Europe),[14] and it is ironically appropriate that a Moor who has converted to Christianity and is now living peacefully in Venice should be co-opted by the Venetians to lead the counterattack on the Islamic intruders. When the Turks' assault on Cyprus simply evaporates after their shipwreck, Othello confronts a more insidious menace. Iago is also a loner, an aberration from the norm in his fierce dedication to revenge after Cassio's appointment to lieutenant excludes him from the office; but his advantage over Othello lies in his operating from within Venetian society. On Cyprus, this worldly-wise European metaphorically takes over the role of the Turkish outsider, as the opening lines of Act 2 subtly convey. After satirically mocking women, Iago responds to Desdemona's "O, fie upon thee, slanderer!" with "Nay, it is true, or else I am a Turk" (2. 1. 112–13). Since Desdemona's purity and absolute devotion to her husband render Iago's misogynistic pronouncements false, the equation of Iago with the Turkish, anti-Christ enemy holds true.[15] Evil Iago is also responsible for the chaotic breach of order in the riot scene that provokes Othello's angry question "Are we turned Turks?" (2. 3. 169).

In the fortified citadel of Cyprus, away from the hierarchies of the metropolis, Othello seems destined to triumph as a free and powerful figure. But Cyprus is still an outpost of Venice, and Iago slyly keeps Othello chained to the prejudices and assumptions of the city-state. In Act 3, he transforms his general into an "erring barbarian" even as he makes Othello believe that Desdemona is a "supersubtle Venetian." This is not a case of Othello reverting to his origins (for he is never presented as a former barbarian, always as a stoical, dedicated warrior), but of his living up to the image of the African outsider that Iago invidiously projects. Only in the finale does Othello go some way toward regaining his stature as an honorary Venetian. In his summation before he commits suicide, he asks that the Senate recall his "service" to the state; yet in refashioning himself, he appears hopelessly split between the "all in all sufficient" warrior revered by the Senate in the past (4. 1. 265) and the stranger who has never truly belonged to Venice. On one level, his suicide is a desperate attempt to reestablish his position within this society, to gain a "passport into the nation" he longs "to call his own."[16] But reenacting his role as a heroic leader who once protected his adopted state by dispatching a "malignant" Turk, he suddenly switches to identify with the outsider when he stabs and kills himself as a surrogate for the treacherous Islamic enemy.[17]

That puzzling allusion in Othello's final speech, whether to the "base Judean" (Folio) or the "base Indian" (Quarto) who throws away a pearl "richer than all his tribe," also conjures up images of the outsider (5. 2. 344).[18] The Judean may recall Judas betraying Christ or the Jew alienated from Christian society, like Shylock from *The Merchant of Venice*. The American Indian—if we take the Quarto reading—almost always appears as an object of wonder or derision in Renaissance contexts, where he is distanced from European explorers and likely to be exploited; when Stephano encounters Caliban in *The Tempest*, his first idea is to take the monstrous native back home to Italy (Naples) as a curiosity that will earn him some money (II. ii. 68–70). Lodovico, spokesperson for Venice in *Othello*, firmly reestablishes the boundaries of the city-state with his curt words after the hero's suicide: "The object poisons sight; / Let it be hid" (5. 2. 360–61). Viewed one way, the "object" is a grotesque tableau of death, the fruits of Iago's evil; but it is also a "loading of the bed" with bodies that include a black foreigner embracing a white European woman. Such a subversive image cannot be countenanced by the ethnocentric world of Venice. Othello accordingly stays locked into the outsider role at the end of the play, his heroic words for the Senate rendered invalid by Gratiano's pronouncement that "All that is spoke is marred" (353).

How does the wider audience react to this presentation of the alien? As a predominantly Western group (in the Globe Theatre of the early seventeenth century, and in many theaters producing *Othello* in subsequent eras), they may be placed in the position of the Venetians who "share a culture the Moor can never understand."[19] As individual spectators, though, they are invited to sympathize with Othello's tragic isolation, challenged to reflect on the predicament of the foreigner who is never fully assimilated and so remains outside the social system, vulnerable to its prejudices.

DOUBT AND FAITH: SEEING AND KNOWING

For whatever reasons—insecurity within an unfamiliar culture, a defensive or overinflated ego, a deep-rooted distrust of women—Othello's faith in Desdemona is not strong enough to resist Iago's insinuations. On a broader level, the play explores two closely related issues: how love is vulnerable to the workings of cold reason, and how carelessness in analyzing testimony and misinterpretation of visual evidence may lead to disastrous errors in judgment. Wrong inferences often lead to "prepost'rous conclusions" (1. 3. 324–25).

Othello's knowledge that Desdemona loves him is intuitive, based on faith rather than empirical evidence; yet Iago, who works by "wit" and is "nothing if not critical" (2. 3. 372; 2. 1. 118), can dismantle that love through what seems, superficially, to be rational proof. He provokes in Othello an epistemological crisis; as Helen Gardner puts it, "Iago ruins Othello by insinuating into his mind the question, 'How do you know?'"[20] Iago's strategy in the temptation scene (3. 3) is twofold. First, he exploits the gap between thinking that something is true and knowing that it is true on a scientific or factual basis; thoughts are subjective, and a person's ideas may not tally with objective reality. Second, having made Othello extremely curious about the ensign's "thoughts" and doubtful about the validity of his own, Iago urges Othello to "see" something that is not there. Love and fidelity are not subject to "ocular proof," but infidelity, Iago implies, can be demonstrated through observable detail; therefore, if Othello has "eyes to see," he can "know" (with a little help from his friend) that Desdemona is false.

As he begins to undermine Othello's faith, Iago interjects "think" and "thought(s)" seven times within sixty lines (3. 3. 95–154), destabilizing knowledge (Cassio is honest "for aught I know" [104]) with pure speculation ("I dare be sworn, I think that he is honest" [125]).[21] More remarkable is how Othello, taking his cue from Iago, comes up with eleven instances of "think" "thinkings," and "thought(s) " in the same sequence. Iago's reluctance to answer questions directly, breaking what H. P. Grice calls the "co-operative principle" within speech acts,[22] becomes a superb strategy to set Othello "in pursuit of the motive behind the question."[23] It prompts a close antiphonal exchange between the two speakers:

Othello	What dost thou think?
Iago	Think, my lord?
Othello	Think, my lord?

> By heaven, thou echoest me,
> As if there were some monster in thy thought
> Too hideous to be shown.   (105–8)

Since Othello suspects that Iago knows more than he is telling, his questions ("Why of thy thought?" [98], "What dost thou think?" [105]) quickly turn into requests and then urgent demands for further clarification of the situation: "If thou dost love me, / Show me thy thought" (115–16), "give thy worst of thoughts / The worst of words" (132–33), and "By heaven, I'll know thy thoughts!" (162).

"Thoughts," as Iago has remarked earlier to Roderigo, may be "villainous" (2. 1. 260–61). Unlike Hamlet, who concludes more neutrally that "there is nothing either good or bad, but thinking makes it so" (*Hamlet* II. ii. 249–50), Iago admits to Othello that his guesswork and his conjectures about human relationships are often "vicious." Now, when Othello prompts him to reveal what is on his mind, Iago tantalizes his general by emphasizing that thought is both "free" (even to slaves) and private ("in my custody") and by offering the disclaimer that his musings—like those of everyone at one time or another—may be "vile" and "false" (3. 3. 135, 164, 136). Such a warning disarms rebuttal and thus furthers Iago's evil purpose. It is because Othello respects Iago's "thoughts" and equates them with factual knowledge ("This fellow . . . knows all qualities, with a learnèd spirit / Of human dealings" [257–59]) that he is eager to listen to his ensign and does not thoroughly scrutinize the evidence offered. And it is because he trusts this male friend, choosing not to put Iago's "My lord, you know I love you" (117) to the empirical test, that he believes what the speaker says and fails to grasp that the "monster" in Iago's thoughts (and then in his own) is a hideous invention.

Iago's next strategy, which begins at "I am glad of this" (193), is to convince Othello that seeing should be equivalent to believing, or that literal vision leads to a kind of knowledge that is superior to faith alone. He has apparently deflected Othello's demand to "know" his "thoughts" by finally giving a name to the hidden topic of their conversation: "O, beware, my lord, of jealousy!" (165). Now he forces his lord to contemplate this monster, all the while warning him to shun the terrible insecurity aroused by it. Othello counters this with confident assurances, telling Iago, "I'll see before I doubt; when I doubt, prove" (190). It is at this point that Iago manipulates references to the visual to point out what Othello might actually see if he looked for it:

> I speak not yet of proof.
> Look to your wife: observe her well with Cassio;
> Wear your eyes thus: not jealous nor secure. (196–98)

Women in Venice let heaven "see the pranks / They dare not show their husbands" (202–3); therefore, Othello should "look to't" if he wants to discover his wife's sexual games with other men. When Iago concludes this speech with a comment on how Venetian wives exert themselves "not to leave't undone, but kept unknown," he is equating what is known (and therefore, by implication, true) with what is visible.

In an especially cunning stroke, Iago alludes to Desdemona's duplicitous hoodwinking of Brabantio—she was able to "seel her father's eyes up close as oak"—when he reminds Othello "She did deceive her father, marrying you" (210, 206). In doing so, he cements the tenuous parallel between betrayed father and husband that Brabantio bitterly insists on in his warning to Othello:

> Look to her, Moor, if thou hast eyes to see:
> She has deceived her father, and may thee. (1. 3. 287–88)

Eyes may dwell on fair, deceiving appearances, or they may pierce through them to grasp the truth. Iago encourages the latter option when he reminds Othello that by holding off on reinstating Cassio, he can "perceive him and his means," adding, "Much will be seen in that" (3. 3. 249–52). As Othello makes his last desperate stab at faith in "I do not think but Desdemona's honest," Iago again exploits the gap between thinking, or hoping, that something is the case and knowing (through factual evidence) that it is actually true. Othello's "but" is too tentative to cancel out the negative formulation ("I do not think"), and Iago promptly widens the crack into a chasm of doubt with "Long live she so. And long live you to think so" (225–26).

In the second part of the temptation scene (3. 3. 330–470), Iago capitalizes on the idea that knowledge depends on personal witness. Earlier in the play, he firmly connected eyesight with proof when telling Roderigo how he failed to gain the lieutenancy even though Othello had seen his prowess as soldier: "And I, of whom his eyes had seen the proof / At Rhodes, at Cyprus" (1. 1. 25–26). Disdaining the handkerchief as a trifle "light as air" (3. 3. 319), he nevertheless plans to use it as the linchpin of his "ocular proof." Arguably, by the time the love token makes its fortuitous appearance onstage in Act 4, scene 1, it has become irrelevant in confirming Othello's doubts; Iago has already fulfilled Othello's demand "Make me to see't" by creating an imaginary vision of Desdemona and Cassio making love.[24] He coarsely reminds Othello of the virtual impossibility of visual "satisfaction" through catching the lovers in the act:

> Would you, the supervisor, grossly gape on?
> Behold her topped? (3. 3. 392–93)

Instead, Iago produces what he earlier referred to as "satisfaction" of "thought" (97); he appeals to the voyeuristic curiosity of the overwrought, jealous husband when he pornographically conjures up the prospect of a debauched encounter through his words "topped," "bolster," "prime," "hot," and "salt." This and his faked but graphic account of Cassio's dream ("plucked up kisses by the roots," "laid his leg o'er my thigh") serve, in lieu of witnessing the adultery firsthand, as "imputation and strong circumstances / Which lead directly to the door of truth" (403–5). The "door of truth" hints at a tantalizing glimpse of forbidden acts that may be going on behind Desdemona's bedroom door. After this, the mere mention of Cassio wiping his beard with the strawberry-spotted handkerchief is enough to seal Othello's devastating delusion: "Now do I see 'tis true" (441). As the victim of Iago's confidence trick, he has, of course, seen nothing literally—only what Iago wants him to visualize.[25] Iago provides the image, and Othello draws the preposterous inference; he even believes that the vividly narrated dream denotes a "foregone conclusion." The kind of concrete description that Iago supplies is termed *evidentia* by classical rhetoricians, but George Puttenham, in his *Arte of English Poesie* (1589), significantly translates it as "Counterfeit Representation."[26]

When the pair next enter together, Iago is inflaming Othello's imagination with an image of Cassio and Desdemona "naked . . . in bed" for "An hour or more" (4. 1. 3–4). Reminding Othello of the handkerchief, Iago encourages him to base his "proof" of Desdemona's guilt on an external token, slyly substituting the concrete, visible object for the unseen, unverifiable abstraction (Desdemona's chastity):

> Her honor is an essence that's not seen;
> They have it very oft that have it not.
> But for the handkerchief—   (16–18)

Again, Othello fails to perceive that invisible "honor," like love, cannot be subject to empirical proof; its presence or absence is emphatically not to be equated with that of a handkerchief that can travel, as Othello has done in the past, "here and everywhere" by chance. Although Iago has to back down from substantiating "What if I had said I had seen him do you wrong?" (24), he successfully stage-manages a surrogate kind of seeing—engineering a "theatrical *trompe l'oeil*"[27] by encouraging Othello (again as voyeur) to "mark the fleers, the gibes, and notable scorns / That dwell in every region of [Cassio's] face" (84–85). Cassio's every "gesture" will seem to point to his sexual intimacy with Desdemona when in fact he is ridiculing Bianca. Never mind that physical gestures—"what you see them act"—are subject to fatal misinterpretation, as Brabantio discovers when Desdemona's demure demeanor belies her real intention to marry Othello (1. 1. 168). By the murder scene, Othello has absolutely convinced himself that the flimsy, circumstantial evidence of Act 4, scene 1 is testimony to his wife's infidelity, for he firmly reiterates to Desdemona, to justify his killing of her, "I saw my handkerchief in's hand" and "I saw the handkerchief" (5. 2. 62, 66). What is more, he has genuinely misinterpreted Iago's staged scenario as proof that Cassio "hath confessed" (68). Othello has made the mistake of "exposing a love based on faith to tests irrelevant to faith,"[28] or, as Winifred M. Nowottny demonstrates in detail, confusing the "kind of belief relevant to the forming of judgments with the other kind of belief characteristic of love."[29]

This has religious implications as well, tying into the play's Christian allegorical weave. In the Gospels, Christ affirms that "all things are possible to him that believeth" (Mark 9:23)—Othello clearly fails in this respect—while St. Paul stresses faith in the mysteries of God that cannot be seen (1 Corinthians 2:9) and how, trusting in salvation, "we hope for that we see not" (Romans 8:25). That wisdom, or applied knowledge, does not always result from literal seeing is also the stuff of many tragic myths; the wise prophet Teiresias is blind in Sophocles' *Oedipus Rex,* while Shakespeare's character Gloucester gains insight into life after he has lost his eyes (*King Lear* IV. i. 18–19). It is no wonder, as Millicent Bell puts it, that "Othello becomes the victim of his desire to know by seeing,"[30] for both he and Iago attach much importance to the organ of sight. Iago insists to Roderigo that Desdemona's "eye must be fed" (2. 1. 224) and later tells Cassio that her eye "sounds a parley to provocation" (2. 3. 21–22), while Othello exhorts Desdemona to treasure the handkerchief and "Make it a darling like your precious eye" (3. 4. 66). Even though Desdemona claims to have moved beyond skin color in her attraction to the Moor—"I saw Othello's visage in his mind" (1. 3. 247)—Othello sets great store by the fact that "she had eyes, and chose me" (3. 3. 189).

In Shakespeare's poem "The Phoenix and the Turtle" (1601), secular love, like divine love, is presented as a mystery that defies rational explanation: "Reason, in itself confounded, / Saw division grow together" (41–42). So, too, the union of Othello and Desdemona is a surprising *discordia concors,* marrying white with black, youth with middle age, the arts of peace with those of war.[31] At first, the union seems remarkably strong, withstanding attacks from a white, insular society. Applying what he considers to be reasonable, even "palpable" standards of judgment (1. 2. 75), Brabantio finds the relationship incomprehensible; his daughter, if not bewitched, would have to be "deficient, blind, or lame of sense" (1. 3. 63) to fall in love with a black man. Iago, too, applies cool reason to deconstruct love when he suggests that Desdemona's "will, recoiling to her better judgment" (3. 3. 236) may reject the aberration of marrying someone so different from herself. Under the tutelage of Iago, Othello mistakenly privileges specious reasoning above intuitive faith.[32]

Iago, as we have seen, preys on Othello's vulnerabilities to arouse in him a jealousy "so strong / That judgment cannot cure" (2. 1. 301–2). With Othello's capitulation to this web of suggestion, the play also suggests how difficult it is for an individual inexperienced in social encounters and linguistic games to pierce through misleading testimony and skewed language.[33] Granted, the mysteries of love should not be submitted to the bar of reason; but once judgment is in play, it is essential to exercise discrimination in evaluating any kind of "proof"—verbal testimony or circumstantial evidence—on which crucial decisions will depend. Othello is unable to do this. Whereas the Duke uses "assay of reason" both to discern the Turks' true intentions in heading for Cyprus and not for Rhodes and to assess the mutual devotion of Othello and Desdemona, Othello is persuaded that fair is foul by Iago's "pageant" to keep him in "false gaze" (1. 3. 18–19)—to make him see what is not really there.[34] Thus he reinterprets Cassio's hasty departure from Desdemona as a lover's furtiveness, sees in his mind's eye his lieutenant making love to his wife, and assumes that Cassio is boasting about his conquest of Desdemona in the eavesdropping scene. Close to the end of the play, Lodovico responds to Iago's question "Are you of good or evil?" with the wisely skeptical "As you shall prove us, praise us" (5. 1. 65–66); Othello, in contrast, is too eager to accept as "truth" what he initially scorns as "exsufflicate and blown surmises" (3. 3. 182).[35] He does just what Iago, playing the concerned friend, warns him not to do, when he builds a coherent (though false) version of reality out of "scattering and unsure observance" (151). In this, Othello is the opposite of the faithful lover Troilus, who, even as he watches Cressida give his token to Diomedes, simply cannot believe what he has witnessed. Continuing to trust in Cressida's loyalty to him, his blind faith becomes "An esperance so obstinately strong, / That doth invert th' attest of eyes and ears" (*Troilus and Cressida* V. ii. 121–22).

MONSTERS AND DEMONS

Sexual jealousy is a particularly unpleasant complex of emotions, humiliating to the individual who experiences it and distressing, sometimes physically dangerous, to the person against whom that jealousy is directed. Renaissance writers viewed it as one of the "Inordinate Passions";[36] Montaigne (in John Florio's 1603 translation of the *Essais*) calls it "the most vaine and turbulent infirmitie that may afflict mans minde. . . . *Of all the mindes diseases, that is it, whereto most things serve for sustenance, and fewest for remedy.*"[37] A disturbing part of the syndrome is a masochistic inclination to imagine the worst (the loved one making love to the rival)[38] that is both horrifying and arousing. Iago fuels this voyeuristic compulsion by encouraging Othello to "behold," in his mind's eye, his wife being "topped" by Cassio (3. 3. 393). In his prurient way, he is providing Othello with what he wants, or, as Iago puts it in Act 4, scene 1, "With her, on her; what you will" (35). Perhaps this is what makes the hero's anguish so degrading—the perversity with which (as Terry Eagleton provocatively notes) Othello "really comes to desire his wife intensely?"[39] only when he becomes jealous, aware that he does not, and cannot, fully possess her. Shakespeare's exploration of jealousy leads to the even more far-reaching theme of the human psyche's predilection for the "monstrous." Monsters of the mind are self-generating, even without the precipitating agent that a depraved manipulator such as Iago supplies.

Desdemona prays that heaven will keep the "monster" of jealousy away from Othello's mind; instead, he succumbs to it. Beyond his vulnerability as a social outsider, several psychological explanations can be offered for Othello's transformation into a jealous man. He may be overpossessive about his wife because he is emotionally insecure,[40] or he may love Desdemona not for herself but narcissistically, because she mirrors and thereby reinforces his favorable image of himself;[41] his excessive pride then refuses to tolerate any apparent falling off in her devotion to him. Perhaps he suffers from what L. C. Knights calls a failure to love with an "outgoing generosity of spirit."[42] More favorably to Othello, readers may decide that any great love produces an equivalent fear that "too much of joy" (2. 1. 195) cannot last and that *Othello* demonstrates how "it is perilous to garner up one's heart in the heart of another human being, and whoever does so loses control of his own destiny."[43]

Ultimately, Othello's destructive passion retains an element of mystery—more unsettling for the audience in its implication that we may all fall prey to jealousy and cannnot simply stereotype and dismiss Othello as a susceptible outsider. To "dote" on someone may mean to "doubt" that person, a semantic connection that Iago forges through phonetic similarity when he evokes for Othello the lover who "dotes, yet doubts" (3. 3. 170). When jealousy is personified as a monster in the play, it is to suggest how human beings can be taken over by a passion that is huge—the sense of "monstrous" evoked in the description of the stormy ocean as a "high and monstrous main" (2. 1. 13)—as well as bestial. Iago defines jealousy as "the green-eyed monster, which doth mock / The meat it feeds on" (3. 3. 166–67), a grotesque parasite that taunts its host. When Emilia describes this passion as a "monster / Begot upon itself, born on itself" (3. 4. 160–61), she underlines its self-generating nature. "Jealous souls" do not need real events to fuel their suspicions because, Emilia explains, they are "not ever jealous for the cause." In the same way, the Jacobean psychologist Robert Burton, author of *The Anatomy of Melancholy* (1621), describes jealous people as "apt to mistake, and amplify . . . without a cause."[44] One of the play's mordant ironies is the echo of Emilia's words in the "It is the cause" speech, where Othello constructs an elaborate rationale for killing Desdemona and yet cannot name the true "cause." Bewildered by the edifice of surmise that Othello has built up, Cassio also protests, near the end of the drama, "Dear general, I never gave you cause" (5. 2. 295).

As Othello's jealousy heightens, it turns the noble warrior into a monster. When Cassio is demoted for drunkenness, he laments how we "transform ourselves into beasts" through an agent, alcohol, that also brings "joy, pleasance, revel" (2. 3. 290–92). Likewise, Othello, once his joy changes into the "misery" of jealousy, is transformed into a "beast that wants discourse of reason" (*Hamlet* I. ii. 150); he threatens to "chop" his wife into "messes" (4. 1. 202). The soldier whose journeys brought him into contact with cannibals and "men whose heads / Grew beneath their shoulders" (1. 3. 143–44) now perceives himself as more monstrous than any of these exotic humans.[45] To be a cuckold—as he imagines himself—is particularly shameful and degrading for him, even subhuman, since "A hornèd man's a monster and a beast" (4. 1. 64). Being a monster implies being put on show (The Latin *monstrare* means to show or point out), as happens to the dead Macbeth, whose severed head is displayed once he has become one of the "rarer monsters" of Scotland (*Macbeth* V. viii. 25). Othello, however, refuses to become a passive spectacle or "fixèd figure" in the face of sexual humiliation (4. 2. 53). Devouring jealousy turns him instead into a violent predator who commits the "monstrous act," as Montano describes it (5. 2. 187), of murdering Desdemona.

How important is Iago in this transformation of Othello? Whereas the jealousy of Leontes in *The Winter's Tale* is purely self-induced, Iago serves as a catalyst to precipitate this monstrous emotion in Othello. Deeply resentful and suspicious himself, he schemes to arouse an equally corrosive jealousy in his master. His words at the end of Act 1, "Hell and night / Must bring this monstrous birth to the world's light" (1. 3. 394–95), clearly establish a connection between the satanic and the monstrous; like the devil at the heart of darkness, Iago will bring to full gestation a monstrous birth.[46] This "civil monster" (4. 1. 66) is all the more pernicious for masquerading as an honest Venetian who is offering worldly-wise advice to help his friend.[47] In urging Othello to "know" with certainty that he is a cuckold rather than live in a fool's paradise, Iago maintains that it is "the spite of hell" to kiss "a wanton in a secure couch, / And to suppose her chaste" (72–74). To the contrary, Iago's hellish spite lies in creating something out of nothing, conjuring up images of an adulterous liasion where none exists. His strategies for doing this are fiendishly clever, so that the temptation scene works as a kind of demonic possession, culminating in Iago's leechlike commitment to Othello: "I am your own forever" (3. 3. 476).

Yet it is also true, as Leslie A. Fiedler comments, that "Iago contributes only one half of the satanic monster."[48] Iago's cynicism is an astringent counterbalance, even a necessary complement, to Othello's idealism, a means whereby the ensign can disable Othello's generous nature and work on the hidden half of his psyche, bringing to the surface a distrust of women and a readiness to believe the worst of people equivalent to Iago's own. When Iago recounts Cassio's "dream," Othello is sure that it denotes a "foregone conclusion" (3. 3. 425). He pictures it as vividly as if he had witnessed the scenario, calling it "monstrous! monstrous!" in the same way that he describes the drunken brawl, which he sees with his own eyes, as "monstrous" (2. 3. 216). Othello has been quick to detect a "monster in [Iago's] thought / Too hideous to be shown" (3. 3. 107–8). But the transference from speaker to hearer is so swift that the audience is left wondering who truly owns the foul creature and thus whether creating and nurturing hideous fantasies should be recognized as a universal human tendency. Iago's metaphor of the human heart as an all-inclusive court of law posits every person as a receptacle for feelings and thoughts that are both impure and pure, illicit as well as legitimate:

> As where's that palace whereinto foul thoughts
> Sometimes intrude not? Who has that breast so pure
> But some uncleanly apprehensions
> Keep leets and law days, and in sessions sit
> With meditations lawful? (137–41)

At the play's conclusion, Iago touches on one grim aspect of reality when he defends what he has done to Othello:

I told him what I thought, and told no more
Than what he found himself was apt and true.   (5. 2. 173–74)

Othello has not found factual or scientific truth; thanks to Iago, he has discovered within himself an aptitude to believe in the fiction of Desdemona's infidelity.
By the murder scene, the "horrible conceit" (3. 3. 115) is so firmly rooted in his
consciousness that, as he tells Desdemona, nothing can "choke the strong conception / That I do groan withal" (5. 2. 55–56). This, *Othello* suggests by extension, is how monstrous the imagination can be. As a parting shot, Iago reminds
his listeners—Othello, the Venetians onstage, and the larger group in the theater—"What you know, you know" (299). This enigmatic statement, gesturing at
a dark, inexpressible kind of knowledge contained within the human mind, posits
a terrible complicity among himself, Othello, and the audience. In Act 2, scene
3, Othello's question about monstrous impulses also resonates beyond its immediate context: "Are we turned Turks, and *to ourselves do that* / Which heaven hath
forbid the Ottomites?" (169–70, emphasis added). The play answers in the affir-
mative.

By Act 4, Othello tells Desdemona that the fountain of his being (the place
where he has garnered up his heart) is now no better than a cesspool, a "cistern for
foul toads / To knot and gender in" (4. 2. 60–61). Is he referring only to Desdemona's body, the pure vessel that has turned foully promiscuous? The syntax also
allows us to interpret the metaphor as akin to Iago's image of the "breast" (or heart)
that contains "uncleanly apprehensions," so that it conveys a sense of Othello's own
center of self having become corrupt, full of perverse, disgusting fantasies. As
Janet Adelman points out, "*Othello* is obsessively about what is hidden away
within the person, the inner, private, and unknowable self that might harbor inac-
cessible desires."[49] This disturbing sense of "inaccesible desires" ties into H. A.
Mason's perception that "for every mind there is something in the play that cannot be faced";[50] and *Othello* does indeed touch on many sensitive issues that will
resonate differently for different readers or audience members. The "foul toads"
that Othello conjures into being in this speech—dark areas of sexual attraction and
repulsion, disgust at the physical side of love,[51] and the spawning of monstrous
thoughts about women—surely constitute one central nexus in the play that is both
tricky to analyze and difficult to confront squarely.

One recent strand of criticism of *Othello* probes more deeply into how the audience is implicated in the "monstrous." Michael Neill analyzes how the play invites
its viewers to indulge their own "obscene desires and fears"—a parallel to what
Othello undergoes but centering instead on deep anxieties about "racial/sexual otherness."[52] Partly guided by Iago, who fantasizes about the "old black ram" tupping
the "white ewe," spectators develop a prurient fascination with what is going on behind the bedroom door of this black man and white woman. Human beings are fascinated by the spectacle of "abomination," as Joseph Conrad reveals in his short
novel *The Heart of Darkness*. *Othello*'s insistent question "What's the matter?" suggests dramatic material "to be both enlarged upon and disclosed";[53] and yet the play

often teasingly withholds information, as about the consummation of the marriage. The marriage bed, hinted at but (by implication) "too hideous to be shown," is fully revealed only in the final scene, which includes the warped eroticism of Othello's kissing Desdemona as a prelude to the consummation of killing her.[54] Samuel Johnson found the murder scene so distressing as "not to be endured."[55] What is most disturbing, thinks Neill, is the way that *Othello* trades on and then satisfies (through the deaths of Desdemona and Othello) the perverse, often racially charged curiosities of the audience.[56] If the play does, by its very dramatic strategies, pander to and even cultivate these monsters of the mind, then it subtly reinforces one of the main dramatic themes. Since none of us is immune to evil suggestions from others (the Iago influence), to fascination with the forbidden, or to destructive jealousy, the real enemy lies within: a predisposition, through our innate sexual, emotional, and psychological makeup, to nurture our own monsters and demons.

NOTES

1. See Derek A. Traversi, *An Approach to Shakespeare* (1938; London: Sands and Co., 1957), p. 127.

2. Pointed out by Harold C. Goddard, *The Meaning of Shakespeare* (Chicago and London: University of Chicago Press, 1951), p. 459.

3. Harley Granville Barker, *Prefaces to Shakespeare* (Princeton, N.J.: Princeton University Press, 1947), vol. 2, p. 118. See also Paul A. Cantor, "Othello: The Erring Barbarian among the Supersubtle Venetians," *SWR*, 75 (Summer 1990): 296–319.

4. David Lucking, "Putting Out the Light: Semantic Indeterminacy and the Deconstitution of Self in *Othello*," *ES*, 75.2 (1994): 110–122, quote at 113.

5. Edward Berry, "Othello's Alienation," *SEL*, 30 (1990): 315–333, quote at 323.

6. Arthur Sewell, *Character and Society in Shakespeare* (1951; Oxford: Clarendon Press, 1965), thinks that part of the tragedy lies in "the reduction of the large spirit of Othello to the petty dimensions" of Venetian society (p. 92). Nick Potter, "*Othello*," in Graham Holderness, Nick Potter, and John Turner, *Shakespeare: The Play of History* (Iowa City: University of Iowa Press, 1987), also finds that pragmatic, commercial Venice is "a world in which there is no place for the high Romance values towards which Othello aspires" (p. 202).

7. Quoted by David C. McPherson, *Shakespeare, Jonson, and the Myth of Venice* (Newark: University of Delaware Press, 1990), p. 73.

8. Jack D'Amico, *The Moor in English Renaissance Drama* (Tampa: University of South Florida Press, 1991), p. 164. James L. Calderwood, *The Properties of* Othello (Amherst: University of Massachusetts Press, 1989), also finds that "when Venetian property rights are threatened, the borders between civilized Christians and barbaric ex-infidels are all too readily erased" (p. 8).

9. Anthony Hecht, "*Othello*," in *Obbligati: Essays in Criticism* (New York: Atheneum, 1986), discusses the possibility that Othello may have converted to Christianity under duress, as "a Morisco, or New Christian, a breed regarded without much trust in the Christian community at that time" (p. 63).

10. In Alvin Kernan (ed.), *Othello, The Signet Classic Shakespeare* (New York: Penguin Books, 1986; 1998), pp. 135, 145.

11. Allan Bloom, "Cosmopolitan Man and the Political Community," in *Shakespeare's Politics* (New York and London: Basic Books, 1964), comments on how Othello, relying on his

reputation as a soldier, "believes that he is universally valued and valuable"; yet "no one can set his roots deeply in a city that is not his own" (pp. 46–47). Margaret Webster, *Shakespeare Today* (London: J. M. Dent and Sons, Ltd., 1957), discusses the way that Paul Robeson, a black outsider in American society, projected Othello's situation: "We believed that he could command the armies of Venice; we knew that he would always be alien to its society" (p. 236). More recently, at The Shakespeare Theatre in Washington, D.C. (1997–1998), Patrick Stewart projected the outsider theme by playing Othello as white in an otherwise nearly all-black cast.

12. Richard S. Ide, *Possessed with Greatness* (Chapel Hill: University of North Carolina Press, 1980), p. 52.

13. Kernan (ed.), *Othello,* comments that "the outer limits of the world of *Othello* are defined by the Turks—the infidels, the unbelievers, the 'general enemy'" (p. lxv).

14. Virginia Mason Vaughan, Othello: *A Contextual History* (Cambridge: Cambridge University Press, 1994), quotes the preface to *The Generall Historie of the Turkes* (1603), where Richard Knolles maintains that the Ottoman Empire has "a full persuasion in time to rule ouer all" (p. 24). Daniel J. Vitkus, "Turning Turk in *Othello:* The Conversion and Damnation of the Moor," *SQ,* 48.2 (Summer 1997): 145–76, discusses the expansion of the Ottoman Empire in the sixteenth century and points out Englishmen's fears of being "conquered, captured and converted" by "Turkish" privateers operating in the Mediterranean and the northeastern Atlantic (p. 147).

15. See Kernan (ed.), *Othello,* p. lxxii.

16. Derek Cohen, "Tragedy and the Nation," *UTQ,* 66.3 (1997): 526–38, quotes at 528 and 535. In "Othello's Suicide," *UTQ,* 62.3 (1993): 323–33, Cohen discusses in more detail how Othello's final act reaffirms the norms of "white civilization" (p. 324).

17. See Vitkus, "Turning Turk in *Othello,*" p. 174.

18. See Leslie A. Fiedler, *The Stranger in Shakespeare* (1973; St. Albans, Hertfordshire: Paladin, 1974), pp. 163–64.

19. D'Amico, *The Moor in English Renaissance Drama,* p. 215.

20. Helen Gardner, "The Noble Moor," *PBA,* 51 (1955): 189–205, quote at 197. Millicent Bell, "Othello's Jealousy," *YR,* 85.2 (April 1997): 120–36, also focuses on how "the torment of Othello is epistemological, a condition of doubt of which sexual jealousy is only a specific illustration or consequence" (p. 123). In "'Preposterous Conclusions': Eros, *Enargeia,* and the Composition of *Othello,*" *Representations,* 18 (Spring 1987): 129–57, Joel B. Altman analyzes how Iago "exploits the eros of knowing, the drive to come to conclusions, in a particularly cunning way" (p. 139).

21. Paul A. Jorgensen, "'Perplex'd in the Extreme': The Role of Thought in *Othello,*" *SQ,* 15 (1964): 265–75, analyzes how Iago replaces "know" with "think" in this scene.

22. H. P. Grice, "Logic and Conversation," in Peter Cole and Jerry L. Morgan (eds.), *Speech Acts, Syntax and Semantics* (New York: Academic Press, 1975), vol. 3, pp. 41–58.

23. Anthony Gilbert, "Techniques of Persuasion in *Julius Caesar* and *Othello,*" *Neophilolog,* 81.2 (April 1997): 309–23, quote at 318.

24. David Bevington (ed.), *Othello, Bantam Classic* (New York: Bantam, 1988), points out that just as Don John in *Much Ado about Nothing* stages an optical illusion to impugn Hero as an adulteress, so Iago can "create illusions to induce Othello to see what Iago wants him to see" (p. xxvi).

25. In "Proof and Consequences: *Othello* and the Crime of Intention," in *Inwardness and Theater in the English Renaissance* (Chicago and London: University of Chicago Press, 1995), Katherine Maus connects the tenuous process of "knowing" in *Othello* with gaps in "evidentiary procedure" revealed in English witchcraft trials: "The process of making the invisible manifest inevitably entails falsification" (pp. 126–27)

26. Discussed by Patricia Parker, "Shakespeare and Rhetoric: 'Dilation' and 'Delation' in *Othello,*" in Patricia Parker and Geoffrey Hartman (eds.), *Shakespeare and the Question of Theory* (New York: Methuen, 1985), pp. 54–74, quote at 64.

27. Michael Neill, "Changing Places in *Othello,*" *ShS,* 37 (1984): 115–31, quote at 125.

28. Norman Rabkin, *Shakespeare and the Common Understanding* (New York: Free Press, 1967), p. 72.

29. Winifred M. Nowottny, "Justice and Love in *Othello,*" *UTQ,* 21 (July 1952): 330–44, quote at 332.

30. Bell, "Othello's Jealousy," p. 124.

31. See Fiedler, *The Stranger in Shakespeare,* p. 146.

32. Terence Hawkes, *Shakespeare and the Reason: A Study of the Tragedies and the Problem Plays* (Atlantic Highlands, N.J.: Humanities Press, 1964), discusses how Othello changes from an "intuitive *consent* of love to a truth which lies beyond the evidence," to a vision of Desdemona in which "reason predominates" (pp. 115, 123). Naomi Scheman, "Othello's Doubt/Desdemona's Death: The Engendering of Scepticism," in Judith Genova (ed.), *Power, Gender, Values* (Edmonton, Alberta, Canada: Academic Printing and Publishing, 1987), also explores how Othello, along Cartesian lines, submits his sense impressions of Desdemona to a "detached and controlling objectivity" (p. 125).

33. Sharon Beehler, "'An Enemy in Their Mouths': The Closure of Language in *Othello,*" *UCrow,* 10 (1990), 69–85, comments on how Othello "stumbles from one erroneous assumption to another," believing "that language can be readily understood" (pp. 71–72).

34. This is explored in detail in Philip C. McGuire, "*Othello* as an 'Assay of Reason,'" *SQ,* 25.2 (1973): 198–209.

35. Joel B. Altman, "'Prophetic Fury': *Othello* and the Economy of Shakespearean Reception," *SLitI,* 26 (1993): 85–113, ingeniously finds a reference here to the "fluttering sibylline leaves" described in Virgil's *Aeneid*—"disconnected inferences" out of which Othello fabricates his own meaning (p. 97).

36. Thomas Wright, *The Passions of the Minde in Generale* (London: Printed by Valentine Simmes for Walter Burre, 1604), p. 72.

37. *Montaigne's Essays,* trans. John Florio (1603), introd. L. C. Harmer (London: Dent, 1965), vol. 3, chap. 5, "Upon Some Verses of Virgil," pp. 88–90.

38. In James Strachey (ed.), *Complete Psychological Works of Sigmund Freud* (London: Hogarth Press, 1953–1974), vol. 18, p. 223, Freud finds homosexual impulses within the triangular relationship constituted by sexual jealousy.

39. Terry Eagleton, *William Shakespeare* (Oxford and New York: Blackwell, 1986), p. 68. See also Joel Fineman, "The Sound of O in *Othello:* The Real of the Tragedy of Desire," *October,* 45 (Summer 1988): 77–96, for an analysis of Othello, through Lacanian psychology, as a "desiring subject."

40. Harold Skulsky, *Spirits Finely Touched: The Testing of Value and Integrity in Four Shakespearean Plays* (Athens: University of Georgia Press, 1976), analyzes how "the flimsiness of Othello's self-esteem strengthens him in his conviction of Desdemona's infidelity" (p. 170).

41. Meredith Anne Skura, *Shakespeare and the Purposes of Playing* (Chicago and London: University of Chicago Press, 1993), points out how jealousy derives from flaws within an intense relationship where "the Other is an adoring object whose function is to serve and mirror one's desires" (p. 293 n.10).

42. L. C. Knights, *An Approach to* Hamlet, in *Some Shakespearean Themes and An Approach to* Hamlet (1959; Harmondsworth: Penguin, 1966), pp. 168–69.

43. Helen Gardner, "'Othello': A Retrospect, 1900–67," *ShS*, 21, (1968): 1–10, quote at 10.

44. Robert Burton, *The Anatomy of Melancholy*, introd. Holbrook Jackson (London: Dent, 1932), vol. 2, p. 391.

45. For a detailed account of the Renaissance association of black men with monsters, which lends resonance to Othello's new perception of himself, see James R. Aubrey, "Race and the Spectacle of the Monstrous in *Othello*," *Clio*, 22.3 (1993): 221–38.

46. See Aubrey, "Race and the Spectacle of the Monstrous," for more analysis of the language of "monstrous childbearing" in the play (p. 234).

47. Edward C. Jacobs and Karen R. Jacobs, "' 'Tis Monstrous': Dramaturgy and Irony in *Othello*," *UCrow*, 9 (1989): 52–62, point out the ironic collocation of "monstrous" and Iago in Othello's response to the brawl, "'Tis monstrous. Iago, who began't?" (II. iii. 216); Iago "is indeed a monstrous villain" (p. 55).

48. Fielder, *The Stranger in Shakespeare*, p. 138.

49. Janet Adelman, "Iago's Alter Ego: Race as Projection in *Othello*," *SQ*, 48.2 (Summer 1997): 125–44, quote at 135 n.21.

50. H. A. Mason, *Shakespeare's Tragedies of Love* (New York: Barnes and Noble, 1970), p. 59.

51. See Edward A. Snow, "Sexual Anxiety and the Male Order of Things in *Othello*," *ELR*, 10 (1980): 384–412. E. A. J. Honigmann (ed.), *Othello, The Arden Shakespeare*, 3rd ed. (Walton-on-Thames: Thomas Nelson and Sons, Ltd., 1997), also discusses the "wide-ranging and deeply probing study of various kinds of sexuality" in the play (p. 49).

52. Michael Neill, "Unproper Beds: Race, Adultery, and the Hideous in *Othello*," *SQ*, 40.4 (1989): 383–412, quotes at 412 and 390.

53. Parker, "Shakespeare and Rhetoric," p. 59.

54. Stanley Cavell, *The Claim of Reason* (Oxford: Clarendon Press, 1979), comments on how "the thing *denied our sight* throughout the opening scene" is "what we are shown in the final scene, the scene of murder" (p. 486). Similarly, Calderwood, *The Properties of Othello*, considers that "grossly gaping on as Desdemona is at last bedded, we are perversely satisfied" (p. 125). In "An Essence That's Not Seen: The Primal Scene of Racism in *Othello*," *SQ*, 44 (1993): 304–24, Arthur J. Little, Jr., notes how the play touches on the notion that "black identity seems all too naturally to find its origins in an imaginary scene of some horrific copulation" (p. 308).

55. Samuel Johnson, *Johnson on Shakespeare*, ed. Walter Raleigh (London: Oxford University Press, 1908), p. 200.

56. Neill, "Unproper Beds," p. 412.

6

CRITICAL APPROACHES

NEOCLASSICAL AND ROMANTIC

Thomas Rymer's lambasting of *Othello* in *A Short View of Tragedy* (1693) was the first piece of sustained literary criticism of the play. The neoclassical standards by which Rymer judged tragic drama called for logic and moral justice in the resolution of the action, decorum in character presentation, and truth to nature; not surprisingly, the critic found the play defective in all these areas. To him it seemed absurd that so much should hinge on a "trifle" like a handkerchief—"Had it been *Desdemona's* Garter, the Sagacious Moor might have smelt a Rat"[1]—and he notes, among other improbabilities, the lack of time during which Desdemona could have pursued an affair with Cassio. The cruel murder of Desdemona flouts all moral "Justice and Reason," raising the question "If this be our end, what boots it to be Vertuous?"[2] So much implausibility, he concludes, vitiates the play's claim to tragic greatness, so that while *Othello* contains some wit and humor, "the tragical part . . . is none other, than a Bloody Farce, without salt or savour."[3]

Rymer is most scathing about the dramatic characters, whom he considers "not less unnatural and improper, than the Fable was improbable and absurd."[4] Desdemona is a "Fool" whose language often violates upper-class norms ("no Woman bred out of a Pig-stye, cou'd talk so meanly")[5] and Othello's character, incompatible with that of a general, fails to convince on two other counts; in the first place, it is unlikely that a "villainous Black-amoor"[6] would be respected by the Venetians (in fact this was historically viable), and then Shakespeare lapses into further inconsistency by giving this "Barbarian" and "Savage" the "soft language" of the "Put out the light" speech.[7] Rymer is most outraged by the "intolerable" presentation of Iago. The ensign is totally unconvincing because he breaks the convention by which soldiers are "open-hearted, frank, plain-dealing"; never "in Tragedy, nor in Comedy, nor in Nature was a Souldier with his Character."[8]

The commentary of this late-seventeenth-century critic, at times maddeningly literal-minded, has nevertheless proved a useful sounding board for later critics.

Any rebuttal of Rymer's judgments requires readers to scrutinize their own responses to *Othello* and to justify the criteria by which they arrive at their evaluations of the drama. Our age is more inclined to defend the logical improbabilities that troubled Rymer in the "fable"—the accelerated time scheme, for instance—as a means of heightening the irrational, all-consuming force of Othello's jealousy. Rather than condemning the handkerchief, as Rymer does, as an absurdly trivial object on which to base a tragedy, twentieth-century critics have justified it as a central symbol of either the "magic in the web of love"[9] or the "privacy of Desdemona made public."[10] Shakespeare's choice of a black protagonist may have been a daring challenge to Renaissance stereotypes that Rymer, with his prejudiced conviction that a "Black-amoor" cannot be "noble," overlooks.[11] And it can certainly be argued that Shakespeare exploits, rather than ignores, the convention of the "plain-dealing" soldier in order to make Iago's hypocrisy all the more far-reaching.

Interestingly, Rymer uses the term "Monstrous" or "Monster" quite often in relation to *Othello;* he calls the foundation of Shakespeare's play "monstrous" and thinks that Othello and Iago, at various times, are unnatural or aberrant enough to qualify as monsters.[12] Critics from the 1980s on have also focused on the play's "monstrous" elements, but whereas the neoclassicist Rymer emphasizes how *Othello* violates what he considers to be the norms of "Humanity and Nature,"[13] modern critics have noted how the play draws on images of miscegenation and invites us to observe, and perhaps to create, monsters of the mind. In other words, late-twentieth-century critics have moved away from concern about dramatic decorum and what Rymer terms "the School of good manners"[14] to a fascination with the dark psychological undercurrents of the play.

Rymer concludes that *Othello* (if we take it seriously) "can produce nothing but horror and aversion."[15] Writing a few decades later, the Augustan critic Samuel Johnson shows no bias against the hero of the play—in place of Rymer's "Jealous Booby,"[16] Othello is now "magnanimous, artless, and credulous"—but he is also shocked by the brutal conclusion of the play. Act 5, scene 1 is a "dreadful scene . . . not to be endured."[17] Judging the denouement by the same neoclassical rules as Rymer did, Johnson thought that it offended against the norms of refined taste and moral propriety to such an extent that he felt compelled to revise it in his careful editing of the play. In the late twentieth century, our tolerance for horror in literature is undoubtedly higher than that of the Augustans, and we are no longer conditioned to expect poetic justice at the end of tragic drama. Nevertheless, it is salutary to remind ourselves of Johnson's honest, highly sensitive reaction to the murder of Desdemona.

Romantic writers, more in tune with Samuel Taylor Coleridge's definition of the poetic imagination as the "balance or reconciliation of opposite or discordant qualities,"[18] were not inclined to attack Shakespeare's tragedies on the grounds of their lack of probability or decorum. Coleridge's criticism of *Othello* is best known for his perceptive comments on Iago's opening soliloquy as the "motive-hunting of motiveless malignity."[19] This opened up the debate on the credibility of Iago's motives (does he have realistically established, deeply felt grounds for hating Othello?)

and the nature of his evil (is he, like the devil, pure "malignity"?). But it is also telling to find this nineteenth-century English gentleman reacting strongly against the blackness of Othello. Instead of relishing the *discordia concors* of the relationship, Coleridge rejects its "monstrous" implications: "It would be somewhat monstrous to conceive this beautiful Venetian girl falling in love with a veritable negro." Unable to accept that there could be such a "disproportionateness" and "want of balance"[20] in Desdemona, he concludes that Othello is an olive-skinned "gallant Moor"[21] who does not have negroid features. Thus begins the controversy, which we now tend to view as racist, on how truly African and dark skinned Shakespeare intended his hero to be.[22]

The nineteenth-century admiration for the inwardness of Shakespeare's characters, or the empathy with which Shakespeare creates them, is crystallized in John Keats's tribute to what he calls the playwright's "negative capability." In a letter written in 1818, Keats further defines the "poetical character" as one that "enjoys light and shade; it lives in gusto, be it foul or fair. . . . It has as much delight in conceiving an Iago [the evil villain] as an Imogen [the pure heroine in *Cymbeline*]."[23] Two years before, the essayist William Hazlitt had offered a sustained analysis of Iago as a brilliantly conceived dramatis persona who fully demonstrates Shakespeare's genius for empathetic creation of character. His starting point is Edmund Kean's depiction of Iago as a "pattern of comic gaiety and good humour,"[24] a performance that Hazlitt admires but ultimately criticizes as "not grave enough."[25] Hazlitt rejects Coleridge's verdict on Iago's "absolute malignity." The keynote of Iago's character, he thinks, is a "want of moral principle"[26] and a "restless, untamable love of mischievous contrivance," which makes him an ingenious plotter, an "amateur of tragedy in real life."[27] What is interesting here is the blend of theatrical commentary (Hazlitt's careful observation of how Kean interprets the role of the villain) and his insights into the character based on a close analysis of the literary text. The two strands are not separated, as they tended to be in the work of A. C. Bradley, the great postromantic critic of the Victorian age.

TRADITIONAL TWENTIETH-CENTURY APPROACHES (1900–1980)

Character Analysis

Traditional Shakespearean critics have, for the most part, taken issue with or blithely ignored the strictures of E. E. Stoll (1933) that Shakespeare was not concerned with character motivation or psychological credibility in *Othello*. Instead, they have analyzed with gusto what Hazlitt refers to as the "range and variety of characters" in the play.[28] Bradley was sensitive to many aspects of this Shakespearean tragedy—he explores its atmosphere of "confinement"[29] and takes Coleridge to task for "blurring" the "glorious conception" of a white woman falling in love with a black warrior[30]—but he was most influential in discussing the play's characters as though they belonged to the world of the realistic nineteenth-century novel or were individuals taken from life. His character study of Iago, which diagnoses Iago's need to heighten his sense of "power or superiority"[31] as the driving force of this individual, is superb of its kind. Bradley's interest in Iago as a realistically conceived creation has continued to flourish. W. H. Auden, for example, sees in him the practical joker or amoral scientist, shoring up his deep sense of personal insufficiency by besting other people,[32] while Michael Neill finds that Iago's behavior is fueled by a seething "resentment."[33]

Despite the inroads of rival schools of criticism, the play—at least until the 1970s and early 1980s—has constantly been mined for what it can offer in the way of realistically conceived characters and their interactions with one another. In *The Characters of Love* (1960), John Bayley unashamedly justifies his approach to Othello, Iago, and Desdemona as psychologically complex characters when he maintains that the substance of *Othello* is the "subject matter of the domestic novel." Because dramatic characters share with the novel "the same mode of individuality,"[34] they can benefit, he believes, from in-depth analysis and moral dissection. Even F. R. Leavis, one of the *Scrutiny* critics of the 1930s who insisted that a play was a dramatic poem and not a "psychological novel . . . draped in poetry," chooses to discuss the "tragic significance" of *Othello* through "character-analysis."[35] His essay "Diabolic Intellect and the Noble Hero: Or, the Sentimentalist's Othello" (1937; reprinted in *The Common Pursuit,* 1952) is a hard-hitting attack on Bradley's romantic assumption that Othello is established as noble. Often overstated and impressionistic, Leavis's discussion of Othello as a deluded, self-idealizing egoist nevertheless proved seminal. For the next twenty-five years or so, camps divided into those who supported the "romantic" view of the the hero and those who, like Leavis, shrank Othello into a "realist" interpretation. More recently, critics have abandoned an approach that treats characters as monolithic, stressing instead how the audience's judgments on them are constantly shifting and being modified as the play proceeds.[36]

Psychoanalytical

Psychoanalytical criticism offers a logical progression from detailed character study; if commentators view Shakespeare's characters as both lifelike and unusually complex, then they may choose to analyze the characters' psychological motivations or neuroses by applying twentieth-century Freudian categories. Occasionally, too, there have been attempts to explore the role *Othello* played in Shakespeare's own psychic development.[37] In this vein, James Joyce (through Stephen Dedalus in *Ulysses*) speculates on how Shakespeare's "unremitting intellect is the hornmad Iago ceaselessly willing that the moor in him shall suffer."[38] More frequently, though, the drive has been to uncover archetypal patterns of human psychology operating within the whole play. According to Jungian theories, the play need not be interpreted as a traditional (Christian) battle between the forces of good and evil; rather, it can represent the universal psychic conflict between the impulse toward cynical negativity and the tendency to romanticize reality.

It was in the 1930s that Maud Bodkin made a strong case for considering the characters of Othello and Iago not in isolation, but as embodiments of opposed impulses within the human psyche. Iago is the devil archetype, or the "spirit of denial of all romantic values,"[39] whereas Othello represents the idealizing principle. In the next decade, J. I. M. Stewart echoes Bodkin's conclusion that Iago projects the "half truths that Othello's romantic vision ignored"[40] when he analyzes how "Iago's villainy draws its potency from Othello's own mind."[41] This vision of master and servant as part of a symbiotic relationship, or Iago as the repressed side of Othello's consciousness, has now become a given of *Othello* criticism. Kenneth Muir, for example, emphasizes in his introduction to the 1968 Penguin edition of the play how the "two main characters exemplify opposing principles which together constitute the human psyche."[42]

Freudian interpreters have also had a field day with the characters of *Othello*. Some interpret Iago's resentment of Othello as repressed homosexuality;[43] although he seems to lust after women, he is really projecting his desire for the Moor onto the female characters of the play. Other critics have analyzed Iago as a sadist, a type of what Karen Horney defines as the vindictive personality, able to prove his own self-worth only by dominating someone else.[44] In a 1997 article that illuminates Iago's destructive impulses, Janet Adelman applies the theories of Melanie Klein on "projective identification" to suggest how Iago projects his own "internal blackness" or "sense of inner filth" onto Othello.[45]

The character of Desdemona, too, has not remained immune to psychoanalysis. According to several critics, it is Desdemona's "oedipal guilt"[46]—her choice of a husband who represents her father (Othello may be nearly as old as Brabantio) or her subconscious desire to punish her father by marrying the Moor—that leads to her self-destructive behavior and then her welcoming of death. Her predicament, according to Stephen Reid, is her "wish for revenge [on Brabantio] and the guilt induced by the achieved revenge."[47]

Othello's jealousy has often been accounted for by deeply rooted psychological mechanisms—childlike narcissism, emotional insecurity (the conviction that he is unlovable), and even repressed homosexuality.[48] In a Freudian reading, Othello's sense of betrayal is "primal."[49] In his reunion with Desdemona on Cyprus, he recreates that symbiotic union with his mother he briefly attained as an infant, the primal relationship in which the object-libido and ego-libido cannot be distinguished. And the destruction of his faith in his wife accordingly precipitates in Othello "profound feelings of betrayal . . . and rage."[50]

Whether or not we accept that oedipal conflicts and fears of desertion by the mother are endemic to the characters of *Othello,* it is clear that the hero enacts "the primitive energies that are the substance of our own erotic lives."[51] And erotic energies can all too easily be dammed up or diverted. Criticism in the 1980s focused on how Desdemona triggers Othello's fear of female sexuality as part of the deeply "misogynist male psychology"[52] of the play. One of the fullest explorations of this issue is provided by the Freudian critic Edward Snow, in "Sexual Anxiety and the Male Order of Things in *Othello.*" Snow finds chronic repression in the male characters, with Iago serving as the "punitive, sex-hating superego";[53] to maintain the "honor" of the male world, Othello must suppress the dangerous sexuality that "has emerged in and through Desdemona."[54]

New Critical and Formalist

The New Critics, who began as a Southern American group in the 1930s,[55] were iconoclastic. Most influential from the 1940s through the 1960s, they turned away from positivist scholarship—source studies and the historical genesis of a literary work—and instead promoted close verbal analysis. Rather than judging poetry or poetic drama as the product of a particular era or an author's intention, or through the traditional lenses of character and plot, they evaluated it as a self-contained linguistic artifact. Their search for unifying principles within literature led the New Critics to focus on the poem's complex structure created by metaphor, symbol, irony, and paradox. In *The Well Wrought Urn* (1947), Cleanth Brooks articulates his method of discerning dramatic and thematic unity through interpreting image clusters: "What is at stake is the whole matter of the relation of Shakespeare's imagery to the total structures of the plays themselves."[56]

L. C. Knights and Leavis, two of the founding fathers of the British journal *Scrutiny,* also advocated a sensitive exploration of the text through close reading. Knights (unlike Leavis) did not single out *Othello* for special analysis,[57] but his 1933 essay "How Many Children Had Lady Macbeth?" was a frontal attack on Bradley's character criticism that sent wide ripples through Shakespearean studies. He reminds readers that "a Shakespeare play is a dramatic poem" whose end is "to communicate a rich and controlled experience by means of words."[58] It is our task to recreate this experience by grasping the "minute particulars"[59] of the play's language. G. Wilson Knight, while not directly associated with either the New Critics or the *Scrutiny* group, furthered this attention to language patterns in his influential *Wheel of Fire* (1930). Rather than extrapolating character or plot for analysis, Knight demonstrates how iterative images and dramatic symbols converge to create the "spatial unity" of the play and organize its themes. Despite its title's gesture toward musical themes and tonality, Knight's piece on "The Othello Music" describes *Othello's* language in predominantly pictorial and spatial terms rather than as a rhythmic, temporal sequence. According to Knight, the play possesses a "unique solidity and precision of picturesque phrase or image, a peculiar chastity and serenity of thought,"[60] and while Othello attains an "architectural stateliness" of speech in his "silver rhetoric," the effect of the Iago-spirit is "like an acid eating into bright metal."[61] Comparable to Brooks and Knight in his approach is Wolfgang Clemen, whose book *The Development of Shakespeare's Imagery* (published in German in 1936 and in English in 1951) traces how, progressively in Shakespeare's mature work, "each image, each metaphor, forms a link in the complicated chain of the drama."[62] Caroline Spurgeon's *Shakespeare's Imagery and What It Tells Us* (1935) combines discussion of iterative imagery (animal images in *Othello*) with some conjectures into the dramatist's interests, likes, and dislikes as deduced from image clusters in the plays.

When Brooks collaborated with Robert Heilman to write *Understanding Drama* (1945), these two advocates of New Criticism extended their close analysis of imagery into an exploration of how characters function in drama. Critics focusing exclusively on language had been accused of bleeding Shakespeare's drama of its "characteristically direct and particular human interest."[63] While Brooks and Heilman are still reluctant to assess characters in terms of mimetic realism, they do encourage readers to see the way that differing viewpoints and values, represented by the dramatic personae, build into disparate perspectives—one balancing another through ironic counterpoint—that constitute the complex, dynamic form of the play. Heilman went on to write an influential book on *Othello, The Magic in the Web* (1956). Its subtitle, "Action and Language in *Othello*," points up the New Critics' concern with imagery and verbal texture and how these features, together with the actional drama, are intimately related to the play's "over-all form."[64] Heilman's study does not shy away from some character analysis but stresses throughout the "complex interconnectedness of the parts."[65]

This concern with "formal order" and thematic unity, often arrived at by tracing image patterns, became traditional in mid-twentieth-century Shakespeare studies. Derek A. Traversi, another *Scrutiny* critic whose *Approach to Shakespeare* was originally published in 1938, echoed the New Critics' concern with "poetic unity . . . in which each event and each character has just its part *and no more* to play in an organic whole which transcends their separate significance."[66] Using Aristotelian rather than linguistic criteria, the formalist Kenneth Burke also examines the "logic of the *action as a whole*" in *Othello* and finds that the categories of plot and character are organized around the idea of "ownership," or "the property in human affections."[67]

Genre

There is no disputing that *Othello* turns into a tragedy. In Aristotelian terms, it traces a fall from happiness to catastrophe through the hero's tragic error; or, exemplifying Northrop Frye's criteria in *The Anatomy of Criticism* (1957), it represents the mythos of autumn. Frye's innovative work on "Archetypal Criticism: Theory of Myths" in the 1950s was, in one sense, a reaction against the "aesthetic view"[68] of New Criticism; instead of isolating the poem or play as self-contained, cut off from its social or historical context, Frye's categories established links between literary works and anthropology, seeing drama partly in terms of social ritual. Critics such as Susan Snyder[69] and Leslie A. Fiedler[70] have subsequently analyzed how the genres of comedy and romance (Frye's archetypal mythoi of spring and summer) also inform or are worked into *Othello*. The opening act, for instance, in some ways sets up audience expectations for a romantic or Roman New comedy, since the blocking figure of the irascible father (Brabantio) is outwitted by the lovers (Othello and Desdemona) who then escape from the city to the unfamiliar society of Cyprus. Unfortunately, Cyprus is not what Frye terms the regenerative "green world"[71] of the comedies, but a claustrophobic fortress. Iago, meanwhile, transforms quickly from the comic trickster to the evil villain, finessing spiteful deception into a game of death.

Again beginning in the 1940s and 1950s, critics debated how far *Othello* is indebted to the genre of the morality play—an early Tudor form in which characters represent forces of good and evil battling for the soul of a Mankind figure. Some commentators, such as Irving Ribner[72] and Kenneth O. Myrick,[73] have felt that *Othello,* with its prominent references to devils and angels, heaven and hell, conforms closely to this homiletic pattern (even though it reverses the usual outcome) and that it raises questions about the hero's eternal damnation. Others, including Sylvan Barnet[74] and Robert H. West,[75] have argued that fitting *Othello* into a morality schema or "Christian teleology"[76] is reductive because it bypasses the rich complexity of character and situation in Shakespeare's play, encouraging too narrow a speculation on issues of salvation and damnation that are finally irrelevant to the tragic experience. Certainly, it is helpful to be aware of the genealogy of *Othello.* It promotes a fuller understanding of Iago's partial function as the morality Vice figure (explicated by Bernard Spivack in *Shakespeare and the Allegory of Evil* [1958]) and of his possible affinities with the devil of the medieval mystery cycles. These vestigial roles, together with his traits as a Machiavellian villain, are all included in Iago's fascinating composite character. Rather than being an end in itself, criticism that discerns the underlying structure of various genres and the "compound of several dramatic traditions"[77] in *Othello* leads to a greater appreciation of how Shakespeare has fleshed this out into naturalistic drama.

Theatrical

Since its debut in the early sevententh century, *Othello* has flourished in the theater. Assimilating the insights of reviewers, scholars have examined the way that actors through the centuries have uniquely fashioned their roles in *Othello* and how successfully directors have transmitted a particular concept of the play. Often, this kind of commentary overlaps with traditional literary criticism that treats the characters as convincing and psychologically coherent creations. The Russian director and proponent of naturalistic acting Konstantin Stanislavsky, writing in 1929–1930, far outdoes Bradley when he fills in the gaps of the courtship between Desdemona and Othello—"I can imagine that she gave him books to read"[78]—and constructs a past for the lovesick Roderigo in which he tossed flowers into Desdemona's gondola.[79] Hazlitt, as we have seen, combines evaluation of how well the roles are performed by nineteenth-century actors with astute character analysis. In his book *The Masks of* Othello (1961), Marvin Rosenberg moves easily from chapters on production history to broader interpretation of the main characters.

Aside from production history and performance evaluation, two major strands of twentieth-century theatrical criticism are relevant to *Othello.* One, a type of historical scholarship, explores how the theatrical-dramatic conventions of Shakespeare's time conditioned his tragedies. The other discusses how Shakespeare's plays come to life as performed drama in any era, privileging their theatrical potential above their literary-dramatic qualities.

Stoll was a formidable presence in the first arena; before he published *Art and Artifice in Shakespeare* in 1933, he had already discussed the significance of certain Elizabethan dramatic conventions in Othello: *An Historical and Comparative Study* (1915). He stresses that Othello is a noble hero, not easily jealous, and that his downfall results from "the convention of the calumniator credited."[80] We should not demand psychological verisimilitude in Othello, complex motivation in Iago, or strict logical probability in the plot; instead, the action and characters are propelled by certain devices tacitly understood by the Renaissance audience. In her *Themes and Conventions in Elizabethan Tragedy*, M. C. Bradbrook, too, is concerned with these agreements "whereby the artist is allowed to limit and simplify his material to secure greater concentration"[81] in the drama. The work of Stoll and his followers was important, like genre criticism, as an antidote to treating the play's characters as "quasi-real people"[82] and as a clarification of some of the stock theatrical assumptions within which Shakespeare worked. But it also had the salutary effect of revealing how little Shakespeare's drama was truly hamstrung by these conventions. Rufus Putney points out that not "deference to theatrical convention" but a "firm basis in reality" is the source of Shakespeare's "unrivalled power,"[83] while three decades later, Christopher Ricks demonstrates that in Shakespeare's drama, unlike that of some of his contemporaries, "The convention vindicates, and is vindicated by, the psychological portrayal."[84] Readers are likely to agree that *Othello,* for all its shortcuts, presents a hero who is "quite in accord with real-life psychological probability."[85]

Research into the actual dimensions of the Elizabethan-Jacobean playhouse has reminded readers that Shakespeare's plays were designed for a theater in the three-quarters round with a large, unlocalized stage. Reacting against excessive spectacle in the Victorian theater, William Poel and the Elizabethan Stage Society (1894) initiated performances of the plays under conditions closer to their original ones. Scholars such as E. K. Chambers, J. Q. Adams, and A. H. Thorndike, followed in the mid-twentieth century by (among others) G. F. Reynolds, Walter Hodges, and Glynne Wickham, worked on reconstructing Elizabethan playhouses and the Globe Theatre.[86] Some aspects of the original staging remain open to conjecture. Was there a curtained discovery space within the tiring-house facade (between the two main doors) and, if so, would Desdemona's bed have been placed there in the final scene of *Othello*? Othello's words "Let me the curtains draw" (5. 2. 103), after he has smothered Desdemona and is about to let Emilia into the bedchamber, suggest that. And although performing the death so far upstage might make it difficult for spectators to grasp its full impact, we know, from a study of prompt-books, that not until mid-nineteenth-century productions was the bed definitely moved farther downstage.[87] J. L. Styan, sensitive to the way that the dramatic "sequence of impressions" might evolve in its original Globe Theatre setting, examines how characters would be positioned on the platform stage at the beginning of the temptation scene when Iago mutters, "Ha! I like not that" (3. 3. 35). Othello and Iago, Styan deduces, have walked downstage from one entrance, while Cassio moves "toward the other upstage door" as Desdemona attempts to restrain him. It is the sheer distance between character groups as they traverse the "diagonal length of the stage"[88] that can fuel, in retrospect, Othello's suspicions. The work of Robert Weimann[89] on *Figurenpositionen* goes further in showing how different parts of the Renaissance stage might correlate with varying levels of mimetic illusion: the *platea,* or forestage, accommodated direct address to the audience, while action on the locus (the main playing area) encouraged a deeper involvement in the realistic spectacle. Quite possibly, Iago's dual roles—on the one hand, the Vice who breaks the dramatic illusion through his rapport with the spectators; on the other, the naturalistically presented individual who deceives those around him—would operate within these differentiated locales.[90]

Styan's enterprising stage-centered criticism, like that of John Russell Brown in *Shakespeare's Plays in Performance* (1967), often goes beyond the historical to assess how Shakespeare's plays achieve their effects in the theater of any age. In *The Elements of Drama* (1960) and *Shakespeare's Stagecraft* (1967), Styan's concern is not with the literary, spatial unity of the play so dear to New Critics and formalists. Rather, he discusses rhythm and tempo in the total "dramatic score" and its "orchestration" to show how the performed play, like music, builds its sequence of impressions through a linear progression and moment-to-moment connections. The "markedly slower pace"[91] of the willow scene (4. 3), for example, is important in varying the tempo and creating a different mood before the frenetic nighttime scene of *Othello* (5. 1). Of course, Styan analyzes visual effects as well—the groupings of characters, the impact of dramatic symbols—but still as part of the kinesthetic experience of the play in performance, for he stresses that "the division between visual and aural elements is, in the nature of theatre, an arbitrary one."[92] Since his work in the 1960s, other critics who concentrate on the text as a blueprint for performance have examined how clues for the actors are built into the verbal score. Interest has also extended, in the work of E. A. J. Honigmann[93] and Jean Howard,[94] into how Shakespeare manipulates and orchestrates audience response through subtle shifts in dramaturgy. Silences can be poignant, as can offstage noises such as the cannon shot and cries of "A sail, a sail" that "wind up the dramatic tension"[95] in the harbor scene. In *Acting and Action in Shakespearean Tragedy* (1985), Michael Goldman includes under theatricality the way that the actor's very "performance," the challenges of presenting a particular role, "constitute an important part of the action of a play."[96] He interprets Othello as a "great self-constructor" who builds the "action of exoticism"[97] into his imaginative construction of himself.

Metadramatic

All the world's a stage, but the stage, too, generates its own self-reflexive world. From *Othello's* theatricality it is a short step to studying the play's metadramatics; that is, ways in which the drama comments self-consciously on its own medium and materials. As well as manufacturing fictions in a realistic-mimetic way, Shakespeare's plays frequently draw attention to the constructedness of their dramatic illusions; one of the dramatis personae, for instance, may function as a surrogate playwright, indirectly commenting on the art of Shakespeare himself. Iago is a supreme example of this. Although they do not pursue the metadramatic implications, Hazlitt and Bradley both note Iago's artistry in evil. As well as being a presenter for the audience, Iago devises and stage-manages various playlets—the rousing of Brabantio (1. 1), the cashiering of Cassio (2. 3), and the eavesdropping scene (4. 1)—but, unlike his creator, he ultimately fails to expunge his own contriving role from the script even though at the end he pledges, artistlike, to maintain silence ("From this time forth I never will speak word"). Commentary on Iago as a playwright-director includes Stanley Edgar Hyman's portrait of him as an artist[98] and Stanley Homan's analysis of him as a "demonic playwright,"[99] a controlling figure who produces a destructive, obscene illusion. James L. Calderwood, one of the pioneers of this type of criticism in *Shakespearean Metadrama* (1971), discusses Iago as a "metacharacter" in his later book *The Properties of Othello* (1989), pointing out how the ensign functions as both a "real" person and an artificial device, using his design (de-sign) as a way of deconstructing meaning for Othello.[100]

Linguistic

The New Critics and G. Wilson Knight sparked interest in poetic language and image patterns in Shakespeare's tragedies; since then, other commentators have focused on *Othello*'s linguistic features as a key to interpreting the drama. They have shown readers that they can learn more about Othello's character by analyzing his speech patterns and more about Iago's ingenious duping of Othello by examining his verbal strategies. From the 1970s on, several critics of style have used the tools of modern linguistics—research into discourse analysis and speech acts—to define more precisely how Iago uses language to manipulate Othello.

William Empson's *Seven Types of Ambiguity* (1930) was a landmark in close textual analysis, a brilliant explication of verbal subtleties in both poems and dramatic verse. In the 1920s, Empson had been a student of the Cambridge scholar I. A. Richards, whose experiment in "practical criticism," encouraging students to respond freshly to poems without knowing their authors or dates, paved the way for close reading techniques similar to those also developed by the American New Critics. Like his mentor, Empson is fascinated by semantic richness and indeterminacy. He notes as one example of the sixth type of ambiguity (where tautology or irrelevance forces the reader "to invent statements of his own")[101] Othello's pronouncement "It is the cause." Because no "primary meaning" of "cause" is given, "we are made to wonder what *it* was that was *causing* the tempest in his mind"; we sense that we are listening to a mind "baffled by its own agonies."[102] Empson's essay "Honest in *Othello*," contained in *The Structure of Complex Words* (1951), begins engagingly with "the fifty-two uses of *honest* and *honesty* are a very queer business; there is no other play in which Shakespeare worries a word like that."[103] Empson goes on to combine highly intelligent inferences on what "honest" means when applied to Iago (it has the double sense of "being ready to blow the gaff on other people and frank to yourself about your own desires")[104] with shrewd cultural commentary. The key word "honest," he maintains, was gradually emerging as part of a "hearty and individualist"[105] ethos, but because it was used patronizingly about social subordinates in the early seventeenth century, Iago probably reacts to the epithet as a social snub. Critics writing in the same decade who look closely at verbal nuances and ambiguities in *Othello* are Molly Mahood, *Shakespeare's Wordplay* (1957), and A. P. Rossiter, who in "*Othello:* A Moral Essay" (in *Angel with Horns*, 1961) examines the implications for the hero of Elizabethan meanings of "jealous," which could mean "suspicious" as well as sexually envious.

Some thirty years later, Martin Elliott committed himself to an "extensive lexical and syntactical analysis"[106] of the text in *Shakespeare's Invention of Othello: A Study of Early Modern English*. Perhaps not surprisingly, he comes to conclusions similar to Leavis's more intuitive observations—along with those of other literary critics analyzing Othello's lexicon—that the hero's patterns of language are often grandiose and self-flattering. Elliott finds that despite Othello's promise to be "free, and bounteous" to Desdemona's "mind," he fails to "maintain such generosity in practice."[107] Many of his longer speeches, too, are devoted to "self-publication."[108] In the 1980s, exegesis of the text through this kind of historical, dictionary-based work became less fashionable than examining deconstructive tendencies within the play's language. Following Jacques Derrida, whose influential *Of Grammatology* was published in 1976, critics interested in deconstructive theory focused on the free play of signifiers in the self-enclosed text. They looked especially at the way that Iago capitalizes on the radical instability within language itself—the gap between signifier and signified, or what Howard Felperin calls "the fallen and irredeemable nature of language as a medium for defining human reality"[109]—in order to break down Othello's certainties about Desdemona and Cassio. Empson had touched on the endless deferral of meaning in the example from *Othello* cited in *Seven Types of Ambiguity;* T. McAlindon, whose *Shakespeare and Decorum* was published in 1973, also commented proleptically on how words lose "all fixity and reliability in the world of Othello and Desdemona."[110] It was left to the full-fledged deconstructionist Terry Eagleton to point out in more detail in 1990 how Othello "conforms himself obediently to Iago's empty signifiers, filling them in with the imaginary signifieds of Desdemona's infidelity."[111] In "Shakespeare and Rhetoric: 'Dilation' and 'Delation' in *Othello*," Patricia Parker provides a more historical discussion of the play's linguistic "instability"[112] and manipulation of meaning by grounding it in the discourse of Renaissance rhetoric.

Deconstructive readings of *Othello* supply provocative insights into the nature of the play's language; they do not, however, provide a practical demonstration of ways in which speakers can manipulate listeners. Dismissing the Derridean free play of signifiers as an "idiosyncratic" dead end,[113] Brian Vickers comments that characters in Shakespeare's plays are "intentional agents" and that "any theory of language helpful to literature should respect context of utterance."[114] Discourse analysis—primarily a study of how speech acts (such as promising or threatening) function pragmatically in conversation—has recently furnished just this: a more exact method for revealing how Iago arouses Othello's jealousy through his verbal tactics. In "The Analysis of Literary Discourse," Malcolm Coulthard (1977) builds on the contemporary work of J. L. Austin and H. P. Grice to show how Iago breaks certain conventions that usually operate between speaker and addressee: of course, Iago violates the "be truthful" maxim of quality, but he also disregards what Grice calls the "maxim of relation," where the onus is on the speaker to "be relevant."[115] Whereas Iago and Cassio generate unproblematic question-and-answer sequences in Act 2, scene 3 (283–97), Iago "deliberately" avoids or sidesteps Othello's questions, parrying them with counterquestions in Act 3, scene 3, "which suggests to Othello that Iago is concealing something."[116] The subsequent breakdown in communication between husband and wife in Act 3, scene 4 is underlined by their "skip-connecting," where they both "stick stubbornly to their own topic."[117] Othello interjects "The handkerchief!" three times while Desdemona continues to defend Cassio as a "sufficient man" (90–96).

Using Act 3, scene 3 of *Othello* as a test case, Vickers deftly shows how discourse analysis can illuminate Iago's exploitation of the way that "honest people rely on the conventions of truth-telling in communication."[118] Juhani Rudanko, in *Pragmatic Approaches to Shakespeare* (1993), also extends Coulthard's work to reveal how Iago, through his utterances, exerts "a surprising degree of dominance over several of the characters."[119] Although Iago is professionally subordinate to Cassio, he issues directives to the lieutenant in Act 2, scene 3 and initiates, and then controls, their conversational topics. Instead of complying with Cassio's directive "We must to the watch" (12), he switches the topic to Desdemona's attractiveness (15–27) and then to an invitation to drink ("Come lieutenant . . . But one cup!" [27–35]). Because Iago is even further below Othello in the social and professional hierarchy (he uses the respectful "you" form while the general addresses his social inferior as "thou"), it is all the more remarkable how skillfully he orchestrates their conversational turns in Act 3, scene 3. His masterful "ability to initiate, develop and close down topics"[120] is part of his subjugation of Othello. It is true that critics who have described and analyzed speech acts and grammatical structures in *Othello* have not come up with significantly new interpretations of the characters or the play. Nevertheless, their work has been useful in verifying the intuitive, less empirically demonstrated observations of literary critics, particularly as they apply to Iago's skills as a controller and verbal manipulator.

RECENT APPROACHES (1980 TO THE PRESENT)

New Historicist

Formalist approaches to Shakespeare's drama, like the linguistic analysis outlined above, bypassed discussion of the plays' historical and cultural contexts or how these plays were implicated in the ideology of their time. But it was only a matter of time before some critics began to theorize about the relation of literature to the material conditions that produced it and advocated reading the literary text as part of the larger text of history—a discourse that itself is open to deconstruction and reinterpretation. Stephen Greenblatt is a key figure in the movement in the United States that subsequently became known as "new historicism." Indebted to Marxism, especially to the theories of the antihumanist Louis Althusser, this movement de-emphasized individuals (the focus of humanist criticism) in favor of the social forces that conditioned them. By the same token, instead of privileging the literary text as a special linguistic form, new historicists treat it as one of a number of competing discourses. In his landmark book *Renaissance Self-Fashioning,* Greenblatt explains how he began by believing in the autonomy of the individual, able to fashion his or her own identity, but became increasingly convinced that the human subject is "remarkably unfree, the ideological product of the relations of power."[121] Consequently, one key emphasis in his work has been on how texts reproduce or contest the sources of Renaissance power. Unlike the old "monological" historicists, Greenblatt and his followers seek out marginalized voices in the texts of the time—the recalcitrant "Other" that is frequently suppressed in discourses that promote the dominant ideology by reinscribing the authority of the ruling class.

One of the instruments of power and repression in the sixteenth century, much discussed by new historicists, was European colonialism. This becomes the starting point of Greenblatt's essay on *Othello* in *Renaissance Self-Fashioning,* titled "The Improvisation of Power." Greenblatt begins with an account of how Spaniard invaders in the 1520s tried to trick New World Native Americans into working in the gold mines of Hispaniola by promising them a version of the paradise in which they believed. The trick demonstrates the Europeans' "ability again and again to insinuate themselves into the preexisting political, religious, even psychic structures of the natives and turn those structures to their advantage";[122] and it is this kind of improvisational skill—a cunning form of empathy—that Iago uses to manipulate Othello. Iago refashions his master by drawing on a long-established Christian attitude toward sexuality: the idea that erotic passion, even within marriage, is somehow sinful. Thus "the dark essence of Iago's whole enterprise . . . is to play upon Othello's buried perception of his own sexual relations with Desdemona as adulterous."[123]

Greenblatt's argument is ingenious and thought-provoking. And although Jacques Lacan is the poststructural psychologist he uses to pinpoint Othello's need to fashion or construct himself in response to "another," his reading of the play ties into Freudian theories about Othello's sexual insecurity. As Graham Bradshaw points out, there is no immediate evidence "that Othello himself tormentedly identifies his own sexual pleasure with sin and 'adultery.'"[124] Yet readers may well feel that a submerged guilt about erotic desire, plus a fear and distrust of female sexuality that Othello can never fully acknowledge, is part of what makes him so vulnerable to Iago. On the historical level, Greenblatt's method has also been criticized for its "bending of evidence, background and foreground" to suit a "one-sided" interpretation,[125] as when he elides important differences within religious texts[126] in an effort to show that Protestant theologians, like the church fathers, frowned on sexual intensity between married couples. In addition, Greenblatt's analogy of colonist exploitation does not quite fit Iago's improvisational tactics. It is true that

Othello's identity in Venice depends on "an embrace and perpetual reiteration of the norms of another culture,"[127] but this means that Iago undermines Othello by playing on the assumptions of his adopted religion and not—as happened with the Native Americans in the colonial analogy—on his indigenous beliefs.

Cultural Materialist

Cultural materialism began as the British counterpart of new historicism. There are numerous overlaps between the two schools; in fact, the 1985 anthology of essays *Political Shakespeare: Essays in Cultural Materialism,* assembled by Jonathan Dollimore and Alan Sinfield, assumes the "shared concerns of cultural materialism and the new historicism as they relate to Renaissance studies."[128] While both movements are influenced by Michel Foucault, who explored discourse as a vehicle of power and subversion, and by Marxist-structuralist theories, cultural materialism owes a special debt for both its name and its philosophy to the work of the sociologist and literary critic Raymond Williams. All of these critics foreground the material constraints on literature; they emphasize how literary texts, as representations of a particular society, both are generated by and contribute to their society's cultural and political contexts. Moreover, "Literary texts are not some static crystalline structure in which we may glimpse a captured immobile past,"[129] for our interest in the past, and what we discover in Renaissance discourses, is frankly determined by our concerns in the present. For many cultural materialists, these concerns are political and left-wing—in part a reaction against the conservative Thatcherite government of Great Britain in the 1980s. Keenly aware of how readers earlier in the twentieth century appropriated Shakespeare's works to bolster a right-wing ideology, the materialists are drawn instead to transgressive elements within the play. In this vein, Sinfield finds that Desdemona's "entirely selfless love" is "subversive" because it challenges contemporary Protestant doctrines of a punitive God.[130] Like Greenblatt, though, cultural materialists admit that the drama's final effect is usually not to demystify the hegemonic Elizabethan-Jacobean status quo but, rather, to reinforce it by containing (and thus neutralizing) groups that transgress it. Nevertheless, Dollimore firmly believes that "the knowledge of political domination" afforded by Renaissance tragedy "*was* challenging"[131] to its audience.

Because *Othello* quickly establishes itself as a domestic tragedy, it has not attracted as much political analysis as have, say, Shakespeare's history plays or *King Lear.* Notwithstanding, cultural materialists have drawn attention to the Christian-Turkish conflict in the play and the role of Venice as a strong commercial center and bulwark against Turkish inroads in the sixteenth century.[132] In her study *Othello: A Contextual History,* Virginia Mason Vaughan reiterates that "cultural contexts are often as important as specific sources in the attempt to understand a particular work"[133] before going on to situate *Othello* in four relevant discourses of the time—global, military, racial, and marital—that would have been available to Shakespeare. Concentrating on "marital" rather than "global" discourse, material feminists have moved beyond a general discussion of the patriarchal constraints on Desdemona to examine how *Othello* presents a "range of ideologies on women and marriage that interact with one another."[134] And Peter Stallybrass encourages readers to see ways in which the treatment of gender overlaps with class distinctions in *Othello,* where both of these hierarchies are interrogated. As an aristocratic maiden who can confer social status on Othello, Desdemona is distinguished by her class but stereotyped by her gender—viewed dismissively as one of the "daughters of Eve."[135] The "subversive intervention" in the play comes from the servant Emilia, a "female grotesque" who challenges the notion of women as the property of men.[136]

Cultural materialists have also questioned how race relations in the early seventeenth century—or the Europeans' perception of the black man at that time—may have affected the presentation of Othello, an African living in the sophisticated society of Venice. Certainly, the issue of Othello's race, and whether Shakespeare's play confirmed or in some ways subverted stock responses to the black outsider, has been canvassed by scholars who do not call themselves cultural materialists. G. K. Hunter's "Othello and Color Prejudice" (1967), for instance, provides an overview of emerging attitudes to blackness in the Renaissance and positions Othello within this debate. Assessing "racist tendencies"[137] in *Othello* criticism, the humanist critic Martin Orkin was one of the first commentators to disparage what he considers the "shocking"[138] remark of M. R. Ridley, in his widely used *New Arden Shakespeare* edition of the play, that a Negro need not look "sub-human"[139] to European eyes. Materialist studies, though, have gone further in suggesting how closely racial otherness is connected with gender issues in this play. Ania Loomba calls it a mistake to address "sexual difference at the expense of the racial,"[140] since the black man (constructed as Other) and the white woman Desdemona (transgressive in her desires) both pose threats to "the racism of a white patriarchy"[141] in *Othello.* Similarly, Karen Newman notes how often black males are associated with "monstrous" sexuality in sixteenth-century discourse while femaleness, too, is regarded as aberrant in this era.[142] The union of the black man with a white, unruly woman in *Othello* is therefore doubly monstrous; yet Shakespeare contests the "hegemonic ideologies of race and gender in early England"[143] by making Desdemona's transgression in choosing a black husband sympathetic to the audience. More recently, Jyotsna Singh has found fault with an approach that conflates "the condition of black masculinity with that of white femininity,"[144] since it elides essential differences between the two marginalized groups. It is true that Othello and Desdemona emerge very differently as the play progresses; the Moor in one sense colludes with white patriarchy while Desdemona remains a victim of it.

Feminist

"Nowhere in Shakespeare are relations between males and females more searchingly, painfully probed" than in *Othello.*[145] Since the dramatic action not only plays men off against women—Othello, Iago, and Cassio are matched with Desdemona, Emilia, and Bianca—but also reveals male attitudes to females in some depth, feminist critics have found this play fertile ground for commentary. Granted, the tragedy centers on Othello, and much of it focuses on the relationship between two men, Othello and Iago. But to balance the exclusively male point of view from which the eavesdropping scene, for instance, is constructed (4. 1), Shakespeare provides an intimate conversation between Emilia and Desdemona in the willow scene, where the women discuss male-female relations (4. 3).[146] The drama, at least, is not written in such a way as to marginalize women. From the mid-1970s on, the gender issues that *Othello* raises have invited a spectrum of feminist criticism, ranging from an "essentialist" approach (that examines the female characters' traits as universal, ahistorical qualities) and psychoanalytic studies to a more historically grounded analysis of how ideas of "woman" in this play are determined by cultural expectations and literary conventions of the time. Feminists have been particularly interested in the way that Desdemona's predicament is presented in *Othello*: to what extent this female is the victim of a repressive patriarchal ideology, or at least the site of competing discourses on the role of wives in late Renaissance society.

Marilyn French's *Shakespeare and the Division of Experience* (1976) adopts the early essentialist approach. French analyzes Shakespeare's plays in terms of the competing masculine and feminine principles. While the masculine principle is associated with order and reason, as well as with negative aggression that leads to killing, the feminine principle is identified with nature—in both its creative, nurturing aspects and its threatening, unruly side. Iago, an "unadulteratedly 'masculine' presence" in *Othello,* shows a clear "contempt for the feminine principle"[147] and works on the hero's vulnerabilities to produce in him the same response. While French is perceptive about how men view women in the play, her work has been criticized as insufficiently sensitive to the way that fictional representations of women in Shakespeare's plays are produced and conditioned by a particular society, by literary sources, and by the demands of the genre in which they appear. Her ahistorical analysis often presents a system of binary oppositions that trap males and females alike in oppressive stereotypes.

At the other extreme from French is the cultural materialist Valerie Wayne, whose "Historical Differences: Misogyny in *Othello*" (1991) carefully situates *Othello* within Renaissance cultural and literary discourses. This feminist critic explores how Iago infects Othello with a "residual Renaissance discourse" (hatred and distrust of women) so that "the misogynist text of the Renaissance is written onto Desdemona's body."[148] Vaughan is also concerned to historicize feminist discussion of the play—to analyze "how Renaissance marital discourse affected the construction of Othello and Desdemona," rather than to use modern psychoanalytic theories to interpret their relationship.[149] But Vaughan's explication of Othello's destructive emotions through a psychological treatise of the time, *The Passions of the Minde in Generale* (1604), somehow diminishes the unique dramatic significance of this jealousy and its impact on Desdemona. Similarly, when Margaret Loftus Ranald uses sixteenth-century courtesy books and ecclesiastical views to argue that Desdemona is "at fault in her wifely conduct,"[150] the effect is to reduce the character's predicament by placing her only within a moral-homiletic context. It means ignoring, among other things, what Wayne calls the "emergent position"[151] of Emilia in the play as she challenges orthodox opinion on wifely submission—a position that partly takes its cue from sixteenth-century Puritan[152] discussions of the mutual rights and obligations of husbands and wives within the partnership of marriage. In feminist criticism, as with new historicism, it has proved difficult (if not impossible) for critics to decide without bias which, among all the competing discourses of the age, most inform the text of *Othello*.[153]

One commentator who has done justice to Emilia's viewpoint in her reading of the play is Carol Thomas Neely ("Women and Men in *Othello*"). Pronouncing this character "dramatically and symbolically the play's fulcrum,"[154] Neely positions herself as "an Emilia critic" to counterbalance those critics who concentrate mainly on the hero. In some ways, her essay is what she terms, in another context, "compensatory" feminist criticism: a way of giving the female characters the kind of attention they have been deprived of in traditional discussions of the play.[155] Concluding that the women "combine realism with romance, mockery with affection," Neely condemns the men, in Emilia's phrase, as "murderous coxcomb[s]."[156] She considers them vain, obsessed with reputation, and "as incapable of friendship as they are of love."[157] Although in the final scene, Othello "does move away from the men and toward the women,"[158] he remains, Neely thinks, essentially unchanged in his passivity and inclination to assign blame elsewhere. While Neely minimizes the tragic impact of Othello's downfall that Shakespeare's play insists on[159]—she envisages the play more as a failed comedy than as a tragedy—her essay does go beyond simply scoring points against the male characters; it was one of the first to illuminate in detail how "the play develops out of the opposition of attitudes, viewpoints, and sexes."[160] There is, after all, no disputing this dialectic in *Othello* or the fact that the men in the play do abuse women.

Neely's essay also contributes to what she terms the "transformational" feminist mode of commentary—a going beyond traditional criticism to examine "the mutually transforming roles and attitudes of men and women in individual plays," including the influence of a female subculture on a "dominant male culture."[161] While Neely discusses how the women in *Othello*, unlike the heroines of Shakespeare's comedies, fail to transform the men by their generosity and realism, much of the emphasis in feminist criticism is on how men reconstruct women. "The men see the women as whores and then refuse to tolerate their own projections,"[162] writes Neely, while Gayle Greene, in a slightly earlier essay, comments on how "defined by men and in relation to men, woman's identity is precarious."[163] The transformational critical mode also interrogates "the relations between male idealization of and degradation of women."[164] In this area, *Othello* reveals the pitfalls of overidealizing women (Cassio's adulation of Desdemona is a dangerous extreme inevitably counterbalanced by his dismissive attitude to Bianca) and emphasizes how quickly the hero, once Iago taps into his uncertainties about women, changes from viewing Desdemona as saintly to interpreting her as a sexual sinner—a whore and devil. That men in Renaissance literature often impose on women a personal construction, imprinting them as their own texts, is underlined in Othello's ironically unselfconscious excoriation of Desdemona: "Was this fair paper, this most goodly book, / Made to write 'whore' upon?" (4. 2. 70–71). Although he is reviling Desdemona for corrupting herself, he is the one who has inscribed her with the name of prostitute.

Feminist exploration of the slide into misogyny—why men in *Othello* (as elsewhere in Shakespeare's tragedies) negatively stereotype or demonize women—is usually conducted in psycholanalytic terms. Critics explain males' ambivalent attitude to females in categories that use and then go beyond the Freudian to explore in some depth the "maternal issues of gender formation":[165] how men are conditioned by their earliest experiences with women (their mothers) and their conflicting infant needs for symbiosis with and separation from the maternal presence. By attempting to deny, or studiously ignoring, the importance of the female in forming masculine as well as feminine identity, patriarchal practices may foster misogyny. In *Man's Estate: Masculine Identity in Shakespeare,* Coppelia Kahn analyzes how Iago uses the male "fear of cuckoldry" as his primary weapon to achieve with Othello a "defensive alliance of men against women as betrayers."[166] Peter Erickson's *Patriarchal Structures in Shakespeare* goes further, finding male bonding in *Othello* a corollary of patriarchal institutions that work to ensure male dominance; what is more, the male bonds "routinely" incorporate "an antifeminist attitude."[167] As Othello switches from idealizing Desdemona to degrading her, he forges instead a "pure bond" with Iago.[168] Other critics have examined in *Othello* what Madelon Gohlke Sprengnether calls men's "vulnerability in relation to women"— their underlying fear of female sexual power and of being "feminized."[169] Marianne Novy also analyzes Othello in these terms, finding that, in Desdemona, the hero entertains an immature "fantasy of love as fusion with a woman both maternal and virginal,"[170] a return to the original symbiosis between mother and infant.

Novy also asserts that the pull toward "mutuality," in tension with the demands of "patriarchy," renders the lovers' relationship vulnerable.[171] Indeed, it is the patriarchal society, with its vested interest in maintaining male authority, that is usually targeted as the ultimate source of "antifeminist" attitudes in Shakespeare's tragic heroes, including Othello. Critics draw on historical evidence for a repressive, paternalistic culture put forward by the historian Lawrence Stone in *The Family, Sex, and Marriage, 1500–1800* (1977). Historians continue to contest or chip away at Stone's thesis; yet we need only look at Capulet's treatment of Juliet (*Romeo and Juliet* III. v. 149–57) or Lear's desire to control his daughter Cordelia (*King Lear* I. i) to appreciate that patriarchal assumptions were an intrinsic part of the literary-dramatic tradition within which Shakespeare worked. Cordelia is presented as daughter and then peripherally as wife in *King Lear,* but it is Desdemona, out of all the women in Shakespeare's tragedies, who is revealed most fully in relation to both her father, Brabantio, and her husband, Othello. Since she is acutely aware of her "divided duty" to these men in Act 1, feminist critics have questioned how far her apparent assertiveness in defying her father is genuinely carried through into the remainder of the play. Does she merely cross from one kind of paternalistic trap into a worse one with Othello? Might her brutal death suggest that, in a broader sense than being killed by a jealous husband, she is being punished as a threatening female who has transgressed the boundaries not only of gender but of class and race, too?

When they regard Desdemona more as a victim than as a challenger of patriarchal norms, commentators engage in the third mode of feminist criticism that Neely outlines. This is the "justificatory" mode: it acknowledges "the existence in Shakespeare's plays and in his culture of . . . the constraints of patriarchy" and then uses this knowledge to justify "the limitations of some women characters" and the "limiting conceptions of women held by male characters."[172] In *Wooing, Wedding, and Power: Women in Shakespeare's Plays,* Irene Dash views Desdemona as victimized by authoritarian marriage conventions. Although at first she is portrayed as an "independent, bright woman," marriage breaks Desdemona's spirit; her tragedy derives from the "testing of premarital ideals" against the reality of married life that inevitably demands more of women than of men. She declines into a woman uncertain of her role as wife who is finally "defeated by marriage."[173] Mary Beth Rose views Desdemona as similarly disadvantaged. Placing her within the historical context of contemporary Puritan tracts that defend the "public dignity and cosmic significance of marriage," Rose argues that Desdemona is initially presented as a "hero of marriage."[174] Yet because Othello privileges his public role as soldier, he fails in the private world of marriage and thus undermines Desdemona's confidence. From being a subject "with her own, distinctive set of actions and priorities," Desdemona inevitably retreats into "victimization" and "passivity" in the last part of the play.[175] To some extent, too, "unresolved paradoxes inherent in the ideals of female equality and wifely obedience"[176]—contradictions contained within the Puritan tracts on marriage—play into Desdemona's destruction.[177] In line with this central paradox, Desdemona's strong self-assertion in explaining who has murdered her ("Nobody—I myself") is simultaneously "an act of self-cancellation."[178] Rose's conclusion that the play grants Desdemona little room in which to challenge the norms of patriarchal society is reinforced by Stallybrass. In "Patriarchal Territories: The Body Enclosed," Stallybrass finds that the play constructs two divergent Desdemonas: the "active agent" in the first half of the play switches in the second part to become passive, her body "interrogated and deciphered" as the object of men's surveillance.[179]

The final movement of *Othello* clearly contains and silences Desdemona in the most drastic fashion. Where feminist critics differ, though, is over how far this protagonist complies with her own subjection and murder. Some discount the possibility of Desdemona's acting autonomously, which might lead to her genuinely challenging her husband, because of the dramatic conventions through which she is presented. The historicist critic Lisa Jardine considers that this character, the product of a male author and the performance of a boy actor, is set up dramaturgically to reflect the condemnation of "sensual," assertive women found in both social and literary contexts of the time. "In the eyes of the Jacobean audience," such women "are, above all, culpable,"[180] and the best Desdemona can do is display "heroic fortitude" in the face of Othello's brutal treatment of her. Jardine's assessment of Desdemona as "Griselda glorious in her resignation in the face of husbandly chastisement"[181] leaves little scope for sympathetic identification with this fictional character. Critics more in tune with the inwardness of Desdemona's portrayal—the way that Shakespeare presents her, naturalistically, as a spirited and then a desperately hurt woman—either champion her as fighting to repair her marriage with Othello up to the end or express disappointment that she capitulates to her abusive husband. Neely maintains that Desdemona's "spirit, clarity, and realism do not desert her entirely in the latter half of the play."[182] Even her final request, "Commend me to my kind lord" (5. 2. 124), Neely interprets as "one final active effort to mend and renew the relationship."[183] For most feminist critics, though, Desdemona's "reluctance to oppose and question Othello"[184] remains a sticking point; they regret the willful, even masochistic, submission suggested by the words of Desdemona's song, "'Let nobody blame him; his scorn I approve'" (4. 3. 53). Thus Greene takes a standpoint contrary to Neely's, finding Desdemona "responsive to and cooperative with" her victimizer,[185] a figure determined by the late-sixteenth-century conception of women as subservient when what is really required of her is "defiance of the role in which Othello has cast her."[186]

Desdemona's declaration to Othello "Whate'er you be, I am obedient" (3. 3. 89) is likely to strike our age as unduly submissive. Indeed, we are predisposed, partly as a result of the women's movement in general, to view Desdemona's predicament as a gender issue—the wife constrained to obey her husband, encouraged to remain silent. This clash between Renaissance and twentieth-century cultural expectations was foregrounded in a 1929 modern-dress production of *Othello* at the Birmingham Repertory Theater, when a reviewer asked whether, in such a contemporary context, "any woman of spirit would continue to consort with her lord instead of smacking his face and leaving him when he had called her a strumpet."[187] But while Desdemona's words may suggest to contemporary audiences a lack of autonomy, they might also be interpreted as the unselfish response of a totally committed love. Desdemona's heart is "subdued / Even to the very quality" of her lord (1. 3. 245–46). Yet such devotion need not be gender-specific; Othello, before Iago's manipulations, seems equally dedicated to Desdemona, promising her "I will deny thee nothing!" (3. 3. 83). In Desdemona's reluctance to "blame" her husband, Shakespeare could be drawing on the New Testament passage from 1 Corinthians that eloquently evokes the long-suffering nature of love that "beareth all things . . . endureth all things" (13:7). His own sonnet 116 also celebrates the kind of love, or "marriage of true minds," that never "alters when it alteration finds, / Or bends with the remover to remove." Unlike Othello, Desdemona refuses to "blow to heaven" her "fond love," even when her husband's feelings toward her change. Pointing out the wider implications of her devotion is not, as some scholars have done, to disparage feminist criticism for concentrating on one element at the expense of others. Rather, it is to emphasize the inevitable partiality of our interpretations.

And even if we regard *Othello* as the work of a creative artist and not merely the site of competing discourses on various Renaissance topics, it is impossible to deduce Shakespeare's intentions in writing the play. Did he set out to portray Desdemona as a spirited woman who challenges patriarchal stereotypes of femininity but is finally trapped within them? Or do we wrongly infer, from the complex dramatic presentation of this woman, that Shakespeare's interest in gender conflicts was similar to our own "intense interest . . . in the family and the sex roles developed within it"?[188] As Linda Woodbridge has pointed out, Shakespeare cannot be regarded as a protofeminist who four hundred years ago miraculously transcended the presuppositions of his age.[189] The label "patriarchal bard" may be more historically accurate.[190] If, like many readers, we decide that *Othello* cannot be read or acted as deeply subversive of the dominant ideological stance on women in the Renaissance—and that even Emilia's oppositional viewpoint is qualified by her subordinate dramatic role and position in the social hierarchy—then the challenge to resist is left up to feminist readers. The onus is on them to uncover, and subvert for themselves, the strategies of the play that are repressive to women.[191]

NOTES

1. Thomas Rymer, *A Short View of Tragedy* (1693; Menston, Yorkshire: Scholar Press, 1970), p. 140.

2. Ibid., pp. 142–43.

3. Ibid., p. 146.

4. Ibid., p. 92.

5. Ibid., pp. 137, 135.

6. Ibid., p. 134.

7. Ibid., p. 138.

8. Ibid., pp. 93–94.

9. Robert Heilman, *Magic in the Web: Language and Action in* Othello (Lexington: University of Kentucky Press, 1956), p. 212.

10. Kenneth Burke, "*Othello:* An Essay to Illustrate a Method," *HudR*, 4 (Autumn 1951): 165–203, quote at 197.

11. Rymer, *A Short View of Tragedy*, p. 102.

12. Ibid., pp. 121, 131, 138.

13. Ibid., p. 143.

14. Ibid., p. 100.

15. Ibid., p. 121.

16. Ibid., p. 128.

17. Samuel Johnson, *Johnson on Shakespeare,* ed. Walter Raleigh (London: Oxford University Press, 1908), p. 200.

18. Samuel Taylor Coleridge, *Biographia Literaria,* chap. xiv, in Donald A. Stauffer (ed.), *Selected Poetry and Prose of Coleridge* (New York: Random House, 1951), p. 269.

19. Samuel Taylor Coleridge, *Shakespearean Criticism,* ed. Thomas Middleton Raysor (London: Dent, 1960), vol. 1, p. 44.

20. Ibid., p. 42.

21. Ibid., vol. 2, p. 223.

22. See Kris Collins, "White-Washing the Black-a-Moor: Negro Minstrelsy and Parodies of Blackness," *JACult,* 19.3 (Fall 1996): 87–101, for a survey of how nineteenth-century stage productions in America also redefined Othello's "color and character" (p. 90).

23. Frederick Sage (ed.), *Letters of John Keats* (1954; London: Oxford University Press, 1965), "To Richard Woodhouse," October 27, 1818, p. 172.

24. Kean's quote is from the *Examiner,* July 24, 1814, in William Hazlitt, *A View of the English Stage,* ed. W. Jackson Spencer (London: George Bell and Sons, 1906), p. 58.

25. Ibid., p. 56.

26. Ibid., p. 38.

27. From the *Examiner,* August 7, 1814, in ibid., p. 59.

28. R. S. White (ed.), *Hazlitt's Criticism of Shakespeare* (Lewiston, Queenston, and Lampeter: Edwin Mellen Press, 1996), p. 91.

29. A. C. Bradley, *Shakespearean Tragedy* (1904; London: Macmillan, 1962), p. 146.

30. Ibid., p. 164.

31. Ibid., p. 187.

32. W. H. Auden, "The Joker in the Pack," in *The Dyer's Hand* (New York: Random House, 1948), pp. 246–72.

33. Michael Neill, "Changing Places in *Othello,*" *ShS,* 37 (1984): 115–31, quote at 121.

34. John Bayley, *The Characters of Love* (New York: Basic Books, 1960), p. 127.

35. F. R. Leavis, *The Common Pursuit* (1952; Harmondsworth: Penguin, 1962), p. 136.

36. See E. A. J. Honigmann (ed.), *Othello, The Arden Shakespeare,* 3rd ed. (Walton-on-Thames: Thomas Nelson and Sons, 1997), p. 25.

37. As in Daniel E. Schneider, *The Psychoanalyst and the Artist* (New York: Farrar, Strauss, and Co., 1950), p. 266.

38. James Joyce, *Ulysses* (1922; Harmondsworth: Penguin, 1969), p. 212.

39. Maud Bodkin, *Archetypal Patterns in Poetry* (London, Oxford, and New York: Oxford University Press, 1934), p. 220.

40. Ibid., p. 223.

41. J. I. M. Stewart, *Character and Motive in Shakespeare* (London: Longman's, Green, and Co., Ltd., 1949), p. 102.

42. Kenneth Muir (ed.), *Othello* (London and New York: Penguin, 1968), p. 39.

43. See Martin Wangh, "*Othello:* The Tragedy of Iago," *Psychoanalytic Quarterly,* 19 (1950): 202–12; and Gordon Ross Smith, "Iago the Paranoiac," *American Imago,* 16 (1959): 155–67.

44. See Leslie Y. Rabkin and Jeffrey Brown, "Some Monster in His Thought: Sadism and Tragedy in *Othello,*" *L&P,* 23 (1973): 59–67.

45. Janet Adelman, "Iago's Alter Ego: Race as Projection in *Othello,*" *SQ,* 48.2 (Summer 1997): 125–44, quotes at 141 and 143.

46. Robert Dickes, "Desdemona: An Innocent Victim?" *American Imago,* 27. 3 (Fall 1970): 279–97, quote at 281.

47. Stephen Reid, "Desdemona's Guilt," *American Imago,* 27.3 (Fall 1970): 245–62, quote at 261.

48. As in Abraham Bronson Feldman, "Othello's Obsessions," *American Imago,* 9 (1952–1953): 147–63.

49. Arthur C. Kirsch, *Shakespeare and the Experience of Love* (Cambridge: Cambridge University Press, 1981), p. 23.

50. Ibid., p. 33.

51. Ibid., p. 39.

52. Meredith Skura, in *William Shakespeare: His Work,* vol. 2 of *William Shakespeare: His World, His Work, His Influence* (New York: Charles Scribner's Sons, 1985), p. 582.

53. Edward Snow, "Sexual Anxiety and the Male Order of Things in *Othello*," *ELR*, 10 (1980): 384–412, quote at 409.

54. Ibid., p. 393.

55. For a full account, see Hugh Grady, "The New Critical Shakespeare: The Tension of Unity," chap. 3 in his *The Modernist Shakespeare: Critical Texts in a Materialist World* (Oxford: Clarendon Press, 1991), pp. 113–57.

56. Cleanth Brooks, *The Well Wrought Urn* (1947; London: Methuen, 1968), p. 24.

57. In *An Approach to* Hamlet (1959), in *Some Shakespearean Themes and An Approach to* Hamlet (1959; Harmondsworth: Penguin, 1966), Knights develops a kinder version of Leavis's thesis when he claims that Othello's "romantic self-dramatization leaves him at the mercy of the 'knowing' man," Iago (p. 168).

58. L. C. Knights, "How Many Children Had Lady MacBeth?" reprinted in *Explorations* (1947; New York: New York University Press, 1964), p. 18.

59. Ibid., p. 9.

60. G. Wilson Knight, *The Wheel of Fire: Essays in Interpretation of Shakespeare's Sombre Tragedies* (London: H. Milford, 1930), p. 97.

61. Ibid., p. 103. Similarly, in *Principles of Shakespearian Production* (Harmondsworth: Pelican, 1949), G. Wilson Knight discusses translation of the text to the stage in spatial terms, as "rather like moving a delicate piece of furniture machinery" (p. 36).

62. Wolfgang Clemen, *The Development of Shakespeare's Imagery* (1951; London: Methuen, 1966), p. 7.

63. J. L. Styan, *The Shakespeare Revolution: Criticism and Performance in the Twentieth Century* (Cambridge: Cambridge University Press, 1977), p. 176.

64. Heilman, *Magic in the Web*, p. 1.

65. Ibid., p. 17.

66. Derek A. Traversi, *An Approach to Shakespeare* (1938; London: Sands and Co., 1957), p. 6.

67. Burke, "*Othello:* An Essay to Illuminate a Method," pp. 182, 167.

68. Northrop Frye, *The Anatomy of Criticism* (Princeton, N.J.: Princeton University Press, 1957), p. 350. See Frank Lentriccia, "The Place of Northrop Frye's 'Anatomy of Criticism,'" in *After the New Criticism* (Chicago: University of Chicago Press, 1980), pp. 3–26.

69. Susan Snyder, *The Comic Matrix of Shakespeare's Tragedies* (Princeton, N.J.: Princeton University Press, 1971), pp. 56–90.

70. Leslie A. Fiedler, *The Stranger in Shakespeare* (1972; St. Albans, Hertfordshire: Paladin, 1974), pp. 117–22.

71. Frye, *The Anatomy of Criticism*, p. 182.

72. Irving Ribner, *Patterns in Shakespearean Tragedy* (London: Methuen, 1960), p. 112.

73. Kenneth O. Myrick, "The Theme of Damnation in Shakespearean Tragedy," *SP,* 38 (1941): 221–45.

74. Sylvan Barnet, "Some Limitations of a Christian Approach to Shakespeare," *ELH,* 22.2 (June 1955): 81–92.

75. Robert H. West, "The Christianness of *Othello*," *SQ,* 15 (1964): 333–43.

76. Barnet, "Some Limitations," p. 85.

77. René E. Fortin, "Allegory and Genre in *Othello*," *Genre,* 4.2 (July 1971): 153–72, quote at 169.

78. Konstantin Stanislavsky, from *Stanislavsky Produces* Othello, trans. Helen Nowak (London: Geoffrey Bles, 1948), in Susan Snyder (ed.), Othello: *Critical Essays* (New York and London: Garland Publishing, Inc., 1988), pp. 69–89, quote at p. 80.

79. Ibid., p. 71.

80. E. E. Stoll, Othello: *An Historical and Comparative Study* (1915; New York: Gordian Press, 1967), p. 6.

81. M. C. Bradbrook, *Themes and Conventions in Elizabethan Tragedy* (1935; Cambridge: Cambridge University Press, 1960), p. 4.

82. Marvin Rosenberg, *The Masks of* Othello (Berkeley and Los Angeles: University of California Press, 1961), p. 227.

83. Rufus Putney, "'What Praise to Give?': Jonson vs. Stoll," *PQ,* 23 (1944): 307–19, quotes at 308 and 319.

84. Christopher Ricks, "The Tragedies of Webster, Tourneur, and Middleton: Symbols, Imagery, and Conventions," in Christopher Ricks (ed.), *English Drama to 1710,* Sphere History of Literature in the English Language, vol. 3 (London: Sphere Books, 1971), p. 335.

85. George Ian Duthie, *Shakespeare* (London, New York, and Melbourne: Hutchinson's University Library, 1951), p. 18.

86. See Styan, *The Shakespeare Revolution,* pp. 4–5.

87. See James R. Siemon, "'Nay, That's Not Next': *Othello,* V. ii in Performance, 1760–1900," *SQ,* 37.1 (1986): 38–51, quote at 40.

88. J. L. Styan, *Shakespeare's Stagecraft* (Cambridge: Cambridge University Press, 1967), pp. 92–93.

89. Robert Weimann, *Shakespeare and the Popular Tradition in the Theater* (Baltimore: Johns Hopkins University Press, 1978).

90. In "'Playing on the Margins': Theatrical Space in *Othello,*" *EiTET,* 10.1 (November 1991): 17–29, Mark Gauntlett also examines how Othello's "annexation" to Iago is "literally enacted as he is 'displaced' into the downstage area so self-consciously defined and commanded by Iago" (p. 26).

91. Styan, *Shakespeare's Stagecraft,* p. 188.

92. Ibid., p. 197.

93. E. A. J. Honigmann, *Shakespeare, Seven Tragedies: The Dramatist's Manipulation of Response* (New York: Barnes and Noble, 1976).

94. Jean Howard, *Shakespeare's Art of Orchestration: Stage Technique and Audience Response* (Urbana and Chicago: University of Illinois Press, 1984). See also Kent Cartwright, "The Scenic Rhythms of *Othello,*" in *Shakespearean Tragedy and Its Double: The Rhythms of Audience Response* (University Park: Pennsylvania State University Press, 1991), pp. 139–79.

95. Howard, *Shakespeare's Art of Orchestration,* p. 11.

96. Michael Goldman, *Acting and Action in Shakespearean Tragedy* (Princeton, N.J.: Princeton University Press, 1985), p. 3.

97. Ibid., pp. 60–62.

98. Stanley Edgar Hyman, "Symbolic Action Criticism: Iago and Prospero, Two Contrasting Portraits of the Artist," in *Iago: Some Approaches to the Illusion of His Motivation* (New York: Atheneum, 1970), pp. 61–100.

99. Stanley Homan, *When the Theater Turns to Itself* (London and Toronto: Associated University Presses, 1986), p. 112. Thomas Van Laan, *Role-Playing in Shakespeare* (Toronto, Buffalo, and London: University of Toronto Press, 1978), also notes how Iago's "calculated" playmaking dislodges Othello's carefully performed identity so that Othello must seek substitute roles (pp. 183–84).

100. James L. Calderwood, *The Properties of* Othello (Amherst: University of Massachusetts Press, 1989), p. 115.

101. William Empson, *Seven Types of Ambiguity* (1930; Harmondsworth: Penguin, 1965), p. 176.

102. Ibid., p. 185.

103. William Empson, *The Structure of Complex Words* (London: Chatto and Windus, 1951), p. 218.

104. Ibid., p. 221.

105. Ibid., p. 218.

106. Martin Elliott, *Shakespeare's Invention of Othello: A Study of Early Modern English* (New York: St. Martin's Press, 1988), p. xv.

107. Ibid., p. 53.

108. Ibid., p. 186 and passim.

109. Howard Felperin, "'Tongue-Tied Our Queen?': The Deconstruction of Presence in *The Winter's Tale,*" in Patricia Parker and Geoffrey Hartman (eds.), *Shakespeare and the Question of Theory* (New York and London: Methuen, 1988), p. 16.

110. T. McAlindon, *Shakespeare and Decorum* (London: Macmillan, 1973), p. 121.

111. Terry Eagleton, *Shakespeare* (Oxford: Blackwell, 1986), p. 67. Thomas Moisan, "Repetition and Interrogation in *Othello,*" in Virginia Mason Vaughan and Kent Cartwright (eds.), Othello: *New Perpectives* (London and Toronto: Associated University Presses, 1991), also analyzes the play's "syntax of indirection" (p. 55) and how Iago's tactics call on the "power of language to create and re-create its own contexts of reference" (pp. 59–60).

112. In Parker and Hartman (eds.), *Shakespeare and the Question of Theory,* p. viii.

113. Brian Vickers, *Appropriating Shakespeare: Contemporary Critical Quarrels* (London and New Haven, Conn.: Yale University Press, 1993), p. 72.

114. Ibid., p. 77.

115. H. P. Grice, "Logic and Conversation," in Peter Cole and Jerry L. Morgan (eds.), *Speech Acts, Syntax, and Semantics* (New York: Academic Press, 1975), vol. 3, pp. 41–58.

116. Malcolm Coulthard, *The Analysis of Literary Discourse* (London: Longman's Group, Ltd., 1977), p. 173.

117. Ibid., p. 178.

118. Vickers, *Appropriating Shakespeare,* p. 91.

119. Juhani Rudanko, *Pragmatic Approaches to Shakespeare* (Lanham, Md.: University Press of America, 1993), p. 36.

120. Ibid., p. 52. In "Complement Extern: Iago's Speech Acts," in Vaughan and Cartwright (eds.), Othello: *New Perspectives,* pp. 74–88, Joseph A. Porter makes the point that Iago exhibits his controlling, manipulative nature through his "performatives" and "directives" as he tells people what to do (p. 85).

121. Stephen Greenblatt, *Renaissance Self-Fashioning: From More to Shakespeare* (Chicago and London: University of Chicago Press, 1980), p. 256.

122. Ibid., p. 227.

123. Ibid., p. 233.

124. Graham Bradshaw, *Misrepresentations: Shakespeare and the Materialists* (London and Ithaca, N.Y.: Cornell University Press, 1992), p. 200.

125. Vickers, *Appropriating Shakespeare,* p. 267.

126. See Valerie Wayne, "Historical Differences: Misogyny and *Othello,*" in *The Matter of Difference: Materialist Feminist Criticism of Shakespeare* (Ithaca, N.Y.: Cornell University Press, 1991), pp. 166–67; and Bradshaw, *Misrepresentations,* pp. 196–98.

127. Greenblatt, *Renaissance Self-Fashioning,* p. 245.

128. Jonathan Dollimore and Alan Sinfield (eds.), *Political Shakespeare: Essays in Cultural Materialism* (London and Ithaca, N.Y.: Cornell University Press, 1985), p. 4.

129. Thomas Healy, *New Latitudes: Theory and English Renaissance Literature* (London, Melbourne, and Aukland: Edward Arnold, 1992), p. 11.

130. Alan Sinfield, *Literature in Protestant England, 1566–1660* (Totowa, N.J.: Barnes and Noble, 1982), p. 126.

131. Jonathan Dollimore, "Shakespeare, Cultural Materialism, and Marxist Humanism," *NLH*, 21.3 (1990): 471–93, quote at 482.

132. Touched on in Nick Potter, "Epilogue: 'This Is Venice,'" in Graham Holderness, Nick Potter, and John Turner, *Shakespeare: The Play of History* (Iowa City: University of Iowa Press, 1987), pp. 204–9, and covered more fully in Virginia Mason Vaughan, Othello: *A Contextual History* (Cambridge: Cambridge University Press, 1994), chap. 1.

133. Vaughan, Othello: *A Contextual History*, p. 3.

134. Wayne, "Historical Differences," p. 153.

135. Peter Stallybrass, "Patriarchal Territories: The Body Enclosed," in Margaret W. Ferguson, Maureen Quilligan, and Nancy J. Vickers (eds.), *Rewriting the Renaissance* (Chicago and London: University of Chicago Press, 1986), pp. 123–42, quote at p. 137.

136. Ibid., p. 142.

137. Martin Orkin, "*Othello* and the Plain Face of Racism," *SQ*, 38.2 (1987): 166–88, quote at 166.

138. Ibid., p. 183.

139. M. R. Ridley (ed.), *Othello, The New Arden Shakespeare* (London: Methuen,1958), p. li.

140. Ania Loomba, *Gender, Race, and Renaissance Drama* (Manchester and New York: Manchester University Press, 1989), p. 41.

141. Ibid., p. 49.

142. Karen Newman, "And Wash the Ethiop White: Feminity and the Monstrous in *Othello*," in *Fashioning Femininity and English Renaissance Drama* (Chicago and London: University of Chicago Press, 1991), pp. 73–93. In another link, Dympna Callaghan points out that African men and white women, as cultural Others, were both literally excluded from the Renaissance stage ("'Othello Was a White Man': Properties of Race on Shakespeare's Stage," in Terence Hawkes [ed.], *Alternative Shakespeares* [London and New York: Routledge, 1996], vol. 2, pp. 192–215). Kim F. Hall discusses the "crucial interrelationship between race and gender" in *Things of Darkness: Economies of Race and Gender in Early Modern England* (London and Ithaca, N.Y.: Cornell University Press, 1995), p. 2.

143. Newman, *Fashioning Femininity*, p. 93.

144. Jyotsna Singh, "Othello's Identity, Postcolonial Theory, and Contemporary African Rewritings of *Othello*," in Margo Hendricks and Patricia Parker (eds.), *Woman, "Race," and Writing in the Early Modern Period* (London and New York: Routledge, 1994), pp. 287–99, quote at p. 290. In "Circumscriptedness and Unhousedness: *Othello* in the Borderlands," in Deborah Parker and Ivo Kemps (eds.), *Shakespeare and Gender: A History* (London and New York: Verso, 1995), pp. 302–15, Carol Thomas Neely also emphasizes the "mutually constitutive categories of gender, race, and sexuality" (p. 303).

145. Marilyn French, *Shakespeare's Division of Experience* (New York: Summit Books, 1976), p. 204.

146. Discussed in Eamon Grennan, "The Women's Voices in *Othello*: Speech, Song, Silence," *SQ*, 38 (1983): 275–92; and Evelyn Gajowski, "The Female Perpective in *Othello*," in Vaughan and Cartwright (eds.), Othello: *New Perspectives*, pp. 97–114.

147. French, *Shakespeare's Division*, pp. 207, 209.

148. Wayne, "Historical Differences," p. 154.

149. Vaughan, *Othello: A Contextual History*, p. 74.

150. Margaret Luftus Ranald, "The Indiscretions of Desdemona," *SQ*, 14 (1963): 127–39, quote at 139.

151. Wayne, "Historical Differences," p. 168.

152. See Juliet Dusinberre, *Shakespeare and the Nature of Women* (London and Basingstoke: Macmillan, 1975), pp. 1–2.

153. In *Broken Nuptials in Shakespeare's Plays* (London and New Haven, Conn.: Yale University Press, 1985), p. 20, Carol Thomas Neely comments on the "precisely contradictory theses encompassing the period, the drama, and Shakespeare" arrived at by Dusinberre, who thinks that much Renaissance drama was "feminist in sympathy" (*Shakespeare and the Nature of Women*, p. 5), and Lisa Jardine, *Still Harping on Daughters: Women and Drama in the Age of Shakespeare* (New York: Columbia University Press, 1983), who finds in the drama attitudes repressive toward women.

154. Carol Thomas Neely, "Women and Men in *Othello*," in Carolyn Ruth Swift Lenz, Gayle Greene, and Carol Thomas Neely, *The Woman's Part: Feminist Criticism of Shakespeare* (Urbana, Chicago, and London: University of Illinois Press, 1980), pp. 211–39, quote at p. 213.

155. Carol Thomas Neely, "Feminist Modes of Shakespearean Criticism: Compensatory, Justificatory, Transformational," *WS*, 9 (1981): 3–15.

156. Neely, "Women and Men," pp. 218, 216.

157. Ibid., p. 224.

158. Ibid., p. 232.

159. In *Comic Women, Tragic Men: A Study of Gender and Genre in Shakespeare* (Stanford, Calif.: Stanford University Press, 1982), Linda Bamber states that centering the play on Emilia tends to make Othello "exasperating, his story tedious, and his death good riddance to bad rubbish" (p. 13).

160. Neely, "Women and Men," p. 214.

161. Neely, "Feminist Modes of Shakespearean Criticism," pp. 9, 10.

162. Neely, "Women and Men," p. 228.

163. Gayle Green, "'This That You Call Love': Sexual and Social Tragedy in *Othello*," *Journal of Women's Studies in Literature*, 1 (Winter 1979): 16–32, quote at 25.

164. Neely, "Feminist Modes of Shakespearean Criticism," p. 9.

165. Lynda E. Boose, "The Family in Shakespeare Studies; or—Studies in the Family of Shakespeareans; or—The Politics of Politics," *RenQ*, 40 (1987): 707–42, quote at 714.

166. Coppelia Kahn, *Man's Estate: Masculine Identity in Shakespeare* (Berkeley, Los Angeles, and London: University of California Press, 1981), pp. 140, 144.

167. Peter Erickson, *Patriarchal Structures in Shakespeare* (Berkeley, Los Angeles, and London: University of California Press, 1985), p. 7.

168. Ibid., p. 97. Jonathan Dollimore, *Sexual Dissidence* (Oxford: Clarendon Press, 1991), also stresses the "primacy and tenacity of the homosocial bond" between Iago and Othello (p. 159).

169. Madelon Gohlke Sprengrether, "'I Wooed Thee with My Sword': Shakespeare's Tragic Paradigms," in Lenz, Greene, and Neely, *The Woman's Part: Feminist Criticism of Shakespeare*, pp. 150–70, quotes at pp. 152 and 162.

170. Marianne Novy, *Love's Argument: Gender Relations in Shakespeare* (Chapel Hill and London: University of North Carolina Press, 1984), p. 133.

171. Ibid., p. 128.

172. Neely, "Feminist Modes of Shakespearean Criticism," p. 7.

173. Irene Dash, *Wooing, Wedding, and Power: Women in Shakespeare's Plays* (New York: Columbia University Press, 1981), pp. 116, 126.

174. Mary Beth Rose, *The Expense of Spirit: Love and Sexuality in English Renaissance Drama* (London and Ithaca, N.Y.: Cornell University Press, 1988), pp. 119, 138.

175. Ibid., pp. 146, 154.

176. Ibid., p. 146.

177. In *Broken Nuptials in Shakespeare's Plays*, Neely also remarks that "even those parts of the ideology of marriage that might have been expected to alter and enhance women's status engendered demands for their subordination" (p. 13).

178. Rose, *The Expense of Spirit*, p. 152.

179. Stallybrass, "Patriarchal Territories," pp. 141, 136.

180. Jardine, *Still Harping on Daughters*, p. 75. Jardine's more recent essay, "'Why Should He Call Her Whore?': Defamation and Desdemona's Case," in *Reading Shakespeare Historically* (London and New York: Routledge, 1996), pp. 19–34, grounds Desdemona's behavior in a social "event" of the time—public defamation. Jardine argues that once Desdemona has been publicly slandered (for Emilia has repeated Othello's charge to Iago), she would have been expected to counter this "substantial defamation" (p. 33). Unfortunately, this again has the effect of blaming Desdemona for not taking an action that, given her circumstances in the play, would have been virtually impossible.

181. Jardine, *Still Harping on Daughters*, pp. 185, 184.

182. Neely, "Women and Men," p. 220.

183. Ibid., p. 227.

184. Jane Sturrock, "*Othello:* Women and Woman," *Atlantis,* 9 (Spring 1984): 1–8, quote at 7. See also Gajowski, "The Female Perspective in *Othello*," p. 100.

185. Greene, "'This That You Call Love,'" pp. 18–19.

186. Ibid., p. 26.

187. From the *Birmingham Gazette,* February 25, 1929, quoted by Julie Hankey (ed.), Othello: *Plays in Performance* (Bristol: Bristol Classical Press, 1987), pp. 98–99.

188. Boose, "The Family in Shakespeare Studies," p. 708.

189. Linda Woodbridge, *Women and the English Renaissance: Literature and the Nature of Womankind, 1540–1620* (Urbana and Chicago: University of Chicago Press, 1984), p. 222.

190. See Kathleen McLuskie, "The Patriarchal Bard: Feminist Criticism and Shakespeare: *King Lear* and *Measure for Measure*," in Dollimore and Sinfield (eds.), *Political Shakespeare*, pp. 88–108.

191. This is what McLuskie (ibid.) recommends, as she urges feminist critics to exercise the "power of resistance, subverting rather than co-opting the domination of the patriarchal Bard" (p. 106).

7

THE PLAY IN PERFORMANCE

This chapter focuses mainly on twentieth-century filmed performances of *Othello*. In covering the earlier theatrical history of the play, I have had to rely on detailed studies of *Othello* on the stage, as well as on commentators who were writing at the time of the major performances. Reactions to the same piece of work, based on individual taste and perception, of course vary widely, and performances, too, may change subtly from night to night or evolve in new directions if the production enjoys a long run. But where the productions are enshrined on videotape, viewers can and should make independent judgments on them; my commentary is intended only as a guide.

OTHELLO ON THE STAGE

Othello is a passionate play. G. B. Shaw dismissed it as "pure melodrama" while conceding the "passion and splendor of its word music";[1] Verdi responded to its rich tones when he turned it into a highly successful opera, *Otello,* in 1887. It is indicative of the physical power of the play that two actors who were stunning as Othello, the Italian Tommaso Salvini (1870s and 1880s) and Frederick Valk, a German Czech (1947),[2] were nonnative speakers, able to use gestures, facial expressions, and vocal power rather than the nuances of the poetry to convey the hero's extremes of feeling. As well as attracting virtuoso actors, this tragedy has always elicited strong affective responses from audiences. Henry Jackson, who watched the King's Men perform the play in Oxford in 1610, noted how Desdemona "moved us especially in her death," for "as she lay on her bed, her face itself implored the pity of the audience."[3] Fifty years later, just before actresses began to take on the roles of the female characters in the 1660s, Samuel Pepys also recounted how a "very pretty lady that sat by me, called out, to see Desdemona smothered."[4] Iago, too, has drawn strong responses from spectators. When the Victorian Othello Charles Macready collared his Iago in Act 3, scene 3, a gentleman in the upper boxes of a Liverpool theater stood up and encouraged him to "choke the devil."[5]

Because of its power to trigger strong emotions, *Othello* has never fallen out of favor in the theater. After the London playhouses reopened at the Restoration of Charles II in 1660, *Othello* was one of the first of Shakespeare's tragedies to be revived. Although the text was trimmed to excise anything too shocking or offensive to neoclassical tastes[6]—Othello's fit, Desdemona's willow scene, and Iago's sexual imagery were notable casualties, not routinely restored until this century—*Othello* was never substantially rewritten, as were *Macbeth* and *King Lear.* In the eighteenth and nineteenth centuries, the part of Othello continued to attract luminary actors whose technical skills could encompass the extraordinary transitions within this demanding role.

It is these extremes, from inner harmony to chaos, that have proved so difficult for a single actor of Othello to master. In the second half of the play, the hero must run through a gamut of emotions as he whips from regret to anguished shame to stormy fury and then back again, often within a few lines. Ideally, actors can suggest some continuity between the dignified warrior of the play's opening and the savagely jealous husband in Act 4, but frequently they are more adept at one facet of Othello than the other. John Philip Kemble, who acted the role in a classical style from 1785 to 1805, was better at portraying the noble Moor than the profoundly disturbed one. The silver-voiced Spranger Barry, dominant in the second half of the eighteenth century, excelled as a tender lover when he "gushed into tears"[7] following "Ah, Desdemon! Away! Away! Away!" (4. 2. 40). Performing the role entirely in Italian, the nineteenth-century actor Salvini was most renowned for his tigerish ferocity, as when he pounced on Iago with "Villain, be sure thou prove my love a whore" or, growling, hurled Desdemona onto her deathbed.[8] Another challenge for the actor of Othello has been to decide how quickly the "mine is sprung within him"[9]—the point at which he first succumbs to jealousy. Edmund Kean (playing the role most successfully from 1814 to 1817) responded fairly early in the temptation scene, with a "sudden spasmodic contraction of the body, as if he had been stabbed" when Iago interjects, "O, beware, my lord, of jealousy!"[10] The American Edwin Forrest, acting in the mid-nineteenth century, was even more susceptible, rising to the bait at Iago's first suggestion that Cassio has retreated "guilty-like."[11] More effective were the Victorian Edwin Booth's calm imperviousness until Iago's trump card, "I know our country disposition well," and Salvini's incredulity up to the point where Iago reminds Othello of how adroitly Desdemona deceived her father.[12]

Consistently low-key acting, however, has rarely produced convincing Othellos. The text itself provides clues for a strongly gestural performance rather than restraint, as when Desdemona recoils from the "bloody passion" that shakes her husband's "very frame" (5. 2. 44).[13] Indeed, one constant in reviews from the end of the seventeenth century through the nineteenth has been an interest in how much passion the lead actor can generate. Despite the heroic stateliness of Restoration acting, Thomas Betterton's Othello was praised for generating a "variety and vicissitude of passions."[14] The Augustans, too, appreciated what the poet-critic John Dryden termed "excellent Scenes of Passion"[15] in Shakespeare's tragedies. Macready admitted that he could never master both the "real pathos and terrible fury"[16] of the role—an insight corroborated by William Hazlitt, the great romantic reviewer, who commented that Macready never generated a "deep and accumulating tide of passion"; instead, he "goes off like a shot, and startles our sense of hearing."[17] Even the restrained Booth rose to "thrilling bursts of passion,"[18] whereas Charles Fechter's naturalistic presentation, also in the Victorian era, was judged to lack fire. Booth's contemporary Salvini was positively cataclysmic. A raging beast in his jealousy—igniting what Henry James, who found in Salvini a "complete picture of passion," termed "black insanity"[19]—he varied the pulse of feeling by counterpointing volcanic moments with gentler ones.

Possibly the most acclaimed interpretation of Othello in nineteenth-century London was that of Edmund Kean at the Drury Lane Theatre. Referring to Kean's galvanizing performance in Act 5 of the play, *Blackwood's* magazine called it the "most terrific exhibition of human passion that has been witnessed on the modern stage."[20] Contemporary poets and critics, even those who preferred to stage Shakespeare in the theater of their own imaginations, found this actor extraordinary. Lord Byron saluted him as a kindred spirit, while Samuel Taylor Coleridge compared watching Kean act to reading Shakespeare by "flashes of lightning."[21] The actor exploited his physical agility, the unusual expressiveness of his face with its brilliant dark eyes, and what John Keats called the "indescribable gusto"[22] of his voice, to produce riveting effects. His transition from the quiet exhaustion of "What sense had I of her stol'n hours of lust?" to a startling frenzy of disgust at the thought of "Cassio's kisses on her lips"[23] produced one flash of lightning. Another memorable sequence was the superb, melodic invocation of sadness in the farewell to war elegy—its "long, lingering tones," wrote Leigh Hunt, "like the sound of a parting knell."[24] Although Hazlitt initially thought that Kean's Othello was "too often in the highest key of passion, too uniformly on the verge of extravagance, too constantly on the rack,"[25] he later conceded that Kean's early interpretation of the part (culminating in 1817) was the perfect way of playing Othello.

In our own century, the tempestuousness of the role has often been muted. Godfrey Tearle, playing Othello at various times between 1921 and 1950, perfected the image of the hero as a "deeply-grieved and highly-civilised, very English" gentleman-poet,[26] a tradition that continued with the Othello of Brewster Mason (1972), who was "serene and slow to jealousy."[27] Ralph Richardson (1938), John Gielgud (1961), and Paul Scofield (1980), all subtle actors, seemed defeated by the role. One of the few who played it with tumultuous energy was Richard Burton (1956),[28] while Anthony Quayle, also in the 1950s, successfully balanced dignity with ferocity.[29] Although his multifaceted impersonation contained some deliberately histrionic, even ironic, elements, Laurence Olivier in 1964 was praised as the most intense, emotionally volatile Othello since Salvini.

Through much of the nineteenth century, Caucasian men continued to play the black Othello. Shakespeare had designed the role for his colleague, the great tragedian Richard Burbage, whose funeral elegy (1618) recalls what an impact he made as the "Greued Moor."[30] White actors in succeeding ages, donning blackface for the part, have wondered how dark to make the Moor, whether to wear military uniform or oriental robes, and what gestures to include without falling into racial parody. David Garrick (1745) felt that for this tragedy of jealousy, and in order to "paint" the passion of jealousy "in all its violence," Shakespeare had chosen to depict "an African in whose veins circulated fire instead of blood."[31] Kean, though, decided to make Othello's color brown, not black, just as his contemporary Coleridge was strongly averse to the idea of Othello being a "veritable negro."[32] This nineteenth-century tradition of whitening the hero has sometimes persisted, as with Anthony Hopkins (the BBC's 1981 Othello), who could easily be mistaken for a suntanned Caucasian.

Inevitably, there is a distancing effect, an added dimension of role-playing, when a white actor portrays a black man. It would seem logical to have Othello played by a person of African descent. Yet because of the color barrier and a history of suppression of blacks in the centuries following Shakespeare, the nineteenth-century African American actor Ira Aldridge created a stir when he took on the role. His performances in provincial theaters in England in the 1820s and 1830s attracted racist commentary—the *London Times* (October 11, 1825) sneered that the "shape of his lips" made it "utterly impossible" for him to pronounce the verse properly—but in the 1850s, he triumphed on the European stages and in Russia.[33] Ninety years later, Paul Robeson's commanding Othello in the Broadway box-office smash of 1943–1944 was a breakthrough for black artists in the segregated United States, at a time when many Americans considered it shocking for a colored man to kiss a white woman onstage. In the 1930 production at the Savoy Theatre in London, Robeson had been criticized for playing Othello too much as the Negro "underdog";[34] but in 1943, he used his imposing physique and resonant baritone voice to create a charismatic Moor. Indeed, his performance convinced the scholar J. Dover Wilson that only a black man could do justice to the role.[35] Robeson's gentle majesty worked best in the first half of the play, however; in subsequent acts, he fell short of passionate fury and of projecting Othello as a convincing murderer, just as James Earl Jones's 1982 Broadway Othello was judged to be too restrained because he underplayed the racial elements and came across as "gentle" and "very humane."[36] Ironically, it was Fechter, the white Victorian actor, who overemphasized Othello's sensitivity to his color when he glanced ruefully in a hand mirror to proclaim, "*It* is the cause,"[37] skewing the meaning of the line to make his darkened skin the reason for Desdemona's supposed infidelity!

Janet Suzman's *Othello,* filmed in South Africa in 1988, made a locally groundbreaking antiapartheid statement by casting the black actor John Kani opposite a white Desdemona.[38] In Europe and the United States, the choice of a black artist for the lead role has now become fairly routine. Contemporary movie audiences expect realism and will find authenticity of character flouted and racial tensions falsified when a white man parades in blackface; they are also likely to feel uneasy about the potentially racist stereotyping of such an impersonation. Martin Wine tries to level the field when he insists that "black actors have not been notably more successful than white ones [in playing Othello], and the real test lies in the individual performance—whether it works or not."[39] On the stage as well as on the screen, however, at the end of the twentieth century (and presumably beyond), British and American theaters heavily favor a black actor for Othello.[40]

Each player of Iago must discover for himself what makes the character tick. The challenge for the villain has been twofold. Iago should seem credible, since a heavy-handed scoundrel will make Othello appear a gullible dupe; yet he risks eclipsing the hero if he becomes too fascinatingly brilliant or steals the lion's share of the audience's attention through his soliloquies. In Shakespeare's time, Iago may have been tilted toward the comic trickster,[41] and certainly in the Restoration, he was portrayed as a relatively one-dimensional, pantomime villain. Thomas Rymer comments on the "Grimaces, Grins and Gesticulation"[42] that characterized the temptation scene, and Colley Cibber describes Samuel Sandford, who played Iago to Betterton's Othello near the end of the seventeenth century, as "masterly" in portraying "characters of guilt" because of his "low and crooked person."[43] In the 1730s, we find Cibber himself mugging to the audience, portraying Iago as a melodramatic villain who "shrugs up his shoulders, shakes his noddle," and "drawls out" his words.[44] But ten years later, Charles Macklin, despite his hoarse voice and sinister appearance ("shaggy-browed" and "hook-nosed"),[45] broke away from the stereotyped villain with his more naturalistic style of acting. Discarding the traditional black costume, he took care to accentuate both Iago's obsequiousness toward the Moor and the subtlety of his evil, for he delivered the soliloquies in a thoughtful rather than gloating fashion. Early in the nineteenth century, Kean also accentuated the gap between the jovial "honest Iago" in public and the clever, vindictive villain revealed in the soliloquies.

It was in the Victorian era that the actor of Iago sometimes garnered more applause than the lead who performed Othello; both Henry Irving and Edwin Booth won acclaim when they turned their talents to portraying the villain. Irving introduced some startling mannerisms and stage business into his debonair Iago. In the quayside scene, he was the epitome of cynicism, slowly eating grapes and spitting out the seeds, "as if each one represented a worthy virtue to be put out of his mouth."[46] Then, in Act 5, scene 1, he brilliantly evoked Iago's cavalier callousness by turning over the body of Roderigo with his foot "in indolent and mocking curiosity."[47] Deeply moved by the pleading of Ellen Terry's Desdemona, "What shall I do to win my lord again?", Irving even turned genuine emotion into what appeared onstage to be crocodile tears, as he ostentatiously dashed them away and then blew his nose "with much feeling, softly and long."[48] Playing Iago to Salvini's Othello, Booth was an even more ingratiating incarnation of diabolical hypocrisy. His advice to actors was to maintain Iago's plausible but vigilant exterior: "Be genial, sometimes jovial, always gentlemanly."[49] For Othello he donned as his mask the "grave, sympathetic, respectful, troubled face that was composed for him to see";[50] only to the audience did he offer "a quick, fiendish smile of triumph and a rapid clutch of the fingers, as though squeezing [Othello's] very heart"[51] as he left the stage after Othello's "Set on thy wife to observe" (3. 3. 240). Iago's kinship with the "divinity of hell" can be suggested in this way to the audience, but, like the stereotyped image of the stage villain, it must be carefully concealed from the hero if Iago is to remain convincing.

Earlier in the nineteenth century, Macready began the trend of playing Iago as a blunt, honest soldier[52]—one who trades on his down-to-earth military persona—that has permeated twentieth-century interpretations of the role. This concept shaped the Iago of Frank Finlay in 1964, who, clad in a leather tunic, played the "solid, honest-to-God NCO"[53] that Olivier deemed appropriate if the villain is to remain a character secondary in importance to Othello. The Iago of Emrys James (Royal Shakespeare Company [RSC], 1971) was a disgruntled noncommissioned officer in a nineteenth-century military setting, a psychotic joker who blended the very mundane with the mentally twisted.

In Trevor Nunn's 1989 RSC production (later televised), Ian McKellen perfected Iago as a regular army man who forges strong bonds with his companions in the barracks and at times caresses Roderigo with a more than soldierly sensuality. Other twentieth-century Iagos have hinted at an underlying homosexual streak, implying that Iago's apparent hatred for Othello is really frustrated desire. Following Freudian theories in 1938, Laurence Olivier tried to project an Iago attracted to Othello (Ralph Richardson), but his flirtatious gaiety only confused the audience.[54] Although Olivier later repudiated this concept as unworkable in the theater, Finlay (1964) incorporated several details that point to the ensign's latent homosexuality. When Olivier's Othello falls in a fit, Finlay's Iago straddles him and pushes his dagger between the general's teeth; then, in the final scene, he faces Othello with arms raised, passively welcoming the thrust of his master's sword. It is unlikely that an openly gay Iago will be forthcoming, even as we move into the twenty-first century, since the text does not encourage such a clear-cut interpretation. Yet our post-Freudian age often searches for a psychological subtext as the basis for character. In the RSC production of 1985, David Suchet left open the question "Is Iago . . . a homosexual, bisexual, or what?"[55] but created an Iago who was deeply tormented by his love-hate feelings for Othello. Jealous of those close to the Moor (played by Ben Kingsley), he was so troubled by Othello's marriage to Desdemona that he felt compelled to destroy it. To some extent, Othello was complicit with Iago's homoerotic feelings for him, for at the end, given the opportunity to dispatch his ensign, "Othello literally *can't* kill the man who loves him."[56]

While the character of Iago has been deemed "actor-proof," playing Desdemona offers no such security. As Wine comments, "to turn innocence and uncomprehending suffering into an active and convincing stage presence offers a tremendous challenge to an actress."[57] Accounts of Anne Bracegirdle, who played Desdemona to Restoration audiences, suggest that the character was initially played for her "pathetic" rather than heroic qualities.[58] Desdemona's role as uncomplaining victim was enhanced by some of the cuts in the Dublin Smock Alley Theatre script that has survived from the 1660s—in particular, Desdemona's spirited argument to reinstate Cassio ("Why, this is not a boon"), her admission that she briefly thought ill of her husband (3. 4. 146–54), and her opportunity for introspection in the willow scene. In the Restoration, her death may have been staged as a prurient bedroom scene; the frontispiece of Nicolas Rowe's 1709 edition of Shakespeare (possibly modeled on actual performances) depicts Desdemona with one breast fully exposed as she is about to be smothered by a pillow.[59] Eighteenth-century Desdemonas infused the role with feeling. Mrs. Cibber, who played Desdemona to Spranger Barry's Othello, "excelled in the expression of love, grief, tenderness,"[60] while Sarah Siddons, awe inspiring as the evil Lady Macbeth, surprised audiences by her sweetness and warmth, coupled with moral integrity, as Desdemona.[61]

This moral strength was stressed by the Desdemonas of the nineteenth century. Even though she "was frightened to death"[62] of Macready's Othello in the death scene, Fanny Kemble resolved to put up a courageous fight. While there was no question of Desdemona's becoming a Victorian virago, Helen Faucit also rejected the notion of Desdemona as a "merely amiable, simple, yielding creature."[63] Courageous in the opening scene and passionate in her final self-defense, she found it unthinkable that Desdemona would submit to her death with decorous female passivity; as she put it, "How could I be otherwise than 'difficult to kill'?"[64] Ellen Terry, the most renowned Desdemona of the Victorian age, conveyed the heroine's warm tenderness but also her tough, unconventional assertiveness, insisiting that the character is not a half-baked "ninny."[65] It appears that this difficult combination—what Marvin Rosenberg calls "equal parts of softness, passion, and strength"[66]—is essential if the actress is to bring out the full complexity of Desdemona's character and avoid being eclipsed by the two great male roles. Twentieth-century Desdemonas have reaped the advantage of a fuller text and the restored willow scene to convey this complexity. Peggy Ashcroft, who played opposite Robeson in 1930, gave an "intensely moving"[67] performance in that scene and was judged "exquisite"[68] overall. Among fairly recent stage Desdemonas, Maggie Smith stands out for successfully negotiating the delicate balance between spiritedness and warm responsiveness. Rising to the occasion with Olivier's Othello, she became heroic in a minor key.

This growing repertoire of possibilities for bringing characters to life in the theater extends to conventions of staging. G. H. Lewes points out how Fechter (1861), proponent of the naturalistic detail that was gaining ground in French theaters, staged the hero "seated at a table reading and signing papers"[69] at the opening of the temptation scene. In such a professional setting, he was at first unfazed by Iago's suggestions. Salvini followed Fechter's lead in this. Once alone, Salvini's Othello tried to continue writing after reflecting "This fellow's of exceeding honesty," but then he "dashes the pen upon the table"[70] at "O curse of marriage"—a piece of business echoed by Willard White in Nunn's RSC production. Later in this scene, the handkerchief is lost. But how, exactly?[71] Because there is no clear stage direction to indicate who drops it, actors must decide whether Desdemona lets the token fall once she is preoccupied with her husband's discomfort or whether Othello actively pushes it away. Edwin Forrest (1836) thrust it aside with an emphatic "Your napkin is too little,"[72] an interpretation that Anthony Hopkins (1981) endorsed when he angrily snarled, "Let it alone!" Booth and Salvini, in contrast, returned the handkerchief gently so that Desdemona was the one who made the fatal move by dropping it.

The deaths of Othello and Desdemona in the final scene of the play pose several technical difficulties for directors and actors. Once he is disarmed of his second weapon (the "sword of Spain"), where does the hero find a blade with which to kill himself? Kean recovered a dagger from the side of Desdemona's bed; Junius Brutus Booth (father of Edwin) had one concealed in his turban;[73] Olivier deftly pierced his jugular with a small blade he flicked out of his bracelet. Eighteenth-and nineteenth-century actors often decided to use a dagger to finish off Desdemona quickly[74] once Othello decides not to let her "linger" in "pain." Salvini, though, shocked audiences by kneeling on Desdemona's chest for the final asphyxiation. Most earlier actors (Garrick, Kemble, Macready) had used a pillow to smother Desdemona; the Italian Ernesto Rossi broke with tradition when he strangled her with his bare hands.[75] Perhaps in an effort to minimize Othello's brutality, the actual murder was sometimes concealed behind the bed drapes, which gave rise to the "thrilling effect" that Macready achieved by thrusting his "dark despairing face"[76] through the curtains to face the audience once the deed was done. This is the only scene in Shakespeare where a woman is violently killed in a prolonged stage sequence. As James R. Siemon points out, decisions over how to downplay the horror of Desdemona's death in the eighteenth and nineteenth centuries reveal "a culture trying to control a text that it desires to experience in the theatre but that it also strongly disapproves."[77] Twentieth-century Othellos, respecting Othello's stated resolve "I'll not shed her blood" (5. 2. 3), have dispensed with the dagger for killing Desdemona and have either strangled or smothered her (Olivier does both). And since the texts of *Othello* clearly state "Let me the curtains draw" *after* the murder (5. 2. 103), modern actors have refused to titillate the audience by concealing the actual killing of Desdemona.

OTHELLO ON FILM

We are fortunate to have a permanent record, on film and videocassette, of some great twentieth-century Shakespearean actors and the productions in which they shine. Inevitably, some intensity is lost when what was manufactured for the big screen in a darkened cinema is viewed on the scaled-down "box" in the living room. Nevertheless, the fact that these films are accessible, and can be viewed long after they have left the local cinema or arts festival, is a great boon. Repeated viewing can confirm or subtly modify onetime impressions.

Of course there is no substitute for live performance. Things can go wrong "on the night," or the actors can be inspired to fresh configurations and new heights. On the screen, though, the circuit between audience and actors is cut, and we know that the performance and mise-en-scène—for better or worse—are fixed forever. The camera work, as Anthony Davies puts it, can be "intensely selective,"[78] pushing us into the actors' faces when we may prefer to choose our own angle or to perceive, as we do when sitting in the theater, the whole dynamic of a group picture onstage. But it can also give us great variety of viewpoint and image, since the camera takes us beyond the architecturally defined space of the playhouse. The director of Shakespeare on film often chooses large-scale, actual locations for the settings of the plays, buildings and landscapes that supply what is only hinted at in the play-text. Orson Welles (1952) and Oliver Parker (1995) both capitalize on this, using inner and outer settings to intensify the play's symbolism and heighten its dramatic and psychological tension. Serge Yutkenvich's *Othello* (1955) similarly turns the natural features of sea, sky, and stone into a kind of "dramatic chorus"[79] to the tragedy. While the camera directs our gaze and may at times seem coercive, the director can compensate by varying the distance from long shot to close-up and by creative editing. Unique patterns are established by the "shapes, colors, and textures" of cinematic images, often sharply juxtaposed through montage and counterpointed by music and "nonverbal sounds."[80] A film that exploits this multilayered but predominantly visual medium will tend to cut portions of the text and rearrange the play's action; thus its product is more properly called an "adaptation" of Shakespeare than a faithful rendition of the play.

Orson Welles's *Othello* (1952)

Orson Welles's *Othello,* one of Welles's first independent European ventures, is just such an adventurous, bravura film. Because Welles ran into financial difficulties, it had to be shot piecemeal over a period of almost four years, partly in studios in Rome but mainly on location in Venice and at the sixteenth-century Portuguese fortress in Mogador, Morocco.[81] Despite these vicissitudes, the movie impressed many critics as a highly imaginative piece of art and was awarded the Grand Prix at the Cannes Film Festival of 1952. To capture Othello's nightmarish fall from greatness, the film fully exploits the resources of cinema. Its flamboyant variety of camera shots and angles, montage of haunting images, and metamorphosis of architecture and landscape into powerful psychological symbols all convey the disintegration of Othello's romantic, heroic world once he is entrapped by Iago.

While it cuts the text quite heavily in the process of adaptation, Welles's *Othello* gives the spectator a glimpse of several key incidents that are only reported in Shakespeare's play. In a striking opening, we are shown what might happen immediately after the play concludes. A slow funeral procession along the ramparts of the castle at Cyprus, with monks carrying the biers of Othello and Desdemona, is intercut with shots of a chained Iago being pulled through jeering crowds and thrown into a narrow cage to be hoisted up to the top of a tower. Voice-over narrative then takes us back to the beginning of the action. What remains concealed in Shakespeare's play—the wedding ceremony—is shown in long shot through the jaundiced eyes of Iago and Roderigo, who then watch the couple escaping by gondola. At the conclusion of Act 1, Othello actually visits Desdemona in her bedchamber and passionately kisses her on "We must obey the time"; from this, we infer that the marriage is consummated even before the couple leaves for Cyprus. When the Venetian embassy arrives in Cyprus (Act 4 in Shakespeare), overhead shots of foot soldiers swarming to greet the ship at the harbor, with packhorses following behind them, serve as a prelude to Othello's plaintive "farewell to war" speech.

In the text, Othello delivers these lines in the second half of the temptation scene (3. 3). Welles, however, not only streamlines the script, but rearranges several sequences and key speeches. While this cut-and-paste approach assumes some familiarity with the play on the part of the audience, it does not destroy narrative continuity overall, as some critics have suggested,[82] since the high moments arise in logical sequence from their new contexts; Othello is overcome by the loss of his military "occupation" when he looks down and actually sees all the trappings of glorious war congregating on the island. Similary appropriate, in cinematic terms, is the transposing of Othello's highly charged speech "If it were now to die, / 'Twere now to be most happy" (2. 1. 187–88) to a voice-over accompanying the shadows of the lovers on their bedroom wall as they celebrate their reunion in Cyprus—an image juxtaposed with flickering shadows of reveling soldiers and their female companions on the street walls outside. Act 4, scene 1, which in Shakespeare begins with Othello's fit and progresses to the eavesdropping scene, is restructured in the film to make the fit the climax of Othello's anguished loss of control. Act 5, scene 1, a violent street scene in Shakespeare's text, is converted in the movie to mayhem in the Turkish baths. Making a virtue of necessity because most of the cast's costumes had not yet arrived, Welles inventively filmed this as the very first sequence in Morocco![83] The arrival of Lodovico and Gratiano is cut; instead, the new arrangement furnishes a touch of black humor when Cassio, reclining in a steam room, is alerted to the knife-brandishing Roderigo by the presence of the fop's fluffy white lapdog.

Less successful in maintaining psychological continuity is Welles's decision to shift Othello's strong speeches of remorse—"Cold, cold, my girl? Even like thy chastity" and "Whip me, ye devils"—from their usual position into a spot immediately after the murder of Desdemona. It is absurd for this self-recrimination to precede Othello's gradual recognition, precipitated by Emilia, that he has made a terrible mistake in judging Desdemona disloyal. Whereas Othello is deprived of his sword twice in the play-text of this final scene, he is not disarmed at all in Welles's version—a technical simplification that comes at the expense of Othello's rich self-dramatizing in the final moments of Shakespeare's play. And instead of wounding Iago and killing himself as a surrogate for the "turbaned Turk," Welles's Othello stabs himself with a dagger at "Behold, I have a weapon" before lurching, mortally wounded, down to the bedchamber vault to deliver a truncated version of the final speech. It is regrettable, too, that Iago must lose his soliloquies, and thus a window into his compulsions, in the interests of cinematic realism. Since characters in this film are not allowed to step out of the dramatic illusion to address the camera directly, Iago must now confide all his thoughts and plans to Roderigo. As a result, Iago's motive of sexual paranoia, divulged in his second soliloquy (2. 1. 286–312), disappears completely.

Even more damagingly for the lead actors, the movie stifles any opportunity for boldly variegated performances. As James Naremore comments, at times "the camera tends to serve as a substitute for acting,"[84] making us constantly aware of how the characters contribute to beautiful and disturbing compositions rather than of how they evolve psychologically. This is especially true of Desdemona. Played by Suzanne Cloutier, she is presented as an icon of female chastity, a beautiful creature whose bright face maintains an expression of guileless purity. Twice she registers righteous indignation, once when Othello calls her "strumpet" in the brothel scene (4. 2) and again when she springs out of bed (5. 2) to contest Othello's assertion that she has given Cassio the handkerchief. On the whole, however, she exhibits sad incomprehension and passivity. Much of her spirited badgering of her husband as she first defends Cassio is cut, and in the final scene, she is presented more as "monumental alabaster" than as living woman;[85] she even shuts her eyes, pretending to be asleep, when Othello makes his loud entrance. Earlier, several low-angle shots of Desdemona on the castle heights, always dressed in pale colors, present her as almost ethereal. In one memorable shot, she walks to the edge of the parapet just before pleading Cassio's cause and looks down to see what we are shown through reverse angle: massed soldiers all gazing reverentially up at her. She is objectified in a more sexual way when Othello laments how he has lost the "fountain" from which his "current" runs, and the camera tracks his hand as it runs down her lower body. The camera also lingers on her muffled, drowning features as Othello pulls a sheet over her face to smother her and, perversely, kisses her through the cloth.

Iago is similarly muted. When he is shown in close-up, his dark, hooded eyes remain cold, his hatchet face drained of all emotion save watchful bitterness. Iago's merriment with Cassio in the eavesdropping scene is very forced, for this stiff, spidery man with the straggly dark hair rarely laughs or even smiles—a deliberate strategy to excise all the devilish glee from the role. Welles's guideline for the character, adopted by the Irish actor Micheál MacLiammóir, was that "no single trace of the Mephistophelian Iago is to be used." Instead, Iago is a "common man, clever as a waggonload of monkeys . . . a business man dealing in destruction with neatness."[86] The keynote of his character is emotional deadness; when Othello embraces Desdemona after "I will deny thee nothing," a reaction shot shows Iago lowering his eyes in cool distaste. According to Welles, Iago hates life because he is sexually impotent, and certainly MacLiammóir's villain reveals no passion and avoids any display of physical affection. Persuading Roderigo to pick a fight with Cassio, he jabs him with a stick as a paltry way of asserting power over him. The closest this "cold adder" comes to touching the "virile lion"[87] Othello is when he helps him off with his armor (symbolically unmanning him) in the second part of the temptation scene, and he neither kneels to his master nor embraces him when he vows to help "wronged Othello." MacLiammóir's voice is usually an insinuating purr, as when he patiently tells Roderigo, "as though explaining to a child why it should brush its teeth,"[88] that he must knock out Cassio's brains.

The restraint of Orson Welles's performance as Othello conveys an impression of nobility brought low rather than savagery unleashed. Welles is gifted with a rich baritone voice and an imposing physique. Yet because he seems concerned not to sabotage each meticulously composed frame or to ruffle the sound track, we miss what MacLiammóir calls the stage actor's opportunity to stand up on an "honest wooden stage" and deliver the "great organ-stop speeches" from the "wild lungs and in the manner intended"[89]—something that Laurence Olivier nevertheless managed to do in his 1944 film of *Henry V.* In the event, the actors' voices were dubbed, and in the 1992 restoration of the film (released by Castle Hill),[90] the dialogue had to be digitalized and then resynchronized with the visuals; the result is a clear but fairly uniform delivery of the lines, with little variation in pitch and volume. Some of Othello's strongest stage moments are also killed by minimizing shots and bizarre editing choices. "Keep up your bright swords" is virtually lost as the camera flashes for a moment on the tiny figure of Othello on a balcony overlooking the canal, and nine of Othello's lines demonstrating leadership when he stops the drunken fight—commanding his associates to "put by this barbarous brawl"—are cut or given to others. His climactic Pontic Sea speech is awkwardly delivered with the camera at Othello's back. When the camera for once holds steady on Othello's face for his long aria to the Senate (1. 3), Welles remains "muffled and remote."[91]

In general, Welles's Othello is best at creating a sense of pathos and regret; he delivers the calm "It is the cause" speech beautifully, his anguished eyes contemplating Desdemona through the darkness. When he confronts Desdemona in the brothel scene, he generates some depth of feeling—scorn and bitterness, but mainly the sorrow of betrayal. Briefly he registers anger when he amplifies her word "committed," and he is passionate in the scene where he strikes her in public. But his growing sense of chaos and disorientation is suggested less by physical and vocal changes than through camera techniques—tilted angles as Othello stalks through pillared arcades—and expressive shots of his environment, both inside and outside the fortress. What stands out most in the central temptation scene is not Othello's gradual build to fierce jealousy or his quicksilver changes of mood, but the symbolic use of space and setting as he and Iago walk briskly along the parapet in an extended tracking shot.[92] The sturdy fortress, with its symmetrically placed cannon ports staving off enemies and its solid walls holding back the wild ocean, correlates with the sight of Othello briefly warding off the insinuations of Iago. Once inside the garrison, a self-questioning Othello peers into mirrors,[93] pondering Desdemona's possible defection.

One of the movie's great strengths is the way that actual settings—architecture and landscapes—acquire this symbolic dimension, reflecting characters' moods and mental states. Early in the movie, Othello's noble, romantic nature is suggested by the splendid symmetry of the Palace of the Doge and the glory of St. Mark's piazza, as well as the graceful image of him gliding down the canal in a gondola with Desdemona. After such formal beauty, we switch to the stormy ocean lashing the rocky shore of Cyprus. Shot in Morocco, these Cyprus scenes center on the huge, windswept fortress stretching down to the sea and up to the expansive sky where gulls wheel in the harsh sunlight. As Philip Kemp notes, "The wide-open settings make this a painfully unprivate *Othello*."[94] In contrast, the inside of the fortress, developed through shots of twisting stairways, corridors, and alcoves leading inexorably toward grilled gates and latticework windows, creates a pronounced labyrinth effect, a psychological prison for the hero. During the drunken fight, Cassio and Montano splash around in the cellars of the castle, recalling the play's images of the "dungeon" and "cistern for foul toads." The bedchamber of Othello and Desdemona is also situated down in the castle vaults—a choice that makes for some complicated choreography and jump cuts in the final sequence (actually filmed partly in Rome studios), where Othello has to move from the large antechamber and its iron gate back to the bed on the lower level.

As Jack Jorgens comments, while the film's "vast spaces, monumental buildings," and "crowds of soldiers" represent Othello's heroic nature, "tortured compositions, grotesque shadows, and insane distortions" distinguish the "Iago style."[95] This second, baroque style also expresses Othello's riven psyche once he comes under Iago's control. Often, Iago and Othello appear crammed together in confined spaces, with Iago assuming a position above Othello in the frame. To convey the growing distance between Othello and Desdemona, Welles films them at opposite ends of the vaulted chamber, separated by rows of pillars. In a series of quick reverse-angle shots, Desdemona hurries after and seems to pursue her faraway lord, until he escapes through a door and shuts it with a resonant clang.[96]

The marriage bed at Cyprus, hinted at pruriently by Iago but never revealed onstage until the denouement, makes several appearances in the film. First seen during the night of revels, it reappears a short while later when Othello, in a crane shot, abruptly opens the canopy to leave Desdemona once the sounds of the street brawl reach him. After Iago's suggestions take root, Othello strides through the vault to the bedchamber, again sharply drawing aside the curtains to stare at what he now believes is a violated sanctum. In a dramatic moment soon after the murder, Desdemona's body tumbles off the bed. When Othello returns mortally wounded, he lifts her up so that after his closing speech, they fall together onto the bed; an overhead shot then lingers on the chiaroscuro pattern of the two entangled bodies.

Since the movie is made in black and white, Welles takes every opportunity to elaborate on the play's reiterated imagery of light and darkness.[97] Monks clad in black carry Othello's funeral bier while white-robed ones transport Desdemona's. Unlike Bianca, who is dressed mainly in a "bunched" and "puffed"[98] black Renaissance-style costume, Desdemona is clad in pale, flowing robes, her face always softly lit. Othello appears in a dazzling white shirt to reprimand Cassio after the fight and wears a white burnoose (Moorish hooded cloak) to contrast with Iago's dark cap and tunic; but as the action intensifies, he moves into deepening darkness, his huge form throwing shadows on pallid walls. In a sinister image, he slides into the murder scene as a grotesque shadow before his bulk fills the screen, which stays totally black throughout the opening of his "It is the cause" speech.

In addition, the film introduces several thematically charged visual motifs that do not appear in the play. Iago's treachery, for instance, is linked to the instability of water. First glimpsed as a dark shadow reflected in a Venetian canal, Iago walks off into pouring rain on Cyprus after promising to be Cassio's "undertaker." The startling shot of water cascading down after Roderigo is murdered in the bathhouse also suggests Iago's sudden flood of malice. Final pictures of the stalwart tower and the ship, their reflections now quivering in water as the credits roll, emphasize the lasting impact of Iago's corrosive treachery. Welles extends the play-text's imagery of trapping—the net and the web—into the visual motif of the cage[99] and its confining bars. The cage in which Iago is to die is prominent in the opening sequence, as the villain is hoisted up for a bird's-eye view of his deadly handiwork; in one clever linking frame, the cross held by the monk leading the funeral cortege merges with the crisscross bars of the cage through which Iago watches the procession.[100] This cage appears, unobtrusively, five more times during the course of the film. Silhouetted hanging next to the dark tower with its single point of light—a symbol of Othello and his bright center of love for Desdemona—it represents Iago's threatening of that love. And it ironically appears above Iago himself in a long shot after he has walked off gloating about the net that "shall enmesh them *all*" (emphasis added).

Net and cage imagery pervades the action of the film. Longing to escape from her father's house in Venice, Desdemona opens a latticed window to look down at the canal and then, in a closely adjacent frame, dashes up to an iron trellis to catch another glimpse of the Moor. For her final conversation with Emilia, she sits behind diamond-shaped latticework, while Othello views her through a triangular grating as she lets down her hair in preparation for bed. The grille motif is reiterated in the squares of Desdemona's ornate hair net and in one arresting overhead shot of her tiny figure crossing a scallop-patterned courtyard between confining pillars. It is echoed, too, in shots of the Venetian ship's square rigging and checkered sail. Even the oval skylight through which the Venetians view Othello's death has squares painted on its underside. The recurring net traps Roderigo too, for he frantically tries to claw his way through a grating in the bathhouse before hiding, to no avail, under the floor slats through which Iago stabs him.

Increasingly after the temptation scene, Othello, too, is photographed next to, or behind, railings and barred windows, trapped in his own nightmare fantasies. The most intense arrangement of jagged diagonals and verticals appears as a latticework roof of branches above Othello and Iago and then to their side in tangled shadow as they proceed through the streets, Iago torturing Othello with images of Cassio and Desdemona in bed together. It is as though Othello's thoughts are now jagged and distorted; shortly afterward, he loses consciousness in an epileptic fit.

Underlying these visual images are sounds that intensify the nightmarish sense of impending tragedy. Earlier commentators complain of the "occasionally garbled and poorly dubbed soundtrack"[101] in versions of the film released in 1952 and 1955, but this distortion was eliminated when the film's sound was remixed and considerably sharpened in the 1992 restoration. This revamped sound track offers a striking complement to the film's developing visuals.[102] The thudding heartbeat of a single bass string, counterpointed by sinister chords from an amplified harpsichord, introduces the somber funeral procession. The cortege then moves in a dead march to the sounds of a tolling bell and solemnly chanting choir, interrupted by sharp, arrhythmic notes as Iago suddenly breaks into the ceremony, dragged across in chains.[103] Throughout the film, a ghostly chorus underscores moments of crisis. It gives a sudden roar at the passionate reunion of Othello and Desdemona in Cyprus; it gasps, too, as Desdemona's smothered face writhes helplessly beneath the sheet in the murder scene. The harpsichord remains a dominant instrument, either to suggest doom through its amplified low chords as the drama progresses toward tragedy or, played much more softly, to convey the tranquillity of Venice. Other instruments contribute to the emotional tone of rising conflict. Trumpets sound as Othello appears on the ramparts to end the brawl; tremulous violins blend with a somber French horn as Desdemona tries but fails to close the distance between herself and her husband; a muffled drum rolls after the death of Desdemona. In the bathhouse, the accelerated twanging of a mandolin points up the macabre killing of Roderigo.

In Venice the background noises are subtle. Distant organ music complements the wedding shown in long shot, while church bells ring out mockingly as Brabantio rushes to try to intercept the lovers and toll again after his broken exit from the Senate chamber. More harsh are the sounds on Cyprus—cannon shots, bugles and flapping pennants, echoing footsteps, doors slamming, and rings clashing together when Othello tears open the curtains around the bed. Especially in the original version, these noises often become "surreally loud."[104] The roar of the ocean underscores Othello's passion as he threatens Iago on the cliffs ("Villain, be sure thou prove my love a whore!"), and a gull shrieks at Iago's first mention of the handkerchief. This leads into a strong image of paranoia created through a montage of images and sounds—the mewing of gulls blending with the imagined tittering of figures (made tiny through reverse zoom) on the parapet above, offset by Othello's rhythmic, labored breathing as he emerges from his swoon. The muffled howling of the wind punctuates Desdemona's killing and its aftermath. Just occasionally the noises and music become a distraction—that heavenly choir, for example, may carry too much of the emotion in the murder scene where Othello and Desdemona should be at the center—but Othello's major speeches are delivered against a backdrop of silence. Such a complex, dynamic sound track is a fitting counterpart to the film's succession of powerful visual images, underscoring the effect of action moving inexorably toward a tragic climax.

The film also gains cohesiveness through a number of "rhyming" or echoing shots.[105] The slow movement of the funeral procession, as vertical shapes of monks carry horizontal biers from the left to the right of the screen, is mirrored in the horizontal gliding of the gondola that transports Othello and Desdemona along a Venetian canal framed by upright pillars. The spiraling of servants down from Brabantio's house in search of the lovers is reversed when Othello, newly arrived in Cyprus, leaps up a tower staircase to greet Desdemona triumphantly at the top. Cannons explode to celebrate this joyous reunion, just as they thunder, ironically, after Othello's outburst "Cuckold me?" A crowd peering down through a well to watch the drunken fight in the crypt foreshadows the eerie upward shot of Venetians witnessing Othello's death through an oval skylight. The overhead shot of Othello's still, upturned face when he lies in a swoon recalls the image of his tilted visage, surrounded by darkness, as he lies dead on the bier. The suddenness with which Desdemona is slapped in the embassy scene—she comes right up to the camera on "Why, sweet Othello," and we see a quick flash of Othello's hand striking her at the left of the frame—is mirrored in the murder of Emilia, stabbed from behind in a sneak attack by her husband.

Despite its artful mirrorings, the movie has sometimes been accused of excessively virtuoso imagery and camera work, of failing to build up a coherent narrative and concentrating, rather, on "moments within the incidents" and "the opportunity they offer for arbitrary effects, visual and auditory."[106] Incredibly, this film that runs for only ninety-one minutes contains some five hundred different frames,[107] leading André Bazin, who nevertheless admires it, to compare the movie's "fragmented" editing to a mirror "relentlessly struck with a hammer."[108] This is the effect, for example, of the rapid intercutting among various parties (Brabantio and his followers, Desdemona, and Othello) as they converge on the Senate chamber in Venice. Yet collage also works brilliantly to suggest the vulnerability of the marriage as the action moves from Venice to Cyprus. Iago's sinister face as he declares "I am not what I am" fades into a close-up of iron figurines striking the bells of St. Mark's Cathedral.[109] This, in turn, dissolves into a midshot of Othello kissing Desdemona as she lies in bed; then a cut into darkness is followed by long shots of a sky torn by lightning and waves crashing on the rocky shore of the Mediterranean island. Threatening chaos is superimposed on a harmonious relationship.

Granted, the film occasionally overplays its visual motifs; there is something very contrived about the way that Othello is locked out of the antechamber in the final scene, when Lodovico and the rest arrive, so that he can be photographed yet again gazing ruefully out from behind railings. But the movie's discontinuities and dizzying perpectives, rather than exhibiting "formalistic decadence,"[110] can usually be justified in terms of its unifying concept: a visual and aural enactment of the collapse of Othello's once civilized and orderly world. Thus the spinning shot of Iago's sword slashing at Roderigo through the floorboards conveys the surrealistic horror of this barbaric treachery, while a parallel whirling shot of the ceiling of the bedchamber (created by a low-angled camera panning rapidly around with Othello) captures the hero's reeling, chaotic senses as he lurches toward his violent death. More than just a fragmented succession of images that are "hauntingly beautiful,"[111] Welles's movie builds into a convincing interpretation of Shakespeare's play as an eloquent "portrait of Othello's heroic world in disintegration."[112]

Stuart Burge's *Othello* (1965)

Whereas Orson Welles's movie is a baroque, expressionistic version of *Othello,* Stuart Burge's film presents the play in classical style. Critics who complain about its uninspired shooting and editing—the failure of this production to exploit its new medium fully—have ignored Burge's intention. The film is not a stained-glass artifact drawing attention to its own beauty, but a transparent window into a landmark piece of theater: namely, John Dexter's 1964 stage production. One of the producers, Anthony Havelock-Allen, defined his wish "to capture the absolute magic of the theater on this occasion" by presenting *Othello* "more or less . . . as one might have seen it at the National Theatre."[113] Granted, it is a fallacy to think that a film can "preserve and enhance" the ephemeral magic of the theater; Olivier himself has remarked that no one can ever capture the smell of adrenaline on celluloid.[114] Inevitably, too, there are some clashes between the strengths of the two media. Olivier's performance is the opposite of that of Welles in being highly physical and often very loud, pitched to an audience who may be sitting fifty yards or more away, rather than geared to the close scrutiny of the camera. Nevertheless, any attempt to provide a record of a great actor's performance for future generations is admirable; as Ronald Bryden remarked when he heard about the film project, "It couldn't save the whole truth, but it might save something the unborn should know."[115]

The costuming and choreography, as well as details of acting, remain essentially unchanged from Dexter's original production. William Kellner's stylized studio set is also closely based on Jocelyn Herbert's design for the theater—simple colonnades for Venice and two large columns backed by steps for most of the Cyprus scenes. Burge's film crew used three Panavision cameras in order to maintain the continuity of the actors' performance. Since the characters, especially Othello, move around a good deal on the set, a few "awkwardly angled and framed shots"[116] seem inevitable. Sometimes, too, compulsive cutting between close and midlength shots breaks the sustained rhythm of bravura speeches, such as Othello's elegiac farewell to war, that are boldly designed for theater audiences. But close-ups clarify details that might be lost on much of a theater audience. No movie spectator can miss the way that Othello commits suicide by piercing his jugular with a sharp blade that he flicks out from his bracelet—a concealed weapon the camera has already focused on when Othello kneels over Iago and threatens to kill him at "Villain, be sure thou prove my love a whore!" While the camera's prying eye is not always kind to this Othello—blackface cannot conceal that the actor was close to sixty years old—Iago benefits greatly from the film's frequent use of close-ups. In contrast to MacLiammóir's distant villain in Welles's movie, Frank Finlay's Iago establishes a strong relationship with the camera and delivers his soliloquies front on, with relish. His sneering "I am your own forever," as he twists and knots the handkerchief at the end of the temptation scene, gains an extra nuance from being addressed more to the audience than to Othello.

Although Burge's stylized studio set lacks the compelling "architectural realism"[117] of Welles's movie, this production creates a more sharply defined social context than does Welles's timeless tragedy. Tension flares up between the natives on Cyprus and their Venetian overlords; during the drunken revelry, a Cypriot spits in Bianca's face because she is fraternizing with the enemy.[118] When another woman is slashed across the face by Cassio's careless dagger, the brawl almost becomes a mutiny. Derek Jacobi's carefully nuanced presentation of Cassio[119] points up not simply the divide between Cypriots and Venetians—he is not about to defend Bianca from the Cypriot's insult—but also the caste system within the army. With his long, curled-under hair and his flounced sleeves, the lieutenant insultingly underlines his "breeding" as his excuse for kissing Emilia on the lips at the quayside. Excessively courteous, as when he kneels to Desdemona in Act 3, scene 1, he is offended by Iago's down-to-earth, salacious attitude toward the woman whom Cassio regards as "exquisite." His tongue loosened by alcohol, this callow social climber gives a nasty, snobbish edge to "any man of quality," seeming to exclude Iago from that category before pointedly reminding him that the lieutenant is to be "saved" before the ancient. Later, he is frankly surprised that a mere noncommissioned officer would want to help him regain his position.

The other white European males also appear lightweight in contrast to the commanding black man in their midst. The Duke is elderly and slightly effeminate, while in the Senate scene, Lodovico appears excessively eager to maintain a good relationship with the Moorish warrior who is protecting Venice's economic interests. From the start, this boldly African Othello is no underdog; he holds center stage in the Senate chamber. Whereas Welles depicts a black Everyman whose racial difference is downplayed, Olivier's Othello proudly flaunts his otherness. His appearance as he strolls onto the stage provides an immediate frisson. In addition to the finely buffed ebony skin, crimped hair, and graceful hand gestures, Olivier cultivates a relaxed, barefooted prowl, "like a soft, black leopard."[120] To lower his natural tenor voice a full octave into a rich baritone, he took voice lessons. Critics note how easily this "eye-rolling . . . tongue-thrusting coal-black Pappy" with the "sexily indolent face"[121] could turn into a racial caricature, "excruciatingly like something out of the *Black and White Minstrel Show.*"[122] Yet Olivier avoids crude stereotyping partly by making Othello a man proud of his race who self-consciously exploits his exotic presence for the white Venetians. Slightly condescending as he recounts his outlandish adventures to the admiring Senators, he is nevertheless delighted to accept the Duke's mandate as evidence of acceptance into this community and even tries to share a joke with Brabantio about his travels. As the performance progresses, Olivier digs deep into the passion of this African warrior whose recent conversion from paganism is signaled by the huge metal cross he wears over his tunic. He does this not to create a racist portrait of a "self-ignorant barbarian"[123] but, rather, to uncover a highly emotional man who is more vulnerable than he realizes, both to the wiles of the supersubtle Venetian Iago and to the destructiveness of jealousy.

Conceived in the 1960s, an era that promoted desegregation and the civil rights movement in the United States, this production does not try to tone down the "color difference"; Olivier acknowledges that the "whole play seeps through with it."[124] Race hatred—the "small white man's sexual jealousy of the black"[125]— seems part of what drives Iago to treachery, combined with class envy and the bitterness of the "noncommissioned officer type"[126] toward his superiors. With his metal-studded tunic and cropped hair, this hard-bitten soldier stands out like a sore thumb among the Venetian aristocrats, with their sumptuous red gowns, and the long-haired "darlings" such as Roderigo and the lieutenant Cassio. After the drunken brawl, where he appropriates both Cassio's sword and his embroidered sash of office, Iago lightly caresses the sash in a gesture that perfectly conveys his malicious delight at having ousted the officer.

There is fire in Finlay's Iago, though it burns deep. In his opening soliloquy, he reveals his brooding malevolence to the audience, pausing thoughtfully at "Let me see now" and only gradually discovering the most promising scheme to execute his revenge. Glimpses into this Iago's dark inner self counterbalance his more theatrical moments as an adroit villain who stage-manages Roderigo (literally pushing him forward to converse with Brabantio in the opening scene) and jauntily claps and rubs his hands together when he briskly determines "Two things are to be done" at the end of the cashiering scene.

While his usual expression is a cold sneer, his mobile features convey a brooding sensuality. The subtext that Iago is impotent[127]—adopted by Finlay, perhaps in response to Orson Welles's concept—emerges in the ensign's disgust when Emilia desperately kisses him after surrendering the handkerchief. His imagination, if not his body, is fired by the seamy side of sexuality. He accompanies lewd suggestions with obscene gestures, as when he tells Roderigo that "the woman hath found him [Cassio] already" and holds up his forefingers to simulate horns, braying rudely in anticipation of how Othello will react to Cassio "soliciting his wife." What sensuality he does express is reserved for men. Iago paddles in Roderigo's palm and kisses the top of his head after tending to his nosebleed (2. 3). At first reserved with Othello, he becomes more demonstrative once his psychological power over the general increases, so that after the fit (4. 1), he massages Othello's shoulders as he alludes to the "yoke" of cuckoldry and solicitously removes a fleck of foam from Othello's tongue to spruce him up for the Venetian embassy. In the finale, the complexity of Iago's sadomasochistic feelings for Othello is strongly signaled when he capitulates to the rage of his master, holding up his arms to receive the Moor's deep sword thrust and yet gloating, "I bleed, sir, but not killed."

Only in this final scene does Finlay's Iago fully reveal his manic streak. The audience briefly glimpses it in Iago's sudden burst of rabble-rousing craziness when he shouts, "Diablo, ho! / The town will rise" during the brawl. For the most part, though, he has been carefully controlled. Now, as Emilia questions him, he behaves like a cornered animal—two close-ups focus on his desperate expression, eyes glinting with fear—and he shrieks, "What, are you mad?" to try to restrain her. His manic fury has been more carefully disguised than his furtiveness. One valid criticism of Finlay's Iago is that he does not show to the world a sufficiently bluff or disingenuous exterior. He fails to play the perfect hypocrite, which Edwin Booth insisted was essential to the role; instead, in the Senate scene, he looks very much the "furtive slyboots"[128] even while Othello is commending him as "honest" Iago.

The reptilian slime and slyness of Finlay's Iago throws into relief the candor, warmth, and sensitivity of Maggie Smith's Desdemona. With Othello she radiates the passion of their relationship, for when she arrives in the Senate chamber, they become instantly absorbed in each other ("the sexual promise between them is electric")[129], and she uses the Quarto's frank "My heart's subdued / Even to the utmost pleasure of my lord" instead of the Folio's tamer phrase ("very quality") to justify her accompanying Othello to Cyprus. Meeting there, Desdemona and Othello exchange a long look of ecstatic wonder before they can express their joy in words. This Desdemona is determined but never shrewish in her firm defense of Cassio, flustered by the loss of the handkerchief, and deeply hurt and embarrassed, though capable of maintaining a gracious dignity, when her husband strikes her in public. Smith projects a young woman who must grow up quickly. There is sad realism in her discovery that "men are not gods" and a brave attempt to stand up to Othello, to discover what is wrong, in the highly physical brothel scene (4. 2) where he twice flings her to the ground after half-embracing her. This Desdemona's spiritedness (counteracting the slight whininess that sometimes creeps into Smith's voice) is marked in her angry "By heaven, you do me wrong!" and again in the death scene, where she makes a wonderful transition from sleepy lack of comprehension to the wide-awake appeal of "let me live tonight!" Smith's Desdemona will not be smothered quietly. Arms flailing, she fends off Othello, protesting and gasping for breath under the pillow before she is finally still.

Though he is flanked by a very strong cast, Olivier's "stunning virtuosity" as an actor puts his Othello at the absolute center of this production's design. It is difficult to do justice to all the bravura moments of this performance; Olivier himself complained that the role of Othello provides "too many climaxes . . . all beckoning you on to scream your utmost."[130] The underlying principle that unifies the performance is Olivier's vision of the hero as a proud man destroyed by "self-delusion," for his Othello believes that he is "impervious . . . to all ordinary passions,"[131] particularly jealousy. Once Iago opens the floodgates, Othello discovers, in a terrifying, humiliating fashion, that he is wrong about himself.

As he prepared them for the 1964 stage production, John Dexter urged the cast to envisage Othello as a "pompous, word-spinning, arrogant black general . . . a man too proud to think he could be capable of anything as base as jealousy."[132] Both director and lead actor had studied F. R. Leavis's essay debunking the hero as "noble" and had decided to present him, with unflattering realism, as a man flawed by pride. Accordingly, this Othello reeks of self-confidence when he first lolls on to the stage chuckling and sniffing a rose, daring anyone to demote him. But he also supports Leavis's concession that the hero is at times "truly impressive, a noble product of the life of action."[133] For Olivier's Othello commands respect by his very tone of voice in "Hold your hands," and it is noticeable that none of Brabantio's followers dares lay a finger on him, just as all the Senators except Brabantio bow to him when they leave the Senate chamber. Othello's egotism is dominant again in his self-flattering speech assuring Iago that he would never succumb to jealousy, followed quickly in stage time by the shrieked "to *me*?" when he contemplates Desdemona being "false" to him. His renunciation of his profession is both a moving cry of pain and a self-indulgent aria, bolstered by histrionic arm

1. Orson Welles's 1952 film of *Othello*: Iago (Micheál MacLiammóir) arouses suspicion in Othello (Orson Welles). Courtesy of Castle Hill Productions, Inc.

2. The 1964 National Theatre production of *Othello* (basis for Stuart Burge's 1965 film): Iago (Frank Finlay) arouses suspicion in Othello (Laurence Olivier). Angus McBean photograph, © The Harvard Theatre Collection, The Houghton Library.

3. The 1964 National Theatre production of *Othello* (basis for Stuart Burge's 1965 film): Othello (Laurence Olivier) holds the murdered Desdemona (Maggie Smith). Angus McBean photograph, © The Harvard Theatre Collection, The Houghton Library.

4. Oliver Parker's 1995 film of *Othello:* Iago (Kenneth Branagh) arouses suspicion in Othello (Laurence Fishburne). Photo by Rolf Konow, courtesy of Castle Rock Entertainment.

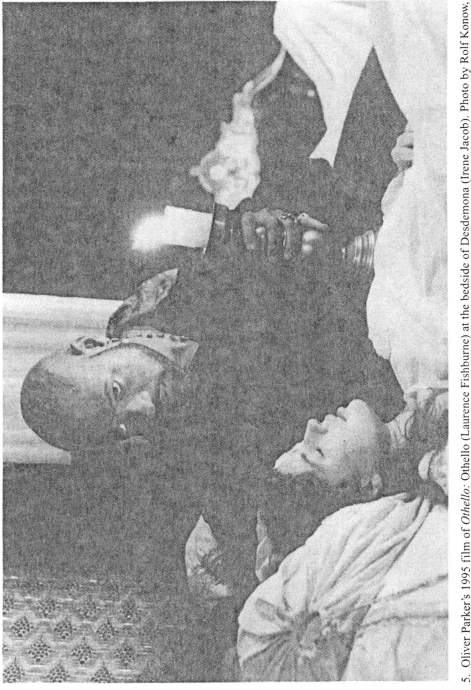

5. Oliver Parker's 1995 film of *Othello*: Othello (Laurence Fishburne) at the bedside of Desdemona (Irene Jacob). Photo by Rolf Konow, courtesy of Castle Rock Entertainment.

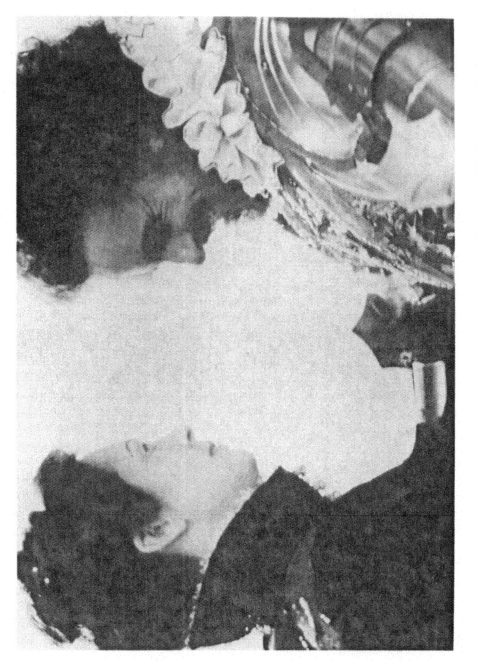

6. Jonathan Miller's BBC/Time Life televised production of *Othello* (1981): Othello (Anthony Hopkins) greets Desdemona (Penelope Wilton). Copyright © BBC, BBC Photograph Library.

7. Jonathan Miller's BBC/Time Life televised production of *Othello* (1981): Iago (Bob Hoskins) arouses suspicion in Othello (Anthony Hopkins). Copyright © BBC, BBC Photograph Library.

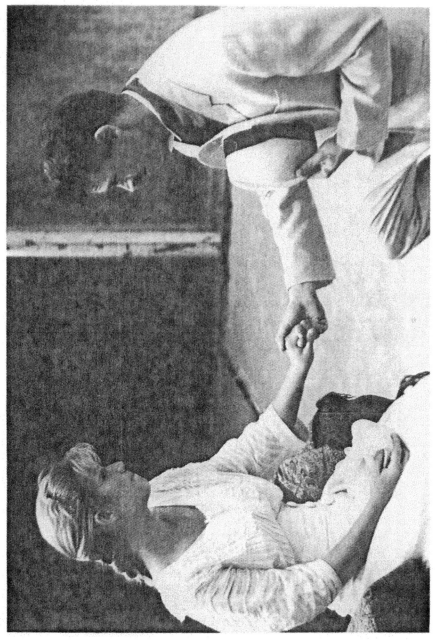

8. The Royal Shakespeare Company's production of *Othello* (directed by Trevor Nunn, 1989): Cassio (Sean Baker) kneels to Desdemona (Imogen Stubbs). Courtesy of Shakespeare Centre Library: Joe Cocks Studio Collection.

9. The Royal Shakespeare Company's production of *Othello* (directed by Trevor Nunn, 1989): Iago (Ian McKellen) arouses suspicion in Othello (Willard White). Courtesy of Shakespeare Centre Library: Joe Cocks Studio Collection.

gestures on "pride, pomp, and circumstance of gl-oor-ious war!" The Pontic Sea speech, culminating in the fierce yelp of "Now by yond m-aar-ble heaven" when Othello tears off his cross to pledge vengeance, is similarly flamboyant. His melo-dramatic self-condemnation after the murder is an all-out performance as he bel-lows "roast me in sulphur" and wails (with West Indian inflection and an extra repetition of "dead") "Dade, Des-dee-mohn, dade, dade!" This speech alone would support Leavis's verdict that Othello's "habit of self-approving self-dramatization . . . remains so at the very end."[134]

But whereas Leavis's interpretation robs the tragic hero of most of his nobility and thus his ability to inspire "sympathy, even admiration"[135] in the audience, Olivier defies "the weight of acting intuition"[136] and manages to have it both ways. His inventive interpretation of the temptation scene (3. 3) avoids making Othello too quick a prey to jealousy. True, the "essential traitor is within the gates," as Leavis puts it,[137] but this Othello is not absurdly eager to swallow Iago's bait. Far from suspecting sexual wrongdoing in Cassio, he takes the opportunity to redirect Iago's evasions into an inquisition of his subordinate.[138] Initially, Othello takes control of the conversation by establishing close physical contact, chucking Iago under the chin at "What didst not like?" and firmly clapping an arm around him, pulling him down to his level as he asks, with exaggerated patience, "What dost thou mean?" He is frankly bored by Iago's disquisition on "good name"—what rel-evance do these generalities have for Othello, with his solidly established reputa-tion?—but Iago's desperately sincere "O, beware, my lord, of jealousy" catches his attention. This becomes a crucial turning point. Drawing on the confidence bor-dering on arrogance displayed early in the play, Othello assures Iago that he is im-mune to hasty inferences. But as the ensign rushes on with more insinuations, Othello becomes perplexed and disturbed, beginning to feel the stab of jealousy but trying to conceal and master it in the proud, muffled pain of "Not a jot" and "No, not much moved."

Once the seed is sown, it quickly sprouts. The handkerchief interlude shows Othello briefly relapsing into tender affection for Desdemona, for he chuckles and almost weeps with relief when she offers to bind his head but then stiffens with sudden supicion as he bends to kiss her. When he returns to the stage, he is "like a lion caught in a cruel trap."[139] Gone is the loose, slightly swaggering gait, for now this Othello walks hunched over and "on the rack," his body suddenly arthritic as it registers the terrible emotional pain that becomes the keynote of his performance until the beginning of Act 5. At times almost paralyzed with grief and mounting hysteria (listening to Iago recount Cassio's dream), at other times he releases his tension in frenetic motion, hurling his racked body from pillar to steps to pillar in the strangled rage of "blood, blood, blood!" Olivier's vocal range in these two acts is extraordinary. To his natural trumpet clarion, he adds several more notes: the somber bass of "'Tis gone" after renouncing his "fond love," the sobbed shriek of "Goats and monkeys," and the howl turning to a jackal yelp in "Desdemon! Away! Away!" Using the violin of tender regret, he pauses in his trumpeting Pontic Sea speech to recall and renounce humble "love." This same tremulous moan is crystallized forever in the utter pathos of his lament "But yet the pity of it, Iago. O Iago, the pity of it, Iago."

Olivier's performance perfectly balances the gentler "pity of it" with the "monstrous" rage of fierce jealousy. In the final scene, Olivier somehow pulls off the almost impossible feat of presenting Othello as an "honorable murderer" who kills Desdemona, not driven by savage, self-centered rage, but filled with a sense of loss and inspired by sacred duty. Disputing A. C. Bradley's assumption that Othello retains his nobility at the end of the play, Leavis is convinced that "self-deception" precludes tragic self-discovery. In Olivier's representation of the character, however, it is more the case that a chastened Othello regains a "humbler, more mature version of his original style."[140] He shows immense dignity when he simply drops his sword after "Where should Othello go?", refusing to intimidate Gratiano with physical prowess. During his tender final speech, he rocks Desdemona in his arms, admitting (his voice high, broken with tears) that he is "perplexed in the extreme."

By taking his cue from Leavis—Olivier describes Othello as "only a goodish fellow who had merely fixed the earmark of nobility upon himself"[141]—the actor risked fatally diminishing the play's tragic impact. Yet Othello soon emerges as a titan in passion. And since we never doubt his deep love for Desdemona and the rightness of his dying on a kiss, he qualifies in part as Bradley's romantic hero, too. This varied portrayal of the role springs from Olivier's creative insights as an actor combined with the hard-won technical skill in which he reveled; he claimed that his life's ambition was to inveigle the audience into coming "not only to see the play but to watch acting for acting's sake."[142] Admittedly, some viewers find this consummate and often self-conscious technique—Olivier's audacious quest for ever higher peaks to scale, akin to someone "racing up a down escalator"[143]— distancing and off-putting. Already his Othello, which Kenneth Tynan in 1964 applauded as the work of "a great classical actor in full spate,"[144] may seem dated to television audiences less attuned to the bravura style. It is nevertheless a theatrical landmark, like Kean's Othello in the second decade of the nineteenth century or Salvini's in the 1880s. And it is thanks to Burge's unpretentious filming that this record of Olivier's virtuoso performance, the centerpiece of a production distinguished by strong ensemble acting, comes across so lucidly today.

Oliver Parker's *Othello* (1995)

Cutting Shakespeare's text to the bone, Oliver Parker's Technicolor adaptation of *Othello* aims to appeal to commercial audiences of the 1990s; yet it makes a strong artistic statement as well. With its choice of settings that enhance the play's imagery and symbolism, quick cuts from one locale to the next, and repeated cinematic motifs, the movie is closer overall to Welles's creative adaptation of *Othello* than to Burge's filming of a theatrical event. So, too, are the actors' performances, which are honed to the demands of the camera, not the stage. The keynote of this sharply edited, strongly paced film is tragic waste. Since Laurence Fishburne's Othello is presented without an obvious flaw, the emphasis falls on two exceptional individuals who are destroyed by the utter malice of Kenneth Branagh's fiendishly cunning, multifaceted Iago.

After Burge's restraint, it is refreshing to find the potential of the cinema so fully realized in this *Othello*. A sense of space is immediately established through the depth of opening shots, as a gondola glides forward over the moonlit lagoon and a tiny figure hurrying up an arcade where two men (Iago and Roderigo) lurk at the top materializes as Desdemona. In addition to the actual streets and canals of Venice, the film introduces a medieval romance setting when it accompanies Othello's long account of how he won Desdemona with a flashback of the Moor strolling with Brabantio to a garden pavilion; here we see Desdemona stroking the scars on Othello's shaved head and his hand, her tears of "pity" wiped away by the strawberry-embroidered handkerchief. The arrival at the garrison on Cyprus, filmed at Castle Bracciano near Rome, downplays the storm—there is one quick shot of a windblown Desdemona gazing out to sea—and instead focuses on the colonizing Venetians trundling their carts and provisions up to the fortress through the sun-drenched streets of the town. We miss the tension, generated by the play-text, of Othello's friends anxiously awaiting his arrival. To compensate, however, Parker provides the fuller social realism of the Venetians settling into a foreign island and an inventive shot of Cassio gallantly helping Desdemona down from her carriage that is mirrored in Iago's paring knife as he plans to "ensnare" the lieutenant.

Parker's movie follows Welles in using several different locales, within the castle and its surroundings, for the temptation scene. Iago's insinuations begin after a friendly pole contest on the castle grounds and continue down in the armory, as Othello cleans and checks his pistol. After the interlude where Desdemona drops her handkerchief and Emilia passes it on to Iago, the conversation between Othello and Iago continues on the beach at a later, unspecified time. But where Welles cultivates a certain impressionistic fragmentation, Parker's smoother shifts from one location to the next help to convey subjective time—Othello is traveling huge psychic distances within a brief duration—and thus solve the problem of the play's "double time" that has bothered some critics. Through well-paced editing, the temptation sequence maintains momentum; yet in chronological terms, its events might stretch over twenty-four hours or even a few days.

The first part of the temptation scene also incorporates a peculiarly filmic device: Othello's fantasies of sexual betrayal once Iago has sown the seed of doubt. A close-up on Iago's mouth muttering poisonous words in Othello's ear leads into a flashback of Cassio dancing with Desdemona during the wedding celebrations. This begins as an accurate memory shot (one the film audience has seen) but becomes elaborated as Othello's imagination adds the intimacy of his wife whispering to his lieutenant and their laughter together. Soon afterward, we cut to Othello in front of transparent bed curtains, parting them with his sword as he glimpses, entwined on the bed, two lovers who quickly turn around to reveal that they are Desdemona and Cassio, surprised and then mocking. When Othello proclaims, "I'll not believe it" immediately after wondering "If she be false," we infer that he has shaken off this false vision. Some doubt still remains, however. Othello's verbal act of faith is followed by a flashback to Brabantio's warning, "She has deceived her father, and may thee"—an image now distorted into the huge face of the gloating father-in-law.

While this inventive montage of images conveys Othello's burgeoning jealousy more directly than a stage production can, it could, like some of the swift changes of location, prove confusing to moviegoers not well acquainted with Shakespeare's play. They might wonder, initially, if Othello is actually surprising the lovers in his bed. There are no immediate clues, such as extrasoft focus, to signal that the sequence is a fantasy. Similarly, the visual sequence that replaces Othello's verbal breakdown just before he goes into a fit—instead of hearing the words "Noses, ears, and lips" we are shown a montage of legs, hands, thighs, lips, and mouths as Cassio makes love to Desdemona—may make the fantasy of adultery disturbingly literal for the spectators, turning them into voyeurs and muddying their image of Desdemona's purity.

Arguably, this device is legitimate in a film that highlights the erotic images. Determined not to let the relationship between Othello and Desdemona be upstaged by the "fascinating" character of Iago,[145] Parker resorts to Hollywood tactics in his decision to show the consummation of their marriage. Thus Othello's line "the fruits are to ensue" (2. 3. 9) is accompanied by rhythmic Eastern music, Othello unbuckling, and Desdemona, having retreated into long shot, slipping off her gown and sliding naked behind the transparent curtains. When Othello joins her, they make love on sheets covered with rose petals reminiscent of the strawberry-spotted handkerchief. To underscore the ubiquitous current of sex, this union is juxtaposed with other less savory ones. Iago brutally "tops" Emilia in his quest for the handkerchief, and Desdemona's graceful wedding dance for her husband segues into an overhead shot of a couple crudely copulating in a cart, underneath which Iago assures Roderigo that Desdemona and Cassio are also headed for an "incorporate conclusion." The gasps above complement Iago's meditation on the "history of lust" as he urges Roderigo, who is both excited and frustrated by the coupling in the cart, to do whatever is necessary to displace Cassio.

Parker's treatment of sexual relationships is much franker than Welles's shadows on the bedroom wall. Other sequences, however, suggest that Parker is paying tribute to his predecessor through careful allusion. As in Welles's movie, Brabantio is shown asleep in bed and then on his balcony when Iago and Roderigo shout to him across the canal. On Cyprus, Welles's Othello rushes up a spiral staircase to embrace Desdemona; in Parker's version, an overhead shot captures Othello riding a splendid horse up a massive stone staircase to greet his wife in the upper courtyard. In a clever extension of Welles's movie, where Othello threatens Iago on top of the cliffs ("Villain, be sure thou prove my love a whore!"), Fishburne's Othello pushes his ensign under the waves and almost drowns him. One of the central devices in Welles's temptation scene, the long tracking shot of Othello and Iago walking along the castle ramparts, is echoed in the later film when Othello paces to and fro on the parapet before kneeling with Iago to vow "black vengeance." Just as Welles shrouds Othello in darkness as he prepares for murder, Parker intercuts shots of Othello silhouetted against the moonlit ocean, contemplating the terrible deed he must perform, with Desdemona's moving willow song.

The "grille-and-bar motif,"[146] so dominant in Welles's movie, finds its way more subtly into Parker's. The secret wedding ceremony is again framed through the viewpoint of an envious Roderigo, now spying through a latticed window. When Fishburne's Othello claims that he is "not much moved" during the temptation scene, he is gazing through vertical swords arranged in a horizontal wooden rack; in the eavesdropping scene, set in the castle crypt that serves as a prison, he peers through bars at Cassio joking with Iago. Dismissing Desdemona to bed, Othello wears a cream burnoose patterned with small brown squares. And finally, as the claustrophic action ends, Lodovico opens a latticed window in the chamber so that the tableau of death is suddenly bathed in sunlight.

This kind of "cinematizing"[147] offers seasoned moviegoers the pleasure of recognition; but Parker goes beyond it to create original visual motifs that underline significant themes in the tragedy. Othello blows out the lighted candles before the consummation of his marriage and again (more loudly) as a prelude to snuffing out Desdemona's life. To the black-and-white imagery prominent in Shakespeare's play and elaborated in Welles's production, Parker adds the image of clasped black-and-white hands. A close-up shot focuses on the ringed hands of Othello and Desdemona sealed in marriage and then bitterly joined by Brabantio in the Senate scene, with a reaction shot of Roderigo horrified by this publicly ratified miscegenation. Tightly clasped hands revealed at the climax of lovemaking symbolize the couple's commitment to each other—a union destroyed by Iago's blood pact with Othello, which is also symbolized by clasped hands. At the end of the cashiering scene, Iago has picked up a smoldering log and smeared on his hand the "pitch" into which he plans to turn Desdemona's "virtue." Now, for the pledge of vengeance, each man pierces his palm and then grasps the bloodied hand of the other, sealing a pact that has in effect replaced that of husband and wife. About to be murdered, Desdemona ironically reaches for Othello's hand as she wakes up and he moves away from the bedside. In an eerie, lingering shot during the final death struggle, we watch Desdemona's white hand frantically cover Othello's black face and then appear limply to caress it as she loses consciousness.

The movie's beautiful closing image of burial at sea, when the shrouded bodies of the lovers shoot gracefully down into the ocean, leaving a trail of bubbles, is foreshadowed by the two chess pieces—black king and white queen—that Iago sweeps off the wall into the water after resolving "This is the night / That either makes me or fordoes me quite." At the end of the first act, Iago used these chess pieces, placing a white knight between them on the board, to formalize his plan for "double knavery" against Othello and Cassio. Just as Iago travesties the gesture of clasped hands, so this villain moves people around like game pieces.

Costume colors in Parker's production are subtly emblematic, underlining passion and jealousy. Othello is first dressed in black blouse, pants, and boots, with a splash of red on his cloak that is picked up in the flame-colored shirt he wears at his wedding celebration. Desdemona is glimpsed wearing a red slip—the scarlet woman!—when Othello imagines her in bed with Cassio. After the first half of the temptation scene, we cut to Iago fastening Othello's cravat, which is yellow—the color of jealousy. Desdemona wears a yellow velvet coat in the Venice scenes, signaling that Othello will eventually see her through jaundiced eyes, and she wears a black-and-white brocaded dress with bright yellow sleeves when she defends Cassio on Cyprus. Masquerading as the homespun soldier, Iago stands out in his brown leather tunic and trousers, contrasting with Roderigo's costlier black clothes and jewelry. The only variation in the ensign's costume is a blue lieutenant's sash, which Iago dons instead of Cassio after his pact with Othello. Whereas Olivier's Moor initially wears a white tunic and switches to a black one, complemented by a black and yellow cloak, for the temptation scene, Fishburne's Othello starts in black but switches to a cream burnoose when he is with Iago on the shore, as does Welles's Othello. For the act of murder itself, Fishburne is appropriately dressed all in black.

The play's minor characters are carefully conceived. The most unusual and illuminating character portrayal is that of the gull Roderigo, usually depicted as a fairly weak and harmless dupe. In this production, Michael Maloney's Roderigo is a walking time bomb, a desperately unstable man continually on the verge of detonating. Branagh's Iago has to work hard to turn Roderigo's shuddering hysteria into hope and then manic joy after the brawl. By the end of Act 4, though, this worm almost turns. He shocks his mentor by savagely pointing his sword at Iago's eye to demand satisfaction until Iago somehow manages to rechannel Roderigo's craving for violent resolution into the plan to kill Cassio. In contrast, Nathaniel Parker plays Cassio as an easygoing, fairly shallow man-about-town. More the lover than the experienced soldier, he suddenly matures in the final scene and, thanks to skillful makeup, looks much older. Anna Patrick, who presents Emilia as a sadly embittered wife, proves that a low-key performance can work well for this character. Whereas most actresses use full lung power for Emilia's dressing-down of Othello—in Burge's version, Joyce Redman is hoarse from shouting in the final scene—Patrick remains quietly intense. She is stunned by Iago's treachery, even though she has no illusions about his merits as a husband; earlier, her Emilia stares reproachfully at Iago (who is standing just outside the chamber door) to deliver a clear-eyed verdict on husbands who "eat us hungrily" and then "belch us."

Some of the ambiguities in Desdemona's behavior that have troubled feminist critics—her self-abnegation and possible complicity with Othello's violence toward the end—are flattened in this production. Partly because her erotic appeal is highlighted in the added scene showing the consummation of her marriage, partly because of her attractively sensual features, Irene Jacob's Desdemona is far from embodying the image of chaste saintliness that Suzanne Cloutier projects in Welles's movie. Lines that suggest extreme passivity, or superhuman altruism, such as "his scorn I approve" in the willow song and Desdemona's dying words, "Nobody—I myself. Farewell. / Commend me to my kind lord," are all cut. And Jacob's Desdemona dies fiercely trying to push off her attacker, not drowning under a sheet. On the other hand, since most of her lines urging Othello to reinstate Cassio are edited out and the brothel scene is played more for pathos than as an angry confrontation between two individuals, her active challenge to her husband is muted. Above all, she projects a strong visual image of frankness and integrity. Although Jacob's Swiss-accented English is initially a distraction—one critic comments that it tends to make Desdemona "more of an outsider"[148] or foreigner than Othello—she delivers her much trimmed lines with freshness and conviction.

There are no such distractions in listening to Branagh's Iago. Branagh handles Shakespeare's blank verse with a suppleness and colloquial vigor that makes its meaning crystal clear to the audience, and he is versatile enough to do justice to the many dimensions of the villain. His tight-lipped "I am not what I am," emphasized in close-up, gains particular resonance because his Iago is so consummate a chameleon. It is fascinating to watch Branagh's villain in the act of switching faces. When Roderigo disturbs his cool reverie at the end of the Venetian Senate scene, Iago transforms into the reassuring, avuncular friend, tenderly chiding Roderigo as a "silly gentleman," graciously seeming to decline his offer of a purse, and warmly clasping his hand to encourage him. Once Iago is alone again, his features set hard in icy contempt, and the pace slows noticeably as he confides, in clipped tones, "I hate the Moor." He continues to reveal this face of diabolical evil whenever he delivers his soliloquies to the camera/audience, while concealing it flawlessly in public. During his voice-over aside, "O, you are well tuned now!", when he watches Othello kissing Desdemona on Cyprus, he is smiling cherubically. With Cassio before and after the drinking scene, he maintains the easy bonhomie of a fellow soldier, belied only by the cold face we glimpse over Cassio's shoulder when they embrace. To Othello Iago is the respectful but sincere subordinate, hesitant to hurt him or to implicate his "worthy friend" Cassio, pacing nervously as he seems to shy away from the topic of infidelity in the temptation scene. In his solicitousness, he appears less the accomplished matador toying with a bull than a leech stealthily sucking out Othello's lifeblood under the guise of helping him. Only at the play's finale, after the Moor wounds him deeply, does he reveal his true malice with the sneering insolence of "I bleed sir, but not killed." He is much colder with Emilia, even sexually brutal, when, turned on by the prospect of acquiring the handkerchief, he slides on top of her and then abruptly withdraws to rejoice at how "trifles, light as air" may destroy Othello's equanimity.

Given this edge of brutality, his sudden bursts of violence are not out of character. Still, it is shocking to see him suddenly rush over to stab Montano from behind under cover of the riot; it foreshadows his stabbing Emilia in the back in the final scene. When he murders Roderigo, he raises up the injured man with a show of tender commiseration, even stroking Roderigo's cheek, but then plunges a dagger into his guts and turns it repeatedly, covering his victim's mouth to silence any squealing.

Yet for all his calculated malice, Branagh's Iago displays a less confident side. He is wide-eyed and breathing hard as he discloses his plan to question Cassio in the castle vaults while Othello looks on, dizzy with his own brinkmanship when he realizes that as soon as Othello sees Cassio "smile," he "shall go mad." He is also strangely unnerved by Roderigo at the end, for when the dying man on the operat-

ing table slowly opens his eyes and reaches out a hand to his betrayer, Iago frantically tries to escape from the room. Is there, then, some emotional vulnerability in
this Iago, despite his depth of evil? Most telling is his reaction to the blood pact
with Othello. He delivers the line "I am your own forever" in a voice strangled
with emotion, and this time, the face the camera catches over Othello's shoulder as
they share a long embrace is contorted with tears. Obviously, Branagh's Iago is im-
mensely relieved at the success of his plan, but he also seems, drawing on a homosexual subtext for the character, to have surprised himself with strength of
feeling for his master. The closeness appears to be reciprocal. As they kneel facing
each other after the final showdown in Act 5, their eyes remain locked; and when
Iago vows he will never speak again, Othello reassures his ensign, in a line often
addressed to Gratiano, "Well, thou dost best."

Branagh's Iago needs to be much more than what Leavis terms a necessary "dramatic mechanism,"[149] since Laurence Fishburne plays Othello without any obvious
character flaw. This Moor is a noble, handsome warrior who sports a pearl earring,
confident of his worth but neither egotistical nor self-dramatizing. His charismatic
presence makes him the center of attention. In the armed confrontation with Brabantio, he takes command, raising his sword to the older man's throat in warning,
just as he does with Emilia in the final scene. His suddenly slapping Cassio across
the face to make him an "example" in the drunken brawl lessens the shock of his
striking Desdemona in the embassy scene, for this, too, can be seen as an instance
of Othello's military discipline. Fishburne's Othello never flaunts his race, as
Olivier's does, nor does he seem embarrassed by it. Because he is relatively close
to Desdemona in age, not "declined Into the vale of years," both this line and
"Haply for I am black" are cut from his "Why did I marry?" speech. The director's
decision to capture a long kiss between Othello and Desdemona in the flashback
wooing sequence, as well as his screening of the consummation and Othello's jealous imaginings, might suggest the stereotype of a voluptuous black man, and Fishburne's Othello, as critics have noted, "looks every inch the warrior sex symbol."[150]
Yet he is no "old black ram" lasciviously pawing his white ewe.

In fact, this Othello is consistently low-key. Laurence Fishburne had made his
name, not as a Shakespearean actor, but in commercial movies (*Boyz N the Hood*
and *What's Love Got to Do with It*), and he gears his performance to the silver
screen. Incited by Branagh's nervously edgy Iago, he internalizes Othello's emotions, projecting sadness and brooding menace rather than the "enormously big"[151]
rage of Olivier. His deep, mellifluous voice barely rises in the scene where he
strikes Desdemona, and in the second part of the temptation scene, his acting becomes two-dimensional rather than admirably restrained. What remains of the
trimmed-down farewell to war speech is delivered matter-of-factly, and he shows
little more passion in asking for "ocular proof" than a businessman checking with
his broker on how far stock prices have fallen. When he shouts, his voice is a
hoarse monotone; we miss Olivier's startling vocal inflections here. As the action
progresses, this Othello acts more in sorrow than in anger. He begins to weep in
the brothel scene, and both before and after the murder, his tears flow freely, al-

though the warrior in Othello flashes out once more when he jostles aside the Venetians, glaring at them to insist, "I have done the state some service" and when he stoically commits suicide by stabbing himself in the stomach with the dagger Cassio has secretly slipped him.

Fishburne's performance, in which gentleness and regret override violence, emphasizes the "pity" of it—the destruction of an extraordinary union of opposites (black warrior and white lady) and the tragic waste of their untimely deaths. As with Othello's excessively graphic fantasies of betrayal, the movie becomes overblown when it pushes this pity to the point of sentimentality. The musical score, composed by Charlie Mole, successfully builds dramatic tension; occasionally, though, a strings and woodwind arrangement rises under a speech in such a way as to artifically foreground the moment and detract from the poetic impact of the words themselves. Thus, when Desdemona is assuring Iago that she would never "trespass" against her lord, the music swells into what is later isolated as the "willow song" theme. The effect, providing easy pathos, is slightly soap opera-ish. And the presentation of Othello's "Had it pleased heaven" speech as voice-over counterpointed by romantic violin and harp diminishes the dynamics of his stormy confrontation with his wife. Why should Desdemona not hear this Job-like cry from Othello's heart? Instead, to fill the gap of apparent silence, she must preoccupy herself with caressing her husband's face.

These Hollywood moments of milking emotion aside, Parker's film adaptation of *Othello* captures the excitement of the play through its strong pacing and its creative, symbolic images. Current audiences attuned to underpowered movie techniques are likely to prefer the emotional restraint of Fishburne's authentic black Moor to the flamboyant theatrics of Olivier's stage-based performance. In a strong cast, Branagh's mutifaceted, searching presentation of Iago stands out, as is appropriate in an interpretation of the play that foregrounds the hero as a noble character who can be brought down only by an artist of evil. On one level, Othello does reveal insecurity; his graphic fantasies of sexual betrayal suggest what Freudian critics of the play have argued: that he is unnerved by female sexuality and quick to demonize his wife. Yet it takes a skillful Iago to activate this vulnerability, so that the main impression we draw from this film is that Othello and Desdemona have become victims of a creature who combines mundane nastiness with devilish cunning. While the final shot of burial at sea crystallizes the tragic waste of two vibrant lives, the immediately preceding shot emphasizes the indestructibility of evil. Having crawled onto the bed to join the trio of bodies in the carnage he has orchestrated, Iago stares insolently into the camera, defying the audience to pierce the mystery of his malice.

OTHELLO ON TELEVISION

Televising Shakespeare's plays poses a different set of challenges from putting them on the big screen. In the intimate medium of television, everything is scaled down and compressed. Producers usually opt for studio sets rather than real locations, and (of necessity) they favor mid- and close shots over the panoramic breadth and depth of shot, or zooming in for extreme close-up, afforded by movie cameras. What is lost in spatial freedom and quick intercutting among locales is, however, compensated for by TV's focus on the naturalistic details of performance. It is also the case that televised Shakespeare carefully emphasizes the actors' words, the nuances of language in a text that remains relatively uncut. The tyranny of the visual persists, of course; but since, as Peter Hall observes, Shakespeare's drama relies heavily on the "associative and metaphysical power of words," his plays turn out to be in some ways "uncinematic,"[152] and usually productions designed for "the box" do greater justice to the subtlety and complexity of the verse than full-scale films are able to do.

Jonathan Miller's BBC/Time Life Production (1981)

It is true that tailoring Shakespeare to the constraints of the TV screen has sometimes deadened rather than released the plays' creative power; Jack J. Jorgens, reviewing the first six plays of the BBC/Time Life series, complains about "nervous, ill-defined images" and "sloppy editing and compositions" instead of the "fine image-and sound making" of "good films."[153] Jonathan Miller's *Othello,* made for the British Broadcasting Corporation in 1981 as part of the Shakespeare Plays series, did not escape some of the problems that dogged that entire series. Committed to televising all of Shakespeare's dramatic works with financial backing from Time Life, the BBC initially settled for producing the plays in a fairly traditional, "stylistically safe"[154] way. But the adventurous Miller, who wanted to use the medium creatively to shake up orthodox interpretations of Shakespeare, went out on a limb with *Othello.* He claimed that Othello's blackness was not at the heart of the play—that *Othello* was "about jealousy" and not about color[155]—and chose as his Moor Anthony Hopkins, a Caucasian actor whose white skin barely changes for the role.

Miller, though, may partly have been making a virtue of necessity. At the start of the series (1979), the heads of BBC Drama wanted James Earl Jones, a black actor experienced in the role, to play Othello. But because the British actors' union, Equity, was adamant about using only its own actors in the series, Jones was never hired.[156] Not only does Miller rob the play of its racial tension by choosing the minimally darkened Hopkins for the role—more than one student watching the BBC version and not paying close attention to the words has come away thinking the hero is white—but Miller's choice of this actor also refines out of existence the soldierly dimension of the role. To put it bluntly, Hopkins lacks the warrior's physique. An actor need not be especially tall and physically imposing to play Othello well; one of the best, Edmund Kean, was below average height. But Miller accentuates Hopkins's unathletic stature by giving him an absurd costume on Cyprus: a ruff framing his head seems to enlarge it while emphasizing his narrow shoulders; tights with inward-pointing silver stripes make him look knock-kneed; and an exaggerated codpiece in the murder scene turns him into a parody of the frustrated husband.

Miller's idiosyncrasy, his deliberate casting against the grain of the play, also emerges in his choice of actors for some of the minor characters. Why, when Othello commends Montano for the "gravity and stillness" of his "youth," should he be played as a white-haired man well past his prime? The BBC's Gratiano—presumably close in age to his brother, Brabantio—turns out to be much more youthful in appearance than either Desdemona's father or the gray-bearded Lodovico. And although Penelope Wilton is a commanding actress who produces a sensitive Desdemona, she looks much too matronly and sensible for the role; she might be part of a couple entering early middle age, not a passionate young woman in love with a significantly older man.[157]

Static camera work during the opening and closing scenes is one of the weaker points of this production. Since Miller wanted to capture the detail and tones of Renaissance painting through his set and costumes,[158] Othello stands immobile at the Duke's table, framed by back-lit red and gold hangings. Instead of the three-camera format that affords quick shifts in perspective and reaction shots, for the most part a single camera holds steady on Othello,[159] who irritatingly cuts up the blank verse rhythms of his defense to the Senators into short phrases, all ending in rising inflections. At the end of the play, Othello's death is also filmed in one shot as part of a carefully composed group picture: in the background, Iago is being restrained by Montano and Gratiano while Cassio peers out from behind Lodovico. Othello claims to "die upon a kiss," but we never see it. He simply slips out of the frame while the camera closes in on the shocked expression of Cassio before he is helped off down the hallway. The object that "poisons sight"—the bed with the corpses of the lovers embracing—remains totally "hid."[160]

In general, however, the production's choreography becomes less torpid in the Cyprus scenes. Miller heightens the sense of *Othello* as closet drama by situating most of it "within doors," in a set closely modeled on a palace in Urbino. Instead of simulating an open-air harbor, Act 2 begins in sterile white corridors where Iago conducts his jests tête-à-tête with Desdemona, while she glances from time to time at the storm outside the window. The world outside is also heard but not seen during Othello's farewell to war speech, when the sound of horses' hooves echoes in the street below the window. The drunken brawl is crammed into a smallish room, and the street scene (5. 1)—one of the few using a stylized, moonlit exterior—is confined to a narrow colonnade out of which Roderigo and Cassio confusingly duck into dark alleyways. More successful is the fluid movement of characters along the interconnecting hallways and then through huge wooden doors when one sequence ends and the next begins. This depth of shot, as characters confined within these interiors move forward or retreat, is used to advantage in the eavesdropping sequence (4. 1). Othello peers around a door to where Cassio and Iago sit at a distance in one of the window alcoves. Since they are almost out of earshot, the audience, along with Othello, catches only scraps of the dialogue: "customer" and "marry" are two key words that emerge from the laughter. When he advises Othello to "strangle" Desdemona, Iago pushes his master back through doors that lead into his private chambers so that he can point to the marriage bed itself. The most gripping depth of shot comes in the final scene when Emilia races down the hall away from Othello, crying out, "Murder!" Her tiny figure suddenly stops short at the end, frozen in disbelief, as soon as she registers Othello's "Thy husband knew it all"; then she slowly turns around, retracing her steps to question him further.

To give adequate texture to shots within these otherwise chilly Renaissance interiors, Miller uses rich lighting effects. The first close-up of Desdemona in the Senate scene captures her face rosily lit from the side, lending a warmth to her character that might otherwise be muted by her ornate black-and-white costume. (In this production, even the strawberry-covered handkerchief, like the checkered floor of the Cyprus castle, remains black and white.) The same warm lighting, contrasting with the "metallic silver"[161] light that often surrounds Iago, is employed for the wedding banquet that opens Act 2; it complements Othello's convivial mood as he amuses the company with conjuring tricks before leading Desdemona off to bed. In the same scene, Iago, remaining at table to plot Cassio's drunkenness, signals his attraction to danger by brushing his hand over a candle flame. Desdemona's drained face is framed behind a cluster of candles at the evening meal the following day; afterward, in the softly lit willow scene, she sits at her dressing table gazing wanly at a lighted candle behind which is propped a skull, a traditional Renaissance emblem for meditating on death. After the murder, when Othello moves out of the glow of the bedchamber into the darker vestibule to let in Emilia, we watch, in long shot, Emilia's discovery of the dying Desdemona reflected in the vestibule mirror while Othello stands to one side.

This is another of Miller's carefully lit, studiously composed perspectives. In most of the Cyprus scenes, however, dynamic interaction among characters is not sacrificed to static visual beauty. The director's preference for capturing key moments on one camera, which makes for some tedium in the Senate scene and in Othello's closing speech, is far from "deadly"[162] in the central temptation sequence. By tracking Iago and Othello with a single camera instead of intercutting between them, Miller conveys the closeness of personae who often function not in isolation, but as facets of the same psyche. We view them as we would do onstage, but with the added benefit of closer angles and microphones that pick up every nuance of sound—Othello's groans and gasps as Iago loudly justifies his "proof." After Othello tries to throttle Iago at "Death and damnation!", they remain locked together; Iago then holds his general around the neck and chest in a viselike grip to seal their joint vow of vengeance.[163]

For two of the secondary characters, Miller's habit of going out on a limb also proves illuminating rather than merely quirky. David Yelland's Cassio is by no means as subtly nuanced as Jacobi's portrayal of the lieutenant, but he emanates a tight-lipped reserve and a carefulness about appearances that perfectly match his austere Puritan costume and what Lynda E. Boose calls the "Dutch Calvinism" of the cool interiors on Cyprus.[164] Even his effusions on Desdemona are restrained, and he politely backs away from Iago's coarse insinuations about her at the beginning of Act 2, scene 3. All this throws into relief his sudden burst of anger, a frightening loss of control, when he shrieks that the ensign Iago is not to be "saved" before him. Bianca is similarly repressed when she first appears on the stage. Rather than flouncing in and aggressively challenging Cassio in Act 3, scene 4 (as most Biancas do), she is subdued, deeply pained that he has been ignoring her. The hurt she has held in then spills over into unbalanced hysteria, a loss of control intensified when, discovering that her lover has been wounded, she weeps forlornly (5. 1).

This mounting tension, as strong emotions swell and then smash through the individual's public facade, affects the major as well as the minor characters. An increasingly edgy Emilia, played superbly by Rosemary Leach, switches in the final scene from horrified incredulity ("My husband?") to outrage, flailing at Iago with her fists to denounce his "villainy." Her pent-up feelings—disgust at Iago and Othello, anguished grief over Desdemona's death—are fully unleashed when she sobbingly defends her mistress as the "sweetest innocent" and insists "I *will* speak." Penelope Wilton's Desdemona, in particular, becomes a study in nerves tightly strung to the breaking point. While she obviously adores her husband, her indignation at his unfair accusations flashes out in "No, as I am a Christian!" (when Othello asks if she is a whore) and in her angrily insistent "I never gave him token," when he accuses her of giving the handkerchief to Cassio. But her most impressive moments come in Act 4 when Othello publicly strikes her—shockingly choreographed as a hard blow to her face, on which the red marks of violence remain clearly visible afterward—and she falls forward, convulsed with sobs. To add to her humiliation, this "obedient" wife feels compelled to return, still bowed down and clutching her face, as soon as Othello summons her back. She weeps uncontrollably when he spins her around like a puppet to demonstrate to Lodovico how she can "turn" and "turn again," and we hear renewed sounds of her anguish even after she has left the stage. Following Othello's accusations in the brothel scene (4. 2), she is utterly stunned, almost catatonic; all the more poignant, then, is the moment when, believing she is beyond tears ("I cannot weep"), she finds that she must again struggle to subdue them once Iago arrives to comfort her. And when Iago questions why Othello would call his wife "whore," the emotional floodgates open again and she sobs brokenly, "I do not know." Unlike the commercial films of the play, this televised *Othello* has no musical score to enhance the emotional tempo. Instead, sudden outbursts of wordless grief or hysteria—Desdemona's desolate sobbing, Othello's throaty snarls, Iago's tittering that builds to a final crescendo of laughter—work with the intimacy of the medium to underscore each violent release of tension.

Othello himself is portrayed as an individual whose carefully controlled demeanor at the opening of the play masks hidden depths of "chaos and horror"[165] that Iago activates. Not a swaggerer like Olivier's rose-sniffing, arrogant Moor, Hopkins's Othello nevertheless is fully self-possessed as he casually adjusts Iago's collar (1. 2) and unruffled to the point of becoming monotonous in the Senate scene. Because Miller aimed to portray the "very ordinariness"[166] and fallibility of Othello, Hopkins's reading of the role stays close to Leavis's unromantic conclusion that Othello is undermined by deep character flaws. Close-up camera angles capture the realistic course of his degeneration in almost embarrassing detail. His fit is a genuine convulsion, preceded by shaking and choking as Othello's eyes dilate and his tongue and jaw become locked in paralysis. In front of the Venetian embassy, his loss of control is terrifying; he growls and snarls as he strikes Desdemona and spits after the deadly serious "Goats and monkeys!" Similarly, he hawks out his disgust in the final scene when he insists that Cassio has "us'd" Desdemona.

Since this Othello's opening scenes are so low-key, it is fascinating to watch him build to climaxes of "energy and rage."[167] Often these arrive where the viewer least expects them, as if Hopkins, who later became an Oscar winner in his own right, wanted to escape the long shadow cast by Olivier's Moor. Hopkins's spirited victory jig to celebrate "the Turks are drowned" works well as an impromptu release of emotional tension after his breathless reunion with Desdemona. He is tetchy rather than deeply "moved" in the first half of the temptation scene; his first real lapse in temper comes, surprisingly, with the snarled "Let it alone" when Desdemona tries to comfort him with the handkerchief. Instead of presenting the farewell to war speech, in Olivier's vein, as a strongly pointed aria of grief, he turns it into a gentle moment of self-discovery. It is the effort to bridge incompatible views of Desdemona that truly unnerves him; he saves his explosion of rage for "By the world, / I think my wife be honest, and think she is not; / I think that thou art just, and think thou art not." Like Olivier, he conveys "the pity of it" in a high-pitched sob, but he also conducts most of the brothel scene in tears, weeping through his "Had it pleased heaven" speech. Vocally, Hopkins's Moor has considerable range, so that a sensitive but strongly passionate rendering of the verse counterpoints what J. C. Bulman calls the "domestic, intimate style."[168] But once we have heard as well as seen this Othello's breakdown in such painful, minute detail, it is difficult for him to salvage much tragic dignity.

If the television medium, and the BBC production in particular, tends to diminish Othello, it favors Bob Hoskins's gangsterish and at times diabolical Iago; he expands to fill the vacuum. His soliloquies are private chats with the audience, delivered in a Cockney accent that perfectly suits Iago's earthiness and street smarts. Like all the other Iagos on film apart from MacLiammóir's epicene ensign, Hoskins gives some weight to this character's sexual paranoia; no giggle accompanies his confiding to the audience his suspicion about Emilia's infidelity. Yet his resolve to be "evened" with Othello "wife for wife" lacks the venom of Finlay's suspicious husband or Branagh's icily malicious Iago, since this villain has a broader compulsion to undermine any moral beauty that threatens his own twisted, brutish view of the world. From the start, an unbalanced edge to his malicious laughter reflects his mad urge to destroy whatever opposes him. Even in an early exchange with Roderigo, he giggles conspiratorially before baring his teeth at "I am not what I am." Miller was fascinated by the psychotic nature of "the practical joker,"[169] and this Iago enjoys playing gratuitous pranks on people: under cover of darkness in the opening scene, he flicks water at Roderigo and Brabantio; and in Act 2, scene 3, he mimics Cassio's pompous, drunken gait as he leaves the party, dogging the footsteps of the lieutenant like an impish shadow. His eyes gleam at the "sport" that Roderigo can afford him, and he guffaws heartily at the prospect of the gull selling all his "land." He is even more overcome with laughter near the end of Act 2, scene 3 when he contemplates the "madness" he will inflict on Othello and the way he will "enmesh them all"; only the reappearance of Roderigo sobers him up. The audience hears a sinister echo of his muted laughter in the dark street scene of Act 5, and when Iago is dragged back to face Othello in the finale, he is softly tittering. The last sound that we hear, after he has been led off, is his crescendo of manic laughter.

This Iago's convincing mask of decency in public makes the jokey nastiness that bubbles up beneath it all the more disturbing. Rather than trading on a blunt military persona, he engages people's trust by appearing to be warmly concerned about them. Even Desdemona turns instinctively to him, confiding to Iago alone that she is "not merry" as she awaits her lord's arrival at Cyprus and reaching out to him for physical comfort after Othello has insulted her in the brothel scene. He sounds utterly plausible when he earnestly assures Desdemona that affairs of state are unsettling her husband, or when he feigns reluctance to reveal Cassio's drunkenness (2. 3) and later to tell Othello about Cassio's "dream." When, without prompting, he walks across to offer Othello the quiet advice "O, beware, my lord, of jealousy!" he seems intuitively to gauge and sympathize with Othello's innermost thoughts.

Hoskins's Iago is certainly the strongest part of the BBC production; he is a study in simmering psychosis that feeds off the tensions in the oppressive castle-fortress, where long hallways and alcoves become an "awful prison"[170] for all the characters. Hopkins's Othello, too, offers an intense portrait of the psychology of jealousy—the inner "chaos" of competing emotions once his stoic facade cracks. But Hopkins's unbecoming costume and unheroic appearance, relentlessly exposed in the close-up medium of television, fail to project him convincingly either as a warrior or as a black outsider. Jonathan Miller's production for the BBC sacrifices the specifics of Othello's situation, as Shakespeare presents them in the text, to the universal or "representative"[171] appeal of a domestic study of malice and jealousy.

Trevor Nunn's RSC Production (1990)

On the upper level of the studio set stand gray, shuttered windows; below them a narrow colonnade surrounds a bare, dusty arena. Trevor Nunn had chosen a minimalist stage in a converted tin shed—not the Shakespeare Memorial Theatre but an intimate theater, The Other Place—for his 1989 stage production of *Othello*. Such a closely confined space, where props and carefully chosen details establish Othello's tightly knit military world, translates well to the TV studio and screen. There is nothing metaphysical about this naturalistically conceived *Othello*.[172] Nunn's production is thoroughly modern and postfeminist in brilliantly suggesting how evil can flourish within a structured military community—a world in which genuine intimacy between the sexes, assayed in Othello's brief marriage to Desdemona, more often than not is displaced by male camaraderie.

The virtue of this spare, unlocalized set, as H. R. Coursen points out, is that it can accommodate so much.[173] An opening street scene in Venice below Brabantio's window is followed by the "lamplit council chamber" of Venice, where the Duke's table is set with brandy glasses and a decanter. With a few fresh props, the same set serves for various locales in Cyprus—a "quayside dominated by a giant, brass telescope," a "sun-drenched courtyard," and a "midnight city square."[174] In the eavesdropping sequence (4. 1), Othello looks through the slats on the upper level; he can see but not fully hear the conversation between Iago and Cassio. The "claustrophobic intimacy"[175] of the set comes most fully into its own for the barracks scene in Act 2, where a couple of camp beds covered with gray army blankets conjure up the life of "hardness" for which Othello feels such kinship.

For this *Othello,* we have moved out of the Renaissance period. Nunn situates the play in a nineteenth-century army milieu, so that Iago is clad in a dark uniform and military cap while Othello sports a waistcoat underneath an epauletted jacket adorned with brass buttons. Several critics identify the production's period with that of the American Civil War—raising the question of how exactly a black general would fit into that context[176]—but the milieu could just as easily be the Franco-Prussian War or the Crimean conflict. Nunn's costuming sharply distinguishes the disciplined army men, dressed in dark uniforms and white shirts, from the civilians and women in their pale summer apparel. Before he joins the army under Iago's tutelage, Michael Grandage's Roderigo is a spineless but moneyed Victorian gentleman, sporting a straw fedora and bow tie. After Cassio's cashiering, it is a visual shock to see him, too, appear in a straw fedora and natty cream-colored suit; one of the rank and file, taking over a few of the Clown's lines, mocks the lieutenant's demotion by pointedly addressing him as "sir."

Nunn's Venetian army strictly enforces protocol—saluting, standing to attention, responding to the bugle calls in the background. At the top of the hierarchy, Willard White's Othello commands "like a full soldier"; the vision of housewives making a skillet of his helmet is so ludicrous that everyone laughs when he conjures it up in the Senate scene. It is because the brawl on Cyprus is such a flagrant breach of discipline that it provokes the general into sternly making an "example" out of Cassio. For his part, Sean Baker's dandyish lieutenant Cassio is keenly aware of being a cut above the noncommissioned officers and regular soldiers. During the barracks revelry, Cassio flares into snobbish anger ("I hold him to be unworthy of his place that does those things") when Iago tries to include him in the debagging ritual inspired by the song about King Stephen's breeches. He then insults Iago by loudly insisting on rank: "The lieutenant is to be saved before the ancient." Cassio's snobbishness also extends to women. Although Othello's blackness—in nineteenth-century terms, his racial inferiority and association with slavery—is seemingly effaced by his rank, Nunn's choice of the black actress Marsha Hunt to play Bianca underlines how Cassio publicly sanctifies the upper-class white Desdemona while deriding and exploiting the lower-class black "whore."

Yet even this privileging of the white aristocratic woman becomes tenuous within the all-male world of the barracks. There is a hint that military camaraderie, which tends to exclude and demean women indiscriminately, overrides even Cassio's chivalric loyalty to Desdemona. For not only does Cassio jest about Bianca with "matey coarseness"[177] in Act 4, scene 1, physically acting out Bianca's unwelcome "lolling" about his neck as he fondles Iago in a way that embarrasses even the ensign, but, unlike Jacobi's Cassio in Burge's production or David Yelland in the BBC one, he also fails to distance himself from Iago's salacious description of Desdemona's eye as a "parley to provocation" (2. 3. 22–23). The two soldiers are conversing while lying on their camp beds in the barracks, and although Cassio adds that Desdemona's eye is "right modest," both men appear to be fantasizing about Desdemona in much the same way.

But it is Iago more than Cassio who is disturbed by the breach of military rank that has made the "general's wife . . . the general"; it is an affront to his sense of army decorum. Throughout the action, he is the main promoter of male solidarity. During the storm, he administers strong drink from his hip flask and proffers cigars he has filched from the Senate chamber. When Cassio describes himself as "past all surgery" after the brawl, Iago worriedly checks the lieutenant's torso and head for wounds. He is more uninhibitedly sensual with Roderigo, stroking and occasionally massaging his shoulders, ruffling his hair at the quayside, and tenderly bandaging his head after the beating. Only to Othello does he remain respectfully distant. When Othello puts out his hand to congratulate Iago on becoming his new lieutenant, a deeply moved Iago clasps the hand and then, surprisingly, kisses the one that Othello places on top of Iago's. He remains reverential when Othello briefly weeps on his shoulder after the eavesdropping scene. Whereas he has no such reservations with a woman—when Desdemona breaks down in his arms, he sensuously caresses her hair and neck—this villain must nerve himself to stroke his general's head. Yet he establishes himself as Othello's misogynistic inner voice and white shadow (McKellen's Iago is tall, about the same height as Willard White's Othello) when he sits at Othello's side, his snake eyes never leaving his master's face, to interpret Desdemona in the worst possible light. As Virginia Mason Vaughan comments, the "male bonding" in this military world is "more intense" than any bond between man and woman can be.[178]

At the play's opening, Desdemona seems to be escaping from another insidious feature of the patriarchal society—a claustrophobic father-daughter relationship. Clive Swift, playing a very Victorian father, is the most shaken and distraught of the Brabantios in the filmed versions; he shouts at and threatens Othello, weeps as he contemplates the loss of his daughter. For her part, Imogen Stubbs's intense, instinctive Desdemona seems more drawn toward her father than do any of the other Desdemonas, for she embraces him before her explanation of "divided duty," caresses his arm after he has ruefully abandoned her to Othello, and rushes around the Duke's table to try to reach Brabantio before his broken exit. In another acute detail that might go unnoticed, Desdemona keeps a daguerreotype of her father on her dressing table in Cyprus. Brabantio's brother, Gratiano, is also played by Clive Swift, a doubling that effectively carries the likeness of the heartbroken father, still with claims on his daughter, from the opening into the closing scene.

Desdemona makes her choice, a painful but clear one, in the Senate scene. At first she is spunky, even tomboyish, in her youthful excitement at the prospect of military adventure; she leaps forward, her eyes shining in anticipation when she hears that she and Othello are to leave for Cyprus "tonight," and she joins in Iago's impromptu entertainment at the quayside with unladylike zest. Yet the world of the barracks on Cyprus is not one that welcomes her. Desdemona is shown in long shot curiously testing one of the army mattresses for hardness; her own bed, revealed with its unadorned iron railing in Act 5, looks scarcely less inviting. In the reunion scene on Cyprus, where Desdemona yearns to embrace Othello immediately, he puts her on a pedestal (a luggage box serving as "Olympus high") and circles her, the camera panning around with him, in adoration. In a heartrending echo shot, during the brothel scene, Othello again sets Desdemona high on a chair, but now in order to pillory her as a "commoner." As we spin around sharing his viewpoint, the strong contrast between Desdemona's earlier ecstatic expression and her present incredulous, tearstained face marks how quickly the madonna/whore dichotomy has undermined their union. That she is ultimately "subdued" to the "utmost pleasure" of her lord is signaled in the murder scene when, after desperately trying to escape from the locked room, she takes Othello's outstretched hand as if mesmerized—a "terrible moment"[179] that suggests cooperation between the patriarchal executioner and his victim.

Emilia, played with quiet distinction by Zoe Wannamaker, furnishes a powerful parallel to Desdemona's marital distress.[180] In contrast to the Iagos of Macliammóir and Finlay, McKellen's villain is not envisaged as impotent, for we see occasional moments of sensuality and even affection (though never true tenderness) between this husband and his wife. Yet Iago's sexual current has been diverted into gnawing jealousy; he reacts warily whenever Cassio touches Emilia. Aroused by the passionate reunion of Othello and Desdemona, Iago surprises Emilia by sweeping her into a sudden clinch, but he dismisses her perfunctorily at the end of that scene. After acquiring the handkerchief, he roughly pulls her onto his knee to reward her with a long kiss but then brushes her aside, coldly reaching for his pipe instead.

Wannamaker's Emilia is obviously baffled and hurt by her husband's unpredictable behavior. Yet to please his "fantasy" and prevent his nagging her (Emilia's "Do not you *chide*" is heartfelt), she trusts him with Desdemona's handkerchief. It is her guilt at having done this, along with some residual disapproval of Othello and Desdemona's mixed marriage, that delays a female bonding that might counterbalance the closeness between the males. As Othello explains to his wife the magical significance of the handkerchief, Emilia's face, framed in profile in the foreground, grows increasingly uneasy. Although the women giggle together over Lodovico, their intimacy is held in check at the beginning of the willow scene; Emilia coolly disengages herself from her mistress's parting hug and returns only when Desdemona begs her opinion on whether any women "do abuse their husbands" through sexual disloyalty. After Emilia's admission that she would do so if the reward were high enough, Desdemona runs to unlock her cabinet (the secret drawer to which a frantic Othello, at the beginning of Act 4, scene 2, could not find the key) to retrieve the box of candies that Cassio gave her earlier. Only after the women enjoy the sweets together, while discussing marital fidelity and "these men" in general, does Emilia embrace Desdemona with genuine warmth at "Good night, good night." This strengthening of their relationship paves the way for Emilia's defense of her mistress, and her fierce denunciation of both Othello and Iago, in the final scene. It is she who completes the strangled Desdemona's barely audible last words as she begs her mistress to "speak again"; and when she herself crawls, dying, onto the bed, the camera focuses on Emilia reaching for and grasping Desdemona's hand in sisterly solidarity.

This gesture, though, comes too late. Iago, the man's man, has unleashed in his master an explosive rage against women, a terrible distrust of the unknown territory of female behavior. White builds slowly in conveying the Moor's combustible jealousy, using his opera singer's velvety baritone voice—an "instrument of matchless power"[181]—to craft a realistic metamorphosis from self-contained soldier to husband brutally out of control. We perceive his potential for anger when he has to restrain himself from laying hands on Brabantio in the Senate chamber and in his controlled fury after the drunken brawl. As the performance progresses, White's calm tones break; his Othello sobs and sweats, his eyes narrowing in pain. His Achilles' heel is less his high opinion of himself than his ignorance about Venetian women. When Iago warns "observe her well with Cassio," Othello chuckles incredulously, but he is startled into attention by Iago's "I know our country disposition well." In this temptation scene, his slowly awakened passion is at first contained by his physical position—sitting at a desk signing papers—but then he drums his fists on the table and tears up and scatters the papers to counterpoint his farewell to war speech. Soon, Iago feels the full force of his master's bearish rage; he has to ward off Othello with a chair when his master almost throttles him at "be sure thou prove my love a whore!" and dashes after Iago in another attempt to attack him.

Yet what is remarkable about White's performance is that it steers so clear of self-dramatization; it affords hardly any glimpses of Leavis's egotistical Moor. Instead of ranting when he vows vengeance, this Othello simply puffs his "fond love" to heaven and then buckles over in anguish. Although the turgid style of "Whip me, ye devils" and "roast me in sulphur!" cries out for a show of self-pity and histrionics (Olivier feasted on it), White avoids melodrama and delivers even these lines through subdued weeping. Despite wearing civilian dress—a white caftan edged with black—in the murder scene, this Othello continues to act as a dignified warrior. He combines tenderness ("It is the cause") with his ingrained soldier's habit of intimidating his opponents; he threatens to attack Gratiano during his "Behold, I have a weapon" speech but stops short after rushing to the unguarded door, recognizing that he cannot escape his "fate." His final speech is not an exercise in showmanship or self-aggrandizement, but a profound need to settle the score. The urgency of "Set you down this" matches the intensity of his defense of his actions in the Senate scene. Again, we are encouraged to perceive Othello as a stong, uncomplicated army man whose buried insecurities would never have surfaced so damagingly without the promptings of an Iago.

Ian McKellen's performance as Iago is so riveting that, although the camera does not privilege him above the other characters or insist that "the play belongs to Iago,"[182] it is difficult to watch anyone else when McKellen is anywhere on the screen. His reputation as "honest" seems based less on words than on acting the consummate military man. As Othello's subordinate, he is fanatically proper, clicking his heels to attention, keeping his back ramrod straight as he marches out with arms swinging, grooming his Hitleresque mustache to keep it spruce. Compulsively tidy, he turns down the end of the blanket before he lies on a camp bed with his boots on, stores his half-smoked cheroots in a tin in his breast pocket, and meticulously rinses out the washbasin after Cassio's drunken retching. When a seething Othello begins to tear and scatter documents (3. 3), Iago rushes around to pick up the mess. He is "constantly tending to people and things"[183] and is utterly reliable in a crisis—as when he gets up on his soapbox to entertain the troops who are anxiously waiting for Othello at the harbor or organizes help for the wounded Cassio in the street scene of Act 5. He talks briskly, with a pronounced northern accent that sets him apart from the standard British of those around him but lends an aura of homespun wisdom to everything he says. In this way, he elicits the trust and belief of Roderigo, Cassio, and, most damagingly, Othello.

Iago's soliloquies reveal how much emotional tension this deeply neurotic man must repress in order to maintain his hard-bitten military persona. He assures Roderigo, in a matter-of-fact manner, that he hates Othello; but it is when he is sitting alone, fingers knotting and unknotting, that he suddenly releases the full venom of his feelings in the spewed-up outcry "I h-aa-te the Moor!" He may be partly motivated by racial prejudice[184]—later the camera catches Emilia and Iago exchanging a disdainful glance when black Othello passionately kisses his white bride at the opening of Act 3, scene 3—but the main component of Iago's corrosive hatred is sexual envy and the paranoia it breeds. We perceive the "poisonous mineral" working most clearly in Iago's second soliloquy, where the camera closes in on his hangdog face and bitter eyes as he mutters, "For I fear Cassio with my nightcap too." He really believes he has been, or might be, cuckolded, as witnessed by his edgy response to Cassio kissing Emilia at the quayside and his eyes narrowed in suspicion as the two retreat to fetch Desdemona in Act 3, scene 1, Cassio's arm around Emilia's waist. Warning Othello about the ravages of jealousy ("Good God the souls of all my tribe defend / From jealousy!"), Iago speaks with a fervor that goes far beyond the mere acting of honesty. In a rare public revelation of his aversion to infidelity, he shrieks, as much to Emilia as Bianca, "This is the fruits of whoring" (5. 1. 116).

Although McKellen's Iago rarely shows such emotions to the outside world—in contrast to Hoskins in the BBC production, no manic laughter bubbles up inside him—the audience knows that this sinister character is "eaten up with passion." Operating on deep feeling and instinct rather than intellectual acuity, he is probably the least clever of the Iagos on film. His habit of pointing a finger at his temple and revolving it when he is plotting something indicates mental wheels that are not exceptionally well oiled ("'Tis here, but yet confused"). Methodically working

out his tactics at the end of Act 2, he suddenly realizes, with the force of a revelation—back stiffening, eyes widening as he gasps, "Ay, that's the way!"—how damaging it will be for Othello to find Cassio "soliciting his wife." Ironically, though,
he finds no fulfillment in the havoc he has wrought by the end of the play. The in-
solent stare of Branagh's Iago and the full release of manic laughter in Hoskins's
impish villain suggest at least some measure of triumph. But McKellen's villain
only steps forward at the end to stare blankly, his eyes coldly malevolent, at the trio
of bodies on the bed. As the lights go up on him, the ensign's tightly folded arms
and twisting fingers suggest that his neurotic tension is unassuaged; he still feels
deeply threatened by Othello and by his master's love for Desdemona. Like the tantalizing suggestiveness of Iago's intense "What you know, you know," directed to
the Moor, the "moral vacuum of the murderer surveying his victims"[185] and then
outstaring the audience heightens the mystery of how such consummate evil could
arise from utterly mundane beginnings.

This final scene crystallizes the sense of waste and stymied relationships that
stays in solution throughout Nunn's production. While Iago remains completely isolated, gaining no satisfaction from his villainy, Othello, it seems, finds a perverse
sexual fulfillment both in destroying Desdemona and in kissing her when she is
dead. Not only is the murder staged as a kind of erotic ritual (Othello crushes his
wife and then writhes on top of her)[186], but Othello remounts Desdemona to kiss her
when he is mortally wounded and spasms as he dies—a necrophiliac possession
that is the logical outcome of Othello's need to control the appetite of this "delicate"
creature. In the claustrophobic barracks community on Cyprus, the natural increase
of the married couple's "loves and comforts" is checked as military camaraderie,
traded on by Iago, widens the emotional gap between bridegroom and bride. As
Othello belatedly possesses his "alabaster" Desdemona, the Venetian men "gape"
on. It is appropriate that Lodovico's lines "The object poisons sight; / Let it be hid"
are cut, for the TV cameras linger on the couple embracing in death and over them
the poker face of the agent who has engineered this poisonous spectacle.

NOTES

1. G. B. Shaw, *Dramatic Opinions and Essays* (1907), vol. 2, p. 276, reprinted in
Leonard F. Dean (ed.), *A Casebook on* Othello (New York: Thomas Y. Crowell Co., 1961),
p. 125.

2. Kenneth Tynan, *A View of Our English Stage, 1944–63* (London: Davis-Poynter,
1975), describes Valk's performance as a "transfusion of bubbling hot blood into the invalid
frame of our drama" (p. 157).

3. Jackson's quote is from a letter in Latin, quoted in translation in Geoffrey Tillotson,
"*Othello* and *The Alchemist* at Oxford," *TLS*, July 20, 1933, p. 494.

4. Samuel Pepys, October 11, 1660, in Mynore Bright (ed.), *Diary and Correspondence of Samuel Pepys* (London: Bickers and Son, 1875), vol. 1, p. 198.

5. Cited in Arthur Colby Sprague, *Shakespeare and the Actors* (New York: Russell and
Russell, 1963), p. 199.

6. For a fuller discussion of the cuts in the playhouse text used by the Smock Alley Theatre in Dublin during the 1660s, see Gineo J. Matteo, *Shakespeare's* Othello: *The Study and the Stage, 1604–1904* (Salzburg: Institut für Sprache und Literatur, 1974), pp. 63–74; Marvin Rosenberg, *The Masks of* Othello (Berkeley and Los Angeles: University of California Press, 1961), pp. 20–27; and Julie Hankey (ed.), Othello: *Plays in Performance* (Bristol: Bristol Classical Press, 1987), pp. 25–26.

7. John Bernard, *Retrospections of the Stage* (London, 1830), vol. 1, pp. 28–29, cited in Hankey (ed.), Othello: *Plays in Performance, p.* 42.

8. Recounted in Edward T. Mason, *The Othello of Tommaso Salvini* (New York and London: G. P. Putnam and Sons, 1890), p. 95.

9. Discussed in John Russell Brown (ed.), *Shakespeare's* Othello: *The Harbrace Theatre Edition* (New York: Harcourt Brace Jovanovich, Inc., 1973), p. 50.

10. *Theatrical Journal,* February 19, 1868.

11. In Rosenberg, *The Masks of* Othello, pp. 94–95.

12. Ibid., p. 109.

13. See Daniel Seltzer, "Elizabethan Acting in *Othello,*" *SQ,* 10 (1959): 201–10, quote at 209–10.

14. Richard Steele, *Tatler,* 167 (May 2, 1710).

15. John Dryden, *An Essay of Dramatick Poesie,* ed. James T. Bolton (London: Oxford University Press, 1964), p. 61.

16. Sir Frederick Pollock (ed.), *Macready's Reminiscences* (New York: Harper and Brothers, 1875), p. 342.

17. *Examiner,* October 13, 1816, in William Hazlitt, *A View of the English Stage,* ed. W. Spencer Jackson (London: George Bell and Sons, 1906), pp. 258–59.

18. *Saturday Review of Politics,* 51 (February 5, 1881), 177.

19. Henry James, *The Scenic Art: Notes on Acting and the Drama, 1872–1901,* ed. Allan Wade (New Brunswick, N.J.: Rutgers University Press, 1948), p. 173.

20. Cited in Rosenberg, *The Masks of* Othello, p. 62.

21. In T. Ashe (ed.), *Table Talk,* April 27, 1823 (London: George Bell and Sons, 1905), p. 25.

22. In H. Buxton Forman (ed.), *The Poetical Works and Other Writings of John Keats* (New York: Phaeton Press, 1970), vol. 5, p. 230.

23. *Times,* February 21, 1817.

24. *Examiner,* October 4, 1818.

25. *Examiner,* January 7, 1816, in Hazlitt, *A View of the English Stage,* p. 150.

26. Norman Sanders (ed.), *Othello, New Cambridge Shakespeare* (Cambridge: Cambridge University Press, 1984), p. 46.

27. Martin L. Wine, Othello: *Text and Performance* (Basingstoke and London: Macmillan, 1984), p. 54.

28. Rosenberg, *The Masks of* Othello, p. 147.

29. Sanders (ed.), *Othello,* p. 47.

30. Horace Howard Furness (ed.), *A New Variorum Edition of Shakespeare: Othello* (1886; New York: Dover Publications, 1963), p. 396.

31. Frank A. Hedgcock, *A Cosmopolitan Actor: David Garrick and His French Friends* (London: Stanley Paul and Co., 1912), p. 341, n.1.

32. Samuel Taylor Coleridge, *Shakespearean Criticism,* ed. Thomas Middleton Raysor (London: Dent, 1960), vol. 1, p. 42.

33. See Hankey (ed.), Othello: *Plays in Performance,* pp. 80–83; and Mythili Kaul, "Background: Black or Tawny? Stage Representations of Othello from 1604 to the Present," in Mythili Kaul (ed.), Othello: *New Essays by Black Writers* (Washington, D.C.: Howard University Press, 1997), pp. 12–15.

34. Herbert Farjeon, *The Shakespearean Scene: Dramatic Criticisms* (London and New York: Hutchinson, 1949), p. 166.

35. J. Dover Wilson and Alice Walker (eds.), *Othello, New Cambridge Shakespeare,* 1st ed. (Cambridge: Cambridge University Press, 1957), pp. ix–x.

36. Wine, Othello: *Text and Performance,* p. 55.

37. *Theatrical Journal,* November 6, 1861.

38. Discussed in H. R. Coursen, "The Case for a Black Othello," in *Shakespearean Performance as Interpretation* (Newark: University of Delaware Press, 1992), pp. 157–62.

39. Wine, Othello: *Text and Performance,* p. 48.

40. See Virginia Mason Vaughan, "Paul Robeson's Othello," in Othello: *A Contextual History* (Cambridge: Cambridge University Press, 1994), pp. 197–98. Vaughan cites Sir Ian McKellen's remark in 1987 that in our time no white actor should take on the role of Othello (p. 197).

41. Hankey (ed.), Othello: *Plays in Performance,* p. 12.

42. Thomas Rymer, *A Short View of Tragedy* (London: Richard Baldwin, 1693), p. 119.

43. *Colley Cibber: An Autobiography,* ed. Robert W. Lowe (London: Grolier Society, 1900), vol. 1, p. 192.

44. *Grub Street Journal,* October 31, 1734.

45. Bernard, *Retrospections,* vol. 2, p. 119.

46. Ellen Terry, *The Story of My Life* (London, 1908; New York: Schocken Books, 1982), p. 131.

47. *Punch,* May 14, 1881.

48. Terry, *The Story of My Life,* p. 131.

49. Cited in Furness (ed.), *A New Variorum Edition of Shakespeare: Othello,* p. 214.

50. "Edwin Booth," *Galaxy,* 7 (January 1869): 83.

51. Furness (ed.), *A New Variorum Edition of Shakespeare: Othello,* p. 188.

52. See Rosenberg, *The Masks of* Othello, p. 124.

53. Kenneth Tynan (ed.), Othello: *The National Theatre Production* (1966; New York: Stein and Day, 1967), p. 2.

54. Discussed in Rosenberg, *The Masks of* Othello, pp. 158–59.

55. "David Suchet—Iago in *Othello,*" in Russell Jackson and Robert Smallwood (eds.), *Players of Shakespeare 2* (Cambridge: Cambridge University Press), pp. 179–97, quote at p. 194.

56. Ibid., p. 198.

57. Wine, Othello: *Text and Performance,* p. 67.

58. Vaughan, "*Othello* in Restoration England," in Othello: *A Contextual History,* p. 100.

59. See Hankey (ed.), Othello: *Plays in Performance,* p. 24. Matteo, *Shakespeare's Othello,* disputes the idea that there was a bold display of erotic elements in Restoration performances of *Othello* (p. 33).

60. Thomas Davies, *Memoirs of the Life of David Garrick* (London, 1780), vol. 2, p. 241, cited in Hankey (ed.), Othello: *Plays in Performance,* p. 33.

61. Rosenberg, *The Masks of* Othello, p. 51.

62. Frances Ann Kemble, *Records of Later Life* (New York: Henry Holt and Co., 1882), p. 645.

63. Robert W. Lowe, "Helen Faucit," in Brander Matthews and Laurence Hutton, *Actors and Actresses of Great Britain and the United States* (New York: Cassell and Co., 1886), vol. 4, p. 181.

64. Helen Faucit, *On Some of Shakespeare's Female Characters* (Edinburgh and London: W. Blackwood, 1891), p. 77.

65. In Ellen Terry, *Four Lectures on Shakespeare,* ed. Christopher St. John (London: Martin Hopkinson, 1932), p. 128; reprinted in Susan Snyder (ed.), Othello: *Critical Essays* (New York and London: Garland Publishing, Inc., 1988), p. 61.

66. Rosenberg, *The Masks of* Othello, p. 212.

67. Farjeon, *The Shakespearean Scene,* p. 167.

68. James Agate, *Brief Chronicles: A Survey of the Plays of Shakespeare and the Elizabethans in Actual Performance* (London: J. Cape, 1943), p. 288.

69. Furness (ed.), *A New Variorum Edition of Shakespeare: Othello,* p. 167. Sprague, *Shakespeare and the Actors,* notes that Charles Dillon at the Lyceum (1856) was probably the first Othello to employ this stage business (p. 194).

70. In Mason, *The Othello of Tommaso Salvini;* reprinted in Snyder (ed.), Othello: *Critical Essays,* p. 38.

71. Brown (ed.), *Shakespeare's* Othello, discusses the possible ways the handkerchief can be dropped (p. 54).

72. Sprague, *Shakespeare and the Actors,* p. 196.

73. Ibid., p. 220.

74. James R. Siemon, "Nay, That's Not Next: *Othello,* V. ii in Performance, 1760–1900," *SQ,* 37.1 (1986): 38–51.

75. Sprague, *Shakespeare and the Actors,* p. 212.

76. Westland Marston, *Our Recent Actors* (London: S. Low, Masston, Searle and Rivington, 1988), vol. 1, pp. 83–84.

77. Siemon, "Nay, That's Not Next," p. 39.

78. Anthony Davies, "Filming *Othello,*" in Anthony Davies and Stanley Wells (eds.), *Shakespeare and the Moving Image: The Plays on Film and Television* (Cambridge: Cambridge University Press, 1994), pp. 196–210, quote at p. 199.

79. Ibid., p. 202. Since Yutkenvich's movie in many ways echoes Welles's slightly earlier one, I have not included it for detailed analysis.

80. Jack J. Jorgens, *Shakespeare on Film* (Bloomington: Indiana University Press, 1977), p. 21.

81. See Charles Higham, *The Films of Orson Welles* (Berkeley, Los Angeles, and London: University of California Press, 1971), pp. 135–37, for an account of the genesis of the film, and Micheál MacLiammóir, *Put Money in Thy Purse: The Diary of the Film of* Othello (London: Methuen, 1952).

82. As does Jorgens, *Shakespeare on Film,* p. 175.

83. See MacLiammóir, *Put Money in Thy Purse,* pp. 92–93.

84. James Naremore, *The Magic World of Orson Welles* (1978; Dallas: Southern Methodist University Press, 1989), p. 177.

85. On the significance of these images of Desdemona's body, see Virginia Mason Vaughan, "Orson Welles and the Patriarchal Eye," in her Othello: *A Contextual History,* pp. 199–216.

86. MacLiammóir, *Put Money in Thy Purse,* p. 27.

87. Higham, *The Films of Orson Welles*, p. 138.

88. MacLiammóir, *Put Money in Thy Purse*, p. 27.

89. Ibid., p. 28.

90. See Joseph McBride, *Orson Welles* (New York: Da Capo Press, 1996), p. 124 n.2.

91. Stanley Kauffmann, "Restoring Welles," *New Republic*, March 9, 1992, p. 29.

92. Anthony Davies, "Orson Welles's *Othello*," in *Filming Shakespeare's Plays* (Cambridge: Cambridge University Press, 1988), analyzes in detail both spatial and lighting effects here, finding in the fortress "the confident frontier of solidity and order" while "the enemy strikes from within" (p. 115).

93. The significance of mirror imagery is discussed in Peter B. Donaldson, "Mirrors and M/Others: The Welles *Othello*," in *Shakespearean Films/Shakespearean Directors* (Boston: Unwin Hyman, 1990), pp. 97–107.

94. Philip Kemp, "Perplexed in the Extreme," *Sight&S*, 29 (November 17, 1992): 31.

95. Jorgens, *Shakespeare on Film*, pp. 176–78.

96. In "A Review of *Othello*," in Charles Eckert (ed.), *Focus on Shakespearean Films* (Englewood Cliffs, N.J.: Prentice Hall, 1972), pp. 77–78, André Bazin notes how "these walls, these vaults and corridors echo, reflect and multiply, like so many mirrors, the eloquence of the tragedy" (p. 78).

97. Davies, "Orson Welles's *Othello*," discusses "shadow" effects (pp. 111–12).

98. MacLiammóir, *Put Money in Thy Purse*, p. 13.

99. This cage motif is discussed in Jorgens, *Shakespeare on Film*, p. 183.

100. Donaldson discusses this and other "barred or crossed images" in "Mirrors and M/Others," pp. 112–18.

101. Naremore, *The Magic World of Orson Welles*, p. 176.

102. Purists may disagree. In "Improving Mr. Welles," *Sight&S*, 29 (November 17, 1992): 30, Jonathan Rosenbaum notes that many of "the *precise* elements of music and sound effects as supervised by Welles" have disappeared.

103. William Johnson, "Orson Welles: Of Time and Loss," *FQ*, 21 (1967): 13–24, points out how the "staccato rhythm associated with Iago gradually imposes itself on Othello's stately rhythm" (p. 20).

104. Jorgens, *Shakespeare on Film*, p. 189.

105. Ibid., p. 179.

106. Eric Bentley, "Orson Welles and Two Othellos," in *What Is Theatre?* (Boston: Beacon Press, 1956), p. 69.

107. Peter Cowie, *The Cinema of Orson Welles* (New York: A. S. Barnes and Co., 1965), p. 100.

108. Bazin, "A Review of *Othello*," p. 78.

109. Lorne M. Buchman, "Orson Welles's *Othello:* A Study of Time in Shakespeare's Tragedy," *ShS*, 39 (1987): 53–65, suggests the underlying link between these two shots— that Iago "will achieve his ends through a controlled use of time" (p. 56).

110. Bentley, "Orson Welles and Two Othellos," p. 70. John Fuegi, "Explorations in No Man's Land: Shakespeare's Poetry as Theatrical Film," *SQ*, 23 (Winter 1972): 37–49, also finds that Welles "simply neglects to ally formal discipline with his immense cinematic intelligence" (p. 44).

111. McBride, *Orson Welles*, p. 128.

112. Jorgens, *Shakespeare on Film*, p. 175.

113. Quoted in Roger Manvell, *Shakespeare and the Film* (New York: Praeger, 1971), p. 117.

114. Laurence Olivier, *On Acting* (New York: Simon and Schuster, 1986), p. 369.

115. Quoted in Tynan (ed.), Othello: *The National Theatre Production,* p. 106.

116. Jorgens, *Shakespeare on Film,* p. 202.

117. Davies, *Filming Shakespeare's Plays,* p. 100.

118. Mentioned by Alan Seymour, "A View from the Stalls," in Tynan (ed.), Othello: *The National Theatre Production,* p. 14.

119. James E. Fisher, "Olivier and the Realistic *Othello," FLQ,* 1.4 (Fall 1973): 321–31, analyzes Cassio's role astutely (p. 329).

120. Olivier's own term in "The Great Sir Laurence," *Life,* 56 (May 1, 1964): 88.

121. Seymour, "A View from the Stalls," p. 13.

122. Robert Kee, from the *New Statesman,* in Tynan (ed.), Othello: *The National Theatre Production,* p. 106. In "Three Green-Eyed Monsters: Acting as Applied Criticism in Shakespeare's *Othello,"AR,* 56.3 (Summer 1998): 358–73, Geoffrey Bent notes the danger: that because Olivier "so flagrantly" projects Othello as black, the character's flaws "appear racial" (p. 369).

123. Jorgens, *Shakespeare on Film,* p. 204.

124. "The Great Sir Laurence," p. 88.

125. Ronald Bryden, from the *New Statesman,* in Tynan (ed.), Othello: *The National Theatre Production,* p. 106.

126. "The Great Sir Laurence," p. 88.

127. See Kenneth Tynan, "Olivier: The Actor and the Moor," in Tynan (ed.), Othello: *The National Theatre Production,* p. 8.

128. Alan Dent, from the *Financial Times,* in Tynan (ed.), Othello: *The National Theatre Production,* p. 102.

129. Bamber Gascoigne, from the *Observer,* in Tynan (ed.), Othello: *The National Theatre Production,* p. 107.

130. "The Great Sir Laurence," p. 80A.

131. Ibid., p. 88.

132. Tynan, "Olivier," p. 4.

133. F. R. Leavis, "Diabolic Intellect and the Noble Hero," in *The Common Pursuit* (1952; Harmondsworth: Penguin, 1962), p. 141.

134. Ibid., p. 142.

135. In "Shakespeare and the Included Spectator," in Norman Rabkin (ed.), *Reinterpretations of Elizabethan Drama* (New York and London: Columbia University Press, 1969), Robert Hapgood comments on how Leavis's essay produces a "pitying contempt for Othello's self-deluding folly," whereas Olivier's performance makes us feel "sympathy, even admiration, for this Othello, with all his faults" (p. 130).

136. Rosenberg, *The Masks of* Othello, finds that "the weight of acting intuition rejects an Othello who is deceived about himself and his nobility" (p. 191).

137. Leavis, "Diabolic Intellect," p. 140.

138. Tynan, "Olivier," pp. 7–8. In the *Life* interview, Olivier describes himself as "working on the assumption that Othello's first reaction to Iago is 'Come on, I know you're after Cassio's lieutenancy and I'll get the truth out of you'" ("The Great Sir Laurence," p. 88).

139. Alan Dent, from the *Financial Times,* in Tynan (ed.), Othello: *The National Theatre Production,* p. 102.

140. Jorgens, *Shakespeare on Film,* p. 194. Fisher, "Olivier and the Realistic *Othello,"* also finds that an "idealistic dimension" of Othello's character is superbly conveyed through the "indirection of realism" (p. 331).

141. "The Great Sir Laurence," p. 88.

142. Ibid., p. 94.

143. Alan Brien, from the *Sunday Telegraph*, in Tynan (ed.), Othello: *The National Theatre Production*, p. 104.

144. Tynan, "Olivier," p. 5.

145. James Delingpole, "Upstaged by the Bad Guy," *London Daily Telegraph*, February 16, 1996, p. 24.

146. See Davies, "Orson Welles's *Othello*," p. 106.

147. A term used by Stanley Kauffman, "Shrinking Shakespeare," *New Republic*, February 12, 1996, p. 30. In this vein, the handkerchief floating skyward in slow motion after Iago triumphantly tosses it up seems to echo a shot from Janet Suzman's filmed South African production of *Othello* (1988) described by Davies in "Filming *Othello*," pp. 200–201.

148. Mark Steyn, "High School Shakespeare," *Spectator*, February 17, 1996, p. 42.

149. Leavis, "Diabolic Intellect," p. 138.

150. Delingpole, "Upstaged by the Bad Guy," p.24.

151. Olivier's phrase in "The Great Sir Laurence," p. 88.

152. Peter Hall, from the *Sunday Times*, January 26, 1969, quoted in Manvell, *Shakespeare and the Film*, pp. 126–27.

153. In "The BBC-TV Shakespeare," *SQ*, 30 (1979): 411–15, quote at 415.

154. Richard Last, "'Shakespeare' Creates Boxed-In Feeling," *London Daily Telegraph*, December 11, 1978, p. 11.

155. Quoted by Sylvan Barnet, "*Othello* on Stage and Screen," in Alvin Kernan (ed.), *Othello, The Signet Classic Shakespeare* (New York: Penguin Books, 1986), p. 284.

156. See Susan Willis, *The BBC Shakespeare Plays: Making the Televised Canon* (Chapel Hill and London: University of North Carolina Press, 1991), p. 14.

157. E. A. J. Honigmann (ed.), *Othello, The Arden Shakespeare*, 3rd ed. (Walton-on-Thames: Thomas Nelson and Sons, Ltd., 1997), may go too far in estimating Desdemona's age at fifteen or sixteen (p. 42), but she cannot be envisaged as much older than twenty.

158. In Tim Hallinan, "Jonathan Miller on the Shakespeare Plays," *SQ*, 32.2 (1981): 134–45, Miller discusses how he uses details in his TV productions that will "remind the audience of the sixteenth-century imagination" (p. 136).

159. See Willis, *The BBC Shakespeare Plays*, pp. 122–23.

160. Lynda E. Boose, "Grossly Gaping Viewers and Jonathan Miller's *Othello*," in Lynda E. Boose and Richard Burt (eds.), *Shakespeare, The Movie* (London and New York: Routledge, 1997), pp. 186–97, justifies this as a deliberate "strategy of witholding" to deny the audience sight of the bed—the play's "object of voyeuristic satisfaction" (pp. 194–95).

161. Ibid., p. 188.

162. H. R. Coursen, "The Bard and the Tube," in J. C. Bulman and H. R. Coursen (eds.), *Shakespeare on Television: An Anthology of Essays and Reviews* (Hanover, N.H.: University Press of New England, 1988), pp. 3–10, quote at p. 4.

163. Ibid., p. 123.

164. Boose, "Grossly Gaping Viewers," p. 188.

165. Jonathan Miller's view, in Henry Fenwick, *The BBC Shakespeare Plays:* Othello (London: British Broadcasting Corporation, 1981), p. 18.

166. Ibid., p. 23.

167. Barnet, "*Othello* on Stage and Screen," p. 284.

168. J. C. Bulman, "The BBC Shakespeare and the 'House Style,'" in Bulman and Coursen (eds.), *Shakespeare on Television,* pp. 50–60, quote at p. 58. Bulman finds that the "Othello music" is continually toned down in this production.

169. Cited in R. Thomas Simone, "Jonathan Miller's Iago," in Bulman and Coursen (eds.), *Shakespeare on Television,* p. 278.

170. Fenwick, *The BBC Shakespeare Plays,* p. 19.

171. Miller's phrase, cited in Barnet, "*Othello* on Stage and Screen," p. 284.

172. Stanley Wells, "Shakespeare Production in England in 1989," *ShS,* 43 (1991): 183–203, calls it "a production of almost Ibsenite social realism" (p. 191).

173. Coursen, "The Case for a Black Othello," p. 154.

174. Ibid.

175. Robert Smallwood, "Shakespeare in Stratford-upon-Avon, 1989, Part I," *SQ,* 41 (1990): 101–14, quote at 110.

176. Coursen, "The Case for a Black Othello," envisages a period soon after the American Civil War, when "Reconstruction" failed and the Southern states reverted to racism (p. 147).

177. Trevor Nunn's phrase, cited in Peter Conrad, "When Less Means Moor," *Observer Magazine,* April 29, 1990, pp. 24–26, quote at p. 26.

178. Virginia Mason Vaughan, "*Othello* for the 1990s: Trevor Nunn's 1989 Royal Shakespeare Company Production," in Othello: *A Contextual History,* pp. 217–32, quote at p. 226.

179. Coursen, "The Case for a Black Othello," p. 156.

180. See Vaughan's analysis of her as a psychologically battered wife ("*Othello* for the 1990s," pp. 226–28).

181. Harry Eyres, *Times,* August 26, 1989.

182. Christopher Edwards, "Tragedy in Close-Up," *Spectator,* September 2, 1989, p. 37.

183. Eyres, *Times.*

184. Barbara Hodgson, "Race-ing *Othello,* Re-engendering White-Out," in Boose and Burt (eds.), *Shakespeare, The Movie,* pp. 23–44, argues that Iago's viewpoint, which the camera often shares, frames Othello as the "colonized other" (pp. 31, 34).

185. Michael Billington, *Country Life,* September 7, 1989.

186. Vaughan, "*Othello* for the 1990s," notes that the promptbook to the stage production calls for a long pause as Othello "kills her + writhes" (p. 230).

BIBLIOGRAPHICAL ESSAY

The following survey, which does not attempt to provide an exhaustive bibliography of *Othello,* outlines important critical work on the play, emphasizing books over articles. Readers who would like to pursue in detail topics treated in this book, such as the role of Iago or the play in performance, are encouraged to take their lead from the notes at the end of the relevant chapter.

Virginia Mason Vaughan and Margaret Lael Mikesell have compiled a comprehensive bibliography of publications on *Othello* up to 1990 in Othello: *An Annotated Bibliography* (New York and London: Garland Publishing, Inc., 1990). *Shakespeare Studies, Shakespeare Survey,* and *Shakespeare Quarterly* contain excellent articles on *Othello* and reviews of significant productions and filmed versions of the play; a selection from *Shakespeare Survey* is reprinted in Kenneth Muir and Philip Edwards (eds.), *Aspects of* Othello (Cambridge: Cambridge University Press, 1977). Among the many critical works on Shakespeare's tragedies that contain illuminating sections on *Othello,* I can single out only a few for special mention: Norman Rabkin, *Shakespeare and the Common Understanding* (New York: Free Press, 1967), on the conflict between reason and faith in the drama; Rosalie Colie, *Shakespeare's Living Art* (Princeton, N.J.: Princeton University Press, 1974), on "*Othello* and the Problematics of Love"; Graham Bradshaw, *Misrepresentations: Shakespeare and the Materialists* (London and Ithaca, N.Y.: Cornell University Press, 1993), which fences with ideologists' views of *Othello;* and *Everybody's Shakespeare* (Lincoln and London: University of Nebraska Press, 1993), in which Maynard Mack astutely reminds us of the sense of "irretrievable loss" that the play conveys (p. 132).

THE TEXT: DIFFERENT EDITIONS

The textual authority of the two versions of *Othello*—the Quarto (Q) of 1622 and the play as it appears in the Folio (F) of 1623—is discussed in Chapter 1.

Readers who consult any of the scholarly editions will find in each a summary of the differences between Q and F and which readings the editor has preferred.

Four of the most helpful and accessible of the conflated texts—based on the Folio version but incorporating some Quarto readings—are the *Signet Classic Shakespeare* (New York: Penguin Books), edited by Alvin Kernan in 1963 and updated in 1986 and 1998; the *Bantam Classic* (New York: Bantam), edited by David Bevington in 1988; the *New Folger Library Shakespeare* (New York: Washington Square Press), edited by Barbara A. Mowat and Paul Werstine in 1993; and the *Everyman Shakespeare* (London and Vermont: J. M. Dent and Charles E. Tuttle), edited by John F. Andrews in 1995. The *Signet* edition includes a translation of the play's main source, a tale from Giraldi Cinthio's *Hecatommithi,* as well as excerpts from important nineteenth- and twentieth-century commentary on the play. Like the *Bantam* and *New Folger* editions, it offers an illuminating introductory essay, while the *Everyman* edition ends with a lengthy compendium of critical "Perspectives on *Othello.*" Both the *Everyman* and *New Folger* editions provide notes and glossary on the page facing the text, easier on the eye than consulting the bottom of the page or the back of the book. The second *New Arden Othello,* edited by M. R. Ridley in 1958 and reprinted in 1992 (London and New York: Routledge), is more biased toward the Quarto version than the others are, but Ridley admits that there is no "authoritative" text of *Othello.* His edition was superseded in 1997 by the third *Arden* (Walton-on-Thames: Thomas Nelson and Sons, Ltd., 1997), edited by E. A. J. Honigmann, who justifies his editorial decisions by carefully evaluating the merits and deficiencies of the Quarto and Folio texts. As well as probing anew the manuscript origins and transmission of Q and F, Honigmann provides appendices and a detailed critical introduction, ranging from traditional issues of character, setting, and theatrical history to a short section on "Feminism." The *New Cambridge Othello* (Cambridge: Cambridge University Press), edited by Norman Sanders in 1984, also contains a comprehensive introduction that covers the play's sources; dramatic structure, themes, and language; history of performance; and textual history. It is a frankly eclectic text, making careful choices between Folio and Quarto readings. As with the *Arden,* the student can find Quarto/Folio variants, and glosses on difficult words or phrases, at the bottom of each page of this text. All of these editions are available in paperback.

SOURCES AND ANALOGUES

In *Narrative and Dramatic Sources of Shakespeare,* vol. 2 (London: Routledge, 1973), Geoffrey Bullough discusses in detail the probable sources of *Othello.* Kenneth Muir, *Shakespeare's Sources I* (London: Methuen, 1957), offers an illuminating analysis of the changes that Shakespeare made in remolding his primary source—the tale from Cinthio's *Hecatommithi* (1566)—into *Othello.* From both these source studies, as well as related articles, we can piece together what Shakespeare may have gleaned from books about the contexts that inform his play: accounts of Africa from John Pory's 1600 translation of Leo Africanus's *The History and Description of Africa;* information on sixteenth-century Venice from Lewis Lewkenor's 1599 translation of Gasparo Contarini's *The Commonwealth and Government of Venice;* and concern about the expanding Ottoman Empire from Richard Knolles's *The Generall Historie of the Turkes* (1603).

GENRE, IMAGE, AND THEME

Othello clearly belongs to the genre of tragedy, but G. R. Hibbard defines what kind— apolitical and domestic—in *"Othello* and the Pattern of Tragedy," *ShS,* 21 (1968): 39–46. Shakespeare's indebtedness to comic form and the way that he inverts it after Act I is covered by Susan Snyder, *The Comic Matrix of Shakespeare's Tragedies* (Princeton, N.J.: Princeton University Press, 1979). Several studies, such as Irving Ribner, *Patterns in Shakespearean Tragedy* (London: Methuen, 1960), trace *Othello's* roots in the morality play. Out of many articles, René E. Fortin's "Allegory and Genre in *Othello," Genre,* 4.2 (July 1971): 153–71, is particularly helpful in outlining Shakespeare's unique recombination of traditional elements.

Analysis of Shakespeare's text as poetic drama is currently out of fashion, but two studies that relate *Othello's* image patterns to its themes remain classic: G. Wilson Knight's "The *Othello* Music," in *The Wheel of Fire* (London: Oxford University Press, 1930), and Robert B. Heilman's *Magic in the Web* (Lexington: University of Kentucky Press, 1956).

HISTORICAL AND SOCIAL CONTEXTS

The race issue has become increasingly central to studies of *Othello.* Since the 1960s, several books and articles have focused on images of Africans both in the society and the drama of Shakespeare's time. Eldred Jones, *Othello's Countrymen: The African in English Renaissance Drama* (London: Oxford University Press, 1965), was followed by G. K. Hunter's important essay "Othello and Colour Prejudice" (1967), included in *Dramatic Identities and Cultural Traditions* (New York: Barnes and Noble, 1978). Anthony Barthelemy, *Black Face, Maligned Race: Representations of Blacks in English Drama from Shakespeare to Southerne* (Baton Rouge: Louisiana State University Press, 1987), offers helpful insights into the dramatic and cultural contexts of *Othello,* as does Jack D'Amico's *The Moor in English Renaissance Drama* (Tampa: University of South Florida Press, 1991). Virginia Mason Vaughan's Othello: *A Contextual History* (Cambridge: Cambridge University Press, 1994) devotes a chapter to "Racial Discourse: Black and White," discussing in detail Jacobean attitudes to the black "Other" that inform *Othello.*

From the 1980s on, new historicists have concentrated on how certain ethnic groups were estranged from white Renaissance society. Stephen Greenblatt's essay "Improvisation and Power," in *Renaissance Self-Fashioning* (Chicago and London: University of Chicago Press, 1980), compares Iago's tactics in undermining Othello to those of New World colonizers, and Dympna Callaghan, "Othello Was a White Man," in Terence Hawkes (ed.), *Alternative Shakespeares,* vol. 2 (London and New York: Routledge, 1996), points out how the marginalization of blacks extended to Elizabethan and Jacobean stages. More often, scholars have situated Shakespeare's hero in discourses about the exotic or monstrous. The material feminist Karen Newman, in "'To Wash the Ethiop White': Femininity and the Monstrous in *Othello*" (contained in *Fashioning Femininity and English Renaissance Drama* [Chicago and London: University of Chicago Press, 1991]), was one of the first to link the monstrous otherness of the black man, Othello, with the unruly female, Desdemona, in terms of their power to transgress dominant ideologies. As Ania Loomba also points out in *Gender, Race, and Renaissance Drama* (Manchester: Manchester University Press, 1989), Desdemona defies the conventions of her gender, class, and race to marry Othello. Despite his efforts to discuss Othello as Other rather than as racial subject, Leslie A. Fiedler touches on our fascination with the forbidden (the union of black man with white woman) in *The Stranger in Shakespeare* (New York: Stein and Day, 1972). Recent critics have gone further in exploring how the audience becomes implicated in the spectacle of the "monstrous" in *Othello*. Michael Neill's important article "Unproper Beds: Race, Adultery, and the Hideous in *Othello*," *SQ*, 40.4 (1989): 383–412, and Janet Adelman's psychoanalytical approach in "Iago's Alter Ego: Race as Projection in *Othello*," *SQ*, 48 (Summer 1997): 125–44, best represent this trend, which took its cue from Stanley Cavell's philosophizings, in *The Claim of Reason* (Oxford: Clarendon Press, 1979), on the "thing denied our sight" in *Othello* (p. 488).

Critical Essays on Shakespeare's Othello (Macmillan: New York, 1994), edited by Anthony Barthelemy, includes the essays of Loomba and Neill, while Harold Bloom's critical edition of the play (New York: Chelsea House Publications, 1987) contains excerpts from Greenblatt and Cavell. Comparing these recent collections with earlier essays included in Leonard Dean (ed.), *A Casebook on* Othello (New York: Thomas Y. Crowell Co., 1961), and John Wain (ed.), Othello: *A Casebook* (Basingstoke and London: Macmillan, 1971), reveals just how far criticism of *Othello* has moved away from studies of character and themes to examine instead the social and political issues raised by the play. (An excellent review of this earlier criticism is provided by Helen Gardner, "'Othello': A Retrospect, 1900–67," *ShS*, 21 [1968]: 1–11.) Another newer collection of essays edited by Virginia Mason Vaughan and Kent Cartwright, Othello: *New Perspectives* (London and Toronto: Associated University Presses, 1991), also incorporates current critical approaches to Renaissance drama: feminist, analysis of audience response, and speech act theory.

Inevitably, critics have questioned whether Shakespeare's play, and not just the contexts that inform it, manifests racial prejudice. James L. Calderwood touches on this question in his illuminating poststructuralist study *The Properties of* Othello (Amherst: University of Massachusetts Press, 1989). It is more fully addressed in "*Othello* and the Plain Face of Racism," *SQ*, 38:2 (1987): 166–88, where Martin Orkin exposes racist assumptions among critics of the play but finds that the hero himself escapes racial stereotypes. Orkin's views tally with those of G. K. Hunter, "Othello and Color Prejudice," and G. M. Matthews, "Othello and the Dignity of Man," in Arnold Kettle (ed.), *Shakespeare in a Changing World* (New York: International Publishers, 1964). Most recently, Othello: *New Essays by Black Writers,* edited by Mythili Kaul (Washington, D.C.: Howard University, 1997), addresses the question of the play's racism from the perspective of black creative writers, critics, and actors.

CHARACTER DISPUTES

Although few critics now focus exclusively on dramatic characters, many important studies have treated the play's protagonists in some depth. Othello himself has proved particularly controversial. Is he a noble hero, as A. C. Bradley (following Samuel Johnson and Samuel Taylor Coleridge) maintains in *Shakespearean Tragedy* (1909; London: Macmillan, 1962), or is he a deluded, self-idealizing egoist, as F. R. Leavis trenchantly argues in "Diabolic Intellect and the Noble Hero"? Following Leavis's essay (included in *The Common Pursuit* [1952; Harmondsworth: Penguin Books, 1962]), Helen Gardner's "The Noble Moor," *PBA,* 51 (1955): 189–205, began a mobilization of forces in defense of the hero; Barbara Everett, "Reflections on the Sentimentalist's Othello," *CritQ,* 3.2 (Summer 1961): 127–39, and John Holloway, *The Story of the Night* (Lincoln: University of Nebraska Press, 1963), pp. 37–56, are among them. Those who continued to analyze the hero more skeptically include Robert B. Heilman, *Magic in the Web* (Lexington: University of Kentucky Press, 1956); Matthew N. Proser, *The Heroic Image in Five Shakespearean Tragedies* (Princeton, N.J.: Princeton University Press, 1965); R. S. Elliott, *Flaming Minister: A Study of* Othello (New York: AMS Press, Inc., 1965); and Martin Elliott, *Shakespeare's Invention of* Othello (New York: St. Martin's Press, 1988). Other commentators, such as Jane Adamson, Othello *as Tragedy: Some Problems of Judgment and Feeling* (Cambridge: Cambridge University Press, 1980), advocate a compromise whereby we balance sympathy for the hero against finding him, at times, gravely culpable. Like John Bayley, *The Characters of Love* (New York: Basic Books, 1960), Adamson notes the characters' protective strategies and capacity for misunderstanding one another, as well as ways in which the play encourages in the audience a "wide range of feelings [and] judgments" (p. 19).

Freudian and feminist critics, however, have continued to lambast Othello. In "Sexual Anxiety and the Male Order of Things," *ELR,* 10 (1980): 384–412, Edward A. Snow takes his cue from Greenblatt's idea (in "Improvisation and Power") that Iago encourages Othello to view intercourse even within marriage as sinful. The male characters' misogyny and distrust of female sexuality is also analyzed by (among others) Peter Erickson, *Patriarchal Structures in Shakespeare's Drama* (Berkeley, Los Angeles, and London: University of California Press, 1985), and Valerie Wayne, *The Matter of Difference: Feminist Criticism of Shakespeare* (Ithaca, N.Y.: Cornell University Press, 1991), pp. 153–79.

Almost everyone considers Iago a villain, but critics have accounted for his treachery in various ways. Iago's derivation from the morality Vice figure is explored by Bernard Spivack, *Shakespeare and the Allegory of Evil* (New York: Columbia University Press, 1958). W. H. Auden, "The Joker in the Pack" (in *The Dyer's Hand* [New York: Random House, 1948]), analyzes Iago's warped psychology, while Maud Bodkin, *Archetypal Patterns in Poetry* (Oxford: Oxford University Press, 1934), discerns Iago as Othello's shadow side; Sidney Homan, *When the Theater Turns to Itself* (London and Toronto: Associated University Presses, 1986), views him as an artist-playwright. Stanley Edgar Hyman reviews all these approaches and includes categories on Iago as Machiavel and latent homosexual in his *Iago: Some Approaches to the Illusion of His Motivation* (New York: Atheneum, 1970). William Empson's "'Honest' in *Othello,*" in *The Structure of Complex Words* (London: Chatto and Windus, 1969), analyzes Iago's character in terms of the social connotations of "honest" in the early seventeenth century. More recently, following Malcolm Coulthard's work in *An Introduction to Discourse Analysis* (London: Longman's Group, Ltd., 1977), Brian Vickers has analyzed Iago's linguistic cleverness by way of speech act theory in his *Appropriating Shakespeare* (London and New Haven, Conn.: Yale University Press, 1993).

Feminist critics have taken a fresh interest in the character of Desdemona. While they usually agree that she is more submissive than subversive in the second part of the play, they often account for her roles in terms of the Renaissance discourses in which she is situated. Carol Thomas Neely, "Men and Women in *Othello,*" in *Broken Nuptials in Shakespeare's Plays* (London and New Haven, Conn.: Yale University Press, 1988), links her to Shakespeare's admirable comic heroines. Mary Beth Rose, *The Expense of Spirit: Love and Sexuality in English Renaissance Drama* (Ithaca, N.Y.: Cornell University Press, 1988), allies Desdemona with Puritan tracts advocating mutuality within marriage. In *Still Harping on Daughters* (New York: Columbia University Press, 1983), Lisa Jardine finds Desdemona doomed by repressive attitudes toward unruly women, while Peter Stallybrass, "Patriarchal Territories: The Body Enclosed," in Margaret W. Ferguson, Maureen Quilligan, and Nancy J. Vickers (eds.), *Rewriting the Renaissance* (Chicago and London: University of Chicago Press, 1986), also discusses the final containment of this potentially transgressive character. The Freudian and materialist essays by Snow and Stallybrass are included in Susan Snyder (ed.), *Othello: Critical Essays* (New York and London: Garland Publishing, Inc., 1988), which also looks in some detail at the theatrical legacy of *Othello.*

OTHELLO IN THE THEATER AND ON FILM

Because of *Othello's* unflagging popularity in the theater, it has rarely been treated as a purely literary text. Emrys Jones, *Scenic Form in Shakespeare* (Oxford: Clarendon Press, 1971), examines dramaturgical questions raised by the play, and Harley Granville Barker draws on his stage experience to analyze *Othello* in *Prefaces to Shakespeare,* vol. 2 (Princeton, N.J: Princeton University Press, 1947). Marvin Rosenberg's *The Masks of Othello* (Berkeley and Los Angeles: University of California Press, 1961) explores actors' presentations and relates them to critical interpretations of the characters; he concludes that Leavis's antiheroic reading of Othello is unlikely to work in the theater. Rosenberg's study and that of Arthur Colby Sprague, *Shakespeare and the Actors* (New York: Russell and Russell, 1963), should be supplemented with Virginia Mason Vaughan's illuminating section on "Representations" in Othello: *A Contextual History,* in which she looks at the way that productions through the ages—such as Tommaso Salvini's Othello in the nineteenth century and Paul Robeson's in the twentieth—answer to cultural predilections of the time. Two editions of the play that provide helpful commentary (on facing pages) showing how key dramatic sequences have been performed are John Russell Brown (ed.), Othello: *Harbrace Theater Edition* (New York: Harcourt Brace Jovanovich, Inc., 1973), and Julie Hankey (ed.), Othello: *Plays in Performance* (Bristol: Bristol Classical Press, 1987), which also provides a comprehensive history of Othello's stage productions. Kenneth Tynan's Othello: *The National Theatre Production* (New York: Stein and Day, 1966) is a fascinating account of Laurence Olivier's acclaimed portrayal of the Moor.

Two important movie versions of *Othello,* those of Orson Welles and Stuart Burge, who filmed the production starring Olivier, are sensitively analyzed by Jack J. Jorgens, *Shakespeare on Film* (Bloomington: Indiana University Press, 1977). Anthony Davies includes an essay on Welles's version in his *Filming Shakespeare's Plays* (Cambridge: Cambridge University Press, 1988), while his "Filming *Othello,*" in Anthony Davies and Stanley Wells (eds.), *Shakespeare and the Moving Image* (Cambridge: Cambridge University Press, 1994), provides an overview of important movie presentations of the play. Those wanting to find out more about the BBC/Time Life televised *Othello* should consult Susan Willis's account in *The BBC Shakespeare Plays: Making the Televised Canon* (Chapel Hill and London: University of North Carolina Press, 1991). This *Othello* is also covered in a stimulating collection, *Shakespeare on Television: An Anthology of Essays and Reviews* (Hanover, N.H.: University Press of New England, 1988), edited by J. C. Bulman and H. R. Coursen.

INDEX

Names of characters in *Othello* appear in **bold type**.

ABOUT THE AUTHOR

JOAN LORD HALL is Instructor in the University Writing Program and Lecturer in English at the University of Colorado, Boulder. Her previous books include *Henry V: A Guide to the Play* (Greenwood, 1997).